Chinese Professionals and the Republican State

The Rise of Professional Associations in Shanghai, 1912–1937

Xiaoqun Xu makes a compelling and original contribution to the study of modern China with this book on the rise of professional associations in the Republican era. Xu focuses on their origins and political and sociocultural milieu in Shanghai, the center of their professional activities. This book is rich in detail about the key professional figures and organizations in Shanghai and fills an important gap in the city's social history.

The professional associations were, as the author writes, "unambiguously urban and modern in their origins and functions . . . representing a new breed of educated Chinese" and they pioneered a new type of relationship with the state. In analyzing the relationship between the state and society in this period, a central issue in China studies, Xu proposes an alternative to the Western-derived concept of civil society. This book illuminates the complexity of modernization and nationalism in twentieth-century China and provides a concrete case for comparative studies of professionalization and class formation across cultures.

Xiaoqun Xu is Associate Professor of History at Francis Marion University and a National Endowment for the Humanities Fellow.

Cambridge Modern China Series
Edited by William Kirby, Harvard University

Other books in the series:

Warren I. Cohen and Li Zhao, eds., *Hong Kong under Chinese Rule: The Economic and Political Implications of Reversion*

Tamara Jacka, *Women's Work in Rural China: Change and Continuity in an Era of Reform*

Shiping Zheng, *Party vs. State in Post-1949 China: The Institutional Dilemma*

Michael Dutton, ed., *Streetlife China*

Edward Steinfeld, *Forging Reform in China: The Fate of State-Owned Industry*

Jing Huang, *Factionalism in Chinese Communist Politics*

Edmund S. K. Fung, *In Search of Chinese Democracy: Civil Opposition in Nationalist China, 1929–1949*

David Shambaugh, ed., *The Modern Chinese State*

Chiang Yung-Chen, *Social Engineering and the Social Sciences in China*

Susan H. Whiting, *Power and Wealth in Rural China: The Political Economy of Institutional Change*

Xin Zhang, *Social Transformation in Modern China: The State and Local Elites in Henan, 1900–1937*

Chinese Professionals and the Republican State

The Rise of Professional Associations in Shanghai, 1912–1937

XIAOQUN XU

Francis Marion University

CAMBRIDGE
UNIVERSITY PRESS

CAMBRIDGE UNIVERSITY PRESS
Cambridge, New York, Melbourne, Madrid, Cape Town, Singapore, São Paulo

Cambridge University Press
The Edinburgh Building, Cambridge CB2 2RU, UK

Published in the United States of America by Cambridge University Press, New York

www.cambridge.org
Information on this title: www.cambridge.org/9780521780711

© Xiaoqun Xu 2001

This publication is in copyright. Subject to statutory exception
and to the provisions of relevant collective licensing agreements,
no reproduction of any part may take place without
the written permission of Cambridge University Press.

First published 2001
This digitally printed first paperback version 2006

A catalogue record for this publication is available from the British Library

Library of Congress Cataloguing in Publication data
Xu, Xiaoqun, 1954–
Chinese professionals and the Republican state : the rise of professional
associations in Shanghai, 1912–1937.
p. cm. – (Cambridge modern China series)
Includes bibliographical references and index.
ISBN 0-521-78071-3
1. Professional associations – China – Shanghai – History. 2. Professions –
China – Shanghai – History. I. Title. II. Series.
HD6497.C6 X8 2000
068′.51′13209041 – dc21
00-034256

ISBN-13 978-0-521-78071-1 hardback
ISBN-10 0-521-78071-3 hardback

ISBN-13 978-0-521-02789-2 paperback
ISBN-10 0-521-02789-6 paperback

For Yin and Daniel

Contents

List of Tables	*page* xii
Acknowledgments	xiii
Abbreviations of Frequently Cited Sources	xv

Introduction	1
Professionals and Their Associations in Republican China	3
Professionalization in Republican China	9
State–Society Relationship in Republican China	13

Part I
Professions and Professionals   21

1 Professions in Early-Twentieth-Century Shanghai	23
Modern Sectors of Shanghai's Economy	23
Law, Medicine, and Journalism in Shanghai	39
2 Professionals as Urban Middle Class	50
The Life of Professionals	50
The Career and Identity of Professionals	68
Conclusion to Part I	78

Part II
Social Institutions, State Actions, and Professionalization   79

3 The Republican State and Urban Associations	83
Urban Associations in Late Qing Shanghai	83

Contents

	Urban Associations in the Beiyang Period	87
	Urban Associations in the Nanjing Decade	95
4	The Republican State and the Legal Profession	107
	The Legal Profession in the Beiyang Period	107
	The Legal Profession in the Nanjing Decade	121
5	The Republican State and the Medical Profession	129
	Medicine in the Beiyang Period	130
	Medicine in the Nanjing Decade	142
	Conclusion to Part II	155

Part III
Professionalism, Nationalism, and Politics   157

6	From "Literary Men" to Professionals: Shanghai Journalists	161
	Journalism and Journalists in Shanghai	162
	From "Literary Men" to Professionals	169
	Freedom of Speech and the Journalistic Profession	181
7	National Essence versus Science: The Medical Profession in Conflict	190
	Native Medicine on the Defensive	191
	National Essence versus Science	196
	Toward the Triumph of Native Medicine	204
8	Professionalism and Nationalism: The Shanghai Bar Association (I)	215
	The Organization of the Shanghai Bar	216
	The Efforts at Professionalization	223
	The Shanghai Bar and the Rendition of the Mixed Courts	229
9	Professionalism and Politics: The Shanghai Bar Association (II)	242
	Between Professionalism and Politics	243
	Into the Politics of National Salvation	254
	Conclusion to Part III	268
	Conclusion	271
	Symbiotic Dynamics in the State–Society Relationship	271

Contents

Synthesis of Urban Society and Its Relationship with
 the State 273
From Republican China to Post-Mao China 278

Glossary 285
Bibliography 299
Index 319

Tables

1. Monthly Income Range of Chinese Professionals in Republican Shanghai — *page* 57
2. Monthly Salary Scale for Government Officials in the 1930s — 58
3. Salaries for Chinese Employees of the SMC in the 1930s — 59
4. Monthly Salary Scale in the Chinese Postal Service in 1925 — 60

Acknowledgments

This book is the final incarnation of my Ph.D. dissertation at Columbia University. My interest in China studies started with my taking a class with Madeleine Zelin in the fall of 1989. Professor Zelin's engaging doctoral seminar attracted me to the study of modern Chinese history. Subsequently, as my dissertation adviser, she supported my idea to explore the rise of Chinese professional associations – at the time, a seemingly unpromising topic. During my years at Columbia, the rest of my dissertation committee – Andrew Nathan, Myron Cohen, Robert Hymes, and Michael Tsin – believed in the potential of my work and helped me in various ways.

After completing a Ph.D. degree in 1993, I conducted further research for this study. The efficient service of the staff at the Rogers Library of Francis Marion University made it easier for me to obtain materials even at a relatively isolated location. The Francis Marion University Foundation and the Francis Marion University Faculty Enrichment Committee provided as much financial assistance as a teaching university is capable of providing. Their support allowed me to photocopy a large quantity of select materials and to go to China in the summer of 1994 to collect additional sources.

During my two research trips to China in 1991 to 1992 and 1994, the staffs at the Shanghai Municipal Library, Shanghai Municipal Archives, and Shanghai Academy of Social Sciences helped to make my research as productive as possible. Several Chinese senior citizens accommodated my requests for interviews. Among them were Wu Kaisheng, Wang Baoji, Zhang Zanchen, Zhu Kewen, Xu Jie, Qin Sou'ou, and Lu Yi. Some of them have since passed away. This book is in a sense a record of their times and lives in another era.

The completion of a draft manuscript for this book brought me into

Acknowledgment

contact with three China scholars – Bryna Goodman, Elizabeth J. Perry, and Jeffrey N. Wasserstrom – who kindly took the time to read and comment on the manuscript. They and three anonymous readers for Cambridge University Press offered valuable critiques and suggestions that guided me to improve the manuscript considerably. None of them, of course, is responsible for any defects this book may contain. William Kirby, the editor of the Cambridge Modern China Series, graciously encouraged me along the way, and Mary Child of Cambridge University Press was cheerfully assuring and helpful.

From the beginning to the end, my wife Yin was my most faithful supporter. Without her sacrifices and support, I would not have been able to complete my Ph.D. program at Columbia, let alone this book. Throughout the years she shared my aspirations to scholarship and bore the heavy load of having a professional career and being a wife and mother at the same time. My son Daniel was born when I was writing the first draft of my dissertation. I was unable to take as much care of him as I wanted when he was very young. After finishing my Ph.D. degree, I decided to slow down my research agenda and be with Daniel more. With love and gratitude, I dedicate this book to my wife and son.

Parts of this book originally appeared in the journals identified in the following three paragraphs. I would like to thank the journal editors and publishers for granting permission to use portions of the material.

The bulk of Chapter 9 and several passages in Chapter 8 appeared in "Between State and Society, Between Professionalism and Politics: The Shanghai Bar Association in Republican China, 1912–1937," *Twentieth-Century China* (University of Michigan Center for Chinese Studies), Vol.24, No.1 (Nov. 1998):1–29.

The bulk of Chapter 7 appeared in "'National Essence' vs. 'Science': Chinese Native Physicians' Fight for Legitimacy, 1912–1937," *Modern Asian Studies* (Cambridge University Press), No.31, Part 4 (Oct. 1997): 847–78.

Several passages in Chapters 1 and 4 appeared in "The Fate of Judicial Independence in Republican China, 1912–1937," *China Quarterly* (Oxford University Press), Vol.149 (March 1997):1–28.

Abbreviations of Frequently Cited Sources

CSPSR	*Chinese Social and Political Science Review*
CWR	*China Weekly Review*
DZ	*Dongfang Zazhi*
FP	*Falü Pinglun*
FZ	*Faling Zhoukan*
GZG	*Guomin Zhengfu Gongbao*
MRD	*Minguo Renwu Dacidian*
MSX	*Minguo Shanghai Xianzhi*
NCH	*North China Herald*
QYTZHH	*Quanguo Yiyao Tuanti Zonglianhehui Huiwu Huibian*
SB	*Shi Bao*
SLGB	*Shanghai Lushi Gonghui Baogaoshu*
SnB	*Shen Bao*
STSFH	*Shanghai Tebieshi Shizheng Fagui Huibian*
SWZX	*Shanghai Wenshi Ziliao Xuanji*
SYZ	*Shanghai Yanjiu Ziliao*
SYZX	*Shanghai Yanjiu Ziliao Xuji*
WZX	*Wenshi Ziliao Xuanji*
XYZ	*Xinwen Yanjiu Ziliao*
YC	*Yijie Chunqiu*
YCH	*Yijie Chunqiu Huixuan*
YP	*Yiyao Pinglun*
ZG	*Zhengfu Gongbao*
ZGFH	*Zhengfu Gongbao Fenlei Huibian*
ZMXFD	*Zhonghua Minguo Xianxing Fagui Daquan*
ZXS	*Zhongyi Xin Shengming*

Introduction

DURING the early part of the twentieth century, the city of Shanghai harbored a wide variety of voluntary associations. They ranged from native-place associations, trade guilds, chambers of commerce, professional associations, Christian congregations, secret societies, the criminal underworld, labor unions, and political party organizations, to a host of educational, vocational, academic, athletic, artistic, theatrical, and literary societies, altogether numbering in the several hundreds. Designed for various economic, social, political, intellectual, and cultural purposes, the voluntary associations operated as legitimate or illegitimate, overt or covert, or public or private entities. The associations, and the diverse social groups they represented, created a vibrant urban society with complex social dynamics evident in the city and beyond, and provided much of the drama in Shanghai's political, social, and cultural history at the time. This book examines one important but under-studied type of those social groups and associations, namely, Chinese professionals and their associations.

Scholars of modern Chinese history have used the term "professional association" to refer to chambers of commerce, bankers' associations, educational societies, and lawyers' groups. This book deals with such professionals as lawyers, doctors, and journalists (touching upon accountants) who were collectively identified in Republican China as *ziyou zhiye zhe* (free professionals). The term's origins are obscure. The term is probably a translation of the German word *freiberufler* or *freier beruf*, though it remains to be discovered who first used or translated the term in China.[1] The history of the concept "profession" in China was quite

---

1. I am grateful to Haken Friberg of Stockholm University who suggested to me the possibility of the German words being translated into the Chinese term.

Introduction

similar to that in Germany. For a long time in China there was no word or term to differentiate "professions" from "occupations" – both were called *zhiye*.[2] Not until 1929 was the term *ziyou zhiye zhe* used by the Guomindang (GMD) official documents to identify professional groups, including doctors, lawyers, accountants, journalists, engineers, and professors, and the term *ziyou zhiye tuanti* to refer to their organizations. Thereafter, those groups all called themselves *ziyou zhiye zhe*.[3]

They were not, however, the same. Doctors and lawyers (and accountants) were self-employed or independent professionals, whereas journalists (along with professors and engineers) were professional employees or salaried professionals. The fact that they were identified as one particular social category by 1929 is significant. First of all, it reflected the GMD's scheme to categorize social groups for the purpose of exercising social control with a vision of having a corporatist state. Furthermore, the notion of free professionals that included all these groups indicated its Western origin because the occupations had been recognized as professions in the West.[4] On the other hand, those diverse groups came to be identified as one category because they did share something in common and they were conscious of their commonality. The professional groups had become a recognizable and recognized social type. At the same time, the development of those professional groups may be taken as a measure of China's modern transformation or modernization.[5]

---

2. For the German case, see Konrad H. Jarausch, *The Unfree Professions: German Lawyers, Teachers, and Engineers, 1900–1950* (Oxford, 1990), pp.4–5; "The German Professions in History and Theory," in Geoffrey Cocks and Konrad H. Jarausch, eds., *German Professions, 1800–1950* (Oxford, 1990), pp.10–11; Charles E. McClelland, *The German Experience of Professionalization* (Cambridge, 1991), p.15.
3. GMD documents did not include associations of professors in the category of *ziyou zhiye tuanti*, but when the election of delegates to the Citizens' Congress took place in 1931, professors were allowed to participate in the election as part of the circle of free professionals.
4. The literature on professionalization in the West shows that the process was a continuous one: more and more occupations required specialized training and thus claimed expertise and demanded the recognition as professions. For experiences of professionalization in several Western societies, see Samuel Haber, *The Quest for Authority and Honor in the American Professions, 1750–1900* (Chicago, 1991); Geoffrey Cocks and Konrad H. Jarausch, eds., *German Professions, 1800–1950*; Charles E. McLelland, *The German Experience of Professionalization*; Konrad H. Jarausch, *The Unfree Professions*; Harold Perkin, *The Rise of Professional Society: England since 1880* (London, 1989); Roy Lewis and Angus Maude, *Professional People* (London, 1952); W. J. Reader, *Professional Men: The Rise of the Professional Classes in Nineteenth-Century England* (New York, 1966).
5. Magali Sarfatti Larson points out that for professions, the most significant aspects of

Introduction

The preceding observations bring us to the objectives of this book. Through examining the development of such professional groups as lawyers, doctors, and journalists, and the political and sociocultural milieu within which they emerged and functioned, this study aims to illuminate three issues that bear on our understanding of urban society in Republican China. First, by analyzing professionals' economic conditions, life-style, cultural functions, social identity, and political orientation, this study will show that the appearance of Chinese professionals as a new social category reflected a new kind of class formation in Republican Shanghai in the course of modernization. Second, with critical use of the concept "professionalization" informed by recent scholarship on the subject, this study will demonstrate that professional associations differed from other urban associations in a number of ways. The most important difference stemmed from the professional associations' professional concerns and their efforts at professionalization. That difference further indicates the increasing heterogeneity of urban society and complexity of urban politics at that time. Third and most important, through explicating the role of the Republican state in Chinese professionalization and examining the relationship of professional associations with the state and other urban organizations, this study will propose the notion of a symbiotic dynamics that characterized the Chinese state–society relationship in the Republican era. With a synthesis of urban society in Republican Shanghai and its relationship with the state, this study provides a point of reference for observing the similar and continuing transformation of state and society in contemporary China.

PROFESSIONALS AND THEIR ASSOCIATIONS IN REPUBLICAN CHINA

Although voluntary associations of different sorts had long existed in rural and urban China, professional associations did not appear in Shanghai and elsewhere until after the founding of the Republic in 1912. In several important respects, the rise of Chinese professionals and their associations was a new social phenomenon. Many of the traditional organizations and their twentieth-century incarnations – such as private

---

modernization are the advance of science and cognitive rationality and the related rationalization and growing differentiation in the division of labor. See Magali Sarfatti Larson, *The Rise of Professionalism: A Sociological Analysis* (Berkeley, 1977), p.xvi.

Introduction

academies, lineage, secret societies, criminal gangs, trade guilds, urban gentry-merchant organizations, and native-place associations – have been studied by scholars.[6] In contrast to those organizations, professional organizations were unambiguously urban and modern in their origins and functions. The emergence of professionals as a social type was predicated upon modern education, modern economy and technology, modern mass media, new concepts of the intellectual's role in society, new patterns of career development, and Western influence in general – all elements particular to a combination of urban environment and the modernization process.

The professional was a new breed of educated Chinese. Traditionally, educated Chinese (literati) were Confucian generalists who possessed expertise in the knowledge and presentation of Confucian classics, history, and literature – areas of knowledge that were closely related and technically undifferentiated. By abolishing the civil service examination, establishing Western-style schools, and promoting industry, commerce, and judicial reform, among other things, the New Policy reform (1901–1911) of the late Qing formally triggered a transformation of

---

6. For private academies, see Benjamin A. Elman, *From Philosophy to Philology: Intellectual and Social Aspects of Change in Late Imperial China* (Cambridge, MA, 1990). For lineages, see Mary B. Rankin and Joseph W. Esherick, eds., *Chinese Local Elites and Patterns of Dominance* (Berkeley, 1990). For secret societies, see Jean Chesneaux, ed., *Popular Movements and Secret Societies in China, 1840–1950* (Stanford, 1972); Frederic Wakeman Jr., *Policing Shanghai, 1927–1937* (Berkeley, 1995); Bryan G. Martin, *The Shanghai Green Gang: Politics and Organized Crime, 1919–1937* (Berkeley, 1996). For merchant organizations, see Susan Mann Jones, "The Ninpo *Pang* and Financial Power at Shanghai," Edward J. M. Rhoads, "Merchant Associations in Canton, 1895–1911," David D. Buck, "Educational Modernization in Tsinan, 1899–1937," Shirley S. Garrett, "The Chambers of Commerce and the YMCA," in Mark Elvin and G. William Skinner, eds., *The Chinese City between Two Worlds* (Stanford, 1974); Joseph Fewsmith, *Party, State, and Local Elites in Republican China: Merchant Organizations and Politics in Shanghai, 1890–1930* (Honolulu, 1985); Marie-Claire Bergère, *The Golden Age of the Chinese Bourgeoisie, 1911–1937* (Cambridge, 1989); Marie-Claire Bergère, "The Shanghai Bankers' Association, 1915–1927: Modernization and the Institutionalization of Local Solidarities," in Frederic Wakeman and Wen-hsin Yeh, eds., *Shanghai Sojourners* (Berkeley, 1992); William T. Rowe, *Hankow: Commerce and Society in a Chinese City, 1796–1889* (Stanford, 1985); William T. Rowe, *Hankow: Conflict and Community in a Chinese City, 1796–1895* (Stanford, 1989); David Strand, *Rickshaw Beijing: City People and Politics in the 1920s* (Berkeley, 1989); Xu Dingxin and Qian Xiaoming, *Shanghai Zong Shanghui Shi, 1902–1929* (A history of the Shanghai General Chamber of Commerce) (Shanghai, 1991); Ma Min and Zhu Ying, *Chuantong Yu Jindai De Erchong Bianzhou: Wanqing Suzhou Shanghui Ge'an Yanjiu* (Dual variations of tradition and modernity: A case study of the Suzhou Chamber of Commerce in late Qing) (Chengdu, 1993). For native-place associations, see Bryna Goodman, *Native Place, City, and Nation: Regional Networks and Identities in Shanghai, 1853–1937* (Berkeley, 1995).

Introduction

knowledge structure and its sociocultural meanings. The late Qing already saw the appearance of new perceptions about the educated as enlighteners of the people and arbiters of public affairs by way of writing for popular consumption – a role different from the traditional type of scholar-officials or literati.[7] The first few decades of the twentieth century further witnessed new career paths opened to and new sociocultural roles created for the educated, including working and living as professionals.

Professional associations too represented a departure from the past in some respects. Earlier studies have shown that in traditional or transitional urban organizations (such as the Shanghai General Chamber of Commerce, the Shanghai Bankers' Association, trade guilds, and native-place associations), native-place and familial ties served as important and defining organizational and functional mechanisms.[8] Similarly, native origins were one of the lines along which the working class in Shanghai was divided and its politics defined.[9] In contrast, while individual professionals could and did participate in activities based on native-place ties, such ties were manifestly unimportant to professional associations – providing a new perspective of urban associations and urban politics.[10]

Shanghai professionals were prompted to form their own organizations primarily because of their professional interests or group interests. At the same time, they had wider concerns about national affairs and

---

7. Leo Ou-fan Lee and Andrew J. Nathan, "The Beginnings of Mass Culture: Journalism and Fiction in the Late Ch'ing and Beyond," in David Johnson, Andrew Nathan, and Evelyn Rawski, eds., *Popular Culture in Late Imperial China* (Berkeley, 1985), pp.360–95; Joan Judge, *Print and Politics: "Shibao" and the Culture of Reform in Late Qing China* (Stanford, 1996). For the late Qing reform, see Meribeth E. Cameron, *The Reform Movement in China, 1898–1912* (Stanford, 1931); Douglas R. Reynolds, *China, 1898–1912: The Xinzheng Revolution and Japan* (Cambridge, MA, 1993). For the educational reform in particular, see Marianne Bastid, *Educational Reform in Early-Twentieth-Century China* (Ann Arbor, 1988); Sally Borthwick, *Education and Social Change in China* (Stanford, 1983).
8. For the intricate native-place relationships in the Shanghai business world during the prewar period, see Marie-Claire Bergère, *The Golden Age*, Chapter 3; Marie-Claire Bergère, "The Shanghai Bankers' Association"; Susan Mann Jones, "Ninpo Pang."
9. Elizabeth J. Perry, *Shanghai on Strike: The Politics of Chinese Labor* (Stanford, 1993).
10. The available membership directories of these professional associations show that their members came from different parts of the country. The Shanghai Bar Association, for example, had members from sixteen provinces and from different counties within a province. Its leaders also hailed from different native places. See *Shanghai Lushi Gonghui Huiyuanlu* (The membership directory of the Shanghai Bar Association), 1934.

Introduction

embraced the idea of national salvation through science, education, industry, and the rule of law (*kexue jiuguo, jiaoyu jiuguo, shiye jiuguo, fazhi jiuguo*). Those public-sounding goals also served the professionals' self-interests. To be sure, the traditional or transitional urban elite of industrial, commercial, and banking interests in the city shared some of the nationalistic sentiment and purpose, and their associations had adopted similar democratic organizational principles by the Republican era.[11] But still there was a difference between professional associations that were based on professional interests and other types of urban organizations that were formed on other grounds.

To grasp the differences and connections between professionals and other social groups, one may regard Chinese professionals as an emerging social class – both as an urban middle class and as a professional class – reflecting a new kind of social class formation. In the fields of political science and sociology, there has been no agreement on what constitutes a class or on how to define class, and "middle class" is notoriously elusive to define. Yet the literature on middle class in Western and non-Western societies in the late nineteenth and twentieth century generally includes professionals in the category of middle class, along with civil servants and traditional petty bourgeoisie.[12] In the scholarship on modern China, mention has been made of the appearance in early-twentieth-century China of an urban middle class, an intelligentsia, professional groups, and new urban classes, but none of them is fully analyzed and well understood.[13] An analysis of Chinese professionals as a professional class–cum–urban middle class will provide a concrete case of social class formation in the Republican era.

---

11. Marie-Claire Bergère, "The Shanghai Bankers' Association."
12. For a useful overview of different approaches to class definition, see Albert Szymanski, *Class Structure: A Critical Perspective* (New York, 1983), pp.602–45. For discussions of professionals as middle class in Western and non-Western societies, see Pamela M. Pilbeam, *The Middle Class in Europe, 1789–1914: France, Germany, Italy, and Russia* (Chicago, 1990), especially Chapter 4; Jurgen Kocka and Allan Mitchell, eds., *Bourgeois Society in Nineteenth-Century Europe* (Oxford, 1993); George Lavau, Gerard Grunberg, and Nonna Mayer, eds., *L'Univers Politique des Classes Moyennes* (Paris, 1983); Bhagwan Prasad, *Socioeconomic Study of Urban Middle Classes* (Delhi, 1971); B. B. Misra, *The Indian Middle Classes* (Oxford, 1961); National Institute of Social and Economic Research, *Growth of Middle Class in Pakistan* (Karachi, 1971).
13. Joseph Fewsmith, for instance, used the term "middle class" to "describe a wide range of merchants, from those who were at least fairly substantial on down to the thousands of shopkeepers who participated in the national goods movements and the associated boycotts." Obviously, this was only one segment of the urban middle class. See *Party, State, and Local Elites in Republican China*, pp.9–10.

Introduction

For analyzing where Chinese professionals were socially situated in Republican Shanghai, an eclectic approach to class definition will suffice. Obviously, professionals may be considered middle class due to their position in the productive structure of society (neither capitalists nor workers) à la Marxist theory of class analysis. At the same time, informed by various approaches to class definition, one may point to professionals' income level and life-style, their position in technical division of labor (mental versus manual), and their perception and self-perception in society. Encompassing all the preceding was the professionals' commitment to professionalism as a new value particular to them and to professionalization as an institutional and material process beneficial to them. Indeed, Chinese professionals' efforts at professionalization made perfect sense when professionalization is viewed also as a process of social class formation integrating individuals into one profession and various professions into a professional community or a professional class occupying a middling position or strata in Chinese urban society and between state and society at large.

As might be expected, however, even as a new social class, Chinese professionals as a whole did not form a monolithic entity any more than other social groups and classes in Republican Shanghai.[14] Although professionals constituted a considerable segment of the population in Shanghai and, to some extent, shared a sense of a professional community, they were by no means a homogeneous group, and were differentiated in economic circumstances, social prestige, political attitudes, group identities, and cultural functions. Nor were professionals a self-contained group separate from other social elements in Shanghai. Quite the contrary, they had all kinds of social, cultural, economic, and political connections with other social groups and organizations in the city and beyond. Indeed, the emergence of professionals as a new social class was part of a larger process of social configuration and political formation in Republican China that at once differentiated and connected various social categories.

---

14. The recent scholarship on modern Shanghai has convincingly demonstrated that both the working class and bourgeois class in Shanghai were horizontally stratified along the economic line and vertically separated along the lines of native-place origins, cultural practices, political orientations (or political connections for the bourgeois class), and local circumstances. See Emily Honig, *Sisters and Strangers: Women in the Shanghai Cotton Mills, 1919–1949* (Stanford, 1986); Elizabeth J. Perry, *Shanghai on Strike*; Alain Roux, *Le Shanghai Ouvrier des Années Trente: Coolies, Gangsters et Syndicalistes* (Paris, 1993); Marie-Claire Bergère, *The Golden Age*; Christian Henriot, *Shanghai, 1927–1937: Municipal Power, Locality, and Modernization* (Berkeley, 1993).

Introduction

To capture the dynamics and relationships in that changing urban society, this study places emphasis on the associational activities of lawyers, doctors, and journalists. Associational activism did not necessarily mean political activism. Professional associations started out for strictly professional purposes, which set them apart functionally from other urban organizations. They only gradually became caught up in the tides of political movements, which further linked them socially and politically with other social groups and organizations. Both aspects of associational activism of professionals were important, as they contributed to the complex dynamics of urban politics and state–society relationship at that time.

Over the period of 1912 to 1937, a general pattern of collective action among professionals emerged. Journalists were slow to organize themselves into formal professional associations and engage in regular associational activities. Their professional maturity came with political activism at the time of national crisis in the 1930s. By contrast, Shanghai lawyers were best organized and their bar association functioned most effectively in both professional and political terms. Western-style doctors and native physicians were equally effective in pursuing group interests through their organizations, although they were much less vocal on purely political issues. One of the concerns of this study is to explain the differences in associational behavior of those professional groups.

This study focuses on the professional community in Shanghai for a reason – in that treaty port, Chinese professionals clustered in the largest number and every factor conducive to the rise of professions was most pronounced. Marie-Claire Bergère once forcefully argued that despite Shanghai's foreign concessions, "Shanghai very obviously was Chinese." Representing a modernist, democratic, and international tradition, Shanghai was a China of minority and marginality, "but just as authentic as the rural China."[15] As this study will show, while foreign presence and dominance in Shanghai did affect the behavior of Chinese professionals in Shanghai in some aspects, one may not assume that the general characteristics of Chinese professionals in Shanghai were radically different from their counterparts in the rest of the country. On occasions of national issues and crises, there were close communications between, and concerted actions taken by, professional organizations in

---

15. Marie-Claire Bergère, "'The Other China': Shanghai from 1919 to 1949," in Christopher Howe, ed., *Shanghai: Revolution and Development in an Asian Metropolis* (Cambridge, 1981), pp.13–34.

Introduction

Shanghai and those in other parts of the country, with the former playing a leading role. If the role of Chinese professionals and their organizations in urban society and their relationship with the state can be delineated in the context of Republican Shanghai, the analysis should be relevant to an understanding of professional groups in other Chinese cities as well.

PROFESSIONALIZATION IN REPUBLICAN CHINA

To illuminate and examine in a comparative perspective the professionals' social identity in Republican Shanghai and their interaction with the state, this study employs the concept of professionalization. Shanghai professionals can be identified as a distinct social type in Chinese urban society largely because of their professional concerns. Their associational activities aiming at professionalization most clearly distinguished them from other social groups amidst the seemingly similar institutional features and collective actions of various urban associations.

In describing and conceptualizing the rise of professions and professionalism in the West, sociologists have used two general approaches or models: (1) the "attribute model" and (2) the "process model" (also known as functionalist approach and power-analysis approach). The attribute model applies several attributes as essential to defining a profession. The three most cited attributes are (1) an expertise based on theory and knowledge acquired through higher education, (2) a professed ethics of servicing the public regardless of monetary reward, and (3) an autonomy in and monopoly of the service through self-regulating and controlling the standards for entry into the profession, usually with a professional association. Some scholars identified more attributes, but Ernest Greenwood argued that the preceding three were the essential ones and others were derivative.[16]

The process model was developed as a response to and criticism of the attribute model. It contends that the attribute model accepts at face value certain occupational groups' claims to professional status as defining attributes. The process model says what needs to be done instead is to analyze how the groups made their claims in order to gain legitimacy.

---

16. Ernest Greenwood, "Attributes of a Profession: Revisited," in Sheo K. Lal, et al., eds., *Readings in the Sociology of the Professions* (Delhi: Gain Publishing House, 1988), pp.12–14; Ronald M. Pavalko, *Sociology of Occupations and Professions* (Itasca, IL, 1988), pp.19–29.

Introduction

It further says that the attribute model is flawed for presenting too rigid a picture of professions, while in fact occupational groups could be located along a continuum from nonprofession to profession. Some studies using the process model have proposed patterns of professionalization that indicate the temporal stages at which certain defining attributes would appear, though scholars differ on the specific sequence of those particular stages.[17] As the advocates of the process model have noted, the attribute model is insensitive to how the process by which occupational groups claim professional status is shaped by the nature of class structure and ignores important variables such as the role of the state in professionalization.[18] In short, the process model stresses an analysis of professionalization as a historical process mediated by class structure, the role of the state, and the acquisition and use of power by professions.

While the process model (power-analysis approach) considerably advanced the study of professions, biased by the Anglo-American experience, scholars of that approach also discounted the experience of professional groups in continental European countries. Magali Sarfatti Larson once considered the French and German cases as being closer to a model of civil service than to that of profession and chose to study the "purer" features of professionalization in Anglo-American societies.[19] Similarly, Eliot Freidson argued that "as an institutional concept, the term 'profession' is intrinsically bound up with a particular period of history and with only a limited number of nations in that period of history."[20]

Recent scholarship on professionalization has been correcting that bias. It has been pointed out that using the Anglo-American experience as the standards limited a full understanding of professionalization in continental European countries. Regarding the relationship between professional groups and the state, the old assumptions about the freedom of professional groups from government intervention in Anglo-American societies need to be modified because professional

---

17. Ronald M. Pavalko, *Sociology*, pp.34–35.
18. Ibid., pp.29–38; Terence J. Johnson, *Professions and Power* (Hong Kong, 1972), pp.21–38.
19. Magali Sarfatti Larson, *The Rise of Professionalism*, pp.xvii–xviii.
20. Eliot Freidson, "The Theory of Professions: State of the Art," in Robert Dingwall and Philip Lewis, eds., *The Sociology of the Professions: Lawyers, Doctors, and Others* (London, 1983), p.26; also see Eliot Freidson, *Professional Powers* (Chicago, 1986), pp.30–38.

Introduction

associations in those countries used state power to reinforce their monopoly of services and control their market.²¹ On the other hand, a much stronger role of the state in shaping and regulating professions in countries such as Germany and France should not negate the experience of professionalization there. As Magali Sarfatti Larson has recently observed, "there was and there is more than one model of professionalization."²²

Informed by the scholarship on the subject, this study will show that the concept of professionalization goes far to illuminate the dynamics of the interaction between Chinese professionals and the Republican state. At no time during the period under study did professions in Shanghai exhibit all three major attributes suggested by Ernest Greenwood. They would less qualify to be called professions if measured by more detailed lists of attributes. Yet, viewed from the perspective of professionalization as a process, the emergence and growth of Chinese professions can be properly regarded as the rise of a self-conscious professional community in Republican Shanghai and beyond. All Chinese professional groups under study strove to establish professional standards and obtain professional status and privileges recognized by the state and society at large, which is the essence of professionalization. And they did so by organizing and acting through professional associations, which is often a key feature in professionalization elsewhere. While there are different ways to explore the interaction between the Republican state and professional associations in Shanghai, professionalization was one of the most important elements in the dynamics.

The German experience in professionalization is especially relevant for comparison. Like its German counterpart, the Chinese state in the Republican era played a crucial role in promoting and regulating professions and was instrumental in the professionalization of several occu-

---

21. See Charles E. McClelland, *The German Experience*, p.7.
22. Magali Sarfatti Larson, "In the Matter of Experts and Professionals, or How Impossible It Is to Leave Nothing Unsaid," in Rolf Torstendahl and Michael Burrage, eds., *The Formation of Professions: Knowledge, State, and Strategy* (London, 1990), p.29. Thomas Broman has argued that for German physicians, professionalization was about defending, not gaining, the status and privilege they had enjoyed before the industrialization. Thus the assumption about professionalization as part of modernization needs to be reconsidered. See Thomas Broman, "Rethinking Professionalization: Theory, Practice, and Professional Ideology in Eighteenth-Century German Medicine," *The Journal of Modern History*, 67 (Dec. 1995):835–72. In my view, the German case here only indicates the variations and complexities of professionalization and modernization in different societies.

pational groups. Such a role was fully recognized and appreciated by professionals as indispensable to their goals. During 1916 to 1927 several warlord regimes succeeded one after another to lay claims to the central government in Beijing and none of them was stable. Nevertheless, Shanghai professionals were willing to support the claim to legitimacy by any regime, no matter who was in power at a particular time, in order to establish their own legitimacy and privilege as professionals in society through government sanction.

On the other hand, Chinese professionalization departed from the Western (both Anglo-American and continental European) experience significantly. One important difference is that once the legitimacy of professional associations was obtained, professional power was often used for more than professional purposes. The point is that actions of Chinese professionals were informed and conditioned by an intersection of two historical forces. One was professionalization as part of modernization and the other was a tradition of urban elite associations addressing social and political issues in the public arena, a tradition formed at least since the late Qing.[23]

As professional associations began to function socially and politically, they mediated between the state and societal interests on a different footing from that of traditional elite groups. While the contention of urban elite associations that they represented the public (*gong*) was nothing new in the Republican era, the status of professional associations as public bodies formally sanctioned by the government was vital.[24] That status strengthened the professional associations' position in no small measure to deflect state pressure as they functioned on a wide range of issues in the public arena. That "publicness" was signified by certain key words. In the Republican era, professional associations, along with trade guilds, chambers of commerce, educational societies, and other organizations sanctioned by the government, were subsumed

---

23. I use "public arena" in the sense defined by Rankin and Esherick: "An arena is the environment, the stage, the surrounding social space, often the locale in which elites and other societal actors are involved. Arenas may be either geographical (village, country, nation) or functional (military, educational, political); and the concept of an arena includes the repertory of values, meanings, and resources of its constituent actors." See Rankin and Esherick, eds., *Chinese Local Elites*, p.11.
24. For the shifting meaning of "public" (*gong*) and its contestation in late imperial and Republican China, see William T. Rowe, "Public Sphere in Modern China," *Modern China*, 16,3 (July 1990):314–19; Mary Rankin, "The Origins of a Chinese Public Sphere," *Etudes Chinoises* 9,2 (Autumn 1990):14–15.

Introduction

under the term *gongtuan* (public association) or *fatuan* (legally established association). Furthermore, professional associations always called themselves *gonghui* (public association), a term derived from *gongsuo*, which had long been used by trade guilds and native-place associations. Hence *lushi gonghui* (public association of lawyers) was used for the bar association, *yishi gonghui* for medical association, *kuaijishi gonghui* for accountants' association, and *xinwen jizhe gonghui* for journalists' association. One more term was invented: The amount lawyers and accountants charged their clients was called *gongfei* (public fees). The accentuated publicness came to pass with the unfolding of professionalization – a process by which individuals were recognized as belonging to a professional group, defined as a public-serving and public-minded group. The state and society at large generally acknowledged professionals holding such a status, even though the publicness of professional associations was gained through constant contestation and negotiation with the state. As far as Chinese professionals were concerned, therefore, professionalization was an integral part of state–society interaction.

STATE–SOCIETY RELATIONSHIP IN REPUBLICAN CHINA

In the past fifteen years or so, state–society relationship has been one of the central issues in the study of modern China. While social scientists are interested in the post-Mao reforms and the attendant developments in state–society and central–local relations (see the Conclusion of this book), historians have paid a great deal of attention to the rise of local elite activism in the late Qing (1860–1911) and the Republican era (1912–1949). Scholars have little disagreement on the empirical evidence of local elite activism during the period of 1860 to 1949, but they differ on whether that development should be understood as the rise of civil society and/or public sphere.[25] As Heath B. Chamberlain has summarized, scholars have generally dealt with the dilemma of applying

---

25. See William T. Rowe, "Public Sphere in Modern China," *Modern China*, 16,3 (July 1990):309–29; "Symposium on Civil Society and Public Sphere in Modern China," *Modern China*, 19,2 (Apr. 1993); Mary B. Rankin, "The Origins of a Chinese Public Sphere," *Etudes Chinoises*, 9,2 (Autumn 1990):13–60; Prasenjit Duara, *Rescuing History from the Nation* (Chicago, 1995), pp.147–75; Yves Chevrier, "La Question de la Société Civile, la Chine et le Chat du Cheshire," *Etudes Chinoises*, 14,3 (Autumn 1995):153–251.

Introduction

the Western-derived concepts to the Chinese scene in three ways, "to alter the concept to fit the landscape; to look for changes in the landscape to fit the concept; or to drop the concept entirely."[26] It is the view of this study that when the concept of civil society is defined as societal autonomy vis-à-vis the state, the concept is too limiting to capture the complexity of state–society relations in Republican China; however, an extended definition of the concept may lose its conceptualizing power and analytical rigor. Therefore, this study examines the concrete forms that various social groups adopted and the specific avenues that the social groups pursued to interact with the state. The intent of this approach is to reach a more accurate understanding of state–society relations in prewar China. Specifically, this study looks at the history of professional associations in Republican Shanghai.

First of all, the nature of professional associations in Republican Shanghai needs to be defined. Different from gentry-merchant organizations, professional associations did not belong to the kind of public sphere defined by Mary B. Rankin – "the institutionalized, extra-bureaucratic management of matters considered important by both the community and the state."[27] Professionals as either independent practitioners or salaried employees were individuals who used their expertise to serve the public and made their living as specialized experts. Professional associations were organized to protect a professional endeavor and promote professional interests or group interests. Professional organizations were ultimately important to the community (and the state) for their public functions, but they were not institutions for communal management or mechanisms for social mediation – as were many traditional urban elite organizations.

Shanghai professionals and their associations articulated their views on matters relating to their professional interests and on national issues through such means as newspapers, professional journals, public letters, circular telegrams, formal and informal professional meetings, and public rallies in concert with other urban associations. As those media of expression constituted a sphere of public discourses, one may consider professional associations' activities as a manifestation of a public sphere in the

---

26. Heath B. Chamberlain, "Civil Society with Chinese Characteristics," *China Journal*, 39 (Jan. 1998):69.
27. Mary B. Rankin, *Elite Activism and Political Transformation in China: Zhejiang Province, 1865–1911* (Stanford, 1986), p.15.

sense defined by Jürgen Habermas – if a public sphere can be conceptualized without reference to civil society.[28]

On the other hand, during the Republican period, professional associations were clearly not independent or autonomous institutions. As noted earlier, the rise of professions and professional associations in Shanghai cannot be separated from the role of the state. The characteristics of professional associations and the process of professionalization entailed government regulations aiming specifically at the professional associations. The Beiyang regimes (1912–1927), especially the Yuan Shikai government (1912–1916), did much of the institutional construction that promoted and regulated the legal profession. The GMD government in the Nanjing Decade (1928–1937) continued the Beiyang policy of promoting and regulating professions, though it changed the rules of the game. In Nanjing's drive to assert state power and create a corporatist state – a drive that was mostly felt in urban areas – Nanjing actively sought to mold and control the societal institutions that were emerging in modernizing cities. Public associations were allowed to exist, but only under the condition that they conform to the statutes and regulations issued by the GMD and accept the supervision of the GMD party and government agencies. Professional associations were subject to either professional regulations or generic statutes binding on all public associations.

Professional associations were not paralyzed by government regulation, however. They responded to the Republican state in a way not always shared by other social groups. Thanks to their professional and public status, they often managed to get around the state's efforts of control and manipulation by negotiating and accepting the terms under which they would operate. As a result, professional associations were able to act on a wide variety of issues in the public arena. Furthermore, the relationship between the state and societal institutions was not always a matter of society resisting state power. Professional associations often invited or sought out state intervention for the purpose of advancing their own interests. The interaction between professional groups and the Republican state was therefore multidimensional and sometimes even contradictory.

The dynamics in the interaction lay in the interdependence between the state and professions: A legitimate government could grant the pro-

---

28. Jürgen Habermas, *The Structural Transformation of the Public Sphere: An Inquiry into a Category of Bourgeois Society* (Cambridge, MA, 1989), pp.27–56.

fessional legitimacy, while the support of the professional would in turn help legitimate the state and contribute to its modernizing projects, including modern state building. The very act of professionals seeking their professional status and privileges through state sanction helped legitimate the Republican regimes. The importance of lawyers to the judicial system and of doctors to the public health system – two crucial areas of modern state building – is obvious. The ascendancy of journalism would have been a necessary condition for legitimating the expansion of a modern state even in a different historical context; it figured prominently in the GMD scheme that emphasized awakening and controlling the masses at the same time.[29] The mutual need between those professions and the state shaped the political culture of the time and fostered a negotiated mutual tolerance and cooperation between the Republican state and professions, from which both sides benefited to some degree.

In addition, the interaction between the two sides unfolded in the historical context of an inherent tension between modernization and nationalism in early-twentieth-century China. Shanghai, if not the whole China, was a semicolonial society dominated by foreign powers and divided into the Chinese Municipality, the International Settlement, and the French Concession. The International Settlement and the French Concession were under foreign administrations independent of Chinese authorities. To a certain degree, the rise of professional associations was a result of Chinese professionals consciously following the model of their Western counterparts. At the same time, the foreign privileges that were glaringly displayed in Shanghai conditioned the responses of Chinese professionals to many important issues.

But Chinese nationalism was not always about an "imagined community."[30] For Chinese professionals, nationalist sentiment and behavior were often reactions to the foreign dominance that affected their daily lives and material interests as individuals and as professional groups. The reactions were thus part of their mundane calculus of making a living and getting ahead socially and economically in their immediate social environ. For instance, Chinese lawyers spared no effort to deny foreign lawyers the right to practice in Chinese courts and Chinese cases. In the

---

29. For the "awakening" mission of the GMD, see John Fitzgerald, *Awakening China: Politics, Culture, and Class in the Nationalist Revolution* (Stanford, 1996).

30. This familiar term is from Benedict Anderson, *Imagined Communities: Reflection on the Origin and Spread of Nationalism* (London, 1991).

nationalist struggle against foreign privileges, Chinese professionals could and did work with the state. To complicate the matter further, Chinese nationalism was manifested in conflicts not only between Chinese and foreigners but also between different groups of Chinese affected by the Western presence and the modernization process. A prime example was the protracted battle between native physicians and Western-style doctors in the process of medical professionalization – a struggle that carried profound implications for China's path to modernity.

Modernizing projects (professionalization being one of them) entailed an increasingly insistent invocation by Chinese professionals of Western-derived notions in dealing with human affairs – notions that suited their understanding of professionalism and their agenda of professionalization. The rule of law and judicial independence were the standards that lawyers would carry, while freedom of speech and press was the battle cry for journalists. Conflicts arose when the state ostensibly accepted labels of modernization in rhetoric but denied their applicability to China in practice. Under such circumstances, the politicization of lawyers and journalists and their associations during the Republican era was hardly surprising.

It was, however, the national crisis brought forth by Japanese aggression in the 1930s that most directly prompted political actions of Shanghai professionals through their organizations. At that time there was a different kind of nationalism, one that arose from a sense of the Chinese nation – an imagined community if you will – being threatened. Professional groups' relationship with the state was very much strained by Nanjing's failure to respond to popular demand for anti-Japanese resistance. Yet, disillusioned and alienated as they were, during the period under study Shanghai professionals as a group did not challenge the state in a fundamental way. The overall political culture, social formation, and international environment during the period did not favor a full development of Chinese professionals or other groups in urban society as independent and effective political forces vis-à-vis the state.

It becomes clear by now that a "civil society" analytical framework would not fully account for all the complexity manifested in the history of Republican Shanghai in general and of Chinese professionals in particular. The rise of professional associations and other urban public organizations in the Republican era signified neither the decline of state power nor the growth of an autonomous civil society. Instead, both the state and societal institutions were expanding and interacting with each other in new public forms and representing new social interests in a changing environment. One may conceptualize the relationship between the Republican state and societal institutions as a symbiotic dynamics – an evolving process in which both the state and society were struggling to define themselves in relation to each other with overlapping and shifting boundaries. The story of Chinese professional associations in Shanghai was a meaningful part of the process.

Following this introduction, the rest of this book is organized in three parts and closes with a conclusion. Part I (Professions and Professionals) explores how modernization spawned new occupations and professions, and lays the groundwork for examining the process of professionalization. Chapter 1 describes the historical background for the rise of modern professions in Shanghai and estimates the size of the professional community in Shanghai during 1912 to 1937. Chapter 2 discusses, in comparison with some other social groups, the life experience of Shanghai professionals as an urban middle class–cum–professional class by looking into their income level, life-style, educational attainment, career pattern, social identity, and political orientation.

Part II (Social Institutions, State Actions, and Professionalization) examines the role of the Republican state, viewing state building and professionalization as two intertwined processes. Chapter 3 focuses on the way in which the state treated social organizations in the Beiyang period and the Nanjing Decade. Against the backdrop of the state's hostile attitude toward, and active regulation of, societal institutions, Chapter 4 describes how the state promoted and regulated the legal profession, and Chapter 5 discusses the relationship between the state and the medical profession.

Part III (Professionalism, Nationalism, and Politics) looks into the actions and reactions of three professional groups in their relations with both the state and society at large, unveiling several important elements in the symbiotic dynamics of state–society interaction. Chapter 6 traces how journalists grew out of the traditional category of "literary men" (*wenren*) to become professionals and illustrates how the national crisis of the 1930s not only helped politicize journalists in the national salvation movement but also reinforced their professionalization. Chapter 7 treats the history of medical professional associations in Shanghai by describing the conflict between Chinese native medicine and Western medicine. The tension between modernization and nationalism and the theme of fighting for group interests in the name of national interest

Introduction

figure prominently. Chapters 8 and 9 tell the story of the Shanghai Bar Association. Chapter 8 shows how, by insisting on the rule of law and judicial independence, the Shanghai Bar related the interests of the legal profession to nationalist aspirations and purposes. Chapter 9 explores the possibilities and limitations of the Shanghai Bar playing a political role as a professional association under an authoritarian state – illustrating a particular form of state–society interaction in Republican China.

The Conclusion considers the overall patterns of the state–society relationship in Republican China and highlights the continuity between that era and contemporary China.

This study mentions many social organizations in Republican China. The following rules are applied in translating their names:

1. If an organization used a formal English translation, that translation is used in this study. Hence the Shanghai Bar Association is used for *Shanghai lushi gonghui*, the Medical Practitioners' Association of Shanghai for *Shanghai yishi gonghui*, and the Institute of Chartered Accountants in Shanghai for *Shanghai kuaijishi gonghui*.
2. If an organization did not use a particular English translation, this study uses "association" for *xiehui* and *gonghui*, and "society" for *xuehui*. Hence the Shanghai Journalists Association is used for *Shanghai xinwen jizhe gonghui*, the Native Medical Association for *zhongyi xiehui*, and the Native Medical Society for *guoyi xuehui*. This study uses "society" or "association" for *hui* and *she*. Hence the Citizens' Association is used for *gongmin hui* and the Society for Promoting the Rule of Law is used for *fazhi xiejin hui*.

Part I

PROFESSIONS AND PROFESSIONALS

The story of Chinese professionals and their relationship with the Republican state is ultimately part of what is called China's modernization. One need not imply a grand theory of modernization, and one should be aware of the pitfall of measuring China with the Western experience. The question is not a theoretical question – why China failed to be like the West, or why China need not be like the West – but an empirical question – how China's development in the early twentieth century was conditioned by the China–West encounter regardless of what China would have evolved into without that encounter. In the empirical context, China's modernization refers to the kind of economic and political transformation first seen in the West but with all its complexities and ramifications rooted in the Chinese sociocultural environment.

To appreciate the nature of professionals and their role in urban society of Republican China, it is necessary to examine how the professionals emerged and became recognized as professionals in the course of modernization. Specifically, one needs to know how such professions were created, what institutional innovations were involved, and what kind of functions the professions served in Shanghai's economic, social, and cultural life. The emergence of professional groups in Shanghai had profound social implications far beyond their professional role. As a new social type, the professional represented a new kind of social configuration and class formation – that of a professional class–cum–urban middle class. One needs to place professionals in their social ecology to see their differences from and connections with other social groups and to understand their responses to and relationship with the state. A close look at how professionals lived in Republican Shanghai sheds light on what modernization meant, in concrete terms, for professionals as a social group and how economic transformation resulted in new kind of life chances and experience. What will be examined in Part I of this study will underscore the reason why Chinese professionals identified themselves, consciously and unconsciously, with modernization, and participated in modernizing projects, including state building, in the Republican era. From those efforts emerged conflict, compromise, and cooperation within an increasingly heterogeneous urban society and between that society and the Republican state.

1

Professions in Early-Twentieth-Century Shanghai

ALTHOUGH this book focuses on such professionals as lawyers, doctors, and journalists, the following historical survey includes a broad sketch of modern sectors of urban economy in Shanghai and new occupations associated with them. This sketch will link the growth of the legal, medical, and journalistic professions with the societywide economic transformation – a material foundation upon which the institutions related to law, medicine, and journalism were established. It will also show the economic, social, and cultural connections between the three professions and other professional or occupational groups that, though not *ziyou zhiye zhe*, could be included in the urban middle class, thus providing a wider backdrop to situate the professional groups in whom the study is most interested.

MODERN SECTORS OF SHANGHAI'S ECONOMY

Commerce

The city of Shanghai emerged from obscurity at the mouth of the Yangzi River primarily as a center of commerce. As early as the Song dynasty the commercial tax collected in Huating County – what was to become part of modern Shanghai – had exceeded the commercial tax collected in Suzhou, in addition to the wine and salt taxes that the government received from the area.[1]

To a large degree Shanghai owed its growing prosperity to the booming trade carried on by maritime and riverine transportation. The first government office in the area that was established during the Song

---

1. Tang Zhenchang, *Shanghai Shi* (A history of Shanghai) (Shanghai, 1989), pp.21–23.

period was a branch of the Shipping Administration (*shibo fensi*). More significantly, the maritime transportation of tribute grain was launched during the Yuan dynasty. Shanghai became a county in 1292 because of its pivotal role in that undertaking. From the Yuan period onward, five major shipping routes originated from Shanghai: (1) Ships sailed on the sea from Shanghai to various ports in Jiangsu, Shandong, and Liaoning Provinces to the north; (2) ships sailed on the sea from Shanghai to various ports in Zhejiang, Fujian, and Guangdong Provinces to the south. Ships also carried goods on (3) the Yangzi River and (4) other internal rivers between Shanghai and cities or towns in Jiangsu, Anhui, Jiangxi, Hubei, Hunan, and Sichuan Provinces. (5) Some ships sailed from Shanghai to places as far as Japan, Korea, and the Southeast Asian countries.[2]

The most important shipping business was the transportation of tribute grain by the sea route. The ship was called *shachuan* (sand ship), which cost seven thousand to eight thousand taels a piece to build. Owners of sand ships were the richest men in Shanghai at that time. In the mid-1820s, sand ships gathering in Shanghai each year numbered over three thousand.[3] The sand-ship trade flourished for several centuries until the 1870s when foreign steamships drove the sand-ship trade into a lingering recession and decline.[4] But the decline caused by foreign competition need not be exaggerated.[5]

Domestic trade along the Yangzi River and its tributaries between Shanghai and the interior was also active. Rhoads Murphey long ago pointed out the role of tea and silk, among other items, in traditional trade activity based on water transportation.[6] More recently Hanchao Lu and Linda C. Johnson showed the crucial role of cotton production and cotton trade in the development of Shanghai as a commercial city.[7]

---

2. Liu Huiwu, *Shanghai Jindai Shi* (A history of modern Shanghai) (Shanghai, 1989), pp.23–24.
3. Tang Zhenchang, *Shanghai Shi*, p.236.
4. Ibid., pp.237–39; Zhang Zhongli, *Jindai Shanghai Chengshi Yanjiu* (An urban study of modern Shanghai) (Shanghai, 1990), pp.190–200.
5. Thomas G. Rawski pointed out: "With the business lost to steamships and railways outweighed by new demands arising from expanding domestic trade and the collection and distribution services required by mechanized carriers, the predominant impact of new modes of water carriage was to increase traffic rather than displace unmechanized carriers." See *Economic Growth in Prewar China* (Berkeley, 1989), pp.207–8.
6. Rhoads Murphey, *Shanghai: Key to Modern China* (Cambridge, MA, 1953), pp.92–115.
7. Hanchao Lu, "Arrested Development: Cotton and Cotton Markets in Shanghai,

Long before Shanghai's official opening to Western trade in November 1843 under the Treaty of Nanjing, Shanghai merchants had already engaged in illicit import and export. Opium and other foreign goods were transferred to Shanghai from Fujian and Guangdong to move on to all parts of the Jiangnan region, while tea and silk arrived in Shanghai from neighboring provinces to be taken overseas.[8] The scale of that trade was small, though. After Shanghai opened as a treaty port in 1843, the city soon overtook Guangzhou to become the most important commercial emporium in China. The import and export trade dominated Shanghai's economy for the second half of the nineteenth century and early twentieth century.

The trade was largely in the hands of foreign commercial firms (*yanghang*). But the profit was not for foreigners alone to make. Chinese entrepreneurs quickly learned to take advantage of the difficulties that foreigners encountered in dealing with the Chinese language, especially its dialects, and with Chinese social customs and local markets. The Chinese shared the profit in three forms. First, Chinese compradors (*maiban*) and interpreters (*tongshi*) employed by foreign firms profited as brokers by securing handsome commissions and by using their foreign connections to run their own businesses.[9] Second, Chinese entrepreneurs established Chinese firms called *yangzhuang* (firms dealing in foreign goods) that specialized in wholesale transactions between foreign firms and the Chinese interior and thrived on the steady increase of imported goods and the growing opportunity for export.[10] Third, native banks (*qianzhuang*) that were traditionally important to commerce now found a new role to play. They became intimately involved in the trade between foreign firms and Chinese merchants who bought foreign goods with promissory notes issued by native banks.[11] Chinese native banks were so indispensable that "[n]ative bank paper till 1853, when the [Taiping] rebels came, was the main currency."[12] Ge Yuanxu informed readers in 1876 that there were over one hundred native banks in Shanghai's

---

1350–1843," *Modern China*, 8,4 (Oct. 1992):468–99; Linda C. Johnson, *Shanghai: From Market Town to Treaty Port, 1074–1858* (Stanford, 1995), pp.43–65.
8. Shanghai shehui kexueyuan jingji yanjiusuo, *Shanghai Duiwai Maoyi* (Shanghai's foreign trade) (Shanghai, 1989), pp.27–28.
9. *Shanghai Duiwai Maoyi*, pp.122–42, 149–54; Albert Feuerwerker, *The Chinese Economy, 1870–1949* (Ann Arbor, 1995), p.71.
10. *Shanghai Duiwai Maoyi*, pp.142–49.
11. Andrea L. McElderry, *Shanghai Old Style Banks (ch'ien chuang), 1800–1935* (Ann Arbor, 1976), p.3.
12. G. Lanning and S. Couling, *The History of Shanghai* (Shanghai, 1921), p.426.

foreign concessions and the walled Chinese city and that transactions in all commodities depended upon promissory notes from those banks, without which newly arrived merchants would have difficulty buying goods.[13] In such a pivotal position in Shanghai's commerce, native banks stood to make considerable profits.

By the turn of the century a new type of Chinese *yangzhuang* appeared, engaging in direct import and export, bypassing foreign firms. Small in scale and modest in operation, those firms struggled to carry on by dealing in nonessential goods and targeting secondary markets, in the face of the predominance of foreign firms. By the mid-1930s they numbered around three hundred and accounted for about 30 percent of all import and export firms in Shanghai.[14] They were operated and managed as Western-style enterprises and in accordance with the commercial rules and techniques learned from their foreign counterparts. Their owners were often former *yanghang* brokers, compradors, or old-type *yangzhuang* merchants.[15]

In a fundamental sense, therefore, commerce was the primary generator of Shanghai's modernization and was the main force that gave rise to Chinese modern enterprises and modern business executives. While foreign commercial firms spawned compradors, the Chinese counterparts begot native entrepreneurs. From the compradors and native entrepreneurs evolved an urban bourgeoisie or capitalist class by the early decades of the twentieth century. Less visible and less appreciated, but equally important, was a new social stratum of professional people – managers, technicians, clerks, brokers, accountants – that grew with the economic transformation of Shanghai. The same was true of other sectors surveyed in the following sections.

Manufacturing

Industrial manufacturing in Shanghai was born with the Self-Strengthening Movement in the 1860s. The establishment of the Jiangnan Arsenal (1865), the China Merchant Steam Navigation Company (1873), and the Shanghai Machine Weaving Plant (1878) marked the

13. Ge Yuanxu, *Huyou Zaji* (Random notes of the tour in Shanghai) (Shanghai, 1989), p.27. Ge did not exaggerate the number of *qianzhuang*. Shanghai had 123 *qianzhuang* in 1873 and 105 in 1876. See Sheng Mujie, "Jiu Shanghai Jinrongye Zongshu" (An overview of the finance industry in old Shanghai), *Jiu Shanghai De Jinrong Ye* (The financial world of old Shanghai) (Shanghai, 1988), pp.2–3.
14. *Shanghai Duiwai Maoyi*, pp.202–4, 221–45.   15. Ibid., p.233.

beginning of Shanghai evolving into an industrial city as well as a commercial center.[16] Plagued by poor management and confronted with competition from foreign goods and the foreign commercial establishment in China, the new Chinese manufacturing enterprises registered very few successes. The government-supervised, merchant-managed (*guandu shangban*) enterprises that characterized the early period of China's industrialization were thoroughly discredited with China's defeat in the Sino–Japanese War of 1894 to 1895. Ironically, the disastrous result of that war greatly stimulated China's economic transformation. One the one hand, the Treaty of Shimonoseki allowed the Japanese (and Westerners too, thanks to the most-favored-nation clause in the treaties between China and Western powers) to open factories in treaty ports, which triggered a wave of foreigners opening factories in Shanghai and elsewhere. On the other hand, the military defeat and national humiliation that China suffered in the war stirred Chinese entrepreneurs to build national industry with a new sense of urgency. A nationalist purpose was intertwined with business calculation and was conveniently utilized by Chinese business executives in their competition with imported foreign goods and foreign enterprises in China.[17]

In spite of foreign dominance, Chinese business executives made the best use of their resources (such as lower labor cost, familiarity with local markets, and social networks for financial and other support) to develop their enterprises.[18] In the period of 1895 to 1913, at least 549 Chinese manufacturing and mining enterprises were launched in China, along with 69 foreign-owned and 40 Sino–foreign joint enterprises, all heavily concentrated in Shanghai and Tianjin.[19] The First World War brought forth what Marie-Claire Bergère called "the golden age of the Chinese bourgeoisie," and Chinese business executives did not miss out on the opportunity. During 1914 to 1918, a total of 539 new Chinese enterprises appeared nationwide.[20] In Shanghai alone, 83 new Chinese factories were established.[21] National industrial growth continued well beyond the 1914–1918 period.[22]

16. Tang Zhenchang, *Shanghai Shi*, pp.256–75.
17. For discussions of Chinese nationalist capitalism, see Marie-Claire Bergère, *The Golden Age* and Sherman Cochran, *Big Business in China* (Cambridge, MA, 1980).
18. Marie-Claire Bergère, *The Golden Age*.
19. Albert Feuerwerker, *The Chinese Economy*, pp.44–53.
20. Du Xucheng, *Minzu Ziben Zhuyi Yu Jiu Zhongguo Zhengfu, 1840–1937* (Nationalist capitalism and the government of old China, 1840–1937) (Shanghai, 1991), p.107.
21. Tang Zhenchang, *Shanghai Shi*, p.527.
22. Thomas G. Rawski, *Economic Growth*.

Both Chinese- and foreign-owned enterprises contributed to Shanghai's industrialization. In 1933, out of the national manufacturing output of 2,645.5 million yuan, Chinese enterprises in Shanghai claimed 727.7 million yuan and foreign firms in Shanghai claimed 323.3 million yuan. In other words, Chinese- and foreign-owned enterprises in Shanghai made up 39.7 percent of the national output in manufacturing.[23] A survey published in 1937 showed that out of 2,435 Chinese-owned factories with a total capital of 406,926,634 yuan in the country, 1,186 were located in Shanghai.[24] In 1934 Shanghai had a total of 5,418 factories; 2,540 of them had a combined capital of 478,293,341 yuan and 3,893 of them had a total of 299,585 workers.[25] Another source put the total number of factories in Shanghai's International Settlement and the Chinese sections in 1935 at 6,097 and that of workers at 416,368.[26] The discrepancy in these statistics seems to result from different standards used to determine what size of a manufacturing establishment qualified as a factory. In any case, during 1912 to 1937 Shanghai emerged as the preeminent industrial center in China.

Banking, Finance, and Insurance

From the beginning, foreign trade in China was hampered by the difficulty of obtaining credit. Although Chinese native banks, and to some extent compradors, played a crucial role in facilitating the trade by providing credit for Chinese merchants, they were far from meeting the growing financial needs of foreign business executives. For a while, along with the businesses of wholesale, shipping, and insurance, most foreign commercial firms in Shanghai performed exchange and credit functions. But that situation failed to satisfy the need of the foreign commercial establishment for trade expansion in the latter half of the nineteenth century. In response to that need, the first foreign bank, a branch of the Oriental Banking Corporation, was opened in Shanghai in 1848. Other foreign banks soon followed suit, including a branch of the Hong Kong and Shanghai Banking Corporation that opened in 1865.[27] Around the turn of the century, a number of foreign banks were set up along or near

---

23. Ibid., p.74, Table 2.3.   24. Albert Feuerwerker, *The Chinese Economy*, p.102.
25. *Shanghai Shehui Tongji Gaiyao* (Shanghai, 1935), pp.41–42.
26. Rhoads Murphey, *Shanghai*, pp.167–69.
27. Liu Hiuwu, *Shanghai Jindai Shi*, pp.202–3.

the Bund.[28] Between 1847 and 1911 a total of twenty-seven foreign banks settled in Shanghai.[29]

Chinese financiers too assumed an increasingly important role in Shanghai's economic life. Chinese native banks continued to operate throughout the prewar period.[30] During 1912 to 1927 the number of native banks in Shanghai increased from eighteen to eighty-seven. Native banks' indispensable role in import and export trade, flexibility in transactions, convenient business hours, willingness to deal with small business firms, and long-established credibility with both foreign and Chinese merchants allowed native banks to complement and exist side by side modern banks. Although during the Nanjing Decade native banks experienced difficulty due to several factors beyond their control, they remained a player in Shanghai's economy. The number of native banks was reduced from eighty-five to forty-six during the decade, but the total capital of those banks stayed at over nineteen million yuan. In other words, a process of concentration and consolidation took place in the circle of native banks.[31]

In the meantime, the period from the late Qing to the 1930s witnessed the birth and growth of Chinese modern banks. The Chinese Commercial Bank (*zhongguo tongshang yinhang*) was founded in Shanghai in 1897. The bank strictly modeled itself after the Hong Kong and Shanghai Banking Corporation in its management and operation and hired foreigners as managers at its branches in various cities.[32] In the following thirteen years, sixteen Chinese banks went into business, ten of which had their headquarters or branches located in Shanghai. Among them were the Bank of the Board of Revenue (*hubu yinhang*) (1905) and the Bank of Communications (1908). The former was to become the Bank of China in 1912.[33] From 1912 to 1920 another nineteen Chinese banks were opened in Shanghai.[34] By 1935 seventy-three Chinese banks, twenty-four foreign banks, two Chinese–foreign joint banks, and fifty-

---

28. Tang Zhenchang, *Shanghai Shi*, p.369.   29. Sheng Mujie, "Jiu Shanghai," pp.7–10.
30. *Minguo Shanghai Xianzhi* (MSX) (Gazetteer of Shanghai County in the Republic), Juan 5, pp.7–8; Thomas G. Rawski, *Economic Growth*, pp.140–41; Andrea L. McElderry, *Shanghai Old Style Banks*, Chapter 7.
31. SYZX, pp.691–94; Du Xucheng, *Minzu Ziben Zhuyi*, pp.169–88, 232, 236; Thomas G. Rawski, *Economic Growth*, pp.139–45.
32. SYZ, pp.268–72; Chen Zehao, "Zhongguo Tongshang Yinhang Shimo" (The story of the Chinese Commercial Bank), *Jiu Shanghai De Jinrong Ye*, pp.194–202; Du Xucheng, *Minzu Ziben Zhuyi*, p.202.
33. Tang Zhenchang, *Shanghai Shi*, pp.372–73.   34. MSX, Juan 6, pp.9–13.

four native banks operated side by side in Shanghai. In addition, there were such banking and credit service institutions as trust companies (*xintuo gongsi*), savings associations (*chuxu hui*), silver exchange companies (*yinhao* or *yin gongsi*), public assessment bureaus (*gonggu ju*), and silver-melting firms (*yinlu*).[35] Chinese native banks and modern banks worked together to finance Chinese enterprises and bankers of both types developed close financial and personal relationships between them.[36]

Stock exchanges constituted an important part of the financial enterprise in Shanghai. Chinese entrepreneurs took an interest in stock trade as early as the 1860s. In 1882 the Shanghai Equity and Precision Stock Company (*Shanghai pingzhun gupiao gongsi*) appeared, marking the beginning of Chinese public stock trading.[37] During the first decade of the twentieth century, Chinese enterprises, especially railroad companies born of the Railroad Rights Movement, issued stocks; Chinese brokers in Shanghai had a big time. The brokers traded stocks and other securities every morning at the so-called tea gatherings (*chahui*) in the Huifang Tea House at the intersection of the Fourth Road (later *Fuzhou lu*) and Daxin Jie (*Hubei lu*). By 1914 those brokers had established a trade association: the Shanghai Stock Trade Association (*Shanghai gupiao shangye gonghui*). They dealt in stocks, foreign currencies, railroad bonds, and government bonds, but their trading method remained traditional – working out deals at the tea gatherings. Furthermore, almost all brokers engaged in stock trading as a sideline, while holding other jobs or running other businesses at the same time. Chinese newspapers treated stock trading as shady business, usually refusing to carry reports of stock prices. Chinese stock trading was still in its infancy.[38]

The first formal stock exchange in Shanghai was the Shanghai Shareholders Association established by British merchants in 1891. It changed into the Shanghai Stock Exchange in 1905 and hired 100 brokers including 13 Chinese. It existed until December 1941 when the Japanese took over the foreign concessions at the outbreak of the Pacific War. The next stock exchange to appear in Shanghai was the Japanese-owned Shang-

---

35. SYZX, pp.217–87, 686–91; MSX, pp.8–21.
36. Thomas G. Rawski, *Economic Growth*, pp.132–45.   37. SYZ, pp.283–84.
38. Deng Huasheng, "Jiu Shanghai De Zhengjuan Jiaoyi Suo" (Stock exchanges in old Shanghai), *Jiu Shanghai De Jinrong Ye*, pp.319–22; Chen Zhengshu, "Shanghai Huashang Zhengjuan Jiaoyisho De Chuangli Yu Yinxiang" (The establishment and impact of the Shanghai Chinese Merchant Stock Exchange), *Shanghai Shi Yanjiu* (The Shanghai history studies), No.2 (Shanghai, 1988), pp.254–57.

hai Stock Exchange (*Shanghai quyin suo*), formed in March 1918. It invited Chinese merchants such as Wang Yiting, Jin Xizhi, and Hu Mei'an to sit on the board of directors and employed other Chinese for key positions. Due to competition from the Chinese stock exchanges and government regulation, the Japanese-owned Shanghai Stock Exchange closed its door by 1929.[39]

Although various gentry-merchant groups in Shanghai made plans for establishing formal Chinese stock exchanges, none of those plans materialized before the 1920s. Finally, stimulated in part by the opening of the Japanese-owned Shanghai Stock Exchange in 1918, a group of Chinese business executives launched the Shanghai Stock and Produce Exchange (SSPE) (*Shanghai zhengjuan wuping jiaoyisuo*) in 1920. The SSPE adopted all operating methods and rules from the Japanese-owned exchange and had its brokers trained by two Japanese professionals hired from Nagoya, Japan. Housed in a building at the intersection of Sichuan Road and Edward VII Road (*Yan'an donglu*), the SSPE set up four departments and one general office, with thirty-nine brokers dealing in securities, cotton, cotton yarn, gold, and silver.[40]

The year of 1920 saw the formation of another Chinese exchange, the Shanghai Chinese Merchants Stock Exchange (SCMSE) (*Shanghai huashang zhengjuan jiaoyisuo*). It was an outgrowth of the Shanghai Stock Trade Association. The members of the association founded the SCMSE after rejecting the co-optation attempt on the part of the SSPE. Those old-timers deliberately put the words "Chinese Merchant" (*huashang*) in the name of the exchange to distinguish themselves from the British- and Japanese-owned exchanges and from the SSPE, which had close Japanese connections. Former members of the stock trade association became the shareholders as well as brokers of the SCMSE. Established on the Hankou Road in May 1920, the exchange was open to business in January 1921, with fifty-five brokers.[41]

In addition to the previously mentioned security exchanges, Shanghai boasted several commodity exchanges. Trading in gold started during the Guangxu reign of the Qing dynasty. In 1905 over thirty gold shops formed the Gold Trade Association (*jinye gongsuo*). Due to the speculative activities and resultant bankruptcy among gold shops, trading in

---

39. Deng Huasheng, "Jiu Shanghai," pp.322–23.
40. Deng Huasheng, "Jiu Shanghai," pp.324–27; *Jiu Shanghai De Zhengjuan Jiaoyisuo* (Stock exchanges in old Shanghai) (Shanghai, 1992), pp.339–41.
41. Deng Huasheng, "Jiu Shanghai," pp.332–35; *Jiu Shanghai De Zhengjuan Jiaoyisuo*, pp.341–43.

gold was once banned by the Shanghai authorities in 1907 but apparently survived or revived in the Republic. By 1917 the Gold Trade Association was reorganized under the government regulations on industrial and commercial associations, eventually leading to the formation of the Shanghai Gold Exchange in 1920 (*Shanghai jinye jiaoyisuo*).[42] Other institutions included the Shanghai Chinese Merchant Cotton Goods Exchange on Avenue Edward VII, the Shanghai Flour Exchange, and the Shanghai Provision Exchange (*Shanghai zaliang youping jiaoyisuo*) in the Chinese city (the Flour Exchange and Provision Exchange partially operated on the upper floor of the Cotton Goods Exchange).[43] In October 1929 the Nanjing government enacted the Law on Stock Exchanges. Under the law, one business district could have no more than one exchange dealing in the same kind of commodities and securities. As a result, the SSPE was dissolved and its operations were incorporated into the SCMSE, the Gold Exchange, and the Cotton Goods Exchange.[44]

Throughout the Republican period speculation was a major driving force of the business at all the exchanges. At the Cotton Goods Exchange, for instance, only 10 percent of the transactions were genuine, while the rest were speculative activities. At the SCMSE about 70 percent of the transactions were speculative.[45] Mao Dun (Shen Yanbin), the prominent writer in the Republican era, hardly needed any exaggeration to describe the speculative fever in Shanghai's stock exchanges when he wrote the famous novel *Midnight*.

The description of Shanghai's financial institutions would not be complete without mentioning insurance companies. The earliest foreign commercial firms already provided insurance for business transactions, especially those involving transportation. From the 1880s onward, foreign insurance companies began to appear in Shanghai and expand their businesses to Chinese residents as well as foreign residents.

Chinese insurance business started with the China Merchants Steam Navigation Company in 1875. The company provided insurance for the passengers and cargo carried by its ships in order to compete with foreign shipping companies that offered similar insurance. In 1882 the first private Chinese insurance company, the Shanghai Fire Insurance

---

42. SYZ, pp.281–83.   43. *Jiu Shanghai De Zhengjuan Jiaoyisuo*, pp.343–53.
44. Deng Huasheng, "Jiu Shanghai," p.332; for the law, see *Jiu Shanghai De Zhengjuan Jiaoyisuo*, pp.294–300.
45. CWR, 48,4 (3/23/1929):158.

Company, was launched. It remained the only Chinese insurance company in Shanghai until the first decade of the twentieth century when several Chinese companies went into business. Between 1912 and 1927 twenty more Chinese insurance companies entered the competitive insurance market in Shanghai.[46]

The Chinese Safety United Life Insurance Company (*huaan hequn renshou baoxian gongsi*) was among the most successful Chinese insurance companies in Shanghai. Lü Yuequan, the founder of the company, was born in Nanhui, Jiangsu, in 1877. Initially a salesperson for a British insurance company, Lü quickly rose to the position of the manager at the company's branch in Nanjing. In 1912 Lü quit the British firm to found his own insurance company, with a capital of twenty thousand taels gathered from a number of Shanghai gentry-merchant investors. Due to the lack of trained Chinese experts, Lü initially employed foreigners as managers and appraisers, but by the 1920s he was able to find Chinese experts trained in the United States. Starting in 1924, Lü also trained and selected prospective employees through correspondence courses that reached people in places as far as Yunnan. Over the years the company selected forty-seven people from more than six hundred prospective employees trained through correspondence courses. By 1931 the Chinese Safety United had branches in thirty-five cities across the country and invested in real estate, stocks, and government bonds.[47]

During the Nanjing Decade, a few more insurance companies entered the market. The Great Peace Insurance Company (*taiping baoxian gongsi*) represented the more successful ones. Established by the Jincheng Bank in 1929 with one million yuan as initial capital and joined by five more banks by 1933, the company's capital was expanded to five million yuan. The success of the Great Peace was attributed to four factors. First, the company waged relentless advertising campaigns. The company's branches and their agencies and the company's six mother banks and their agencies, numbering more than nine hundred across the country, all advertised for the company and sold insurance policies. The company logo, the *yinyang* sign, and its commercial slogan, "Great Peace Insurance, Insures Great Peace," were seen everywhere. Second, the company employed respectable and resourceful people in local society as managers at its headquarters in Shanghai and branches in various

---

46. Du Xucheng, *Minzu Ziben Zhuyi*, pp.523–28.
47. Gong Huibai, "Hua'an Hequn Baoshou Gongsi" (Hua'an United Life Insurance Company), *Jiu Shanghai De Jinrong Ye*, pp.294–301.

provinces and cities. Those people were not necessarily experts in the business of insurance, but they had wide connections in industrial and commercial circles to develop profitable clientele. Third, the company devoted attention to recruiting and training capable employees. It selected over one hundred employees from college and middle school graduates by examinations and then put those employees through further training. All of them became key operatives of the company. Fourth, the company aggressively took over other insurance companies. In 1933 and 1934 the company bought three insurance companies at low prices, but kept their names and retained most of their employees. Thus the Great Peace actually operated four insurance companies and utilized one management system to run them all. The Great Peace was said to be the first Chinese insurance company to adopt such a monopolistic approach to business expansion learned from the United States.[48]

Transportation and Communications

In the second half of the nineteenth century, foreign firms in China repeatedly proposed the construction of railroad and telegraph lines. But the Qing government turned down all the proposals and plans. Frustrated, foreign business groups built a telegraph line in 1873 and a railroad between Wusong and Shanghai in 1876 without the permission of the Chinese authorities. Before long the telegraph line was sabotaged by local people who believed the line had a negative effect on their families' *fengshui* (geomancy), while the railroad was purchased for 285 thousand taels and then dismantled by the Qing government.[49]

Not until the 1880s did Chinese officials in favor of Western-style industrialization prevail over the conservatives, and telegraph lines begin to be built. By 1884 telegraph lines had linked twenty-seven cities and the Telegraph Bureau headquarters moved from Tianjin to Shanghai. By the early twentieth century, telegraph lines not only linked most provinces in the country, but also reached Japan, Singapore, the Philippines, the United States, and European countries.[50]

Railroad construction started in 1898 with the rebuilding of the

---

48. Wang Boheng, "Cong Taiping Baoxian Gongsi Dao Taipingyang Baoxian Gongsi" (From the Great Peace Insurance Company to the Pacific Insurance Company), *Jiu Shanghai De Jinrong Ye*, pp.281–83.
49. Zhang Zhongli, *Jindai Shanghai*, pp.236–38.   50. Ibid., pp.242–44.

railway between Wusong and Shanghai.⁵¹ The railroad covered 10,506 kilometers by 1915 and 20,746 kilometers by 1936.⁵² Due to the extensive water transportation system available, railway connections between Shanghai and other parts of the country did not develop in any impressive fashion.⁵³

Maritime transportation remained crucial to Shanghai's economy. In the mid-1920s twenty-five steamship lines served the port of Shanghai with regular services. Seven of these connected with ports in the United States, sixteen with ports in Europe, and two with the Philippines. More lines provided occasional services. In 1924 the port registered over 32.5 million tons of steamships entering and leaving, of which nearly 27 million tons (11,652 ships) were classified as ocean vessels. The cargo moving in and out of the port annually amounted to over 10 million tons.⁵⁴

The development of transportation helped the modernization of postal service. Since the Ming dynasty, traditional China had been known for the extensive courier service (*yichuan*) administered by the imperial government and private letter agencies, but those systems became increasingly inadequate for the Chinese society undergoing modernization. Foreigners in Shanghai and other treaty ports had set up their own postal services under consulates since the mid-1840s. Meanwhile the Shanghai Municipal Council (SMC) of the International Settlement established the Shanghai Local Post in 1864 with branches in other treaty ports and with its own stamps. In addition, the British-administered Chinese Maritime Customs also ran postal departments that issued their own stamps and cooperated with the Local Post in delivering mails.⁵⁵ Not until 1896, after repeated efforts, did the Zongli Yamen and Robert Hart, the director of the Maritime Customs, finally succeed in persuading the Qing court to approve the establishment of a Chinese postal service headquartered in Shanghai.⁵⁶

After the 1911 Revolution the traditional courier service was abolished and the national postal service developed quickly during the fol-

---

51. Zhang Zhongli, *Jindai Shanghai*, pp.236–49.
52. Thomas G. Rawski, *Economic Growth*, p.209, Table 4.7.
53. Rhoads Murphey, *Shanghai*, pp.89–90.
54. "The Port Problems of Shanghai," *The North China Trade Review*, NCH, 3/17/1926, p.25.
55. Ying-wan Cheng, *Postal Communication in China and Its Modernization, 1860–1896* (Cambridge, MA, 1970), pp.52–58.
56. Ying-wan Cheng, *Postal Communication*, pp.98–100.

lowing decades. In 1916 the postal service operated with a profit for the first time, and the revenue continued to increase in subsequent years. The postal service was administered by foreigners who numbered 101 in 1917, along with 25,000 Chinese employees.[57] Since the service was successful, foreign powers agreed to end their separate postal services in December 1922.[58]

In August 1928 the GMD government appointed Liu Shufan as the director-general of the postal service – the first Chinese to hold that position – and issued a new set of regulations on postal service.[59] In April 1929 Nanjing further decreed that Chinese, instead of English, be the official language of the Chinese postal service, effectively ending the dominance of foreigners in the service.[60] Under Chinese management the postal service continued to be the most efficient and financially sound state-run agency. By the mid-1930s the postal service operated 2,469 post offices with 37,036 employees, in addition to 10,183 postal agencies (shopkeepers performing postal duties), and handled 573 million articles of mail matter posted in 1935.[61] The postal service in Shanghai grew at such a quick pace, especially after taking over foreign postal services in 1922, that the old post office building was no longer adequate. In 1924 a new post office building was built at a cost of around 2.25 million taels. The new building, called a "magnificent structure" by the *North China Herald*, was located at the corner of North Suzhou Road and North Sichuan Road on the north side of the Suzhou Creek. The building served as an eloquent testimony to the rapid development of the postal service in Shanghai and in the country.[62]

Professional Employees in Shanghai's Modern Sectors

The institutional and material changes in Shanghai's infrastructure gave rise to new occupations and professions, creating a demand for technicians, engineers, managers, accountants, telephone operators, secretaries, brokers, bank tellers, salespersons, and service personnel of all kinds. By whatever standards one may make the cut, a large portion of the people occupying those positions would qualify as professional employees – some being self-employed professionals – or as white-collar workers who

---

57. NCH, 11/24/1917, p.471; 10/26/1918, p.239.   58. NCH, 8/30/1924, pp.325–26.
59. NCH, 9/1/1928, p.351.   60. CWR, 48,7 (4/13/1929):278.
61. NCH, 5/8/1935, p.205; 7/8/1936, p.81.
62. NCH, 6/21/1924, p.456; 11/22/1924, p.325; 12/5/1924, p.406.

were at the lower end of the urban middle class and blended into the working class. From the preceding survey, it is clear that both Chinese and foreign entrepreneurs were involved in training and developing the work force of professional employees and white-collar workers vital to Shanghai's modernization. The growth of the legal, medical, and journalistic professions would have been unimaginable without the existence of that work force and the modern sector in Shanghai.

While the development of the Chinese working class and bourgeoisie in Shanghai is well documented, information on the growing number of professional employees and white-collar workers in Shanghai's modern sectors is sketchy at best.[63] Having surveyed the economic and institutional transformation, this study now attempts an estimation of the number of professional employees and white-collar workers in those sectors to sense the demographic dimension of the changes outlined.

According to the occupation statistics in the Shanghai yearbook of 1935, which only covered the population of the Chinese sections in Shanghai, among 1,711,983 working people, 23,535 people were employed in the sector of transportation and 185,912 people engaged in commerce. Because transportation and commerce included many occupations, from the number of people in those two sectors this study is unable to tell how many people were merchants or managers and how many were laborers or clerks. But the relative size of the two groups (1.37 percent and 10.86 percent of the active population in the Chinese sections respectively) at least indicates the weight of the two sectors in Shanghai's economy.[64]

For the purpose of this study, the census conducted in 1935 by the SMC of the International Settlement is more useful. It gave a detailed occupational breakdown for the Chinese population in the Settlement. In the sector labeled "trade," the census did not differentiate owners and employees, but did indicate the following: 351 advertising agents; 2,539 commission agents; 5,183 druggists; 401 employment agents; and 3,439 salespeople. In Republican Shanghai those categories may not have been exactly what they would be in the West – the SMC tried to categorize

---

63. One rare study of Chinese professional employees and white-collar workers is Wen-hsin Yeh, "Corporate Space, Communal Time: Everyday Life in Shanghai's Bank of China," *American Historical Review*, 100,1 (Feb. 1995):97–122.
64. *Shanghaishi Nianjian* (Shanghai municipal yearbook) (1935), pp.C24–25; the numbers in the *Shenbao Nianjian* (Shenbao yearbook) of 1935 are slightly different in these categories.

Chinese occupational groups by using Western concepts – but still those groups represented some of the professional employees and white-collar workers in the sector of trade.

Similarly, in the banking and insurance sector the SMC's 1935 census shows 1,439 brokers and 9,165 staff. In the industrial sector the census shows 32 surveyors, 29 statisticians, 918 engineers, and 435 mining engineers; in the transportation and communications sector, 36 aviators, 166 omnibus company staff, 886 railway staff, 342 telegraphists, 311 telephone operators and staff, 359 wireless operators, and about 100 tramway officials (estimated from a total of 1,039 officials and workers). The census shows 1,434 accountants and 3,627 clerks for all sectors.[65] In other words, professional employees and white-collar workers in industry, banking, transportation, and communications added up to no less than 19,579 people, or 9.56 percent of the employed Chinese (204,849) in the International Settlement in 1935. If those in the same occupations who resided in the French Concession and the Chinese sections are added, the number for those occupations in 1935 is around 28,000 people. The amount may not be an impressive number, but the importance of those people to the functioning of the economy in Shanghai was certainly much more than their percentage in the population.

More important, while the dearth of sources on those people does not allow any systematic study of their role in Shanghai's urban life (not in this study anyway), the preceding demographic sketch helps contextualize the professional groups called *ziyou zhiye zhe* and the new social class formation they represented. Because the professional employees and white-collar workers in Shanghai's modern sectors were the closest social and occupational peers to lawyers, doctors, and journalists, the notion of an urban middle class would have to include those people, the internal stratification among them notwithstanding. On the other hand, as the study looks at *ziyou zhiye zhe* as a professional class defined by their professional status and concerns, the difference between that category and other social groups including many professional employees was also obvious. A consideration of the relationship between *ziyou zhiye zhe* and the state must take into account the connections and differences between *ziyou zhiye zhe* and other social groups both within and outside the urban middle class. Bearing in mind these points, the study now turns to the development of law, medicine, and journalism.

65. SMC, *Report for the Year 1935 and Budget for the Year 1936* (1936), pp.56–58.

Professions in Early-Twentieth-Century Shanghai

LAW, MEDICINE, AND JOURNALISM IN SHANGHAI

Judicial System

Traditional China knew no independent judicial system, perhaps with the exception of the central government. Practically every chief administrator at the provincial, prefecture, and county level performed judicial as well as administrative functions. Indeed, there was neither conceptual nor institutional separation between those two functions. Foreign observers had long criticized features of traditional Chinese judicial process, such as bribery, confession through torture, cruelty in the yamen and prisons, and barbaric methods of punishment. Those practices were cited as the justification for extraterritoriality, an important element of the unequal treaties imposed upon China by foreign powers in the nineteenth century.

Toward the late nineteenth century quite a few Chinese reformers proposed legal reform as a way to strengthen the nation. After the Qing court began the New Policy reform in the first decade of the twentieth century, legal and judicial reform was proposed as part of constitutionalism.[66] In 1907 the Qing government enacted the Organic Law of Judicial Courts (*Fayuan bianzhifa*) and the Provisional Regulations on High and Lower Courts (*Geji shenpanting shiban zhangcheng*). In 1910 the Qing enacted the Currently Applied Criminal Code of Great Qing (*Daqing xianxing xinglu*), which was revised on the basis of the Criminal Code of Great Qing (*Daqing luli*).[67] Those reforms marked the beginning of a modern judiciary in China. Under those laws a court system began to be established and judicial process institutionalized. By 1912 a total of 345 courts had been in place nationwide, including a Supreme Court (*daliyuan*) in the capital, high courts at the provincial level, and district courts in major cities, each with their corresponding procuratorates.[68]

The Republic inherited the system and moved further in the direction of reform. The establishment of modern courts and prisons continued, and new laws were promulgated. By 1926 the government had issued

---

66. Marinus J. Meijer, *The Introduction of Modern Criminal Law in China* (Arlington, VA, 1976), pp.38–43; Meribeth E. Cameron, *The Reform Movement*, pp.100–135.
67. Marinus J. Meijer, *The Introduction*, pp.40–41; Yang Honglie, *Zhongguo Falü Fada Shi* (A History of the development of Chinese laws) (Shanghai, 1990), pp.868–1028; Meribeth E. Cameron, *The Reform Movement*, pp.171–75.
68. *China Yearbook, 1913*, pp.396–97.

twelve ordinances concerning the civil code, eight ordinances concerning the criminal code, fifteen ordinances concerning judicial procedures, four sets of regulations concerning judicial administration, and eleven other laws and ordinances. In 1926 there were 995 judges in service in the country and qualifications for such post were rigorously enforced.[69] In September 1912 the Ministry of Justice issued the Provisional Regulations on Lawyers (*Lüshi zanxing zhangcheng*), thus officially establishing the legal profession for the first time in Chinese history. The regulations were amended and revised several times through 1927.[70] During the Nanjing Decade judicial reform continued, but failed to achieve its major goal of establishing courts in all counties through out the country.

At the beginning of the period of this study, Shanghai had three courts: the District Court of Shanghai in the Chinese Municipality and the two Mixed Courts – one in the International Settlement and one in the French Concession. The two Mixed Courts were partially returned to the Chinese authorities in 1927 and the International Mixed Court was reorganized as the Provisional Court. But foreign consuls retained the right to sit at and observe trials in the two Mixed Courts. A further reform took place in 1930. Both the Provisional Court and the French Mixed Court were integrated into the Chinese judicial system, becoming the First Special District Court and the Second Special District Court respectively. At the same time, the Second Branch and the Third Branch of the Jiangsu High Court were instituted as the appellate courts for the two special district courts, while the Jiangsu High Court, located in Suzhou, remained the appellate court for the Shanghai District Court.[71]

Throughout the late imperial period, litigation played an important part in Chinese social and economic life.[72] Lawsuits were especially common in Shanghai – a commercial center and a treaty port. The division of Shanghai into the International Settlement, the French Concession, and the Chinese Municipality provided a safe haven for criminals

---

69. Yao-tseng Chang, "The Present Conditions of the Chinese Judiciary and Its Future," CSPSR, 10,1 (Jan. 1926):163–71; Yang Honglie, *Zhongguo Falu*, pp.1029–1243.
70. Yao-tseng Chang, "The Present Conditions," pp.174–75; Yu-chuan Chang, "The Legal Practitioner in China," CSPSR, 22,2 (July–Sept. 1938):145–48.
71. For more on the evolution of the Mixed Courts, see Chapter 8.
72. See Melissa Macauley, *Social Power and Legal Culture: Litigation Masters in Late Imperial China* (Stanford, 1998); Philip C. C. Huang, *Civil Justice in China: Representation and Practice in the Qing* (Stanford, 1996); Kathryn Bernhardt and Philip Huang, eds., *Civil Law in Qing and Republican China* (Stanford, 1994).

who took advantage of the division among the three jurisdictions. A corrupt police force in each jurisdiction made the matter worse. The division of Shanghai was a major reason why crime abounded and the criminal underworld thrived in Shanghai.[73]

On the other hand, however, within the International Settlement and the French Concession there existed the rule of law and due process close to those practiced in the West. Having been long exposed to those notions and practices, Chinese residents in Shanghai became accustomed to them and those living in the foreign concessions had resorted to lawsuit in a Western fashion before the judicial reform started in 1907. It is no accident that after the founding of the Republic the sole experiment with jury trial in the country took place in the Shanghai District Court in the spring of 1912.[74] It was in this sense that Yao Gonghe observed in 1917:

> The Chinese residing in the International Settlement have numbered 800,000. Although they are still unspeakably low in knowledge and [educational] level, under the influence of British custom, their habit of following the law is superior to [the people in] the interior. For instance, the country began to have courts of justice after the founding of the Republic, but eight or nine out of ten average citizens would be stupefied by the question of what is a civil case and what is a criminal case. Whereas residents in the Settlement, even if women or children, all know that cases of murder, robbery, brawling should be reported to the police, and cases of debt to the Mixed Court.... [In the interior] officials bully the people and the people dare not resort to the law, whereas the residents in the Settlement all know that detaining people without warrant is kidnapping, and a kidnapper, whether an official or a common person, would be punished.[75]

Yao's comments betrayed a sense of superiority as a Shanghai resident over "uninformed" and "unsophisticated" people in the interior, a sense to which Shanghai people, especially the educated, were prone. Never-

---

73. Su Zhiliang and Chen Feili, *Jindai Shanghai Hei Shehui Yanjiu* (A study on modern Shanghai's underworld) (Hangzhou, 1991), pp.46–58; Flederic Wakeman Jr., *Policing Shanghai*; Bryan G. Martin, *The Shanghai Green Gang*.
74. The experiment was found unsatisfactory and trial by jury was abandoned. See NCH, 1/11/1913, p.75; 8/9/1919, pp.326, 369–70; CWR, 21,12 (8/19/1922):451.
75. Yao Gonghe, *Shanghai Xianhua* (Leisured talk about Shanghai) (Shanghai, 1989), p.46.

theless, Yao did point out a fact – the difference between people in Shanghai and those in the interior in understanding the rule of law and the way a modern judicial system operated.

Moreover, the dense population in an urban environment and the hundreds and thousands of financial and commercial transactions taking place in Shanghai every day tended to breed all kinds of civil and criminal cases between foreigners, between the Chinese and foreigners, and between the Chinese. In 1932 the courts in Shanghai accepted a total of 34,985 civil cases and disposed of 27,884, leaving 7,101 cases to be tried. For the same period, the same courts accepted 32,138 criminal cases and tried 30,597, with 1,541 cases left.[76] With a total population of Shanghai in 1932 at 3,063,985 Chinese and 69,797 foreigners, there was an average of 1 civil or criminal case for every 47 people per year or 184 cases a day.[77]

The high frequency of lawsuits meant a big market for law practice. Private legal assistants or pettifoggers (*songshi*) had long existed in China in spite of their proscription by the government.[78] After the Regulations on Lawyers were enacted in 1912, such people remained illegitimate in the judicial process. In their stead, formally trained and officially registered legal professionals arrived on the scene; they were either returned students or graduates from the schools of law and government that mushroomed after the founding of the Republic. In 1914 there were already over two hundred registered Chinese lawyers in Jiangsu Province, including Shanghai.[79] In addition, before 1928 there were several dozen Chinese lawyers who did not join the Bar as required by the law, but were practicing at the Mixed Courts. In 1929 the Shanghai Bar Association had 475 members.[80] By 1937 a total of 1,328 legal professionals – virtually all Chinese lawyers practicing in Shanghai – had joined the Bar.[81]

Medicine

Although Chinese native medicine is as old as Chinese history, the story of medical professionalization has to start with the arrival of Western

---

76. *Shanghaishi Tongji Bucong Cailiao* (Supplement to the statistics of Shanghai) (Shanghai, 1935), pp.13–15.
77. *Shanghaishi Nianjian*, 1937, p.C12.
78. See Melissa Macauley, *Social Power and Legal Culture*.
79. SB, 1914: 5/20, p.7.   80. SLGB, No.26 (Jan. 1930), pp.37–72.
81. *Shanghai Lushi Gonghui Huiyuanlu*, 1937.

medicine in China, introduced by missionaries in the second half of the nineteenth century. From Peter Parker on, missionary doctors labored assiduously to persuade the Chinese to trust Western medicine and treatment in hospitals.[82] Missionary societies established hospitals to practice Western medicine. By 1905 there were 166 missionary hospitals and 241 clinics in China. By 1920 missionary hospitals numbered 250.[83] Missionaries formed medical associations and published medical journals to spread knowledge of Western medicine and to study its application to diseases in China. In 1866 the first missionary medical college was established in Guangzhou to train Chinese students and more were to appear in the following decades.

Shanghai was one of the places where missionary efforts at promoting Western medicine were most strongly felt. Informed by the discussions on medical and sanitary issues in urban centers back in their home countries and sensitized by the miserable conditions of health care and sanitation around them, medical missionaries made tremendous efforts to establish a medical and sanitary infrastructure in Shanghai's foreign concessions, from waterworks to hospitals.[84] William Lockhart, a British missionary doctor, established the first modern hospital serving the Chinese population in Shanghai in 1844 to 1846 just outside the walled Chinese city. Moved to Shandong Road in the International Settlement in 1861, the institution was known in the Republican era as the Shantung Road Hospital (now the Renji Hospital).[85] From 1896 to 1924 missionaries from Great Britain, the United States, and Germany founded six missionary medical colleges in Shanghai that trained the first generation of Western-style Chinese doctors.[86] In general, the very presence of foreign concessions in Shanghai provided the Chinese with a showcase of Western medicine and public health administration. By appointing a commissioner of public health in 1898, the SMC demon-

---

82. Edward V. Gulick, *Peter Parker and the Opening of China* (Cambridge, MA, 1973); G. H. Choa, *"Heal the Sick" Was Their Motto: The Protestant Medical Missionaries in China* (Hong Kong, 1990).
83. Shi Quansheng, *Zhonghua Minguo Wenhua Shi* (A cultural history of the Republic of China) (Changchun, 1990), p.417; G. H. Choa, *"Heal the Sick,"* p.220.
84. Kerrie L. MacPherson, *A Wilderness of Marshes: The Origins of Public Health in Shanghai, 1843–1893* (Oxford, 1987).
85. NCH, 12/9/1934, p.338; Guo Weidong and Liu Yigao, eds., *Jindai Waiguo Zaihua Wenhua Jigou Zonglu* (Shanghai, 1993), p.22; G. H. Choa, *"Heal the Sick,"* pp.24–25. For details about the operation of the hospital, see Kerrie L. MacPherson, *A Wilderness of Marshes*, pp.148–71.
86. Shi Quansheng, *Zhonghua Minguo*, pp.418–19.

strated, somewhat belatedly perhaps, the principle that public health is a responsibility of city administration.[87]

During the Republican period the majority of Western-style Chinese doctors were trained abroad or in missionary medical colleges and hospitals. The first Chinese medical school in Shanghai did not come into existence until 1917 when the Chinese government nationalized the Tongji Medical School established by a German, E. H. Paulum, in 1908. In 1926 the Southeast Medical University was founded in Shanghai, followed by the Fourth Zhongshan University Medical School in 1927. By 1934 Chinese medical schools counted thirty nationwide, including national, provincial, and private schools.[88] Throughout the Republican period, foreign medical schools were superior in facilities and equipment to their Chinese counterparts in Shanghai. Nevertheless, both missionary and Chinese medical schools trained a new breed of practitioners who promoted Western medicine in China.

With the best health care facilities in the country, Shanghai had the largest number of Western-style Chinese doctors and foreign doctors, though not all Chinese residents in Shanghai had access to their care. According to Pang Jingzhou, a Western-trained doctor and the vice-president of the Medical Practitioners' Association of Shanghai, 616 registered Chinese doctors (and 265 foreign doctors) were practicing in Shanghai in 1933.[89] A 1935 survey shows that of 5,390 college-trained Chinese doctors in the country, 1,182 (22 percent) were in Shanghai – almost all of whom resided within the International Settlement and the French Concession.[90] According to the 1935 census of the SMC, among the Chinese population in the International Settlement were 2,859 doctors, 273 dentists, and 234 opticians.[91]

The census found a greater number of Chinese doctors than the survey did, because the former apparently included native medical practitioners in the category of "doctor." Most Chinese, especially the poor, depended on native medical practitioners for curing their ills. Native physicians greatly outnumbered Western-style doctors even in Shanghai, the most Westernized city in the country. Pang Jingzhou confirmed that in the early 1930s licensed native physicians numbered 5,477 in

---

87. For the work done by the Public Health Department of the SMC, see "Growth of Shanghai's P.H.D.," NCH, 10/10/1934, p.56.
88. G. H. Choa, "*Heal the Sick*," pp.226–27.
89. Pang Jingzhou, *Shanghaishi Jinshi Nianlai Yiyao Niaokan* (An overview of Shanghai's medicine in recent ten years) (Shanghai, 1933), p.15.
90. *Chinese Medical Journal*, 49,6:547–48.   91. SMC, *Report*.

Shanghai.[92] The competition between native physicians and Western-style doctors constituted a prominent aspect of medical professionalization in China. In this study native physicians are considered part of the professional community in Shanghai.

Journalism

In early-twentieth-century China, newspapers and periodicals were the main mass media. The missionary community is credited for introducing modern journalism into China.[93] By the late nineteenth century, however, newspapers and periodicals published by foreign entrepreneurs outgrew missionary publications. In the 1890s foreigners were publishing nearly 170 newspapers and periodicals in China (in Chinese and other languages).[94] The most influential of the foreign newspapers was the *North China Daily News*, started in 1864, and its weekly edition, *North China Herald*, started in 1850.[95]

The first Chinese-language newspaper published by the Chinese was the *Zhongwai Xinbao* (Chinese and Foreign News), which appeared in Hong Kong in 1858. More influential was the *Xunhuan Ribao* (Circular Daily) published by Wang Tao in Hong Kong in 1874. It featured commentary on current political affairs.[96] The reform movement of the 1890s spawned a great number of newspapers and periodicals around the country. The years between 1894 to 1900 saw 216 newspapers and 122 magazines published.[97] Although most of those publications did not last long, they ushered in the era of the Chinese modern press.

Shanghai came under the influence of modern press early and remained the center of journalistic enterprises in the Republican era. Because of the legal protection provided by the foreign concessions, journalistic publications in Shanghai enjoyed a relative freedom of expres-

---

92. Pang Jingzhou, *Shanghaishi*, p.17.
93. Ge Gongzheng, *Zhongguo Baoxue Shi* (A history of Chinese journalism) (Shanghai, 1927), pp.64–67; Roswell S. Britton, *The Chinese Periodical Press, 1800–1912* (Shanghai, 1933) pp.17–20; Yutang Lin, *A History of the Press and Public Opinion in China* (Shanghai, 1936), p.80; Fang Hanqi, *Zhongguo Jindai Baokan Shi* (A history of newspapers and magazines in modern China) (Taiyuan, 1981), pp.11–12.
94. Shi Quansheng, *Zhonghua Minguo*, p.359.
95. *North China Herald* was first published in 1850 by Henry Shearman. In 1864 *North China Daily News* was added to the weekly to carry increasing commercial news. By 1867 the *Daily News* became the main paper and the *Herald* its weekly edition.
96. Roswell S. Britton, *The Chinese Periodical Press*, pp.39, 41–44.
97. Leo Ou-fan Lee and Andrew J. Nathan, "The Beginnings of Mass Culture," p.364.

sion and suffered much less from the political vagaries of the late Qing and early Republic. The year 1872 saw the appearance of the *Shen Bao* (Shanghai News) published by British merchant Earnest Major and edited by Jiang Zhixiang. The paper was to be sold to Shi Liangcai in 1912 and become the most influential daily in Shanghai and in the country. Other Chinese newspapers and periodicals followed. By 1912 Shanghai ranked first in the country in number of newspapers with 73 Chinese and 25 foreign newspapers, followed by Beijing (52), Tianjin (44), and Guangzhou (39).[98]

For the purposes of this study, the modern press in Republican Shanghai should include periodicals and mosquito papers (*xiaobao*) as well as daily newspapers. Those types of publications were closely related in their origins and functions: a journalist (*baoren*) working for daily newspapers or mosquito papers was often at the same time or another time a writer (*wenren*) for periodicals. Literary supplements of newspapers, especially serialization of fiction in them, were part of the literary scene (*wentan*) and extension of literary periodicals. Mosquito papers were, in a sense, an extension of both newspapers and literary periodicals. The earliest mosquito papers that appeared around the turn of the century were born of intellectuals' frustration with the political situation and characterized by political satires, though the tendency toward escapist entertainment and sensationalism turned out to be the most salient feature in later varieties of mosquito papers.[99]

During the 1910s and 1920s, newspapers and periodicals, as well as books, continued to proliferate in Shanghai. In 1928 Shanghai had 187 Chinese periodical publications, including daily newspapers, tri-daily mosquito papers, monthlies, quarterlies, bimonthlies, and weeklies, plus 22 periodicals or newspapers in the surrounding counties that belonged to Greater Shanghai. In addition, 53 foreign-language newspapers and periodicals were published in the city.[100] In the Nanjing Decade journalistic enterprise did not take a downturn in spite of government censor-

---

98. *China Yearbook, 1913*, p.662.
99. Leo Ou-fan Lee, *The Romantic Generation of Modern Chinese Writers* (Cambridge, MA, 1973), pp.4–9; E. Perry Link, *Mandarin Ducks and Butterflies* (Berkeley, 1981), pp.117–24, 249–60; Zhu Jundi, "Shanghai Xiaobao Lishi Yange" (The evolution of Shanghai's mosquito papers), XYZ, No.42 (June 1988):163–79, No.43 (Sept. 1988):137–53; Qin Shaode, *Shanghai Jindai Baokan Shilun* (On the history of newspapers and periodicals in modern Shanghai) (Shanghai, 1993), pp.133–55.
100. Huang Tianpeng, *Zhongguo Xinwen Shiye* (China's journalistic enterprise) (Shanghai, 1930), pp.186–98.

ship. By 1936 Shanghai saw 57 dailies, 44 weeklies, 50 biweeklies, 144 monthlies, 7 bimonthlies, 12 quarterlies, and 55 others – all together 369 periodical publications (in Chinese and foreign languages) in a single city. The content of those publications included news reports, political commentary, translation of foreign literature, scholarly discussion, religious preaching, scientific or pseudoscientific knowledge, children's interest, health counseling, popular fiction, and tabloid stories.[101]

The great number of newspapers and periodicals implied a strong publishing industry in Shanghai. The publishing industry came into maturity between 1910 and 1930 with modern printing machines and distribution methods.[102] Not surprisingly, Shanghai claimed the largest number of bookstores in the country, and a bookstore was often at the same time a publishing house known as a book bureau (*shuju*). In 1935 there were 259 bookstores in Shanghai, 131 of which were book bureaus dealing in both sale and publishing of books and periodicals.[103] In the early-1930s Shanghai's bookstores, newspaper publishers, voluntary associations, and educational institutions turned out a total of 215 kinds of periodicals amounting to more than 10,000 pages each month.[104]

These numbers suggest a large reading audience in Shanghai. The readership in the city was such in the 1920s that "[t]he sight of a ricksha coolie poring over a scrap of newspaper while awaiting his passenger is becoming more and more common."[105] Leo Ou-fan Lee and Andrew J. Nathan have estimated that in the first decade of the twentieth century the reading audience in China was 2 to 4 million. They show that in 1907 to 1908 Shanghai was the largest exporter of newspapers and periodicals in the country.[106] While no precise number for Shanghai's readership is available, some estimations for the 1930s may be attempted here. In 1933 each issue of Chinese daily newspapers mailed within Shanghai numbered 57,817, while that of all other Chinese periodicals mailed within Shanghai numbered 205,801.[107] Assuming that these were the numbers of subscribers and that people only subscribed to one periodical or one newspaper (in reality intellectuals often subscribed to several journals and newspapers), this study calculates 263,616 people as subscribers to

---

101. Xu Wancheng, *Quanguo Baokan She Diaocha Lu* (A national survey on publishers of newspapers and magazines) (Shanghai, 1936).
102. Perry Link, *Mandarin Ducks*, pp.79–95.
103. *Shanghai Shudian Diaocha* (A survey of Shanghai's bookstores) (Shanghai, 1935).
104. SYZ, pp.399–401.   105. *Chinese Recorder*, 56,5 (May 1925):293–394.
106. Leo Ou-fan Lee and Andrew J. Nathan, "The Beginnings," pp.368–73.
107. *Shanghaishi Tongji Bucong Cailiao*, p.79.

newspapers and periodicals in Shanghai. To those numbers may be added the people who bought newspapers and periodicals at bookstores and street corners. They would be at least no less than subscribers. Because one copy of a newspaper or magazine usually passed from one person to another, actual readers were several times more than subscribers and buyers, though their numbers are difficult to estimate with any accuracy. One estimation is that the most popular fictions of the Mandarin Duck and Butterfly school reached 400 thousand to 1 million readers in Shanghai during the 1910s and 1920s.[108] Even if subscribers and buyers only are considered, the number (527,232) already amounted to 15.8 percent of the Chinese population in the whole city in 1933 (3,330,931).[109] That number was much higher than the estimated percentage of readers in the population nationwide – 1 percent in the first decade of the twentieth century,[110] and 5 percent in the mid-1930s.[111]

Journalists and writers who served that audience were a small fraction of the population in Shanghai, without counting contributors who were many times more. In 1930 the Chinese section of the city had 83 newspaper reporters. In 1935 the number was 66.[112] In addition, journalists residing in the International Settlement numbered 2,024 in 1935.[113] That number seems to have included writers and publishers of mosquito papers and magazines and those working for foreign newspapers and news agencies, as well as reporters, editors, and owners of Chinese newspapers. In any case, the rise of Chinese journalism as an enterprise and a profession and the transformation of Chinese journalists from "literary men" to professionals remain a fascinating story to be told.

The Professional Community in Shanghai

Having examined the growth of modern professions and the composition of the professional community in Shanghai, this study can begin to estimate the overall size of the professional community and have a better sense of what the size would mean. The Shanghai yearbook of 1937 gave the number of Chinese professionals (*ziyou zhiye zhe*) living in the International Settlement as 14,634 (which was taken from the 1935 SMC census), including doctors, lawyers, engineers, accountants, journalists,

---

108. Perry Link, *Mandarin Ducks*, p.16.   109. *Shanghaishi Nianjian* (1937), p.C12.
110. Leo Ou-fan Lee and Andrew J. Nathan, "The Beginnings," p.373.
111. Yutang Lin, *A History of Press*, pp.148–49.
112. *Shanghaishi Nianjian* (1937), pp.C25–26.   113. SMC, *Report*, p.58.

and "others."[114] That number presumably included native medical practitioners. In 1936 there were 220 registered Chinese doctors, dentists, veterinarians, obstetricians, and native physicians living in the French Concession.[115] If other professionals from lawyers to accountants and journalists are included, the total number of Chinese professionals residing in the French Concession was probably no less than 1,000. Meanwhile professionals living in the Chinese sections in 1936 numbered 2,469, including 1,925 doctors (*yishi*), of whom most were apparently native physicians.[116] Added together, the number of Chinese professionals in Shanghai was about 18,100 in 1936. If professors are included in the category of professionals as the SMC census did, another 1,754 people can be added.[117] Thus the total number of self-employed and salaried professionals (*ziyou zhiye zhe*) as defined by the GMD government amounted to about 20,000 in Shanghai. These numbers speak to the important questions of how modernization changed the population composition in Shanghai, how the process led to a new social configuration and class formation, and how indispensable the functions of those professional groups were in Shanghai and beyond. Such was the demographic dimension of the social ecology within which the legal, medical, and journalistic professions must be examined.

114. *Shanghaishi Nianjian* (1937), pp.U23–24.
115. Ibid., pp.V45–46.   116. Ibid., pp.C25–26.
117. According to one source, faculty and staff in Shanghai's universities and colleges numbered 2,632 and the ratio between faculty and staff was about 2 to 1. This translates into 1,754 professors. See Xu Wancheng, *Shanghai Dazhongxiao Xuexiao Diaocha Lu* (A survey of Shanghai's universities, middle schools, and primary schools) (Shanghai, 1935).

2

Professionals as Urban Middle Class

DURING the period under study a number of social surveys were conducted (some sponsored by the GMD government) on the economic conditions of Shanghai workers. But there has been no systematic collection of data providing information on the living and working conditions of any professional groups. Accordingly, the scholarship on Republican China has been unable to discuss in any detail how those groups variably called "professional groups," "middle class," and "new urban elite" actually led their daily life. This chapter represents a first effort to fill in this blank, though anecdotal information must be used, where systematic data are lacking, in order to get the fullest possible picture of the life experience of Chinese professionals in Republican Shanghai.

THE LIFE OF PROFESSIONALS

Professional Income

Before describing the income and living standards of Chinese professionals in Republican Shanghai, this study briefly addresses the question of what currency was involved. The history of Chinese currency is a complicated subject and obviously cannot be fully treated here. As far as prewar Shanghai is concerned, however, the picture was relatively clear. For the most part the silver dollar (*yinyuan*) and silver tael (*yinliang*) were the basic currency. Foreigners customarily referred to the silver dollar as the Mexican dollar (Mex), although in reality by the 1920s the Yuan (Shikai) dollar (*Yuan datou*) increasingly replaced the Mexican dollar in circulation, because of the former's lower silver content. Paper notes issued by banks in lieu of silver dollars and "small money" – dimes and 20-cent pieces – were used in daily transactions. Copper coins (*tongqian*) – decimal units of silver tael – known as "cash" to foreigners were also used in daily business. Silver tael was usually used in large transactions such as wholesales, insurance premiums, and foreign trade. When various kinds of silver tael were in use in the country, the Shanghai tael was considered relatively stable in value – 523.248 grains of silver 1,000 fine in the 1920s and 518.512 grains 1,000 fine in the early 1930s. The exchange rate between a silver dollar and a silver tael was roughly 1:1.33, with some fluctuation. After the GMD government abolished silver tael as currency in April 1933, silver dollars became the sole basic currency in forms of silver coins and paper notes.[1] As will be shown later, the income of professionals and other social groups was indeed counted in silver dollars during the period under study.

Lawyers. In January 1912 the forerunner of the Shanghai Bar Association – the General Bar Association of the Republic of China (GBARC) – issued a scale for lawyers' fees, probably the first fee scale in the country. In September 1912 the Provisional Regulations on Lawyers enacted by the Yuan Shikai government required that local bar associations set a standard scale of lawyers' fees. In 1913 the Shanghai Bar issued its scale, presumably a reworking of the earlier scale set by the GBARC. The scale was revised in 1927 because of "the rising cost of living in Shanghai." Under the new scale, the fee for consultation was 10 yuan per hour; for reading files or meeting a detained defendant, 20 yuan per visit; and for appearing in court, 100 yuan per appearance. The maximum fee for the first and second trial of a civil case was 2,000 yuan per case, and of a criminal case, 1,000 yuan, but there could be exceptions in very serious cases.[2] In the 1910s and the early 1920s a number of Shanghai lawyers were disbarred or reprimanded for receiving payments beyond the standard fees.[3] That disciplinary action might not have occurred in the late 1920s and the 1930s, however. Several lawyers who

---

1. Qian Jiaju and Guo Yangang, *Zhongguo Huobi Shi Gangyao* (An outline history of Chinese currency) (Shanghai, 1986), pp.177–227; Frederic E. Lee, *Currency, Banking, and Finance in China* (New York, 1982), pp.8–26; C. E. Darwent, *Shanghai: A Handbook for Travelers and Residents* (Shanghai, 1920), pp.v–vii; *All About Shanghai and Environs: A Standard Guide Book* (Shanghai, 1935), pp.103–4; Eduard Kann, *The Currencies of China* (Shanghai, 1927); Holdo Stromwall, "Subsidiary Coins in Shanghai," *The North China Economic Review*, NCH, 3/17/1926, p.13; "Shanghai Tael Defined," NCH, 7/27/1932, p.156; "Abolition of the Tael," NCH, 5/15/1933, p.422.
2. SB, 1927: 9/26, p.7.   3. SB, 1915: 2/8, p.5; 9/17, p.8; 11/28, p.8; 1920: 8/15, p.5.

practiced in the 1920s and 1930s testified that because of virtual nonenforcement, lawyers simply ignored the scale set by the Bar and charged their clients as they pleased.[4]

As early as 1913 the *North China Herald* reported that Chinese lawyers in Shanghai were making "a very good livelihood," and that "fees of as much as Tls 1,000 have been paid for single cases."[5] Indeed, in the famous case concerning Song Jiaoren's assassins in 1913 (see Chapter 8), the wife of one of the accused was charged 5,000 taels by the lawyer she wanted to hire and she agreed to pay 2,000 yuan in advance.[6] In a textbook example provided by an accounting journal, in executing a will that was worth 385,030 yuan, a lawyer's fee was 1,500 yuan.[7] The profits of a law practice, therefore, could be handsome. In addition to practicing law, some lawyers also engaged in a second job, such as running a business, practicing as an accountant, or teaching at one or more colleges. Those lawyers were certainly very well off.

Wu Kaisheng began law practice in 1926 after having received a law degree at L'Université de Lyon. He opened a four-room law firm on Avenue Edward VII of the French Concession with three associate lawyers. The firm's monthly revenue was at least between 1,000 yuan and 2,000 yuan, and sometimes it went as high as 10,000 yuan. Although about half of that revenue went to Wu's associates, Wu's personal income was high by the standard of that time. He made quite a fortune in two years and was able to buy a big house and own a car. He bought a piece of real estate for 3,000 taels in 1927 to 1928 and sold the real estate for ten times as much in 1932.[8] His affluence and social connections may be seen in the fact that when he got married in 1927 at the age of twenty-seven, over five hundred people attended the wedding ceremony.[9]

Wu Jingxiong (John C. H. Wu) graduated from the Comparative Law School of Soochow University in 1920 and went on to earn a J.D. degree from the University of Michigan. After several academic positions at

---

4. Wu Kaisheng, interview with the author, December 30, 1991; Wang Baoji, interview with the author, July 31, 1994; Zhu Zijia (Jin Xiongbai), *Huangpu Jiangde Zhuolang* (The muddy wave of the Huangpu River) (Hong Kong, 1964), p.85.
5. NCH, 8/19/1913, p.182.   6. SB, 1913: 6/26, p.7.
7. *Lixin Kuaiji Jikan* (Lixin Quarterly of Accounting), 2,2:361–63.
8. Wu Kaisheng, interview with the author, December 30, 1991; Wu Lilan and Lin Qi, *Wu Kaisheng Boshi Zhuanji* (A biography of Dr. Wu Kaisheng) (Hong Kong, 1993), p.42.
9. SB, 1927: 9/29, p.7.

Harvard, Northwestern, and Soochow universities, and a stint as the president of the Provisional Court in the International Settlement in 1929, Wu began to practice law in Shanghai in 1930. Because of Wu's fame as former president of the Provisional Court, many clients flocked to him. Within a few months Wu made no less than 40,000 taels and continued to do very well thereafter.[10]

Wang Baoji, also a graduate from the Soochow University Law School, started a law practice in 1931. He took civil cases only, usually involving financial liabilities between business firms. He would make about 10,000 yuan a year, which was above average among Shanghai lawyers. By late 1937 when the Japanese occupied Shanghai, Wang had made enough money to quit the practice to become a partner in starting a bank and an insurance company.[11]

Apparently, however, not every lawyer was able to earn the kind of income that Wu Kaisheng, Wu Jingxiong, and Wang Baoji did. Lawyers' incomes varied from person to person, just as did medical practitioners' incomes. In 1928 the *North China Herald* attacked the Shanghai Bar Association by saying that Chinese lawyers in Shanghai competed keenly for clients and some would spend a whole morning in court for "the paltry sum" of 5 yuan and then go about boasting how they undercut other practitioners.[12] Regardless of the allegations, it would seem that most lawyers who were not famous would probably earn no more than 100 yuan to 200 yuan a month.

Doctors. Before the Nanjing Decade there were no standard guidelines governing the compensation paid to medical practitioners. Traditionally, it was a private matter between the physician and the patient. Only local custom would decide how much was appropriate for a physician to charge a patient or for a patient to pay a physician. When Western medicine came to China, Western-style doctors followed the tradition, varying their charges depending on local custom and patients' circumstances. In the mid-1910s medical advertisements in newspapers indicated that Western-style doctors in Shanghai would usually charge 1 yuan for an office visit (*menzhen*) and 6 yuan for a house call (*chuzhen*).[13]

---

10. John C. H. Wu, *Beyond East and West* (New York, 1951), p.133.
11. Wang Baoji, interview with the author, July 31, 1994.
12. NCH, 8/25/1928, p.330; also see Zhu Zijia, *Huangpu*, p.84.
13. For example, SB, 1915: 10/4, p.7; 10/5, p.7; 1916: 3/15, p.6; 4/20, p.7.

After the GMD came to power, the Shanghai Bureau of Health issued regulations on doctors' fees for the first time as follows: the fee for an office visit was 0.20 yuan to 1.20 yuan; for a house call, 1 yuan to 5 yuan; and for a special examination (*tezhen*), 6 yuan to 10 yuan. A few months later, in response to doctors' complaints, the bureau revised the regulations to increase the fees to 0.20 yuan to 2.20 yuan, 1 yuan to 10 yuan, and 6 yuan to 15 yuan respectively.[14] Of course there is no way to know how many doctors complied with the regulations. There appeared to be no mechanism to enforce the regulations. Pang Jingzhou, a Western-trained doctor practicing in Shanghai, reported in the 1930s that a doctor would usually charge about 4 yuan for an office visit and 10 yuan to 20 yuan for a house call.[15] Those amounts were obviously above the official regulations and seemed to be no secret. Treatment or surgery was much more expensive. As a record of malpractice lawsuits in the 1930s shows, one injection of blood serum cost a patient 22 yuan, and one plastic surgery on breasts cost a patient 400 yuan, which was said to be much lower than the usual rate for such operations.[16]

To know the income of a doctor, of course, the key question is how many patients the doctor would see each day. Pang Jingzhou said that if a Western-style doctor would work thirteen hours a day, the doctor could see at most forty patients, and that at 3 yuan to 4 yuan a patient, the doctor could earn over 100 yuan a day. In reality, however, few doctors could survive such a work schedule.[17] It seems safe to assume that few doctors actually earned more than 100 yuan a day. According to Zhu Kewen, another Western-trained doctor who practiced in the 1930s, on average, doctors would earn several hundred yuan a month and those who made 1,000 yuan to 2,000 yuan a month were considered very successful.[18]

In addition to the fees charged on patients, many doctors received kickbacks by prescribing expensive drugs and referring patients to particular drugstores, a practice that was much criticized but never seemed to cease.[19] Some doctors did so well financially that they became the targets of kidnapping for ransom, one of the most common crimes in

14. SB, 1929: 10/15, p.7.
15. Pang Jingzhou, *Shanghaishi Jingshi Nianlai Yiyao Niaokan*, pp.45–47.
16. Song Guobin, *Yisong Anjian Huichao* (A collection of medical malpractice lawsuits) (Zhonghua yixuehui, 1935), pp.5–7; 21.
17. Pang Jingzhou, *Shanghaishi*, p.45.
18. Zhu Kewen, interview with the author, December 18, 1991.
19. Pang Jingzhou, *Shanghaishi*, pp.52–53.

Shanghai. In March 1918, for instance, a doctor was hoaxed to pay a house call to a "patient" in Hardoon Road (*Tongren lu*) where he, along with his assistant, was held for a ransom of 10,000 yuan. The doctor negotiated with his captors to a compromise for 4,000 yuan, but managed to escape before the money was paid.[20]

As for native medical practitioners, in most cases their fees in the early 1930s would range from 0.2 yuan to 2.4 yuan for an office visit and from 1.2 yuan to over 10 yuan for a house call.[21] Some better-known native physicians would charge more – 2.4 yuan to 8 yuan for an office visit and 6 yuan to 30 yuan for a house call.[22] Other renowned native physicians adopted another strategy to earn more money. They would see no more than twenty patients a day to emphasize the quality of their examinations, but charge 20 yuan to 30 yuan per patient.[23] As for the number of patients that native physicians would receive daily, contemporary estimations seemed to agree. In the opinion of Pang Jingzhou, the native physician's examination of patients (involving essentially looking at the patient's facial complexion and using three fingers to feel the patient's pulsation and interpreting both) was so easy that one physician could see as many as one hundred patients a day.[24] Hu Bang'an provided a more comprehensive estimation: The most successful native physicians would see more than one hundred patients a day in the physician's office; the next successful, several dozens a day; and the less successful, several a day. Such physicians made up about 80 percent of native physicians in Shanghai.[25] If, then, on average, a moderately successful native physician had twenty office-visiting patients at 1 yuan per person and two house-called patients at 5 yuan per person each day, the physician would make about 30 yuan a day or 900 yuan a month.

Journalists. The most common and generic Chinese translation of the word "journalist" in the Republican era was *baoren* (newspaper person), which has a counterpart in the post-1949 era – *xinwen gongzuo zhe* (news workers). The vague term *baoren* could mean people in different positions in a newspaper publisher or a news agency, from copyist to editor in chief, and their incomes varied with their positions. In this book the

---

20. NCH, 3/23/1918, p.708.
21. *Guoyi Minglu* (The directory of native physicians) (Shanghai, 1932).
22. Hu Bang'an, *Guoyi Kaiye Shu* (The art of practicing native medicine) (Shanghai, 1933), p.34.
23. Ibid., p.65. 24. Pang Jingzhou, *Shanghaishi*, pp.64–65.
25. Hu Bang'an, *Guoyi*, pp.6–7.

concern is on news reporters (*xinwen jizhe*) and editors (*bianji*) only. People often worked in both capacities at different times or even at the same time.

Huang Tianpeng wrote the following in 1930: An editor in chief (*zong bianji*) would earn a monthly salary of between 150 yuan and 350 yuan; a chief editor (*bianji zhuren*), from 120 yuan to 200 yuan; an editor, from 60 yuan to 100 yuan and occasionally up to 150 yuan; a reporter stationed in other cities, around 100 yuan plus business expenses; and a local reporter, around 50 yuan.[26] Ge Gongzhen reported about the same salary range for journalists in the 1920s.[27]

As those sources would suggest, the salary of reporters and editors varied considerably with different newspaper publishers. When Xu Zhucheng entered the National News Agency (*guowen she*) in 1928 as a copyist, his monthly salary was 20 yuan. He became an apprentice reporter (*lianxi jizhe*) at the *Dagong Bao* (L'Impartial) in Tianjin, with a monthly salary of 40 yuan. In the third year he was promoted to the position of editor and his salary was raised to 70 yuan. A few months later he got a raise to 100 yuan. When he was assigned as a resident reporter in Hankou, he received 150 yuan for salary plus 50 yuan for business expenses each month.[28] Lu Yi was a primary school teacher with a monthly salary of 80 yuan before he entered the *Xinwen Bao* in 1931 as an apprentice reporter. For his new job he received 50 yuan a month and free lodging provided by the newspaper publisher. The second year he became a reporter with a monthly salary of 80 yuan. When he left the newspaper in 1937, his salary had been raised to 140 yuan.[29] Gu Zhizhong entered the *Shi Bao* in 1924 as a reporter with a monthly salary of 80 yuan, which was considered high among the staff of that newspaper. When he left the newspaper two years later, his salary remained the same.[30]

The highest possible salary for a journalist was about 300 yuan; few people actually got to that salary level. Among the staff of the *Xinwen Bao*, only the editor in chief Li Haoran was able to get close to that

---

26. Huang Tianpeng, *Zhongguo Xinwen Shiye*, p.93.
27. Ge Gongzheng, *Zhongguo Baoxue Shi* (A history of Chinese journalism), pp.244–45.
28. Xu Zhucheng, *Baohai Jiuwen* (Reminiscences of old newspapers) (Shanghai, 1981), p.263.
29. Lu Yi, interview with the author, January 12, 1992.
30. Gu Zhizhong, "Yisuo Bingbu Lixiang De Xinwen Xuexiao" (A not ideal school of journalism), XYZ, No.26 (July 1984), pp.33–50.

Table 1. *Monthly Income Range of Chinese Professionals in Republican Shanghai in the 1920s and 1930s*

	Chinese yuan
Doctors	300–3,000
Lawyers	300–2,000
Journalists	70–300

amount.[31] In addition to salary, however, the publishers of successful newspapers, such as the *Shen Bao*, *Xinwen Bao* and *Dagong Bao*, also provided their employees with benefits, including a year-end bonus or special subsidies for marriage, death of parents, or decennial birthdays. Starting in 1926, the publisher of the *Xinwen Bao* even provided its employees with life insurance, medical leave, medical expenses, and a retirement bonus.[32]

To conclude the discussion of professional income, it may be stated that on average Chinese lawyers, doctors, and journalists in prewar Shanghai received a monthly income between 70 yuan to 300 yuan, as summarized in Table 1.

Income of Other Social Groups

The knowledge of Shanghai professionals' income level alone does not say much about their economic conditions. The key questions are the following: How much was 70 yuan or 300 yuan worth? What kind of lifestyle could be supported by that amount of money? How did that level of income make people urban middle class in material and cultural terms? To answer these questions, the study first takes a look at the income level of some other social groups for comparison. Second, the study examines the cost of living during the period to see the money's worth and the life-style of Shanghai professionals.

A comparison may be made with the income of government officials. Under the GMD government regulations, the monthly salary scale for

---

31. Ibid.; Xu, *Baohai*, p.262.
32. Xu Zhucheng, *Baohai*, p.264; Wang Zhongwei, "Woyu Xinwen Bao De Guanxi" (My relationship with the News Daily), XYZ, No.12 (June 1982), pp.136–37.

Table 2. *Monthly Salary Scale for Government Officials in the 1930s*

	Chinese yuan
Minister (*buzhang*)	800
Deputy minister (*fu buzhang*)	675
Chief secretary (*mishuzhang*)	525–600
Department chief (*shuzhang*)	525–600
Division chief (*sizhang*)	450–600
Bureau chief (*juzhang*)	450–600
Section chief (*chuzhang*)	450–600
Secretary (*mishu*)	300–450
Branch chief (*kezhang*)	250–400
Branch staff (*keyuan*)	60–180

Sources: *Guomin Zhengfu Gongbao* (GZG) (National Government Bulletin), No. 9 (July 21, 1927): 17; *Shenbao Nianjian* (Shenbao yearbook), 1933, p. F28.

officials is shown in Table 2. Obviously, high- and middle-ranking government officials received higher income than average professionals. The income of most professionals was comparable to that of a branch chief (*kezhang*) or branch staff (*keyuan*). Only very successful lawyers and doctors were able to make the same or more money than high officials. This fact, which was very similar to the situations in France and Germany in the late nineteenth and early twentieth century, explains why many educated people regarded a position in government bureaucracy as the best career.

A comparison may be made with the Chinese employed by the SMC (Table 3). Again, the incomes of Chinese lawyers, doctors, and journalists were comparable to those of the Chinese employees who held positions in the SMC that required secondary or higher education. The comparisons with government officials and Chinese employees of the SMC may offer a concrete reason for considering civil servants and professionals as belonging to the urban middle class in Republican China, though it is not a concern of this study.

In Republican China jobs in banking, the postal service, and the railroad were regarded as "gold rice bowl," because they offered better pay and guaranteed relative job security. The employees in those places were typically salaried professionals and white-collar workers. A look at the income of the employees in the postal service and railroad provides a better measure of where "free professionals" stood financially in com-

Table 3. *Salaries for Chinese Employees of the SMC in the 1930s*

	Chinese yuan
Assistant chemist	150–300
Trained nurse	50–110
Senior engineer	300–500
Secondary engineer	120–200
Senior translator	300–400
Secondary translator	125–175
Senior assistant auditor or accountant	400–500
Assistant auditor or accountant	250–400
Assistant secretary	225–300
Head cashier	80–100
First copyist	100–225
Second copyist	60–100
Typist	50–60

Source: "Gonggong Zujia Gongbuju Zhiyuan Jingji Weiyuanhui Baogaoshu" (Report of the committee on the welfare of the employees of the SMC of the International Settlement), in *Shanghai Gonggong Zujie Nashui Haurenhui Zhongyao Wenjian* (Important documents of the Chinese ratepayers association of the International Settlement in Shanghai), 1937, pp.58–78.

parison. The monthly salary scale in the Chinese postal service after the strike of 1925 is shown in Table 4.

In 1928, after another strike by postal workers, the Ministry of Transportation and Communications announced a new salary scale for postal workers, clerks, and officers. Under that new scale the salary for junior postal clerks ranged from 40 yuan to 130 yuan; senior postal clerks, 150 yuan to 500 yuan; deputy postal officers, 550 yuan to 650 yuan; and postal officers, 700 yuan to 800 yuan.[33]

The salary for railroad employees was comparable. Under the regulations issued by the Ministry of Transportation and Communications in June 1927, the salary for railroad clerks ranged from 25 yuan to 800 yuan in a scale of forty-eight ranks.[34] The scales for the railroad and postal service may be visualized as pyramids with more people at the bottom and fewer people at the top. In other words, the majority of employees

33. SB, 1928: 10/16, p.6.   34. SB, 1927: 6/27, p.8.

Table 4. *Monthly Salary Scale in the Chinese Postal Service in 1925*

	Chinese yuan or tael
Mail carrier	19–48 yuan
Sorting person	21–71 yuan
Postal clerk	35–150 yuan
Postal officer (Chinese)	100–600 tael
Postal officer (foreigner)	175–1,250 tael

Sources: *Shi Bao* (SB), 1925: 8/19, p.3; Tang Hai, *Zhongguo Laodong Wenti* (The problem of Chinese labor) (Shanghai, 1928), pp.162–67.

in the postal service were mail carriers, sorting persons, and junior clerks. The majority of railroad employees were workers, clerks, conductors, and technicians. On average, the income of those people was comparable to or lower than that of professionals.

A comparison with blue-collar workers is revealing. According to contemporary surveys, Shanghai workers' daily wages in the 1920s and 1930s were as low as 0.408 yuan a day on average (in silk-reeling industry), which would mean a monthly income of 12.24 yuan if the worker were paid for thirty days a month. The highest paid worker (in the shipbuilding industry) earned an average daily wage of 1.256 yuan, amounting to a monthly wage of 37.68 yuan with a thirty-day pay period.[35] It may be noted that to earn that wage, workers had to work very long hours. Workers in the Shanghai cotton textile and silk-reeling industries, who accounted for 67 percent of all industrial workers in Shanghai, typically worked twelve hours a day. On average, the number of daily working hours for all Shanghai workers was eleven, with an average of merely thirty-three days off per year.[36]

Living Cost in Shanghai

Because systematic data on the living expenses of professionals are lacking, one may gain a rough notion of the living expenses of professionals by a quick look at the living cost and spending pattern of Shang-

---

35. Tang Hai, *Zhongguo Laodong Wenti* (The problem of Chinese labor) (Shanghai, 1928), pp.172–73; *Shenbao Nianjian*, 1933; *Shanghaishi Shehui Tongji Gaiyao*, pp.21–22.
36. *Shenbao Nianjian*, 1933, pp.P8–9.

hai workers. In the 1920s, on average, a single unskilled worker spent 11.85 yuan a month on living expenses, and a five-person family of an unskilled worker spent 21.34 yuan per month. On the other hand, a single skilled worker spent 19.26 yuan a month on living expenses, and a five-person family of a skilled worker spent 35.85 yuan per month.[37] A survey in 1927 to 1928 covering 230 families of Shanghai textile workers found that the average monthly income per family was 31.877 yuan, of which 56.6 percent was spent on food, 9.2 percent on clothing, 6.5 percent on housing, 7.6 percent on fuel and lighting, and 20.1 percent on other items.[38] That level of income and the spending pattern continued into the 1930s.[39]

The price of rice – the most important index of living cost in Shanghai – posted a steady rise from the 1910s to the mid-1920s and stabilized from the mid-1920s through 1937, though not without occasional fluctuation. In 1918 the price for the best quality rice (Jiangsu rice or Chinese white rice) was 8 yuan to 8.20 yuan per picul; for medium quality, 7 yuan to 7.50 yuan; and for the low grade, 6 yuan or less. Those prices represented a 60 percent rise in price over 1908.[40] In the 1920s and 1930s occasional upsurge in the price of Jiangsu rice would exceed 15 yuan (in 1920), 18 yuan (in 1926), 20 yuan (in 1929), and even 23 yuan (in 1930) per picul. The highest price for Saigon and Rangoon rice (cheaper types of rice) was reached between 17.40 yuan and 19.20 yuan per picul in the summer of 1930.[41] Leaving aside any occasional upsurge, however, the price of Jiangsu rice on average was 10.25 yuan in 1920, 10 yuan in 1921, 12.50 in 1923, 13 yuan in 1924, and 12.75 in 1925.[42] In the mid-1920s the British–American Tobacco Company provided its employees with a rice allowance whenever the price of rice jumped over 8 yuan per picul; the Commercial Press adopted a similar policy with a threshold at 9 yuan per picul.[43] Those allowances may suggest that the normal price of Saigon

37. Tang Hai, *Zhongguo*, pp.176–78; CWR, 49,10 (8/3/1929):432.
38. Sheng Jun, Index of Living Cost in Shanghai (Shanghai, 1930), p.9 *Shenbao Nianjian*, 1933, pp.P14–17.
39. *Shanghaishi Shehui Tongji Gaiyao*, pp.26–28; NCH, 6/6/1934, p.349; 12/26/1934, p.503.
40. NCH, 5/18/1918, pp.391–92.
41. NCH, 7/3/1920, p.31; 9/25/1920, p.825; 7/8/922, p.107; 7/10/1926, p.66; 10/5/1929, p.23; CWR, 53,5 (7/5/1930):172.
42. NCH, 6/19/1926, p.538; 4/21/1928, p.103. Kotenev gave a slightly different set of numbers for the period of 1919–1924: 7.48 yuan (1919), 10.26 (1920), 10.43 (1921), 12 (1922), 12.52 (1923), and 12.22 (1924). Presumably he was referring to the price of Jiangsu rice. See A. M. Kotenev, *Shanghai: Its Municipality and the Chinese* (Shanghai, 1927), p.11.
43. NCH, 6/26/1926, p.590; 9/4/1926, p.477.

or Rangoon rice during the 1920s would be 8 yuan to 9 yuan. In the 1930s the retail price of rice remained within the range of 9 yuan to 13 yuan for Jiangsu rice and 7 yuan to 11 yuan for Saigon or Rangoon rice.[44] Sometimes Jiangsu rice was sold as low as 7 yuan per picul, as was the case in early 1931.[45] Contemporaries estimated that a picul of rice was sufficient for one month for a five-person family or four adult male workers.[46] The cost of rice explains how Shanghai workers would be able to survive with a monthly wage of 12 yuan to 35 yuan.

The rent for housing – the second most important index of living cost in Shanghai – was a different story from the price of rice. Thanks to continuous increase in Shanghai's population and thus in the demand for housing, the value of real estate in Shanghai shot up dramatically after the turn of the century. In 1916 the value of land in the central district of Shanghai was 45,000 taels per *mu*. In 1925 the value rose to 85,000 taels and by 1932 to 170,000 taels.[47] A piece of real estate within the International Settlement changed hands in 1921 for 268,000 taels and was again sold in 1924 for no less than 535,000 taels – the value of the land almost doubled in three years.[48] Another example, as mentioned earlier, was a piece of property sold by Wu Kaisheng in 1932 for ten times as much as he bought it for in 1928.

The dramatic rise in land value caused housing rent to climb steadily and sometimes steeply during the period under study. It was reported in 1921 that the rent for Chinese residents in the International Settlement increased between 20 percent and 300 percent and that housing formerly rented for 50 yuan a month was renting on average for 80 yuan to 90 yuan a month.[49] Between 1925 and 1929 the rent for Chinese-style houses in the Settlement and the French Concession again increased 20 percent to 30 percent. Houses rented in 1925 for 65 taels a month were renting in 1929 for 85 taels. In cases where an old building was demolished and replaced by new accommodation, rents went up 75 percent.[50]

The rising rent, along with higher food prices, kept many Shanghai working-class people from residing in the city. According to the *North China Herald*, about one-half of the workers in Shanghai in the early

---

44. NCH, 3/3/1931, p.297; 8/18/1931, p.227; 6/14/1932, p.422; 9/5/1934, p.358; 7/25/1934, p.140; 8/15/1934, p.248; 4/3/1935, p.28; 11/20/1935, p.322; 10/28/1936, p.151; 5/27/1936, p.373; 1/13/1937, p.68; 7/21/1937, p.112.
45. NCH, 2/10/1931, p.197.   46. NCH, 6/26/1926, p.590; CWR, 49,7 (7/13/1929):296.
47. *The North China Trade Review*, NCH, 3/17/1926, p.29; NCH, 10/23/1935, p.170.
48. NCH, 3/15/1924, p.405.   49. NCH, 11/12/1921, p.450.
50. NCH, 1/28/1930, p.163.

1920s were financially unable to reside in Shanghai. "They may lodge, or otherwise exist in the place, but what they mean by home may be in a locality as remote as Ningpo. Girls who work in the Yangtszepoo mills make light of a trudge of five miles over country paths twice a day. Then there is the great band of week-enders. They come from villages lying, for instance, along one of the sea walls on the Pootung littoral, and rumour has it that the steam launches carry two thousand human beings every day between there and Shanghai."[51]

As shown, the workers who did reside in the city spent only a fraction of their low income on housing. That is to say, they could afford only housing of poor quality. Some of the shelters were shacks made of bamboo and mud or were grounded worn-out boats on the periphery of the foreign concessions.[52] In such "squatter villages," no rent was paid but arrangement was sometimes made with the police covering protection and taxation.[53] Most industrial workers in Shanghai, however, did not live in squatter villages or shantytowns. They lived in one- or two-story houses.[54] A 1929 survey found that most of unmarried common coolies in Shanghai slept in night-houses for 0.50 yuan a month (their homes were probably in Subei or Ningbo), while married unskilled workers would spend 1.50 yuan to 3.00 yuan a month on housing.[55] The latter arrangement meant renting one or two rooms in one of the cheapest houses available, as the lowest rent for a house was 6 to 8 yuan a month in 1926.[56]

Looking at the living cost and spending pattern of Shanghai workers, it becomes obvious that the disparity in income between workers and professionals would result in different kinds of life experience. Tang Hai pointed out in 1926 that a five-person family that spent 66 yuan on living expenses was considered *middle level*, while a five-person family that spent 30 yuan was below the middle level.[57] All data sampled by this study confirm that on average a worker's family earned no more than 35 yuan a month, whereas the income of most professionals was well over the level of 66 yuan per five-member family. If a Shanghai worker's family could survive, however miserably, on a wage of 35 yuan a month

---

51. NCH, 2/28/1920, p.516.
52. Jean Chesneaux, *The Chinese Labor Movement, 1919–1927*, pp.102–5; for a brief history of these squatter villages or shantytowns, see Hanchao Lu, "Creating Urban Outcasts," pp.563–96.
53. NCH, 9/4/1926, p.477.   54. Hanchao Lu, "Creating Urban Outcasts," pp.585–86.
55. CWR, 49,7 (7/13/1029):309.   56. NCH, 9/4/1926, p.477.
57. Tang Hai, *Zhongguo*, pp.183–84.

or lower, an income of 70 to 300 yuan for a professional's family would make significant difference in quality of life.

While it is difficult to reconstruct how much average Shanghai professionals would spend on food and what they would actually eat, it is possible and useful to take a look at their housing conditions. Most professionals under study lived in the International Settlement or the French Concession – a situation true for 288 of the 354 members of the Medical Practitioners Association of Shanghai, 392 of the 637 members of the Shanghai Native Medical Society, and 379 of the 475 members of the Shanghai Bar Association in 1929.[58]

Whether one was living in the foreign concessions or in the Chinese sections only tells part of the story. Most Shanghai professionals simply lived in better housing. Wang Baoji rented two rooms in a house on Burkill Road (now *Fengyang lu*) in the International Settlement in the 1930s. When he made enough money by the early 1940s, he saw fit to buy a piece of land in Nanshi and build a big house on it.[59]

When Lu Yi was an unmarried reporter for the *Xinwen Bao*, the publisher provided Lu Yi with lodging free of charge. He would spend eight yuan a month on food by boarding at a nearby eatery. After he got married, he rented two rooms in a house on Medhurst Road (now *Taixing lu*) in the Settlement for twelve yuan a month and spent eighteen yuan a month on food. With such a budget (he was earning more than eighty yuan a month, as noted earlier), he was able to save and sent money to his mother living in Chuansha, a rural county adjacent to Shanghai, while living a simple but comfortable life.[60]

Wang and Lu rented rooms instead of houses in the 1930s because the rising housing rent in Shanghai had an impact on the urban middle class. As early as 1919 the average number of occupants per Chinese house in the International Settlement had reached eleven (the number of occupants per foreign house was six) – apparently more than one family.[61] The crowding probably worsened by the 1930s. Wang Zhongfang (Paul K. Whang), a frequent contributor to the *China Weekly Review*, wrote in

---

58. Compiled from the addresses listed in *Shanghai Shi Yishi Gonghui Huiyuanlu* (The directory of the Medical Practitioners Association of Shanghai) (1936); *Guoyi Minglu* (The directory of native physicians) (1932); and "Shanghai Lushi Gonghui Huiyuanlu" (The directory of the Shanghai Bar Association), in SLGB, No.26 (Jan. 1930), pp.36–72.
59. Wang Baoji, interview with the author, July 31, 1994.
60. Lu Yi, interview with the author, January 12, 1992.
61. NCH, 9/20/1919, p.767.

1931 that "out of the huge army of office workers who constitute the middle class of Shanghai society," no more than 30 percent would earn more than 100 yuan a month. The majority of the middle-class people in Shanghai could not afford to maintain their own houses, because any "livable house" would cost at least 50 yuan a month but middle-class people could spend no more than 20 percent of their monthly income – twenty yuan – on housing. "The only way open to them is to have a house jointly rented by several families."[62] That piece of writing by Wang gives four revealing points. First, Wang considered office workers as part of the middle class in Shanghai. Second, middle-class people aspired to making at least 100 yuan a month. Third, houses rented under 20 yuan a piece per month were considered unlivable by middle-class people in Shanghai. Fourth, middle-class people would spend 20 percent of their income on housing, compared to industrial workers spending under 10 percent of their already low wages on housing.

Culture and Life-Style

The working class and the middle-class professionals were set apart by not only their material life but also their cultural life. Workers did have a cultural life – including the celebration of the lunar festivals and occasional entertainment provided by traditional theater performers – but the urban environment, the routine of factory life, and low income prevented workers from enjoying much cultural entertainment.[63] Spending three quarters of his or her waking time on hard work to survive, the worker simply did not have enough time and money to enjoy the cultural life that the city offered. In contrast, professionals had both time and money for a variety of cultural activities they sponsored or patronized.

The working class and the middle-class professionals were also set apart by different educational attainment. Of all Chinese workers, only about 40 percent were literate[64] – probably just "functionally literate," to use Evelyn S. Rawski's term.[65] In contrast, most professionals were at least educated in middle schools. Many received higher education in

---

62. CWR, 58,2 (9/12/1931):58.
63. Chesneaux, *The Chinese Labor Movement*, pp.105–8.   64. Ibid., p.109.
65. Functional literacy in Qing and Republican China is defined as a reading knowledge of several hundred to two thousand characters, see Evelyn S. Rawski, *Education and Popular Literacy in Ch'ing China* (Ann Arbor, 1979), pp.1–4.

China or abroad. Having higher education might not have been true of all journalists, but was typical of lawyers and Western-style doctors. As this study will show, government regulations on the legal and medical professions stipulated a college education as part of the qualifications. Most professionals in those fields qualified to practice by virtue of such an education.[66] With time, money, and education, Shanghai professionals readily and eagerly partook in the urban culture of Shanghai both as its makers and consumers. They read newspapers and magazines of all kinds; saw Chinese- or foreign-made movies; patronized the opera, theaters, and concerts; danced in ballrooms; and socialized in cafes and brothels. Not insignificantly, to some degree the behavior of professionals in such material and cultural consumption had often been cultivated and conditioned in their college years.[67]

Successful lawyers enjoyed the urban culture in a conspicuous way. Born in a gentry-official home and graduated from the college of Law and Government in Hangzhou, Qin Liankui was a founding member of the Shanghai Bar Association and built a successful practice in the city. In spite of having received a modern education, he pursued the life-style of traditional gentry-literati. He frequented a high-class brothel and patronized one young woman there, eventually taking her as his concubine. He was a fan of the Peking Opera and often went to the theater. He was fond of gambling, which his earnings from his law practice were able to support. On more than one occasion Qin would lose several thousand yuan at one gambling session. On gambling tables he came to associate with Du Yuesheng, the head of the notorious Green Gang, and stayed on good terms with Du. All that activity, however, did not prevent Qin from becoming a leading member of the Shanghai Bar Association and winning a high reputation as a competent lawyer.[68]

After Wu Jingxiong started a law practice in 1930, he earned so much

---

66. One group was an exception: native medical practitioners. Most of them were qualified to practice by virtue of experience through apprenticeship. Many older practitioners did not receive modern education, but had formal or informal traditional education, since serious practitioners in native medicine had to read native medical classics and write prescriptions. During the Republican era a growing number of native physicians were graduates from specialized schools of native medicine where some courses in modern sciences including Western medicine were part of the curriculum.
67. Wen-hsin Yeh, *The Alienated Academy: Culture and Politics in Republican China, 1919–1937* (Cambridge, MA, 1990), pp.205–28.
68. Frank Ching, *Ancestors: 900 Years in the Life of a Chinese Family* (New York, 1988), pp.398–440.

money that he refused to serve as a judge at the Supreme Court in Nanjing. Before he knew it, he lived the life of a "regular play-boy," indulging in "flower houses" every night for seven years. He planned to take a sing-song girl as his concubine, which his sudden awakening to Christian morals prevented.[69]

The life-style of Qin and Wu might not have been typical of average lawyers, but even less successful professionals led a much easier and more enjoyable life than workers and the uneducated. The experience of Huang Yaomian, a writer and school teacher, may not have been untypical. When he began to earn more than one hundred yuan a month, he felt it necessary to frequent coffeehouses where he would leave big tips for happily amazed waitresses – with a satisfied ego thinking of himself an elegant figure in the "Shanghai society."[70]

Another indication of how the life-style of professionals differed from that of laboring people was the way professionals socialized among themselves. The Shanghai Journalists Association, for instance, met monthly in big restaurants for dinner gatherings (*jucan hui*). On each occasion, a few dozen people would show up and take turns playing host and paying the bill. At such gatherings they would exchange news concerning their professions and discuss activities of their associations. Before 1927 the Shanghai Journalists Association's annual meetings featured foreign or Chinese movies or performances of foreign or Chinese music or theater. Other professional associations, such as those of accountants and professors, engaged in similar activities.

Not surprisingly, the places for many journalists to meet privately were Shanghai's brothels, where they socialized and entertained themselves frequently. Many lawyers were regular customers of brothels as well.[71] Those forms of social interaction and material and cultural consumption helped define a particular urban culture of Shanghai. It is those aspects of social and cultural life, perhaps more than anything else, which set professionals apart from laboring classes. On the other hand, their professional careers and pursuits distinguished them from the bourgeoisie and capitalists that shared in the consumption of urban culture.

To be sure, Chinese professionals in Shanghai were not a rigidly confined social group but a fluid one. Differentiation or stratification existed

69. John C. H. Wu, *Beyond East and West*, pp.133–37.
70. *Xin Wenxue Shiliao* (Sources on the history of new literature), No.1 (Beijing, 1988), pp.33–34.
71. Bao Tianxiao, *Chuanying Lou Huiyi Lu Xubian* (A sequel to the memoir from the mansion of bracelet shadow) (Hong Kong, 1973), pp.47–55, 74–76, 105–10.

in income and wealth, social esteem, educational attainment, and lifestyle. The lower tier of the professional class would include white-collar workers (about whom little is known) and blend into the lower classes. Unemployed college graduates or would-be professionals, for example, can arguably be regarded as proletarians rather than middle class, though they were still "intellectuals" by virtue of their education. Yet, to laboring classes toiling in rice fields and in workshops and on factory floors, let alone those pulling rickshaws in the streets, the seeming leisure of those educated people with an urban life-style was an unmistakable sign of being a different social class above them.

THE CAREER AND IDENTITY OF PROFESSIONALS

Education and Career

In traditional China being educated and culturally sophisticated was a valued asset. A classical education leading to a degree in the civil service examination distinguished the gentry-official-literati class from all other social groups. After the New Policy reform of the late Qing, education was no longer necessarily the sole gauge to measure one's success in life, but it was still the only path leading to new careers in modern professions. Furthermore, if education was not the sufficient condition for stepping into the circle of political power, in most cases it was still the necessary condition. The majority of officials in the successive Republican governments reached their positions through (1) serving in the military – the Beiyang Army, the Nationalist Revolutionary Army, and all sorts of military academies throughout the period – or (2) receiving higher education in foreign countries or in China.[72] After the founding of the Republic, college graduates who studied the liberal arts and law outnumbered those studying sciences, engineering, medicine, and business. They competed keenly for offices in successive Republican governments. Returned students too tended to get employment in government bureaucracy. In 1916, for instance, there were 1,655 returned students in Beijing, 1,024 of whom (62 percent) worked in government offices, 132 worked in educational institutions, and 399 were at leisure (*fuxian*), a euphemism for unemployment.[73] Y. C. Wang's detailed study on returned students pointed out the same trend.[74]

72. Wen-hui Tsai, *Patterns of Political Elite Mobility in Modern China, 1912–1949* (Hong Kong, 1983), pp.130–36.
73. DZ, 14,9:197.
74. Y. C. Wang, *Chinese Intellectuals and the West* (Chapel Hill: 1966), p.375.

Some contemporary critics regarded the phenomenon as an evil legacy from the imperial times and evidence of the corruptive nature of the current regimes, because government offices were considered the opportunity to make money. Others pointed to defects in the education system. Too many schools of law and government were established, they maintained, while education in sciences, engineering, medicine, and business was neglected and curricula in those fields were weak. Graduates from those majors found that they were unable to get a job or establish a career based on their education. As a result, government offices became the only possible career for many graduates. Whether the blame was placed on the graduates or on the education system, all critics agreed that when there were not enough governmental posts for all educated people, those who failed to find employment in the bureaucracy became "high class vagrants" (*gaodeng youmin*).[75] In the 1930s unemployment of the college-educated continued to be a problem, and criticism of the failure of modern education remained similar to the criticism voiced from 1910 to 1930. Students undertook education "not to fit themselves as useful citizens of the country but chiefly to obtain comfortable official positions," and there was a "lack of coordination between the school curriculum and social needs."[76] In addition, new kinds of criticism appeared that blamed either foreign imperialism, the class structure of the society, or the failure of students to put their minds to serious learning.[77] For whatever reasons, the problem remained throughout the period. In 1936 the *Shen Bao* reported the presence of 9,622 jobless college graduates in the country.[78]

While job opportunities for college graduates would be fewer still in rural areas, the presence of high-class vagrants in big cities indicated the desire of both returned students and graduates from Chinese colleges, including those coming from a rural background, to seek professional employment in cities.[79] Earl H. Leaf, a correspondent for the United Press, wrote as late as 1936: "A high-spirited young fellow who has had a taste of 'life' in any metropolitan city of the world, now finds existence in Kweiyang or Changsha entirely too prosaic and dull.... It is all too true that most returned students look upon their life in their native vil-

---

75. SB, 1913: 5/3, p.1; DZ, 12,9:18–19; 12,10:46–47; 14,1:23; 14,2:16; L. K. Tao, "Unemployment among Intellectual Workers in China," CSPSR, 13,3 (July 1929):251–61.
76. NCH, 7/25/1934, p.121; 8/8/1934, p.202; 8/29/1934.
77. Yeh, *The Alienated Academy*, pp.186–95; Thomas D. Curran, "Education and Society in Republican China," Ph.D. dissertation, Columbia University, 1986, Chapter 4.
78. SnB, 1936: 5/23, p.15.   79. Y. C. Wang, *Chinese Intellectuals*, pp.367–69.

lages and towns as an exile to be endured only until the first opportunity arrives for getting back to 'civilization'."[80] Of course, a lot of young Chinese educated abroad or in Chinese cities never went back to their native places to endure such an exile. Xu Maoyong recalled that as a primary school teacher, with only a primary education, he had already decided to become a "literary man" (*wenren*) and was unwilling to return to the life of peasants and workers, in spite of a concern about the possibility of unemployment.[81]

The reluctance to leave cities among the educated translated into a high concentration of college graduates in Shanghai either with or without a job. The situation may be glimpsed in one middle school in Shanghai. In 1928 the Daxia Middle School managed by a Dr. Wang Zulian hired nineteen teachers. Among them were three doctoral degree holders, five master's degree holders, and seven bachelor's degree holders.[82] Although the credentials of those teachers are impressive, they only testify to the desire of educated people to live in big cities and the limited job opportunities for them even there. Those who did not find employment still preferred to remain in cities, making use of their skills learned through education in whatever way they could.

It is against the background of unemployment and underemployment of educated people that professionals may be considered a privileged group in more than one sense. They were intellectuals and – more than that – they were professionals. Since by definition professionals were employed or self-employed, they were a group of people who made it. They achieved two related goals to which so many educated people aspired: they both (1) obtained professional jobs and (2) stayed in cities. They were a select group even among educated people and as such constituted a social and cultural elite unlike any other groups.

Professionals, once they got there, enjoyed more opportunities to make career moves. Professionals often took on two or more professional jobs concurrently or consecutively either out of economic necessity or by personal choice. Teaching at college level was the most common second job taken concurrently by such professionals as lawyers, doctors, and journalists. Writing and publishing were other areas for many professionals to dabble in, though not necessarily as a formal job.

---

80. CWR, 78,13 (11/28/1936):449.
81. Xu Maoyong, *Xu Maoyong Huiyi Lu* (Memoir of Xu Maoyong) (Beijing, 1982), pp.36–39.
82. SB, 1928: 1/29, p.7.

In terms of consecutive career moves, lawyers seemed to be the group that contained more job hoppers. Jin Xiongbai, for example, worked as a journalist for nine years before taking up a law practice in 1934, and then again took the position of the acting editor in chief at the *Shi Bao* in 1936.[83]

Career opportunities were not equally open to all professionals and would-be professionals. In the Republican era graduates of colleges and middle schools made up the majority of the staff and functionaries in the government, but important official positions were largely reserved for established professionals. Some professionals moved from professional careers into government, such as Pan Gongzhan and Chen Dezheng, two journalists who became GMD party and government officials in Shanghai. Others shuttled between the roles of professionals and government officials, which was often seen among the legal professionals. Better known among them were Wu Kaisheng, Wu Jingxiong, Zheng Yuxiu, Wei Daoming, Lu Xingyuan, and He Shizhen (see Chapters 4, 8, and 9).

The social differentiation among Chinese professionals in career opportunity (and thus income and prestige) resulted from the modernization process. Experts of specialized knowledge and techniques, such as lawyers and doctors, became important participants in the modernizing projects and the Republican state building and were socially and economically rewarded accordingly. In contrast, people who remained generalists and made a living by writing and who were generically identified as "literary men" (*wenren*) sank to the bottom among all the educated – in terms of receiving social and economic rewards. That is why writers, albeit self-employed and free-lancing, had a hard time being recognized as *ziyou zhiye zhe* and rewarded as such.[84] Journalists fared not much better for the most part of the Republican period.

In another dimension, the differentiation among and within professional groups resulted from professionalization itself. As Harold Perkin

---

83. MRD, p.499; Zhu Zijia, *Huangpu*.
84. Qin Sou-ou, a well-known Mandarin Duck and Butterfly writer, recalled that the social status of writers was so low that writer (*zuojia*) was not even considered an occupation, let alone a profession. (Qin Sou-ou, interview with the author, January 5, 1992.) In early 1937 over eighty Shanghai writers held an informal symposium (*zuotanhui*) to discuss how to unite for national salvation and possibly form a professional association of writers. One of the six organizers, Shao Xunmei, declared that writers had transformed from "literary men" to *ziyou zhiye zhe*. (SnB, 1937: 1/31, p.14.) But no official recognition of such status for writers came from the GMD government.

pointed out in his analysis of a professional society in England, the process of professionalization resulted in an intersection, if not a replacement, of horizontal division of classes with a vertical separation of interest groups (professions) competing for income, power, and status. He also said there is a career hierarchy among and within professions.[85] While Perkin's insight may not fully apply to Republican China, it goes some length to explain the internal differentiation of Chinese professionals as a new social class and their relationship with other social groups in Shanghai and with the Republican state.

Social Identity and Political Role

That professionals moved in and out of the government in the Republican era raises a question about their social identity and political role. Regarding social identity, a distinction may be made between class identity and professional identity, even though they are related. We speak of professionals as urban middle class in terms of their material and cultural life in comparison with other social groups. Professional identity refers to the professionals' identity based on their professional jobs, that is, what they actually did for society to make their living and how society at large perceived what they did. The emergence of professionals was a new kind of social class formation precisely because their professional identity and professional concerns were job defined and job oriented, not shared by other social groups, while their material and cultural consumption might have been shared, say, by the capitalist class or traditional urban elite. The political role and orientation of professionals was contingent more upon their professional identity than their class identity. Their relationship with other social groups and with the state is to be understood in the same light.

From about 1915 to 1925, educated Chinese adopted the term "intellectual class" (*zhishi jieji*) from the Japanese to translate the Russian expression "intelligentsia" and debated what role the Chinese intellectual class should play in shaping the nation's destiny. Writing in 1922, Zhang Guotao and Qu Qiubai, two leading Communists, called on the intellectual class to walk away from single-minded study and research so that intellectuals would be able to shoulder the political responsibility and assume the role of leading China's struggle for a better future.[86] In

---

85. Harold Perkin, *The Rise of Professional Society*, pp.9–11, 455–71.
86. *Xiangdao* (Guide), 1,12:98–100; 1,18:147–48.

Qu's view, the Chinese intellectual class comprised two types: One type was the old gentry class who had once symbolized Chinese culture and now was a social burden incarnated in corruptive politicians – high-class scoundrels. The second type were people baptized by "European wind and American rain" – Western culture, such as students, educators, employees in banks, telegram-telephone services, steamship and railroad transportation – the new intellectual class. Qu envisioned the latter group to be the leader of revolutionary social change.[87]

Others who were not Communists harbored equal passion for the leading role of the intellectual class. One contributor to Beijing's *Chen Bao* (Morning News) argued in 1925 that the intellectual class should unite with the laboring class because the former was a class selling its mental labor just like the latter was a class selling its physical labor. The intellectual class should be aware that it was a dominated class as well.[88] The contributor opined in a separate piece that although Liang Qichao and others placed China's hope on the high-mindedness (*juewu*) and ability of the intellectual class to organize better government, the performance of the intellectual class was disappointing. Members of the intellectual class either were concerned with power and wealth or were prejudiced against people of different views and indulged in forming small cliques.[89] Another contributor deplored that the intellectual class had abandoned its social responsibility of leading the masses and that members of the intellectual class either withdrew into the unreal world of empty talk or were going after power, wealth, and private interests.[90]

In this discourse about the intellectual class the educated Chinese were confronted with two choices: either (1) seek a political career to lead the country or (2) join revolutionary forces to change the society – both were considered a continuation of the traditional role of the educated leading the society. Certain educated Chinese did make political choices as the lives of some professionals would suggest. This, however, was by no means representative of all educated Chinese in the Republican period.

Although during the May Fourth era Chinese intellectuals (students, professors, and writers) consciously played a role of awakening and enlightening the people, by 1927 the "intellectual class" itself had come

---

87. *Xiangdao*, 1,18:148.
88. *Chengbao Fujuan* (Morning News Supplement), 1925: 1/6, p.1.
89. *Chengbao Fujuan*, 1924: 11/23, p.4.   90. *Chengbao Fujuan*, 1925: 1/14, p.4.

under attacks. As a result, a less pretentious term was invented to describe educated Chinese – *zhishi fenzi* (knowledgeable elements).[91]

By the 1920s the choice between the two political roles had become a false one, and even the very notion of educated people being political and intellectual leaders of the nation had been outlived by the changing social reality. On the one hand, politicians and military leaders had become the force dominating the political scene. On the other hand, modernization had created new occupations, new careers, and new lifestyles. New possibilities were open for educated Chinese to live their life in accordance with their social ideals and personal tastes.[92] As noted earlier, professionals may be included among intellectuals (meaning the educated), but all intellectuals were not professionals. That is to say, professionals began to have a distinctive identity. What Qu Qiubai called the new intellectual class clearly included professional employees associated with modern institutions and modern economic sectors. Many free professionals and professional employees chose to stay aloof from politics and officialdom and even from the role of enlighteners. Most of them preferred to contribute to China's modernization and national salvation in their job-defined roles. As early as the mid-1910s, perceptive foreigners observed that "a new class of professional Chinese," quite apart from politicians, had appeared in China. "Young doctors, engineers, and lawyers have been and are being trained abroad and in the modern centres of high learning in China, and the numbers are growing each year."[93]

How did the professionals perceive themselves? One example may be sufficient here: In 1924 a group of Chinese accountants in Shanghai established the Institute of Chartered Accountants of the Chinese Republic (later changed to the Institute of Chartered Accountants in Shanghai). In a letter to the Ministry of Agriculture and Commerce asking for official approval, the accountants stated their professional status and function as follows:

> The system of accounting is the product of economic evolution. As business organizations are getting ever more complex in this age of industrial and commercial growth, the design for starting [a business], the regular auditing, and the liquidation at the foreclosure – all depend upon the arrangement and advice of accountants. Like

---

91. Vera Schwarcz, *The Chinese Enlightenment: Intellectuals and the Legacy of the May Fourth Movement of 1919* (Berkeley: 1986), pp.184–91.
92. Y. C. Wang, *Chinese Intellectuals*, p.365.   93. NCH, 11/17/1917, pp.380–81, 428–29.

lawyers and doctors, they appear where needed and are in a detached position with an independent spirit to verify the true conditions of the financial world, to build society's confidence, and to provide services to the public.... One must have three indispensable qualifications to become an accountant. The first is knowledge, the second, experience, and the third, ethics.[94]

The preceding document clearly established the self-perception of lawyers, doctors, and accountants as public-serving professionals with independent spirit, specialized knowledge, and professional ethics. The professionals projected that image to the public, asking to be recognized as such by the state and by society at large. When the Chinese term *ziyou zhiye zhe* was coined in 1929 to give professionals a new identity that distinguished them from such ambiguous categories as "intellectual class" and "knowledgeable elements," it was but recognition of a social reality that had been taking place for some time.

Professionals as a whole refused to be political activists per se. As Jerome Grieder said, "The [Chinese] liberals persisted in the view that their civic status was not to be determined or valued exclusively, or even primarily, in terms of its public dimension. They thought of themselves not as public men, but as private individuals with a legitimate claim to be invited to influence public life."[95] The liberals to whom Grieder referred were mainly professionals, either independent or salaried.[96] Here the experiences of professionals in their material life, cultural life, and career – that is, both their class and professional identities – were intimately relevant to professionals' preference in this regard. The combination of comfortable urban life-style and self-gratifying professional pursuit tended to keep more successful and accomplished professionals away from becoming political agitators and rebels or political careerists. It is no accident that revolutionaries and political activists in the 1920s and the 1930s tended to be people with less educational attainment or professional accomplishment. There was also an inverse correlation between the degree of professionalization and that of political alienation

---

94. SB, 1924: 7/28, p.5; *Shanghai Zhonghua Minguo Kuaijishi Gonghui Nianbao* (Annual report of the Institute of Chartered Accountants in Shanghai of the Chinese Republic) (1926), pp.3–4.
95. Jerome B. Grieder, *Intellectuals and the State in Modern China* (NewYork, 1981), p.341.
96. Jerome B. Grieder named teachers, writers, journalists, publishers, doctors, lawyers, technicians, engineers, bankers, military personnel, and a large number of civil servants in public health, transportation, communications, mining, trade, finance, and Customs. Ibid., p.338.

and rebelliousness among professional groups. In the 1920s and 1930s, for instance, Communists and their sympathizers were more easily found among the educated who were the least professionalized, such as school teachers, students, and writers, than among lawyers, doctors, journalists, and accountants.[97]

The professional identity of *ziyou zhiye zhe* and their role in society were well recognized by the 1930s. Hu Yuzhi was a left-leaning intellectual who joined the League for Protection of Civil Rights in 1932 and the Chinese Communist Party (CCP) in 1933. Writing at the height of the national salvation movement in 1936, Hu observed, "to ask university professors to paint posters, writers to shout slogans in the street, lawyers or poets to fight in the battle field, is to forget the division of labor in the struggle for national liberation." Professionals, whom Hu called "intellectuals," had their important tasks. "A novelist could use his works to arouse the masses; a journalist could use his speech to promote resistance; a lawyer could defend arrested patriots according to the law; even civil servants could make use of their positions to push for resistance [against Japanese aggression] and national salvation. We do not need all novelists, all journalists, all lawyers, and all civil servants to participate in direct struggle of resistance against the enemy as we do masses of workers and peasants."[98] Leaving aside the political role Hu assigned to professionals, it is clear that he perceived professional jobs as important in their own right and pertinent to the nation's well-being.

Yet, government activities and policies were an important concern for professionals and often led to friction between the government and the professional community. One source of friction was the professionals' demand for professional privilege and autonomy. A second source of friction stemmed from the failure on the part of the government to deliver an honest and efficient government and to resist foreign imperialism – conditions under which professions would prosper.

In the matter of the GMD–CCP conflict, professionals as a social group or class appeared to be neutral, wishing to see an end to the civil wars that ravaged the country for so many years. Primarily for that reason, the organized political expressions of professionals were called at the time the third force. In his study of the third force in Republican China, Takaharu Kikuchi covered widely diverse political and social

---

97. Xiaoqun Xu, "The Making of Chinese Communists, 1921–1935: A Biographic Study," *Chinese Historians*, 4,1 (Dec. 1990):34–61.
98. *Shenghuo Ribao Xingqi Zengkan* (Sunday Supplement to Life Daily), 1926: 7/26.

movements, including Deng Yanda's Third Party, Huang Yanpei's Vocational Education Movement, Du Zhongyuan's nationalistic commentary, Zhang Junmai's Nationalist Socialist Party, Liang Shuming's Rural Reconstruction Movement, Shen Junru's activity in National Salvation Society, Zheng Qi's Chinese Youth Party, and the Chinese Democratic League.[99] Kikuchi held that the social basis for those movements were urbanites, national capitalists, intellectuals, and middle or rich peasants. The scholars in the People's Republic of China (PRC) described the same movements as "modern bourgeois democratic revolutionary movements." They define those movements as bourgeois by referring to the movements' ultimate political goal – a bourgeois democratic republic.[100] Westerners often regarded the "third force" as expressions of Chinese liberalism essentially for the same reason, though not all those forces or groups advocated liberal or democratic programs.[101] Whatever the case, those movements were almost all initiated and championed by professionals whom this study would define as urban middle class. Those better-publicized political and social movements, however, did not exhaust the ways in which professionals expressed themselves and interacted with the state on social, political, and professional issues. As will be shown in the following chapters, professional associations were potentially useful vehicles for professionals to pursue professional and political agendas.

99. Takaharu Kikuchi, *Chugoku Daisan Shili Shiron* (A historical treatise on the third force in China) (Tokyo, 1987).
100. For example, see Wang Jinwu, *Zhongguo Xiandai Zichan Jieji Minzhu Yundong Shi* (A history of bourgeois democratic movement in modern China) (Changchun, 1985).
101. Roger B. Jeans, ed., *Roads Not Taken: The Struggle of Opposition Parties in Twentieth-Century China* (Boulder, CO, 1992), pp.7–8.

Conclusion to Part I

CHAPTERS 1 and 2 have demonstrated how China's modernization actually effected socioeconomic transformation and affected people's lives in the process. The emergence of professions and professionals obviously represented an important aspect of the modernization process. The emergence led to the more pronounced external differentiation of social groups or classes from one another and at the same time to the more intricate internal stratification of each group or class into more stripes and shades than ever before. It both complicated and simplified the ways in which social groups related to and communicated with each other, because the socially more differentiated groups were functionally more integrated in an urban environment than in traditional times. The emergence also resulted in increasingly necessary but increasingly complex interaction between the state and society. In the case of professionals, despite an internal stratification among themselves, professionals constituted a particular social category or class that grew out of modernization. In terms of their life-style and material and cultural consumption characteristic of an urban elite culture, they were in the company of transitional urban gentry-merchants and capitalists in Shanghai and a world apart from working-class people. On the other hand, as this study will show, their professional concerns and commitments distinguished them from the bourgeoisie, but sometimes coincided with the latter's agenda, especially when acting for nationalist causes or confronting expanding state power. It is in the midst of these complex relationships that the Chinese urban society in the Republican era continued (from late Qing) to grow more heterogeneous, with increasingly pluralistic social interests. More importantly, these interests were articulated and defended in the public arena in collaboration with or in opposition to the state.

Part II

SOCIAL INSTITUTIONS, STATE ACTIONS, AND PROFESSIONALIZATION

The story of Chinese professions and professional associations in Republican China cannot be adequately told without first examining the crucial role of the state. Historically, the Chinese state was always suspicious of voluntary associations, both elite and nonelite varieties, seeing them as representing private interests and subversive to both the state authority and the general harmony of the society. Yet voluntary associations were always part of the Chinese social landscape throughout the ages. They thrived when the political order broke down and maintained a tenuous, often surreptitious existence when the political order was stable. In the late imperial period, rural and urban elite associations gained increasing prominence and legitimacy.

From the late nineteenth century onward many societal organizations began to take on a new character. The quickened pace of modernization in the Republican era brought forth more diverse social interests and public issues than ever before and gave rise to new forms of societal organizations and collective actions that sought to address the diverse interests and issues. Many of the issues were articulated and the interests defended in the public arena for the first time, which involved constant interaction between the state and society as well as among social groups. Some of the traditional urban elite associations that had long existed adapted to changing economic and political conditions and managed to find new roles for themselves and operated in new forms.[1] Others were born of the socioeconomic transformation in early-

---

1. Studies on these organizations have been cited in the Introduction. For the Shanghai General Chamber of Commerce, see Marie-Claire Bergère; Joseph Fewsmith; Xu Dingxin and Qian Xiaoming. For native-place associations in Shanghai, see Bryna Goodman. For the Green Gang, see Bryan G. Martin.

twentieth-century Shanghai and in turn contributed to the process. Professional associations belonged to the latter category.

During the Republican period the role of the state in relation to urban associations assumed a different character from the role in traditional China. On the one hand, the state continued to be wary of voluntary associations in society and tried to exercise a firm control over social forces that could be potentially subversive to the state and disruptive to social and political order. On the other hand, the state had an ambivalent policy toward social organizations. After the Qing government sanctioned chambers of commerce, educational societies, agricultural societies, and provincial assemblies during the New Policy reform (1901–1911), other urban associations not specifically sanctioned by the state also acquired considerable vitality.[2] The founding of the Republic promised an even greater public role for urban organizations, including professional associations. A key strategy for urban associations to gain legitimacy was to assume publicness by claiming to be public associations (*gongtuan*) even when they were not legally established associations (*fatuan*).

During the Nanjing Decade the GMD expounded the theory of three-staged revolution to qualify the Three Principles of the People and justify the GMD monopoly of political power and its dominance over society during the tutelage period. Engaging in a corporatist social engineering, Nanjing sought to organize society into functional groups supervised by the party-state. Yet, the regulations and statutes enacted by the GMD to control urban associations also lent the associations legitimacy at the same time.

From late Qing through the Nanjing Decade, the line between public and private associations was never clearly established by law. Various social groups chose to interpret the publicness as defined not by government sanction, but by a purpose of serving public good because that was the professed purpose of those state-sanctioned institutions. The publicness thus defined was often grudgingly and tacitly recognized by the Republican state. During the Nanjing Decade, therefore, as people's associations (*renmin tuanti* or *minzhong tuanti*), those organizations continued to claim that they represented public opinion and possessed civic

---

2. About the late Qing reform and the Qing-sanctioned societal institutions and their local ramifications, see Joseph W. Esherick, *Reform and Revolution in China* (Berkeley, 1976), especially pp.107–12; R. Keith Schoppa, *Chinese Elites and Political Change: Zhejiang in the Early Twentieth Century* (Cambridge, MA, 1982), especially pp.72–76.

power or civil rights (*gongquan*). The ambiguity of what was or was not public thus provided room for urban elite associations to claim a public role, but also gave the state the opportunity to categorize groups and organizations it wanted to suppress as private associations serving private interests. The contestation over publicness versus privateness in the nature of urban associations became a key feature in the state–society interaction in the Republican era.

3

The Republican State and Urban Associations

THE RELATIONSHIP between voluntary associations and the Chinese state from the late Qing through the Republican era can be traced along a trajectory showing that the state was assuming increasingly modern characters – the trajectory of modern state building. At the same time, the trajectory projects a Chinese urban society growing more and more diverse and heterogeneous, engaging the state in a variety of new ways and for newly emerging societal interests. This chapter will sketch briefly various urban associations in Shanghai during the Qing dynasty and then examine in more detail the urban associations that proliferated, and the state policies toward them, during the Beiyang period and the Nanjing decade. The chapter thus provides a necessary background to the analysis offered in Chapters 4 and 5 of the role of the Republican state in promoting and regulating Chinese professions and professional associations.

URBAN ASSOCIATIONS IN LATE QING SHANGHAI

Various urban associations had long existed in Shanghai just as in the rest of the country. While Shanghai was gradually becoming an important commercial center in the eighteenth and nineteenth centuries, and especially after Shanghai's opening as a treaty port in 1843, migrants from other parts of the country made up the majority of the Shanghai population. Following a familiar pattern seen elsewhere, Shanghai residents organized themselves in native-place associations, trade guilds, labor gangs, secret societies, and gentry-merchant organizations.

The earliest elite associations that appeared in Shanghai were *huiguan* dominated by ship merchants. In 1715 ship merchants from Shanghai and Chongming counties formed the first native-place trade association in

Shanghai – the Merchant Ship Association (*shangchuan huiguan*). The association worshiped the guardian deity for sailors – the Mother Queen of Heaven (*tianhou shengmu*) – and held regular drama festivals and extravagant celebrations every year on her birthday, March 23.[1] Other merchants soon followed suit. In 1754 merchants from Huizhou and Ningguo of Anhui Province organized themselves in the Huizhou-Ningguo Native Association (*huining huiguan*). Three years later merchants from Quanzhou and Zhangzhou of Fujian Province founded the Quanzhou-Zhangzhou Native Association (*quanzhang huiguan*), followed by the Chaozhou Native Association (*chaozhou huiguan*) (1783) and Ningbo Native Association (*zhening huiguan*) (1819).[2]

Other trade guilds, which were often based on native-place origins, appeared as well. The Fresh Meat Trade Guild (*xianrou ye gongsuo*) was formed in 1771, and the Drug Trade Guild (*yaoye gongsuo*) in 1788. During the Qianlong reign (1735–1795), 8 huiguan and gongsuo were established in Shanghai; during the Jiaqing and Daoguang reigns (1796–1850), 12; during the Xianfeng and Tongzhi reigns (1850–1874), 14; during the Guangxu reign (1874–1908), 28; and during the Xuantong reign (1908–1911), 7.[3] These figures are not complete. As other sources indicate, the Qing period saw at least 124 native-place or trade-oriented merchant associations in Shanghai.[4] Linda C. Johnson has referred to the organizations as "the guilds that built the city [of Shanghai]."[5]

The proliferation of merchant associations manifested the importance of commerce and the dominant position of merchants in Shanghai. The enduring dominance culminated in the formation of the Shanghai Commercial Consultative Association (*Shanghai shangye huiyi gongsuo*) in 1902. The organization was changed into the Shanghai General Chamber of Commercial Affairs (*Shanghai shangwu zonghui*) in 1904 and then the Shanghai General Chamber of Commerce (*Shanghai zong shanghui*) in 1912.[6] By that time it had come to represent the interests of not only commercial but also banking and manufacturing elite in the city.

The commerce in Shanghai, especially the shipping business, depended not only on merchants but also laborers and boat operators. During

1. Tang Zhenchang, *Shanghai Shi*, p.102.   2. Ibid.
3. *Shanghai Xian Xuzhi* (Sequel to the gazetteer of Shanghai County).
4. SYZX, pp.143–53.   5. Linda C. Johnson, *Shanghai*, pp.123–54.
6. Xu Dingxin and Qian Xiaoming, *Shanghai Zong Shanghui Shi, 1902–1929* (A history of the Shanghai General Chamber of Commerce, 1902–1929) (Shanghai, 1991), pp.37–66, 179–87.

the Qianlong and Jiaqing reigns boat operators in Shanghai already numbered between sixty and seventy thousand, and dock laborers between ten and twenty thousand. Dock laborers divided Shanghai's docks into monopoly territories and prevented outsiders from competing for their jobs.[7] Because the dock laborers, boat operators, and a large number of the unemployed were mostly migrants from other parts of the country, they naturally formed gangs for mutual aid along native-place ties.

The laboring class also brought preexistent secret societies into or created new ones in Shanghai and found ready recruits. At least four secret societies were active in late Qing Shanghai: the Heaven and Earth Society, the Small Knife Society, the Red Gang, and the Green Gang.[8] The Heaven and Earth Society and the Small Knife Society responded to the Taiping Rebellion with an uprising in 1853. As a result, they were suppressed and disappeared as organizations from the Shanghai scene thereafter.[9] The forerunner of the Green Gang proved to be the most adaptive secret society. It absorbed elements of other groups and evolved into what became known as the Green Gang in the 1890s. During the Republican period, it was to grow into a mafia-like criminal organization dominating the Shanghai underworld.[10] Membership in the Green Gang and other minor labor gangs or mutual-aid groups was the primary form of association among members of the emerging working class in Shanghai. The appearance of well-organized labor unions in modern form had to await the mobilization of the GMD and the CCP in the early 1920s and beyond. Even then the traditional forms of association would remain important to workers, especially unskilled workers.[11]

Political organizations appeared in Shanghai toward the end of the nineteenth century, as Shanghai played an important part in the upsurge of reformism in the aftermath of the Sino–Japanese War of 1894 to 1895. The creation of the Society for Strength and Learning (*qiangxue hui*) in Beijing in 1895 was followed by the appearance of a branch society in

---

7. Tang Zhenchang, *Shanghai Shi*, pp.101–2.
8. Su Zhiliang and Chen Feili, *Jindai Shanghai Hei Shehui Yanjiu*, pp.21–22; Bryan G. Martin, *The Shanghai Green Gang*, pp.10–18.
9. Zhou Yumin and Shao Yong, *Zhongguo Banghui Shi* (A history of Chinese secret societies) (Shanghai, 1993), pp.187–200.
10. For the Green Gang's activity in the Republican era, see Zhou Yumin and Shao Yong, *Zhongguo Banghui Shi*, pp.476–82, 528–62; Bryan G. Martin, *The Shanghai Green Gang*; Frederic Wakeman Jr., *Policing Shanghai*.
11. Elizabeth J. Perry, *Shanghai On Strike*; Emily Honig, *Sisters and Strangers*; Alain Roux, *Le Shanghai Ouvrier des Années Trente*.

Shanghai within two months – the first reform organization in Shanghai. In 1902 Wu Jinghen, Cai Yuanpei, and Zhang Binglin founded the Patriotic Study Society (*aiguo xueshe*), an association that openly promoted new learning and secretly aided the anti-Qing revolution. In 1905 the Study Society of Shanghai (*huxue hui*) and the Society for Educational Research (*jiaoyu yanjiu hui*) were founded. By 1908 they merged into the Shanghai County Educational Society (*Shanghai xian jiaoyu hui*).[12] Members of these associations were mostly local gentry-merchants and gentry-managers. They agitated for educational reform and directly undertook such reform programs at the local level – a typical kind of elite activism in the late Qing.

During the last years of the Qing dynasty, Shanghai became one of the centers for the promotion of constitutionalism. In 1906 the Association for Preparing a Constitution (*yubei lixian gonghui*) was founded in the city. Its members included many prominent gentry-merchant-officials and transitional intellectuals in Shanghai. In February 1908 the Political Information Society (*zhengwen she*), founded by Liang Qichao in Tokyo six months earlier, moved to Shanghai to intensify its propaganda drive for a constitution, only to be banned by the Qing government within six months. In addition to those two well-known associations, Shanghai saw another constitutionalist organization, the Research Society for Constitutional Government (*xianzheng yanjiu hui*). Formed before 1906, it was composed of a small group of intellectuals such as Yuan Xitao, Shen Enfu, Huang Yanpei, Shi Liangcai, Chen Leng, and Di Chuqing.[13] All those people were to become influential figures in the educational-cultural circles in Republican Shanghai.[14]

Competing with Constitutionalists, anti-Qing revolutionaries also arrived in Shanghai. Bent on overthrowing the Qing government, revolutionaries were outlaws themselves. They took advantage of the political shelter provided by the foreign concessions in Shanghai to establish both revolutionary organizations and revolutionary propaganda organs

---

12. Hu Daojing, "Shanghai de Xueyi Tuanti" (Shanghai's learning and art associations), *Shanghai Tongzhi Guan Qikan* (Journal of the Institute of Shanghai General History) (Shanghai, 1935), pp.833–42.
13. Tang Zhenchang, *Shanghai Shi*, pp.421–26.
14. Yuan Xitao and Shen Enfu were active in the Chinese Society for Improving Education. Huang Yanpei was known for his role in founding and operating the China Vocational Education Society, among other things. Shi Liangcai became the owner of the *Shen Bao* (Shanghai News). Di Chuqing was the publisher of the *Shi Bao* (Eastern Times), of which Chen Leng was a chief writer.

such as the *Su Bao* (Jiangsu news), the *Minhu Bao* (The people's voice), and the *Shenzhou Ribao* (China daily). Revolutionary organizations, from a branch of the Self-Reliance Society (*zili hui*) to that of the Revolutionary Alliance (*tongmeng hui*), operated energetically in Shanghai. Even some overt Constitutionalists, such as Cai Yuanpei and Huang Yanpei, took part in revolutionary organizations.

This cursory sketch shows that in the centuries before the Republican period there was already a long and rich tradition in Shanghai, as in the rest of the country, of people in different social strata organizing themselves in voluntary associations for various purposes. The proliferation of urban associations, especially political organizations, in late Qing was indicative of profound changes in the political culture and intellectual life of the time.[15] The changes were in part the paradoxical result of the late Qing reform initiatives. Designed to strengthen the state capacity to control society and direct modernization, the reform initiatives encouraged societal organizations and activities in the public arena, which the Qing state was simply unable to control. An important development was that while the state only recognized those organizations sanctioned by the state as public ones, participants in activities directed at changing the political system regarded their organizations as no less public in that they were serving the ultimate public good. The changing and contentious political culture prepared the fertile ground from which more urban associations, including professional organizations, were to spring up in Shanghai in the Republican era.

URBAN ASSOCIATIONS IN THE BEIYANG PERIOD

Urban Associations in the Early Years of the Republic

The year of 1912 and after witnessed an explosion of urban public associations in China, a reflection of an extraordinary outpouring of popular enthusiasm for public action and political participation in the early years of the Republic. The idea that popular initiative and activism was a source of the nation's strength had been publicized and widely accepted by educated Chinese years before the 1911 Revolution. The liberal ideas borrowed from the West in the late nineteenth and early twentieth cen-

---

15. Frederic Wakeman Jr., "The Price of Autonomy: Intellectuals in Ming and Ch'ing Politics," in S. N. Eisenstadt and S. R. Graubard, eds., *Intellectuals and Tradition* (New York, 1973), pp.55–67.

turies were sinicized or distorted to accommodate a Chinese environment. Nevertheless the general thrust of prevailing ideas about constitutionalism favored the expression and representation of the people's will (*minyi*) or public opinion (*yulun*) and the exercise of the people's rights (*minquan*) or civic power (*gongquan*), for the sake of strengthening the nation (*guojia*).[16] The fall of the Qing dynasty and the founding of the Republic further aroused popular enthusiasm and heightened expectations, among the urban population in particular, about the role of the people in the republican political process and in the reconstruction of the nation. The enthusiasm and expectations were not necessarily associated with a commitment to such Western-derived values as "the rights of the individual, the tolerance of varieties of thought and behavior, and belief in electoral control over executive and legislative government."[17] It was generally assumed, however, that people could and should choose whatever means appropriate to their taste and ability to contribute to the rejuvenation of China. The result was a mushrooming of all kinds of urban associations and a dramatic rise of popular activism from 1912 onward.

A staggering number and a wide variety of social organizations sprang into life in Shanghai during the immediate post-Revolution years. Many of them were short-lived and of little consequence, and thus are difficult for the historian to trace. Many others, however, became active and effective political or quasi-political or nonpolitical bodies representing the interests of diverse social groups in the city. Among them the Shanghai General Chamber of Commerce was certainly one of the most important and its story has been told adequately elsewhere.[18] Professional associations were part of the phenomenal rise of urban organizations, but had different origins and purposes from other types of voluntary associations, as will be shown in the following chapters.

One type of associations – citizens' associations – is noteworthy. The Zhabei Citizens' Association (*zhabei gongmin hui*) was formed in March

16. Benjamin Schwartz, *In Search of Wealth and Power* (Cambridge, MA, 1964), pp.68–73; Michael Gaster, *Chinese Intellectuals and the Revolution of 1911* (Seattle, 1969); Andrew J. Nathan, *Chinese Democracy* (Berkeley, 1985), pp.45–66. This strand of thought has endured in China for a century, to the day of June 4, 1989. See Guang Lei, "Elusive Democracy: Conceptual Change and the Chinese Democracy Movement, 1978–79 to 1989," *Modern China*, 22,4 (Oct. 1996):417–47; Joan Judge, *Print and Politics: "Shibao" and the Culture of Reform in Late Qing China*, pp.63–67.
17. Ernest P. Young, *The Presidency of Yuan Shih-k'ai: Liberalism and Dictatorship in Early Republican China* (Ann Arbor, 1977), p.81.
18. Xu Dingxin and Qian Xiaoming, *Shanghai Zong Shanghui Shi*.

1912 by residents in Zhabei, one of the two major areas of Shanghai under Chinese jurisdiction (the other being Nanshi – the formerly walled Chinese city). At the founding meeting of the association, Zhang Zijun, the chairperson, stated that the opinions of Zhabei citizens were extremely important to the interests of Zhabei, and that "we citizens have rights to speak about, discuss, and deal with all local administrative orders [and measures], [the rights] that nobody should give up."[19] Six months later another association of the same sort, the Southern District Citizens' Association (*nanqu gongmin hui*), appeared in Nanshi. At the founding meeting of that association, it was announced as a rationale for the organization that in the Republican era all local affairs should be taken care of on the basis of consensus and collective wisdom and efforts.[20]

Although sources are silent on the intriguing question of what kind of people were leaders and participants of the associations, it may be safely assumed that many would have been local merchants who had the greatest stake in keeping local order and controlling local public affairs. The obscurity of the leaders and members of the associations may have also reflected a trickling down of public activist spirit from the more elite elements to the more common or nonelite elements among the Chinese population in Shanghai. It is equally significant that the associations were based on residence in a particular district of the city rather than on native-place origins or occupations. Such organizational principles pointed to the urban and modern characters of the associations, which of course did not replace but supplemented traditional ones that operated at the same time. The use of political vocabulary indicated the degree to which the urban population understood the ideas about Republicanism and popular participation in public affairs, especially the notion of local self-government (*difang zizhi*), at that time. The very name of the associations – citizens' association – marked a clear departure from the old form of local elite organizations such as native-place associations and trade guilds.

Yuan Shikai's Efforts to Control Voluntary Associations

The popular enthusiasm for public action and political participation was antithetical to the political order envisioned by Yuan Shikai, the president of the Republic. Yuan's main agenda was to strengthen the power

---

19. SB, 1912: 3/18, p.5.   20. SB, 1912: 9/22, p.5.

of the central government – his presidency in particular – and to limit the power of the parliament in Beijing and of provincial governments in the rest of the country. Firm control over social organizations was a necessary part of that scheme. Yuan adopted a policy of restricting and suppressing, whenever and wherever possible, voluntary associations and other expressions of popular activism.

As early as May 1912 Yuan Shikai ordered that all private associations (*sili tuanti*) not interfere in the affairs of judicial and administrative organs.[21] In July 1912 the Ministry of Agriculture and Forestry issued a similar order to all voluntary associations in agriculture, forestry, husbandry, and the fishing industry.[22] In September 1912 a presidential order from Yuan Shikai banned all "secret associations" (*mimi jieshe*).[23] The order was duly transmitted through Cheng Dequan, the governor of Jiangsu, to Wu Xin, the Shanghai civil administrator (*minzheng zhang*), who then passed it to Mu Xiangyao, the Shanghai police commissioner.[24] Within one month Yuan Shikai and Cheng Dequan reiterated the order.[25] In December the Ministry of the Interior ordered a ban on an allegedly anarchist organization and the order was carried out in Shanghai.[26] Meanwhile Cheng Dequan proceeded to have the Shanghai Merchant Volunteer Corps (*Shanghai shangtuan*), which had taken part in the Shanghai Uprising during the 1911 Revolution, make written reports about their organizations. Two months later the volunteer corps was disarmed.[27] Such actions signaled that the Yuan Shikai government wanted to quickly put a lid on popular activism, especially activism in the form of societal organizations.

After the failure of the Second Revolution in 1913 and the dissolution of the parliament and provincial assemblies by Yuan Shikai in 1914, the pressure on voluntary associations increased. One of the organizations in Shanghai that suffered from the pressure was the Zhabei Citizens' Association. That association had been concerned mainly with matters that had an impact on the local life in Zhabei. In April 1912, for example, it discussed the boundary dispute between Zhabei and the International Settlement that had caused conflicts between the police forces of the two jurisdictions.[28] In December 1912 it sent a telegram to the Jiangsu gov-

21. ZGFH, No.36, p.1. 22. SB, 1912: 7/3, p.5. 23. ZGFH, No.36, p.2.
24. SB, 1912: 10/20, p.5. 25. ZGFH, No.36, pp.2–3; SB, 1912: 11/19, p.5.
26. SB, 1912: 12/16, p.5; 1913: 8/15, p.8. 27. SB, 1912: 12/31, p.6; 1913: 3/9, p.7.
28. According to the *North China Herald*, a police officer of Zhabei tried to cut the queue of a ricksha puller inside the International Settlement and the man resisted. The police

ernor and the provincial civil administrator requesting that the provincial assembly members from Zhabei be disqualified, because they were not elected by Zhabei citizens, whose civil rights (*gongquan*) were thus violated.[29] In the wake of the Second Revolution, the association passed a resolution asking the Chinese Municipal Government to negotiate with the Shanghai Municipal Council of the International Settlement for the withdrawal of armed foreigners from Zhabei and to order municipal agencies to resume normal functions. It blamed Mu Xiangyao for abandoning his responsibility as police commissioner and causing disorder in Zhabei during the turmoil. It petitioned the Jiangsu governor demanding that a new election be held for the administrators of Zhabei and that a branch of the police department be established in Zhabei.[30] Its demands all addressed local affairs in Zhabei and were generally in favor of law and order. Nevertheless, the implications of a voluntary association taking an active and independent role in public affairs were no longer tolerated after the failure of the Second Revolution. Just a few days after the association petitioned Governor Cheng Dequan, it was banned by a presidential order that accused the organization of using false pretenses to form a private clique.[31]

Another organization that suffered the same fate was the National Citizens' Association (*quanguo gongmin hui*) (NCA). Emerging in Shanghai in the aftermath of Song Jiaoren's assassination in March 1913, the NCA was vocal in criticizing the Yuan Shikai government for its role in the assassination and for its acceptance of the "reorganization loan" (*shanhou dajiekuan*).[32] In June 1914 the association was banned by the order of Li Yuanhong, the vice-president of the Republic. Li justified the ban by saying that "although the Provisional Constitution (*Linshi Yuefa*) allows [freedom of] association and assembly, [associations] with pre-

---

officer was arrested by the police of the Settlement. As a retaliation, the police of Zhabei arrested two police officers of the Settlement. NCH, 5/4/1912, p.291.
29. SB, 1912: 12/8, p.5.
30. SB, 1913: 3/11, p.7; 8/5, p.8; 8/12, p.8.
31. SB, 1913: 8/17, p.7.
32. The $25 million loan was made by an international consortium composed of British, French, German, Russian, and Japanese banks. It carried a 5-percent interest and was guaranteed by China's tariff and salt tax. The agreement provided that the Chinese government would invite foreigners to manage the collection of salt tax. Without the consent of the parliament, Yuan Shikai had his prime minister and two other officials sign the loan agreement on April 26, 1913. This loan greatly boosted Yuan's military strength for cracking down the political opposition and the Second Revolution.

posterous aims must be disciplined according to the law," and that the association in question did not register with the government and acted like a secret society.³³

It was probably true that the NCA and the similar organizations did not register with the government, but at the time there was no explicit law or regulation requiring registration of voluntary associations. The citizens' associations were obviously not secret societies, because they had held meetings publicly, issued open statements, and telegraphed the government on political issues. The real reason was simple – the government wanted no interference in political affairs from independent social organizations. In August of that year, the newly appointed Shanghai governor (*zhenshou shi*) Zheng Rucheng made the message clear by a notice to the Shanghai county magistrate stressing that no voluntary associations should be established without official permission.³⁴ Thus under the Yuan Shikai government, voluntary associations not formally sanctioned by the government were treated as private ones and were liable to be identified as secret societies and suppressed as such.³⁵

Warlord Regimes after Yuan Shikai

The state's efforts to subdue popular activism during the Beiyang period were most vigorous and successful under Yuan Shikai. After Yuan's death in 1916, the state's control over society became less effective, as the central government was preoccupied with and disrupted by factional strife and civil wars. Besides, from about 1915 to 1925 an increasingly acute sense of national crisis gripped the urban Chinese population and spurred popular activism in a way not seen before. The Beiyang regimes repeatedly proclaimed that voluntary associations should not interfere in political affairs, to no apparent effect. In the spring of 1918, for instance, the Chinese government and Japan engaged in secret negotiations to sign a mutual defense pact that would allow Japanese forces to enjoy privileges in China. The news of the negotiations precipitated a wave of protest, especially among Chinese students in Japan and in the country. In response to the student protest, the Ministry of Education issued an order to provincial departments of education (*jiaoyu ting*)

---

33. SB, 1913: 6/20, p.7; ZGFH, No.36, p.3.   34. SB, 1913: 8/26, p.7.
35. The suppression extended to religious groups as well. In October 1914 the Ministry of the Interior issued an order banning private religious proselytizing on the grounds that such activities tended to create religious schisms among believers and thus impede freedom of belief. See SB, 1914: 10/18, p.6.

saying that the Sino–Japanese agreement under negotiation was a security matter, with which no faculty, staff, or students of schools or universities should interfere, and that rallies and statements with regard to that issue were prohibited.[36] The Ministry issued another order urging Chinese students who had returned from Japan in protest against the agreement to go back to study in Japan.[37] The orders were ineffectual.

It is well known that Shanghai was a major center of popular political actions from the May Fourth Movement to the May Thirtieth Movement and that public associations were active in those movements. What should not be overlooked is that the political activism of the urban associations did not subside with the passing of the May Thirtieth Movement in 1925. From late 1925 to the spring of 1927, Shanghai remained the scene of political mobilization and popular activism involving many public associations. The issues that prompted different groups into public action varied. Among them were the aftermath of the May Thirtieth Incident, the status of the Mixed Court, labor movement and unrest, the abolition of the Publication Law, Japanese military actions in Manchuria and North China, and the dispute with Russia on the issue of the Chinese Eastern Railway.[38] In October 1925 warlord Sun Chuanfang took control of Shanghai.[39] Alarmed by the continuous political mobilization of societal organizations, Sun ordered a ban in May 1926 on political activities of voluntary associations, accusing them of inciting the people on political issues by such activities as circulating inflammatory telegrams and staging protest rallies.[40] The order and the events that prompted it illustrate the widespread involvement of urban associations in political affairs and their modes of public action.

The Weakness of the Beiyang Government

Three factors circumscribed the Beiyang government's control over society. (1) The civil wars and factional strife among warlords following the death of Yuan Shikai were an obvious reason for the less-than-effective intervention by the state in society. (2) The rising nationalist

---

36. SB, 1918: 5/31, p.5.   37. SB, 1918: 6/8, p.5.
38. Ren Jianshu, ed., *Xiandai Shanghai Dashi Ji* (A chronicle of modern Shanghai [1919–1949]) (Shanghai, 1996), pp.247–316.
39. Lai Xinxia, *Beiyang Junfa Shigao* (A draft history of Beiyang warlords) (Wuhan, 1983), pp.320–21.
40. SB, 1926: 5/21, p.4.

sentiment among the Chinese urban population that accompanied the protest against the Twenty-One Demands, the May Fourth Movement, the May Thirtieth Movement, and the Northern Expedition also encouraged and protected the political actions of public associations. During the Republican era, nationalism repeatedly served as the motive for popular activism and the legitimate defense of the people against the state suppression. (3) The Beiyang government faced ideological and institutional constraints. Unlike the GMD government that would come later, the Beiyang government did not have an ideological and institutional framework within which to deal with societal organizations. Ideologically, the government professed allegiance to the ideal of constitutionalism (even Yuan Shikai's monarchial ambition did not exclude the role of a constitution) and to the respect for freedom of assembly, association, and speech spelled out in the Provisional Constitution. The successive warlord regimes that succeeded Yuan were not prepared to abandon the facade of republican ideals. On the contrary, they each claimed to be the legitimate protector of the constitution. Political and military battles for power were fought under the pretense of protecting or restoring constitutional government.[41] In such a political environment, the government was ideologically on the defensive when it attempted to crack down on societal organizations and popular activism.

Institutionally, the Beiyang government did not have systematic regulations dealing with all societal organizations. During the Qing dynasty, before the New Policy reform, the government did not institute any regulations requiring trade guilds and native-place associations to register with local or central authorities. But those groups often asked to be placed on the record (*zai'an*) with local authorities as a form of acquiring official sanction[42] – which essentially remained to be the case in the Beiyang period. The government accepted as legitimate the late Qing creations of chambers of commerce and educational societies and the time-honored trade guilds and native-place associations. Certain professional associations were regulated with specific laws and ordinances (see following chapters). They were recognized as *gongtuan* (public associations) and *fatuan* (legally established associations). The prevalent popular consensus, to which the Beiyang government seemed to have subscribed, was that once an organization was recognized as *gongtuan*

---

41. Lai Xinxia, *Beiyang Junfa Shigao*; Andrew J. Nathan, *Peking Politics: 1918–1923* (Berkeley, 1976).
42. William T. Rowe, *Hankow: Commerce and Society in a Chinese City*, p.257.

or *fatuan*, it had the right to play a role in the public arena. But it was not clear what qualified an organization as public, because the Beiyang government never established a legal-institutional procedure for any and all voluntary associations to formally acquire such a status.

Because of those constraints, the Beiyang government turned to tradition to find an ideological rationale for suppressing undesirable societal associations. Yuan Shikai trumpeted his opposition to secret societies as soon as he secured the presidency. Traditional types of secret societies had indeed become more active before and after the fall of Qing. What the government tried to do, however, was to identify any societal associations it wanted to eliminate as secret societies (*mimi jieshe*) or private associations (*sidang*) or rebels (*luandang*) or bandits (*fei*) and thus justify their suppression. The government targeted political opposition in particular and reserved the harshest treatment for such groups.[43] It was equally intolerant of groups that were deemed subversive to general social and political order, such as real religious sects, secret societies, and bandits. But within the political framework of a republic with constitutional rights for citizens, there were limits to the state's efforts to ban or restrict all voluntary associations, since many of them were clearly neither political, nor secret, even if their publicness was not formally established. Thus many urban associations managed to delineate a public role for themselves and win considerable ground by asserting their publicness in terms of their goals and purposes.

URBAN ASSOCIATIONS IN THE NANJING DECADE

A Changed Political Environment

In early 1927 a new wave of association building surged up in Shanghai. Aroused by the victorious Northern Expedition launched by the GMD from Southern China against warlords and the radical rhetoric that accompanied it, the people of Shanghai greeted the political change with a host of new voluntary associations. Conspicuous among them were many labor unions, either under the auspices of or independent of the Shanghai General Labor Union that had organized three armed uprisings in anticipation of the arrival of the Nationalist Revolutionary Army

---

43. Following the failure of the Second Revolution in mid-1913, newspapers reported almost daily the arrest and execution of the so-called partisans (*dangren*) who had allegedly participated in the Second Revolution.

(NRA). New merchant associations popped up in large numbers, adding to the existing ones. Many cultural and educational societies and a number of professional associations came upon the scene as well. Among them were the Federation of Universities in Shanghai, the University Professors Association, the Shanghai Middle School Teachers and Staff Association, the Shanghai Primary School Teachers and Staff Association, the Shanghai Writers Association, and the Shanghai Journalists Association.

The Shanghai people mistakenly thought that they were entering a new era of popular activism and participatory political process. Before long they were rudely awakened to the reality of party rule (*dangzhi*) under the GMD.

Chiang Kai-shek's conquest of Shanghai was not a military conquest but a political conquest. Before the NRA entered Shanghai on March 22, the uprising organized by the Shanghai General Labor Union – led by the CCP – had driven warlord forces out of the city. What Chiang Kai-shek faced in Shanghai was not a warlord regime, but a Provisional Municipal Government and a GMD Shanghai Municipal Party Headquarters under the control of the GMD left and CCP members, backed by strong popular support. The GMD scheme for the political conquest of Shanghai was to eliminate political opposition first and deal with other societal organizations later. The first step was completed in the coup on April 12, 1927, and the subsequent anti-Communist purging (*qingdang*). Chiang Kai-shek's force took over the Municipal Government and the Municipal Party Headquarters on April 14, two days after the onset of the White Terror.[44]

With labor unions crushed in their members' blood, the Labor Union Unification Committee (*gonghui tongyi weiyuanhui*) – controlled by the GMD – was put in place. But the corporatist attempt of the GMD to control labor unions was less than entirely successful. After a succession of party-controlled organizations to preside over labor unions, the MPH and the Bureau of Social Affairs became the agencies with which labor unions were required to register. Yet the GMD had to work with the Green Gang to have any real grip of the labor movement in Shanghai.[45]

---

44. Harold R. Isaacs, *The Tragedy of the Chinese Revolution* (Stanford, 1961), pp.175–82; Jean Chesneaux, *The Chinese Labor Movement*, pp.362–71; Bryan G. Martin, *The Shanghai Green Gang*, pp.99–111.
45. Elizabeth J. Perry, *Shanghai on Strike*, pp.89–108.

In the wake of the April 1927 coup, the GMD proceeded to rein in the Shanghai General Chamber of Commerce and the Federation of Street Merchant Associations. In spite of resistance by the two organizations, by 1929 the GMD had reorganized the former and disbanded the latter, placing Shanghai's commercial and industrial elite under its control.[46] The only remaining source of power held by Shanghai capitalists – financial power – was finally taken away from them by the GMD's banking coup of 1935.[47] A small group of Shanghai capitalists managed to find ways to play some political role in Shanghai.[48] On the whole, however, the political prominence and economic dominance that Shanghai's commercial, banking, and manufacturing elite had enjoyed from 1910 through the 1920s were forever gone.[49]

The Framework of State Control over Society

Unlike the Beiyang regimes that were struggling between traditional patterns of behavior and the impulse to modernize, the GMD had a distinctive party doctrine or ideology (*dangyi*) to guide its revolutionary actions and state building. As John Fitzgerald has demonstrated, the ideology of party rule and the vision of corporatist politics were largely the legacy of Sun Yat-sen.[50] The ideology included the Three Principles of the People (*sanmin zhuyi*) and the theory of a three-staged revolution. While one of the three principles was *minzhu* (democracy), it was qualified by the theory of a three-staged revolution: The nationalist revolution had to move from (1) military government (*junzheng*), through (2) tutelage government (*xunzheng*), to reach (3) constitutional government (*xianzheng*). The establishment of the National Government (*guomin zhengfu*) under Chiang Kai-shek in mid-1927 was proclaimed as the transition from the military government to the tutelage government. During

---

46. Xu Dingxin and Qian Xiaoming, *Shanghai Zong Shanghui Shi*, pp.390–401; Joseph Fewsmith, *Party, State, and Local Elites in Republican China*.
47. Parks M. Coble Jr., *The Shanghai Capitalists and the Nationalist Government, 1927–1937* (Cambridge, MA, 1980), pp.161–204.
48. Christian Henriot, *Shanghai, 1927–1937*, pp.53–82, 271–84.
49. The Shanghai capitalists were smarting under the GMD rule so much so that they were almost relieved to see the victory of the Communists in 1949 and embraced the new regime. See Marie-Claire Bergère, "Les Capitalistes Shanghaiens et la Période de Transition entre le Régime Guomindang et le Communisme (1948–1952)," *Etudes Chinoises*, 8,2 (Autumn 1989):7–30.
50. John Fitzgerald, *Awakening China*.

that stage, the GMD would exercise state power on behalf of the people and rule the country through the party (*yidang zhiguo*).

Even with the unequivocal doctrine of party dominance, only gradually did the GMD develop the regulations dealing with nonpolitical voluntary associations. The earliest measure in that regard was a set of regulations drafted by the GMD Central Department of Organization and issued by the National Government in August 1927. The document defined the relationship between the GMD party organization and people's associations (*minzhong tuanti* or *renmin tuanti*) as follows: The organization and activities of people's associations were subject to the supervision and guidance of the GMD party headquarters at each level. The party headquarters at all levels were to warn against, correct, and when necessary, with the help of the military and the police, stop inappropriate activities of any association, though the association would be allowed to appeal to the superior party headquarters for its case.[51] Such a measure put voluntary associations under the surveillance of the GMD party apparatus, but it did not address the legitimacy of voluntary associations in society. A more systematic control mechanism was yet to be designed.

In June 1929 the GMD Third Central Committee Second Plenum adopted a resolution on the Procedures for Establishing People's Associations (*Renmin tuanti sheli chengxu an*). It classified voluntary associations into two categories: (1) occupational associations (*zhiye tuanti*) and (2) social associations (*shehui tuanti*). Occupational associations included groups such as agricultural societies (*nonghui*), labor unions, and chambers of commerce. Social associations included groups such as charitable societies, student associations, women's associations, and cultural associations.[52] The brief resolution was too vague and too general to be a useful guidance in practice. It reflected the general impulse of the GMD to regulate societal organizations, but also indicated that the regime had not figured out a rational way to do so.

In December 1929, taking a step on its own initiative, the Ministry of Education issued the regulations on scholarly associations (*xueshu tuanti*). The regulations defined scholarly associations as those that were privately organized for the purpose of scholarly research. Such organizations were subject to the supervision of educational administrative

---

51. GZG, No.10 (1927: 8/1), pp.36–37.
52. *Renmin Tuanti Fagui Huibian* (A compilation of the regulations on people's associations) (Wuxian, 1930), p.1; GZG, No.336 (1929: 12/4), p.12; SB, 1920: 1/20, p.6.

offices of provincial and special municipal governments. They were forbidden to violate party doctrine, to impair public security, to corrupt good social customs, to involve themselves in superstition, to interfere in administrative affairs or matters other than scholarly matters, and to amass wealth in the name of promoting scholarship. They were required to report to the educational offices about their finances and personal information on their leaders and members, and to be inspected by the educational offices of the government.[53]

From 1929 to 1931 the GMD's efforts to regulate voluntary associations were institutionalized step by step. The state adopted a series of regulations and ordinances on organizing, reorganizing, and supervising various associations, from educational societies, agricultural societies, labor unions, student associations, women's associations, cultural associations, to charitable organizations. The regulations and ordinances constituted the legal-institutional framework with which the GMD monitored, controlled, and suppressed, when necessary, voluntary associations of all kinds. In March 1930 the GMD Central Executive Committee ordered that the new regulations supersede fourteen earlier sets of regulations on organizing voluntary associations.[54]

An important document to examine in this study is the Amended Procedures for Organizing People's Associations (*Xiuzheng renmin tuanti zuzhi fang'an*) adopted by the GMD Central Executive Committee in July 1930. Under the guidelines of that document, the procedures for organizing voluntary associations were elaborate and strict. To initiate an occupational association (*zhiye tuanti*), there had to be fifty members; to initiate a social association, there had to be thirty members. All associations had to apply for permission to organize and to make the application to the GMD party headquarters. All associations had to receive an inspection by a GMD director. In addition, the associations had to follow the Three Principles of the People, accept the direction of the GMD, abide by the law, and obey government orders. Occupational associations should admit no one but true members of their trades, and social associations should admit no one but people who had legitimate jobs. Any person who had committed "reactionary deeds" or was deprived of civil rights or had been expelled from the GMD party could not join any

---

53. Shanghai Shi Jiaoyuju Dang'an (The archives of the Shanghai Municipal Bureau of Education) (Dec. 1929–Apr. 1930), the Shanghai Municipal Archives (SMA), file number 235-1-42.
54. Ibid. (Apr. 1930–June 1931), SMA, file number 235-1-44; GZG, No.429 (1930: 3/27), pp.2–4.

associations. The meetings of any association, except routine meetings, should be approved in advance by party headquarters and concerned government agencies.[55]

Justifying the party's control over societal organizations, the document asserted that not having enough political consciousness or legal knowledge and not knowing how to organize themselves, people were prone to manipulation by "reactionaries" (*fandong fenzi*, a GMD code word for Communists or any political dissidents) whose goal was to harm the Republic. Now that the party's political tutelage had begun, the government was to punish or reward people according to the law and the party was to show the lawful way for people to organize in accordance with the party's principles.[56] That Leninist proposition was all that the GMD party-state considered necessary to offer as justification for imposing itself upon society.

The document provided the GMD's vision of a corporatist party-state in which important social groups and sectors were organized into associations, only to be supervised and directed by the party. Conflicts in society and between society and the state would be mediated; societal initiatives would be channeled into serving the purpose of the party-state. The vision laid down an ideological framework – something the Beiyang government lacked – for the GMD to perceive and use to deal with societal organizations and popular activism. It was under that framework that a whole range of legal or regulatory arrangements were invented to supervise the whole society, or at least urban society. Later chapters of this book will show how the GMD party and government enforced its regulations and rules.

One development indicative of changes during the Nanjing Decade was the terms "public association" (*gongtuan*) and "legally established associations" (*fatuan*) falling into disuse and being replaced by the GMD vocabulary "people's association" (*renmin tuanti* or *minzhong tuanti*). That change would allow the GMD to avoid the issue of voluntary associations' publicness and deny their independent public role; as people's associations, they were supposed to be guided and supervised by the party. Equally significant, there appeared to be efforts to revive the old vocabularies. In 1933 it was necessary for the Judicial Council (*sifa yuan*) in Nanjing to give an official definition of the term *fatuan* in response to an inquiry from the Guangxi Provincial Department of Civil Affairs. The Judicial Council's Conference on Uniform Interpretation of Laws and

---

55. GZG, No.429, pp.2–4.   56. ZMXFD, p.1335.

Ordinances decided that *fatuan* referred to "associations that are established under laws or regulations and in accordance with the Organizing Procedures for People's Associations."[57] In 1934, pressed by an inquiry from the GMD Hunan Provincial Executive Committee, the GMD Central Committee on Directing Mass Movement (*minzhong yundong zhidao weiyuan hui*) asked the Judicial Council to define the term "public and legally established associations" (*gong fatuan*). The Judicial Council replied that *gong fatuan* should refer to "associations that are organized in accordance with the law and had the purpose of serving public interests in society."[58] The stories behind the inquiries are obscure but intriguing. They may suggest that certain social organizations in different parts of the country were trying to seek larger roles in the public arena by appropriating the terms that had connoted legitimacy in the Beiyang period but were not used by the GMD. For its part, the GMD government would often deny societal associations a public role by identifying them as "private associations" (*siren tuanti*), even if they were legally established ones (see Chapter 5). The usage of language (or particular words) regarding social groups' status and legitimacy therefore appeared to be one of the arenas where the state and social organizations contested for their respective roles in society. It is in this light that the disuse of *gongtuan* and *fatuan* and the inquiries about them may be understood.

Interestingly, the GMD was quite tolerant of one type of voluntary organization whose primary function was to serve narrow group interests, that is, the native-place association. As Bryna Goodman's study has shown, native-place organizations proliferated in both the old *huiguan* form and a new organizational form, *tongxiang hui*, from the Beiyang period well into the Nanjing Decade.[59] Those associations were able to flourish even under the GMD rule, in no small part because Nanjing defined that type of association as a public beneficence association (*gongyi tuanti*) and explicitly adopted a "neither encourage, nor prohibit" policy toward native-place associations.[60] The rationale for this definition was not explained, but remains rather intriguing. In any case,

---

57. *Sifa Yuan Gongbao* (Bulletin of Judicial Council), No.75 (1933: 6/17):3–4.
58. *Sifa Yuan Gongbao*, No.127 (1934: 6/16):2.
59. Bryna Goodman, "New Culture, Old Habits: Native-Place Organization and the May Fourth Movement," in Frederick Wakeman and Wen-hsin Yeh, eds., *Shanghai Sojourners* (Berkeley, 1992), pp.76–107.
60. *Renmin Tuanti Fagui Shili Huibian* (A compilation of the interpretations of the laws and regulations on people's associations) (Nanjing, 1937), pp.590–98.

because native-place associations were treated leniently and because they could in effect be used for purposes other than strengthening group solidarity based on native-place ties, people found it desirable to form and join native-place associations. Hence the proliferation of *tongxiang hui* during the Nanjing Decade.

Finally, to make the framework of control complete, the GMD government enacted in January 1931 the Emergency Law on Crimes against the Republic (*Weihai minguo jinji zhizui fa*) with which to crack down any real or imagined enemy to the government. The offenses under the law that would condemn perpetrators to fifteen years of imprisonment included the use of associations to harm the Republic.[61] With that instrument in place, not even native-place associations were free from all constraints.

The GMD Control in Shanghai

In Shanghai public associations were numerous and their influence was widely felt. The GMD party apparatus and government agencies in the city were not only vigorous in implementing the regulations on voluntary associations decreed by Nanjing, but also active in imposing restrictions on popular activism on their own initiative.

In June 1928, before any regulations were enacted by Nanjing, the Committee on Party Affairs and Mass Training (*dangwu yu minzhong xunlian weiyuanhui*) of the GMD Municipal Party Headquarters (MPH) issued the Regulations on the Registration of Mass Associations (*minzhong tuanti dengji tiaoli*). That document stipulated detailed requirements for any association to be eligible to register with the committee. The requirements included supporting the GMD and the Three Principles of the People. Only after registering with the committee could any association register with proper government offices to become legal. The materials to be submitted to the committee for registration were to include the bylaws of the organization, résumés of its leaders, and a list of its members with their personal information. After registration, associations were to give monthly reports on changes in leadership and membership, financial status, internal affairs, and any unusual situations concerning the organization. When an association wanted to dissolve, it had to report the reason to the committee and cancel its registration officially. The committee ordered that all associations register by the end of

61. See Chapter 9 for detail.

July.[62] From August 1928 to December 1931 the Shanghai-Wusong Garrison Headquarters (*songhu jingbei silingbu*) and the Shanghai Special Municipal Government (*Shanghai tebieshi zhengfu*) issued several notices urging all associations to register with the party and government offices or be banned.[63] In the fall of 1928 the Shanghai Municipal Bureau of Social Affairs issued regulations on registration of labor unions, agricultural societies (*nonghui*), and industrial and commercial organizations (*gongshang tuanti*).[64]

The announced party supervision was no idle gesturing. On September 11, 1927, before any regulations were issued, the MPH Provisional Executive Committee discussed how to deal with organizations that had not been approved by the MPH. Two cases were on the table: (1) the Shanghai Women's Association (*Shanghai funu xiehui*) and (2) the Shanghai Revolutionary Comrade Association (*Shanghai geming tongzhi hui*). The former was said to be disobeying the directives of the MPH; Zhu Jianxia, presumably the head of the organization, was accused of soliciting donations for personal use and of trying to undermine the unity of the GMD. The committee resolved that Zhu be expelled from the GMD party and the Women's Association dissolved. In the case of the Comrade Association, the committee identified its members as Communists and opportunists and was to ask the Shanghai-Wusong Garrison Headquarters and the Bureau of Public Security to shut down the organization.[65] The situations with the Women's Association and the Comrade Association are just two examples of the vigilance of the GMD party organ in Shanghai over societal organizations it did not control.

The policies and practices of the GMD authorities in Shanghai reflected a general distrust of any spontaneous public actions on the part of urban associations. In October 1929 the Bureau of Social Affairs ordered that public beneficence associations (*gongyi tuanti*) could not meet without getting the permission of the bureau first.[66] The regulation covered native-place associations, which might indeed have been the target. In April 1934 the MPH and the Municipal Government prohibited various trade associations (*tongye gonghui*) from holding joint meetings.[67] In January 1930 the Garrison Headquarters and the MPH issued a notice that labor–management disputes should be mediated and

---

62. SB, 1928: 6/29, p.5; 6/30, p.5; 7/1, p.5.   63. SB, 1928: 8/26, p.6; SnB, 1931: 12/25, p.9.
64. SB, 1928: 8/29, p.6; 9/3, p.6; 9/4, p.7.   65. SB, 1927: 9/12, p.5.
66. SB, 1929: 10/22, p.6.   67. SB, 1934: 4/30, p.10.

arbitrated by the concerned government offices and labor should not threaten strikes. One month later the Municipal Government announced that labor–management disputes were to be mediated by the Bureau of Social Affairs and no other organizations should interfere.[68] When a private Rent Disputes Mediation Board appeared in August 1930, it was banned by the MPH within two days.[69] The authorities appeared anxious to prevent any social actors outside the government from competing with themselves for the authority to mediate conflicts within society.

The efforts to regulate societal organizations even caused friction between agencies within the Shanghai Municipal Government. In February 1931 the GMD Central Executive Committee adopted the Specifics of the Organizational Guidelines for Cultural Associations (*Wenhua tuanti zuzhi dagang shishi xize*). That document defined cultural associations as those promoting scholarship and education, to be supervised by offices of education, and social associations as those improving social customs, to be supervised by offices of social affairs.[70] In early May the Shanghai Bureau of Social Affairs asked the Bureau of Education to hand over the files of associations improving social customs, in accordance with the Specifics. A clerk in the Bureau of Education indicated to the bureau chief that it was difficult to distinguish between associations improving social customs and those promoting education and scholarship. The bureau chief turned to the Municipal Government for instruction and was told to wait for further clarification from the Executive Council (*xingzheng yuan*) in Nanjing. At the same time, in deference to the regulations on cultural associations, the Ministry of Education revoked its 1929 regulations on scholarly associations. Finally in September the GMD Central Department of Mass Training (*zhongyang minzhong xunlian bu*) ordered that the Bureaus of Social Affairs and Education, along with the MPH, jointly examine the bylaws of various cultural associations to determine their nature and decide which office should supervise which organizations. The practice was thus established that the Bureaus of Education and of Social Affairs would meet and examine registered cultural associations one by one to distinguish between the two types of organizations.[71]

In September 1934 under a directive from the GMD party center, the MPH undertook a systematic survey of all public associations in Shanghai. The survey covered a long list of items: the association's name,

---

68. SB, 1930: 1/7, p.7; 2/12, p.6.   69. SB, 1930: 8/19, p.5.   70. ZMXFD, p.1343.
71. *Shanghai Shi Jiaoyuju Dang'an* (Apr. 1930–June 1931), SMA, file number 235-1-44.

address, telephone number, and founding date; the governmental office the association registered with; the number of members and of GMD party members; the names and responsibilities of past and present officers and of association employees; financial sources and financial status; certificates of permission from the MPH and the Bureau of Social Affairs; any internal problems; the plan, recent implementation, and emphasis of the association's work; members' political attitudes; and the dates of meetings.[72] Although how the survey was implemented is unknown, the kind of thoroughness with which the GMD exercised its surveillance over societal organizations is striking.

The Limits of State Control

No doubt the GMD government did a much more thorough job than the Beiyang regimes in attempting to control societal organizations and popular activism. The suppression of independent social and political activities was institutionalized in the form of the regulations on all types of public associations. The regulations were designed to demobilize popular initiatives and activism, especially in the political sphere, and to put all associations under the close watch of the GMD party-state. Guided by a Leninist-fascist theory, the GMD was ideologically capable of envisioning a corporatist state and laying down specific rules and systematic regulations to control voluntary associations, which was quite a departure from the Beiyang regimes. More importantly, it possessed greater state power than its Beiyang predecessors to enforce its rules and regulations in a more effective fashion, at least in urban society. The ubiquitous surveillance and control over society by the GMD state was truly unprecedented and to be surpassed only by the Chinese Communist Party after 1949.

Yet, the efforts of the state, either the Beiyang or the GMD, at a total control over society had limits. For one thing, public and covert associational life in Shanghai was never entirely stifled even under the GMD rule. If anything, old urban associations continued to function and new ones appeared throughout the period of 1912 to 1937. While a complete count of public associations in Shanghai during the Beiyang period is lacking, the number of merchant associations may give a sense of their proliferation. Before 1929 there were 261 large and small merchant (trade) associations in Shanghai. After the reorganization under the

---

72. SnB, 1934: 9/28, p.10.

direction of the MPH that year, the number of merchant associations was reduced to 170, which was not a small number in itself. Moreover, merchant associations were reduced in number largely due to a consolidation of small organizations into larger ones within certain trades. In other words, the number of people involved in merchant associations and associational activities was hardly reduced.[73]

For all the vigorous actions of the GMD to control society, voluntary associations continued to multiply, even though within the boundaries set by the government. In 1934 a GMD document gave a count of public associations in Shanghai as follows: 1 agricultural society and its 14 branches, 94 labor unions, 65 trade associations, 19 college student associations, 40 middle school student associations, 89 cultural associations, 8 religious associations (exclusive of Christian organizations), 8 professional associations (*ziyou zhiye tuanti*), 97 charitable organizations (including some traditional *gongsuo*), 38 public benevolence societies, 65 native-place associations, and 52 less easily classified associations – a total of 525 officially recognized public associations.[74] The number was incomplete for all voluntary associations, since it only referred to registered and government-sanctioned associations. It excluded politically oriented organizations such as various national salvation societies that appeared in the 1930s and discounted secret societies, labor gangs, religious sects, and other illicit associations.

The number of government-sanctioned public associations is suggestive of the vitality and resilience of a society of urban public associations that stubbornly protected its functional space, in spite of government intent to control and contain it. But the number in and by itself could also be deceiving, because, with a corporatist vision of state–society relationship, the GMD itself required the formation of public associations in industrial, commercial, educational, and other sectors under state regulations. The real question, therefore, is how the social organizations actually functioned and for what purposes. In addition to the earlier studies on labor unions, merchant organizations, native-place associations, and student unions in Shanghai, the story of Shanghai professional associations speaks exactly to this question. But before turning to that story, this study examines how the Republican state treated professions and professional organizations.

73. Xu Dingxin and Qian Xiaoming, *Shanghai Zong Shanghui Shi*, p.397.
74. *Quanguo Minzhong Yundong Gaikuang* (A national overview of mass movement) (Nanjing, 1934), pp.36–116.

4

The Republican State and the Legal Profession

CHAPTER 3 illustrates the persistent suspicions the Republican state held toward voluntary associations from the Beiyang period through the Nanjing Decade. It is against that background that the policies of the successive Republican governments toward professions and professional associations are to be examined. Of all social organizations, professional associations appeared to be the most legitimate ones because their publicness was asserted by themselves and assumed by the state and the general public. To effect a modern state, the successive Republican governments paid a great deal of attention to the reforms in the judicial system and engaged in the construction of its institutional infrastructure. In so doing, the state promoted the legal profession and accepted bar associations as legitimate institutions.[1] This chapter will take a close look at the ways the Republican state promoted and regulated the legal profession.

THE LEGAL PROFESSION IN THE BEIYANG PERIOD

The Regulations on Lawyers

The judicial reform that had begun in the late Qing prepared the ground for the development of a modern judicial system in China. The draft

---

1. Alison W. Connor's studies have provided a useful overview of how the legal profession started and developed under government regulation and how Chinese lawyers were trained under Western influence in the Republican era. See Alison W. Connor, "Lawyers and the Legal Profession during the Republican Period," Kathryn Bernhardt and Philip Huang, eds., *Civil Law in Qing and Republican China* (Stanford, 1994), pp.215–48; Alison W. Connor, "Legal Education during the Republican Period: Soochow University Law School," *Republican China*, 19,1 (Nov. 1993):84–112.

criminal code issued in 1910 provided for the practice of legal representation by lawyers on behalf of both the defendant and the plaintiff. When the Republic of China was founded, there were already some lawyers in Shanghai and elsewhere. In January 1912, a number of bar associations, including a General Bar Association of the Republic of China in Shanghai, were established by lawyers on their own initiatives.

The Yuan Shikai government, inaugurated in mid-1912, had the option to ignore the spontaneous establishment of bar associations in the country or to take action to regulate the profession. It chose to act. In the spring of 1912 certain lawyers requested that the Ministry of Justice recognize the bar associations that were being established in various parts of the country. The Ministry of Justice responded that a set of regulations on lawyers was under preparation and that the Ministry of Justice would evaluate those bar associations for recognition after the regulations were enacted.[2] In September 1912 the Ministry of Justice issued the Provisional Regulations on Lawyers (*Lüshi zanxing zhangcheng*), thus formally establishing the legal profession.

Modeled after the Japanese counterpart, the Provisional Regulations on Lawyers specified lawyers' qualifications, licensing procedures, obligations, and disciplinary procedures. Under the regulations, male citizens could be lawyers with one of the following three qualifications: (1) having studied law (*falu*) or law and government (*fazheng*) for more than three years in, and graduated from, universities and specialized schools (*zhuanke xuexiao*) in China or foreign countries; (2) having served as chief justice or chief procurators or taught law and government for three years in universities or specialized schools; and (3) having studied law and government in foreign specialized schools for eighteen months with certificates and then served as judges or procurators or police chiefs (or taught law in universities or specialized schools) for one year. Men could apply for taking the examination to qualify as lawyers with one of the following five credentials: (1) having graduated from schools of law and government after three years of study; (2) having studied law and government for two years in Chinese or foreign specialized schools; (3) having studied law and government for eighteen months in Chinese or foreign specialized schools; (4) having taught law and government for eighteen months in universities or specialized schools; and (5) having served as judges or procurators. The regulations provided that a bar association should be formed in each area under the jurisdiction of a district

2. ZG, No.16 (1912: 5/16).

court. Article 30 of the regulations prohibited bar associations from taking actions in matters other than judicial issues or issues concerning the common interests of lawyers.[3]

By August 1913 the Ministry of Justice had issued licenses to 1,520 lawyers around the country.[4] In Jiangsu Province 124 lawyers had registered with the Jiangsu High Court to practice by March 1913. They all qualified by virtue of having graduated from a law school or a department of law and government in Chinese or foreign universities.[5] Of those lawyers, 22 were members of the newly established Shanghai Bar Association.[6] While the regulations spelled trouble for some self-styled legal practitioners, other lawyers who met the government standards welcomed the government regulation that contributed to the professionalization of their jobs by keeping out unqualified practitioners and legitimizing qualified professionals. Those lawyers' support of government regulation may explain the swift and smooth transition from the GBARC to the Shanghai Bar Association.

Both the state action and the lawyers' response in the matter were noteworthy. The regulation of the legal profession under the Yuan Shikai government was part of the continuation of the late Qing efforts at judicial reform.[7] In the United States and Great Britain, bar associations resulted from lawyers' efforts to protect themselves as a profession. Professional standards in those countries were promoted by bar associations. The Beiyang government, however, followed the example of Germany and Japan and took it upon itself to regulate the legal profession, including administering qualifying examinations. The regulation of the legal profession was envisioned as part of the judicial reform required by the modern-state-building project.

Inasmuch as government regulations made it mandatory for lawyers to form and join local bar associations, the Shanghai Bar was not a voluntary association. Yet the fact that the GBACR and a number of other bar associations had been founded in the country before the enactment of government regulations indicates that lawyers also had the impulse to form self-conscious and self-regulating bodies that would identify themselves as a distinctive profession. At the same time, the lawyers

---

3. ZG, No.142 (1912: 9/19); *Zhonghua Minguo Faling Daquan* (A complete collection of the laws and ordinances of the Republic of China) (Shanghai, 1915), Sec.8, pp. 122–26.
4. ZG, No.457 (1913: 8/13).   5. SB, 1913: 2/10, p.5; 2/28, p.5.   6. SB, 1913: 6/20, p.7.
7. Xiaoqun Xu, "The Fate of Judicial Independence in Republican China, 1912–1937," *China Quarterly*, No.149 (March 1997):1–28.

were willing to seek recognition from an established central government to secure their own legitimacy even if it would entail government regulation. They fully recognized and accepted the trade-off. In late Qing local elite increasingly drew their legitimacy from their own local activities in the public arena rather than their success in civil service examinations or formal ties to the imperial government; now lawyers were once again looking to the state as a legitimizer for their new roles. Such action might well be taken as a measure of the hope lawyers had for the Republican state. The lawyers' action to seek legitimacy from Beijing in turn helped to legitimize the state. As a result, the hybrid nature of the resulting professional associations was neither fully independent nor tightly controlled by the state. It is that ambiguous status that gave the legal profession, particularly the Shanghai Bar, the room in which to maneuver and the position from which to negotiate with the state and mediate between the state and society. The exact nature and content of the relationship between the Republican state and the legal profession, therefore, was not fixed permanently by the government regulations; rather it would be decided by interactions and negotiations between the two.

The Supervision of the Legal Profession

The government regulation of the legal profession did not stop with issuing the Provisional Regulations on Lawyers. It was a continuous process of monitoring, checking up, and correcting. Under the Provisional Regulations on Lawyers, provincial high courts were responsible for supervising and, when necessary, disciplining bar associations. In May 1914 the Jiangsu High Court asked the Shanghai Bar Association (SBA) to submit a list of practicing lawyers who were members of the SBA to see whether there was any change in the lawyers' status over the past year.[8] In November 1914 the Ministry of Justice ordered that all local bar associations evaluate their members' qualifications and make reports thereof.[9] In the next few years the number of lawyers increased quickly, especially in Jiangsu Province, which included Shanghai. Suspecting that unqualified practitioners were among those lawyers, the Ministry of Justice ordered a reevaluation and relicensing of lawyers in October 1917.[10] In 1919 the Ministry of Justice again found the number of lawyers

8. SB, 1914: 5/20, p.7.   9. SB, 1914: 11/10, p.6.   10. SB, 1917: 10/29, p.5.

in Jiangsu too large (around five hundred) and ordered an examination to be held for lawyers in Jiangsu.[11]

The provisions in the Provisional Regulations on Lawyers were rigorously enforced. Under the rules, a lawyer could open only one law firm in the area of the lawyer's district court and bar association. In June 1913 the Jiangsu High Court informed the Shanghai District Court that twenty members of the SBA had opened more than one firm, thus violating the provision. The Shanghai District Court in turn asked the SBA to notify the lawyers in question and rectify the situation immediately.[12]

The Provisional Regulations on Lawyers required that bar associations set a ceiling for the fees (*gongfei*) and gratuities (*xiejin*) that lawyers could receive from their clients. Later the Ministry of Justice prohibited lawyers from taking gratuities at all. In 1915 newspapers reported several cases of lawyers taking unlawful payments from clients. Lu Shangtong's was a typical case. Winning a real estate suit for his client, Lu earned 1,400 yuan as his fees. The client told Lu that to express her gratitude to the judge who tried the case, she would like to send the judge an inscribed plaque saying "benevolent rule." Lu advised that such was not appropriate in the Republic and that donating money would be a more direct token of gratitude. The woman asked Lu to pass three hundred yuan to the judge and later sent another five hundred yuan in a check directly to the judge. When the judge received the check with the message that he was supposed to have gotten eight hundred yuan, he was rather puzzled. After finding out what the matter was all about, he reported it to the Ministry of Justice. Lu was charged with swindling money from a client and was tried and convicted in the Shanghai District Court. He was sentenced to thirteen months in prison and lost his appeal at the Jiangsu High Court.[13]

Similarly, when a lawyer sued his former client in the Mixed Court of the International Settlement for defaulting three hundred yuan the latter had promised as gratuity, the court dismissed the case on the ground that the Ministry of Justice prohibited gratuities.[14] Not surprisingly, lawyers voiced complaints that the Justice Ministry's regulations made life much harder for lawyers than before.[15] As late as 1920 some lawyers were still disbarred by the Ministry of Justice for overcharging their clients, though the enforcement of the rule did not seem to be persistent thereafter.[16]

11. SB, 1919: 2/11, p.6.   12. Ibid.   13. SB, 1915: 2/8, p.5; 9/17, p.8.
14. SB, 1915: 11/28, p.8.   15. SB, 1915: 9/27, p.7.   16. SB, 1920: 8/15, p.5.

In regulating the legal profession, the Beiyang government established an important "rule of avoidance." In 1915 the Ministry of Justice decreed that lawyers who had served as judges or procurators or secretaries at courts and procuratorates could not, within three years of leaving office, practice in the same area over which their former offices had jurisdiction. In 1916 the Justice Ministry revoked the prohibition without explanation.[17] In September 1918, however, the Justice Ministry reinstated the prohibition, pointing out that lawyers who had once served in courts or procuratorates often used their connections with their former colleagues to get inside information and advertised such connections to attract clients. The potential misconduct would be too much to control.[18] Following the directive, the Jiangsu High Court ordered the Shanghai District Court to void the registration of any lawyers who fell into the category in question and urged such lawyers to comply with the rule immediately. At the inquiry of the Shanghai Bar, the Ministry of Justice clarified that the prohibition applied to district courts only and did not cover high courts.[19]

The concept of the rule of avoidance had originated in traditional China where officials from county magistrates to provincial governors were forbidden to serve at their native counties or provinces. Since administrative officials exercised judicial powers in traditional China, it may be argued that even the Republican application of the rule to judicial officers was not entirely novel. On the other hand, in the Republican era, only judicial officers and legal professionals were subject to the rule of avoidance, while administrative officials were not. The rule of avoidance may properly be regarded as a measure specifically to help insure the fairness of judicial process.

The rule of avoidance remained in force until early 1927 when the Ministry of Justice in Beijing repealed it in response to a request put forward by over two hundred judicial officials. The rule did not make sense, argued those officials, because it only covered three years, and because ministers and deputy ministers of justice and the teaching staff of the Judicial Training Institute (*sifa jiangxi suo*) were not subject to the rule while they had much closer connections with judges.[20] That argument won approval, but not for long.

Under the Republican legal codes, litigants who could not afford the expense of legal representation would be provided lawyers free of

---

17. ZG, No.281 (1916: 10/16).   18. ZG, No.942 (1918: 9/8); SB, 1918: 9/16, p.5.
19. SB, 1918: 10/7, p.5; 10/28, p.5; 12/5, p.5.   20. FP, No.185 (1927: 1/16):18.

charge. But there were no specific regulations as to who was supposed to provide that service. The Ministry of Justice simply asked local bar associations to assume that responsibility. While there was no legal basis for the request, the moral force behind the action was strong. As the legal profession claimed to be a profession whose ethics required it to serve the public regardless of remuneration, lawyers could find no excuse to refuse pro bono work. The Shanghai Bar did recommend some of its members to the district court as candidates for the service, and volunteer services were indeed rendered, though it also would happen that appointed lawyers failed to show up at trials.

At first the district court paid volunteer lawyers one yuan per appearance in court as transportation fare, but later the payment was canceled due to the lack of funds in the judiciary. As a result, lawyers appointed by the court as volunteers often failed to show up at trials, causing confusion and contributing to the backlogging of cases in court. To remedy the situation, in August 1924 the president of the Shanghai District Court contacted the president of the SBA. They worked out two alternatives: either (1) all SBA members would take turns to serve as volunteers or (2) the association would recommend two to four members who would take turns to serve on a monthly basis. The plan had to be approved by the SBA's general meeting, however.[21] No formal arrangement for the volunteer service appeared to be finalized. In April 1927, after the rendition of the Mixed Court, the Provisional Court of the International Settlement designated thirty members of the SBA to take turns to render volunteer services in the court.[22] Despite the efforts of the SBA and the government, throughout the period the problem of volunteer lawyers failing to show up in court was never completely solved.

Restrictions on Lawyers

While lawyers were asked by the government to render volunteer service, they were denied opportunity to expand their practice. At issue was whether lawyer could represent litigants and defendants at trials presided over by county magistrates. Under the judicial system at the time, provinces had high courts and major cities had district courts, but most rural counties did not have courts. In rural counties without courts, county magistrates performed judicial as well as administrative functions as their predecessors had done in traditional China. The practice was

21. SB, 1924: 8/5, p.6.   22. SB, 1927: 4/12, p.6.

institutionalized by two ordinances – (1) the Provisional Regulations on County Magistrates' Management of Judicial Affairs (*Xian zhishi jianli sifa shiwu zanxing tiaoli*) of 1914 and (2) the Provisional Regulations on County Magistrates' Disposal of Lawsuits (*Xian zhishi shenli susong zanxing zhangcheng*) of 1923.[23] In 1916 a national judicial conference convened by the Ministry of Justice adopted a resolution that in rural areas county judicial offices (*xian sifa gongshu*) be established, each with one trial officer (*shenpan yuan*) presiding over trials and the county magistrate acting as procurator. The following year saw the enactment of an ordinance to that effect, the Organizational Regulations of County Judicial Offices (*Xian sifa gongshu zuzhi zhangcheng*).[24] But necessary expenditure for the plan was never included in the government budget and the plan remained on paper by 1926.[25]

On the other hand, under the Provisional Regulations on Lawyers, legal professionals could only practice in the area where a district court was located and therefore had no legitimate role in trials held in county magistrate offices. In February 1913 the Ministry of Justice issued a specific order to prohibit lawyers from practicing in counties where no district courts were established. The rationale was that legal defense was one of the three components of the judicial system (the other two being the procurator and the judge) and could function in a balanced way only in a formally established court.[26] The government seems to have feared that if lawyers were allowed to confront county magistrates instead of judges who had formal legal training, they would manipulate laws and outwit magistrates to the advantage of their clients in return for better remuneration.

If the possibility of lawyers manipulating laws existed (which, indeed, may be seen as the function of legal defense), the alternative – a system that gave county magistrates judicial powers, unchecked by the presence of lawyers – resulted in real corruption and miscarriage of justice at the county level. The government was aware of the problem. From 1913 to 1914 the Ministry of Justice issued a series of orders and directives addressing the abuses committed by county magistrates administering county judicial process at various locations. The abuses named in official communications ranged from overcharging litigants for legal complaint

---

23. ZMFD, pp.5555–57.   24. ZMXFD (1934), pp.1127–28.
25. Yao-tseng Chang, "Present Conditions of the Chinese Judiciary and Its Future," CSPSR, 10,1 (Jan. 1926):172–73.
26. ZG, No.280 (1913: 2/16); ZGFH, No.36, p.14.

forms (*zhuangzhi*), systematically using torture, and illegally detaining defendants, to recklessly applying the death penalty and failing to report to superior courts the reasons for such death sentences.[27]

Because the presence of lawyers was not considered an antidote to judicial abuses at the county level and because provincial high court branches did not exist for all counties, the government resorted to administrative supervision to address the problem. It ordered the subprovincial circuit administrators (*daoyin*) – a traditional administrative level revived by Yuan Shikai – to act as appellate court judges for cases tried at the county level.[28] In November 1914 the Office of the Greater Shanghai Circuit Administrator (*huhai daoyin gongshu*) received an order from the Ministry of Justice. There were evil local gentry who controlled county-level judicial power and abused the local people, said the order, and the office should supervise the judicial process at the county level and allow the people to report any injustice they suffered.[29] The administrator was empowered with judicial responsibility to review cases tried in the surrounding counties that belonged to Greater Shanghai. The administrator announced that his office would do its best to detect and punish those who committed corruption and injustice in the counties.[30] At the same time, however, the Ministry of Justice warned all circuit administrators that as their responsibility was to oversee the judicial process at the county level, they should remain within the boundary of jurisdiction and not take over the judicial powers of county magistrates.[31] Leaving aside the fact that those circuit administrators had no legal training any more than county magistrates, the Justice Ministry appears to have intended to balance the powers of the bureaucracy at different levels and prevent any of them from abusing their powers. The net result, as might be expected, was utter ineffectiveness of the supervision over the judicial process at the county level, as revealed by an order of the Justice Ministry in March 1916 that reiterated the prohibition of corruption among county yamen runners (*liyi*).[32] In 1925 a former county magistrate published a pamphlet entitled "One Hundred Abuses at the County Office," exposing all kinds of judicial abuses that occurred at the county level.[33]

The situation at the county level added force to the lawyers' argument that they should be allowed to practice at the county level. When a

27. ZGFH, No.16, pp.4, 14–15; No.17, pp.86–87.   28. DZ, 12,2:2.
29. SB, 1914: 11/5, p.5.   30. SB, 1914: 12/24, p.5.   31. ZGFH, No.17, p.87.
32. SB, 1916: 3/11, p.7.   33. Xiaoqun Xu, "The Fate of Judicial Independence," pp.20–21.

number of county judicial offices were scheduled to be set up in Jiangsu Province in 1922, the Shanghai Bar immediately petitioned the Ministry of Justice and the Jiangsu High Court. It requested that the proposed county judicial offices be turned into branch district courts so that lawyers could appear at trials in those places. At the same time, anticipating the failure of the petition, Zhang Yipeng, the president of the Shanghai Bar, sent a parallel proposal to the Jiangsu High Court asking that lawyers be allowed to appear at the sixteen county judicial offices scheduled to be established in the province.[34]

It was no secret that lawyers wanted to get more clients and expand their practice as a profession. It was equally true, however, that the appearance of lawyers in the judicial process at the county level would aid in controlling corruption there. Yet the Ministry of Justice repeatedly rejected the proposal from lawyers that they be allowed to represent litigants at county trials. In a response to the Shanghai Bar on the matter, the Ministry of Justice overruled the proposal by simply saying that the Provisional Regulations on Lawyers did not have such a provision.[35]

Moreover, the Ministry of Justice prohibited lawyers from writing complaints for cases tried at county offices. In 1918 and 1919 the Ministry of Justice ordered several times that lawyers sign and affix personal seals on any legal complaints they wrote for their clients. Because lawyers were not allowed to appear in trials at the county level, they did not comply with the law when taking fees for such services there. In response to the practice, in May 1920 the Justice Ministry ordered the Shanghai District Court to ferret out such cases and punish the violators severely.[36] Whether those measures were rational may be debatable. The point is that they were part of the state's efforts to regulate the legal profession in the context of judicial reform.

Judges and Courts

The regulation of lawyers under the Beiyang government can be better understood when viewed in a wider perspective, considering the government's attempt to rationalize the court system and its demands on judges. Motivated by a general desire to modernize the nation as they understood it and a particular goal of abolishing extraterritoriality, the successive Republican governments continued to carry out judicial

34. SnB, 1922: 3/27, p.14; 4/10, p.14.   35. SB, 1923: 12/6, p.5.   36. SB, 1920: 5/15, p.5.

reform in terms of the rule of law and judicial independence. From the beginning, the Yuan Shikai government made clear its intention to keep the judiciary out of party politics. The Organic Law of Judicial Courts (*Fayuan bianzhifa*) that the Republic inherited from the late Qing had a provision barring judges from joining political parties and organizations as well as parliament and local assemblies. In December 1912 the Ministry of Justice issued an order invoking that provision and requiring judges who were political party members to renounce their party affiliation.[37] In March 1913, responding to a report that judges in Guangxi Province all belonged to political parties, the Justice Ministry issued an order that the Guangxi High Court make sure those judges quit their political parties.[38] In the meantime the Justice Ministry published a list of all judges who served at the Supreme Court (*daliyuan*), the High Court, and the District Court in the capital, showing that all those judges had quit political parties or never belonged to any party.[39]

From 1913 to 1915 Yuan Shikai personally issued several directives emphasizing the importance of judicial independence and of judges' public-mindedness.[40] In March 1914 Yuan Shikai issued an order, prepared by Sun Baoqi (the prime minister) and Liang Qichao (the minister of justice), prohibiting judges from joining political parties. The judicial system was established to ensure the people's rights, said the order, and judges should rise above personal and selfish opinions and maintain the spirit of judicial independence.[41] In January 1915 the prohibition was extended to cover county magistrates who exercised judicial powers.[42]

The Yuan Shikai government's action was itself partially politically motivated, however. The Justice Ministry's list of judges quitting political parties or never belonging to political parties shows that the parties the judges quit were the GMD and the Republican Party (*gonghe dang*). It would seem that the prohibition of judges from joining political parties served Yuan Shikai's political purposes. For the same reason, the Yuan Shikai government barred military personnel and the police from joining political parties and organizations.[43] From a historical perspective, if the principle had been fully established and maintained, instead of being broken by the GMD later,[44] it would have contributed to the

---

37. ZGFH, No.36, pp.9–10.   38. Ibid., p.11.   39. ZG, No.301 (1913: 3/9).
40. ZG, No.595 (1913: 12/29); No.1069 (1915: 4/30).   41. ZGFH, No.36, p.4.
42. ZG, No.961 (1915: 1/11).   43. ZGFH, No.36, pp.3–4, 9, 12–13.
44. For the GMD practice in this regard, see Xiaoqun Xu, "The Fate of Judicial Independence."

rationalization of the judicial system and the realization of judicial independence. That the prohibition was not extended to lawyers reflected a perception of lawyers' role and status as being different from those of judges. Lawyers had a role in the judicial process but were not an integral part of the judicial system. Simply put, lawyers were not on the payroll of the government as were judges.

Besides a concern to keep the judiciary independent of political influence, the government paid attention to the qualifications and ethics of judges. Starting in 1912 the government implemented new requirements for judges and appointed judges from among candidates who had three years of education in law or law and government and had working experience in the judiciary. At the same time, to ease the shortage of judges, the government also administered examinations for judges who had less formal legal training but had served in the judiciary since the late Qing judicial reform. To ensure smooth working of the judicial system, the Ministry of Justice ordered that judges be treated equally regardless of which route they took to become judges.[45]

While emphasizing the qualifications of judges, the government exalted a spirit of public service and asked judges and judicial personnel at all levels to administer an efficient and honest judicial system. In March 1913 Xu Shiying, the minister of justice, issued directives urging chief justices and chief procurators to be diligent and calling for serious supervision over all judges and procurators in their performance of duties. In a Republic, said Xu, the rule of law was the most important principle to be upheld and judicial officials should neither abandon their duty nor abuse their office. Within four months Xu issued another directive with the same message.[46] Those high-sounding words were rhetoric, to be sure, but the intention of the government to deliver an efficient and honest judicial system should not be viewed as false, even though its capability to achieve the result was very much in question.

The way in which cases were handled in courts was another concern to the Beiyang government. The Ministry of Justice required courts to give monthly reports on how many cases were disposed and how many were left. The reports indicated that there was a large backlog of cases pending trial in many courts. Yuan Shikai personally urged courts to speed up judicial process and ease the backlog so as to relieve the people's grievances and suffering.[47] In April 1914 Zhang Shizhao, the

---

45. ZG, No.142 (1912: 9/18).
46. ZG, No.302 (1913: 3/10); No.446 (1913: 7/31).   47. ZG, No.1240 (1915: 10/21).

minister of justice, appointed a lawyer to Shanghai to help dispose of cases left by the Chinese and Foreign Court (*huayang caipan suo*), an institution that had been set up in 1912 and dismantled within a few months. It was announced that poor litigants would be spared court fees.[48] In June the Ministry of Justice further ordered that to ease the backlog, cases that were received by May 31 and needed to be tried jointly by district and high courts be tried instead by district court alone as a temporary expediency.[49] Just one year later, however, the Ministry of Justice again found it necessary to set deadlines for courts to dispose of backlogged cases.[50]

The same occurred at the county level. In March 1913 the Ministry of Justice ordered all provincial judicial preparation offices (*sheng sifa choubei chu*) to investigate the backlogging of cases at county magistrate offices. Within three weeks the Justice Ministry again issued an order that assistant trial officers (*bangshen yuan*) be swiftly appointed to speed up the disposal of backlogged cases at the county level.[51]

Despite the best intentions and efforts on the part of the central government, the limited number of courts and the increasing number of lawsuits made the problem a perennial one. As seen in Chapter 1, by the mid-1930s the three district courts in Shanghai were capable of disposing of about 87 percent of cases received each year and the remaining 13 percent represented more than eight thousand cases. As of 1936 the Ministry of Justice in Nanjing was still calling for a speedy end to the backlog of cases in court.[52]

It is clear that the government regulation of lawyers during the Beiyang period was part of an overall endeavor by the state to rationalize the governmental institutions in general and the judicial system in particular. The government, especially under Yuan Shikai, made strenuous efforts to bring efficiency and fairness into the system. Although the efforts were not altogether successful, they were not in vain either.

An Evaluation of the Beiyang Regimes

Scholars in the past often cited the frequency with which the heads of government changed during the Beiyang period to argue that it was a "confused and destructive" period.[53] The prevailing stereotypes were

---

48. SB, 1914: 4/14, p.7.   49. SB, 1914: 6/16, p.4.   50. SB, 1915: 6/27, p.7.
51. ZGFH, No.15, pp.125, 133.   52. SnB, 1936: 2/2, p.15.
53. Hsi-sheng Ch'i, *Warlord Politics in China, 1916–1928* (Stanford, 1976), pp.1–2; James

that the Beiyang government was little more than a bunch of warlords who did all harm and no good to the country and that the central government was completely ineffective during the period of warlordism (1916–1927). Recent scholarship on Chinese warlordism tends to problematize such stereotypes, but understanding of the Beiyang period remains inadequate.[54] In a small way this study tries to balance the earlier conclusions with such evidence as presented in this chapter.

The point is that the state was not just the head of the government, be it president or prime minister, nor was it only the central government. It was a whole range of institutions, the whole structure of the administrative bureaucracy, the armed forces, the judiciary, the police, and even public health agencies, from the national capital to the county level. When a part of the structure broke away from the center, in the form of one or more provinces, the effect was not necessarily a total disintegration of the whole structure. Nor did a change of government heads signify a change of the whole system. In June 1917, during one of the political crises in the central government that resulted in the imperial restoration farce staged by Zhang Xun, the Ministry of the Interior issued an order. The order said that administrative, military, and police offices at all levels should not stop their work just because of the political upheaval in the capital; otherwise things would be piled up and difficult to handle in the future. "The state and the locale, like a man's torso and his members, are connected by veins and are extremely important [to each other]."[55] The order seems to have reflected the attitude of most officials and functionaries within the state system: Political upheaval would subside sooner or later and administrative duties would still have to be performed by the bureaucracy.

That attitude partly stemmed from the situation that there was little turnover in administrative officials and functionaries, from deputy ministers down, in the Beiyang government, in spite of frequent changes in the offices of president and prime minister.[56] That situation lent some continuity and consistency in the implementation of government policies and the enforcement of government regulations. In retrospect, although the political turmoil of the period affected the normal functioning of the

---

E. Sheridan, *China in Disintegration: The Republican Era in Chinese History, 1912–1949* (New York, 1975), pp.18–21.

54. See, for example, Arthur Waldron, *From War to Nationalism: China's Turning Point, 1924–1925* (Cambridge, 1995); Edward A. McCord, *The Power of the Gun: The Emergence of Modern Chinese Warlordism* (Berkeley, 1993).

55. SB, 1917: 6/11, p.5.   56. Andrew J. Nathan, *Peking Politics*, pp.72–74.

state in some aspects and to some degree, the impact need not be exaggerated. During the period of 1912 to 1927, continuity existed between the Yuan Shikai government and those that followed, especially in the routine operations in the administrative and judicial organs of the state system. For all the defects people may find in the Republican judicial system, the records of the Beiyang government in carrying on judicial reform and in regulating the legal profession should be evaluated in more positive terms than they have been. The political motives in the actions of the government did exist, but the significance of what was actually done went beyond those motives. The major institutional groundwork had been laid down for a modern judiciary when the GMD took over state power in 1927 to 1928.

From the perspective of state–society relations, during the Beiyang period the state system on the whole did not cease to function. The state and society constantly interacted with each other in a meaningful way. For the areas that recognized the central government in Beijing, – no matter who was in power at a particular time – the lines of communication and the chain of command between them and Beijing did not break down for the most part, and subnational and subprovincial state apparatus usually functioned as they were supposed to, despite political changes at the national level. Shanghai was precisely one of such areas. It was at least partly due to the direction and regulation of the ministries in Beijing that the legal profession in Shanghai was established and developed during the Beiyang period. The Beiyang government's attitude toward bar associations was positively different from its attitude toward other urban associations. It never perceived bar associations as political or subversive, even after they expressed political views at the height of the nationalist movement. The Beiyang government regulated the legal profession on professional issues and from a professional perspective. To that extent the Beiyang government fostered the legal profession in the country and the SBA in particular.

THE LEGAL PROFESSION IN THE NANJING DECADE

The term "occupational association" (*zhiye tuanti*) in the GMD documents included but did not specifically refer to professional associations. In May 1929 the Legal System Committee (*fazhi weiyuanhui*) discussed at a meeting whether regulations on professional associations (*ziyou zhiye tuanti*) should be formulated. That discussion was the first reference to the term by the GMD officials. By June the committee decided that if *ziyou zhiye tuanti* referred to trade union or chamber of commerce, there was no need to issue separate regulations; if the term referred to organizations of lawyers, doctors, or other such occupations, respective regulations should be issued.[57] By 1930 *ziyou zhiye tuanti* became a category separate from *zhiye tuanti* in the GMD documents and it included associations of lawyers, doctors, accountants, engineers, and journalists.[58] In the preparation for the Citizens' Congress (*guomin dahui*) in 1931, professors were included in the category of *ziyou zhiye zhe* to elect their delegates to the congress.

This newly created term – *ziyou zhiye zhe* – helped several occupational groups to regard themselves as a professional community sharing similar professional values and interests. Meanwhile, the GMD institutionalized new ways to regulate and control professional associations more systematically than the Beiyang government. As far as Shanghai lawyers were concerned, the pressure was felt immediately when Chiang Kai-shek consolidated his control over the city in mid-April 1927.

The Legitimacy of the Legal Profession

The establishment of the National Government in Nanjing on April 18, 1927, signified a change of government, a government upon which the legitimacy of the legal profession depended. The change touched off a crisis for the SBA. The date of April 24, 1927, was the day originally set for the spring general meeting of the association. A district procurator was present at the meeting, as stipulated by the 1912 Provisional Regulations on Lawyers. The GMD Shanghai Municipal Party Headquarters also sent a representative there, simply because of the party's decision to supervise all public associations. Zhang Yipeng, the president of the SBA, however, did not show up. Instead, he sent a person to deliver an official notice saying that according to the chief district procurator's instructions, the SBA's general meeting was temporarily suspended because the National Government had not enacted new regulations on lawyers. At the time sixty-seven members were present, not enough for

---

57. *Lifa Yuan Gongbao* (Bulletin of Legislative Council), No.6, p.28; No.7, p.24.
58. "Shanghaishi zhengfu zhiling" (The Shanghai Municipal Government Directive), No.7994, April 18, 1931, *Shanghaishi yiao yu ju dang'an* (Archives of the Shanghai Bureau of Education), SMA, file number 235-1-44; *Renmin Tuanti Fagui Shili Huibian*, pp.588–89; FZ, No.38 (1931: 3/25). In the document lawyers, doctors, journalists, engineers, and accountants were identified as *ziyou zhiye zhe*.

a quorum. Yet, in protest against Zhang's notice, those members continued the meeting anyway. They resolved that the association established under the Beiyang government had lost its legitimacy to exist and should be reorganized under the National Government. They elected thirty members to form a reorganization committee and decided to let the MPH pick fifteen of them as formal committee members, with the other fifteen being alternate members.[59]

What transpired on April 24 amounted to a coup. The group that staged the coup was apparently backed by the GMD Political Council Shanghai Branch (PCSB) and the MPH. Approving the group's action, the MPH named fifteen formal members of the reorganization committee and ordered Zhang Yipeng and Zhang Jiazhen, the president and the vice-president of the SBA, to hand over the association business to the new committee.[60] Zhang Yipeng and Zhang Jiazhen were unwilling to be pushed aside just like that, however. On April 30 they wrote to the PCSB and the chief district procurator to argue their case. If the SBA were to be reorganized, they said, one first had to establish whether the Provisional Regulations on Lawyers and the bylaws of the association were still in effect. If not, the National Government had to enact new regulations. Before new regulations were enacted, it was not appropriate to invalidate the existing ones, although their effectiveness might be limited at the moment. Zhang Yipeng and Zhang Jiazhen requested that the government give clear instructions so as to prevent a minority from usurping the organization illegally.[61] In the meantime more than one hundred SBA members published a public letter to Zhang Yipeng and Zhang Jiazhen, asking them not to hand out the association as if it were a private possession before the government enacted new regulations and formal elections were held.[62] Facing opposition, the reorganization committee chose not to confront Zhang Yipeng, Zhang Jiazhen, and other SBA members directly. The reorganization committee went to meet with the MPH and the PCSB instead.[63]

The outcome of the conflict was predictable. The reorganization committee received the full support of the MPH and the PCSB. The MPH and PCSB issued the reorganization committee written directives to take over the SBA. Armed with the directives, the committee simply informed Zhang Yipeng and Zhang Jiazhen of the date for handing over the association business. By that time Zhang Yipeng and Zhang Jiazhen must

---

59. SB, 1927: 4/25, p.6.   60. SB, 1927: 4/28, p.8.   61. SB, 1927: 5/1, p.8.
62. SB, 1927: 5/4, p.8.   63. SB, 1927: 5/2, p.7; 5/3, p.8.

have realized that under the circumstances arguing legal points was useless and possibly dangerous. They decided to comply with the directives of the MPH and PCSB. The transfer of the SBA's business was completed on May 15. Within one week the reorganization committee sent copies of a reorganization agreement (*gaizu guiyue*) to the MPH, PCSB, and Jiangsu Department of Justice.[64] It should be noted that all the aforementioned activities took place before the GMD promulgated any regulations on public associations.

The reorganization was significant in three respects. First, it suggests that there had been friction within the SBA before the arrival of the GMD regime. Some members of the association seem to have harbored discontent with Zhang Yipeng and Zhang Jiazhen all along and simply took this opportunity to force them out. Second, the lawyers in the reorganization group were probably GMD party members who took full advantage of their political connection to take over the association. Third, the GMD was obviously eager to shake up the SBA that was founded under the Beiyang government. It seemed eager to exercise a measure of control over the SBA at a time when regulations on all public associations had not been in place. It also wanted to reserve the power to confer legitimacy upon the SBA – a power full of symbolic meaning. The reorganization meant that the legal existence of the legal profession in Shanghai was henceforth identified with the GMD state and in return lawyers would be expected to support the GMD. From the perspective of the average member of the SBA, the GMD regime had come to stay. It would be the government under which Shanghai professionals were to live and upon which the association depended for its own professional privileges – which is why Zhang Yipeng and Zhang Jiazhen eventually complied.[65]

To completely change the foundation of the legal profession's legitimacy, the GMD announced in June 1927 that lawyers' licenses issued by the Ministry of Justice in Beijing (which was still in existence) were no longer valid and new licenses were to be issued by the Nanjing government.[66] It asked lawyers to apply for new licenses with proper credentials and old licenses.[67]

---

64. SB, 1927: 5/11, p.7; 5/14, p.8; 5/16, p.5; 5/22, p.7.
65. The MPH's interest in controlling professionals was not limited to lawyers. In late April 1927 the MPH approached members of the Institute of Chartered Accountants in Shanghai to invite them to join the party. See SB, 1927: 4/27, p.7.
66. SB, 1927: 6/22, p.7; NCH, 5/28/1927, p.375.   67. SB, 1927: 8/1, p.8.

Regulations on Lawyers

Urged by the reorganized Shanghai Bar, the Ministry of Justice in Nanjing enacted the new Regulations on Lawyers (*Lüshi zhangcheng*) on July 23, 1927.[68] Based on the 1912 regulations, the new ones had only a few minor changes, the most important of which was to allow women to join the legal profession. Enacted at the same time were the Regulations on Registration of Lawyers (*Lüshi denglu zhangcheng*).[69] In December 1928 the Ministry of Justice issued the Regulations on Lawyers' Selection Committee (*Zhenba lüshi weiyuanhui zhangcheng*). The committee would determine the qualifications of lawyers.[70]

Both the old and the new regulations on lawyers provided for the regular attendance of the district procurator at bar associations' meetings, but neither said anything about other forms of supervision. In reality, however, the MPH's officials regularly attended the general meetings of the SBA and other professional associations, in accordance with the regulations on people's associations. In the fall of 1930, the SBA denied the MPH's authority to supervise it on the grounds that the SBA was part of the judicial system and not an ordinary social association. But the Ministry of Justice ruled that although the bar association was different from other voluntary associations, it was subject to the direction of the GMD party headquarters in the matter of carrying out the party doctrine (*zhixing dangyi*).[71] That form of supervision was in sharp contrast to the practice of the Beiyang government. Professional associations were treated by the GMD in the same way as other public associations and placed under the direct surveillance of the party-state.

For years local bar associations drew up their bylaws in accordance with the Regulations on Lawyers. But controversies arose in areas not covered by the Regulations on Lawyers. Some local bar associations provided in their bylaws how lawyers and judges should treat each other in court. The Ministry of Justice objected to such provisions and the bar associations insisted on them. To solve the problem once and for all, in February 1936 the Justice Ministry issued a model of bylaws for bar associations. Citing the problem posed by local variations, the Justice

---

68. ZMXFD (1936), pp.5629–32; FP, No.215 (1927: 8/14):9–13.
69. FP, No.215 (1927: 8/14):9–13.   70. ZMXFD (1936), pp.5631–32.
71. Guo Wei and Zhou Dingmei, *Lushi Banshi Shouxu Chengshi Huishu* (An annotated compilation of the procedures for lawyers' practice) (Shanghai, 1937), p.33.

Ministry ordered all local bar associations to copy the model for their bylaws, filling in local differences in such areas as public fees, admission fees, membership fees, and the number of officers.[72] The measure was the culmination of the state's efforts to set a national norm for the legal profession.

Restrictions on Lawyers

The GMD state continued reforms in the judicial system and monitored the legal profession on a regular basis. In several respects the GMD government followed the rules set by the Beiyang government, a testimony to the Beiyang government's achievements. For example, the rule of avoidance was revived. On February 28, 1929, the Ministry of Justice issued a directive that any lawyer who was a former judge or procurator could not practice in the same district where the lawyer had served within one year of leaving the office. On July 30, 1932, the restriction was expanded to cover all former court officers including court interpreters. One year later the restriction period was extended to three years. In February 1932 the Justice Ministry further prohibited the lawyer from practicing in the area where the chief justice or chief procurator or county chief judicial officer was a close relative. Another directive prohibited lawyers from serving as judges in the same area within one year of ceasing practice.[73] The regulations by the Beijing and Nanjing governments pointed to the situation that during the Republican era lawyers frequently moved in and out of the government bureaucracy, that is, taking and leaving positions of judges and procurators. That situation was another dimension of the divide between the state and society being blurred, as those same people changed roles back and forth between regulators and the regulated, between agents of the state and actors in society.

The GMD government continued to allow county magistrates to preside over the judicial process and to prohibit lawyers from practicing there. In August 1928, responding to an inquiry from a local bar associ-

---

72. FZ, No.295 (1936: 2/26); SLGB, No.34, p.53; Guo Wei and Zhou Dingmei, *Lushi Banshi Shouxu Chengshi Huishu*, pp.22–30.
73. SB, 1929: 10/6, p.6; Liu Zheng, *Lushi Daode Lun* (On the ethics of lawyers) (Shanghai, 1934), pp.35–37; *Shanghai Lushi Gonghui Huiyuan Yingxing Zhuyi Shixiang* (Handbook of guidelines for members of the Shanghai Bar Association) (1936), pp.13–16, 18; SLGB, No.25 (July 1929), pp.8–9, 16; No.30 (Apr. 1932), p.42; No.34 (July 1936), pp.112–13; FZ, No.82 (1931: 1/27); No.83–86 (1931: 2/24); No.168 (1933: 9/20); NCH, 9/13/1933, p.402.

ation, the Supreme Court ruled that lawyers could not appear at trials held at county judicial offices. In January 1932 and April 1933 the Ministry of Justice repeated the same order. In addition, it reiterated the rule that lawyers sign and affix personal seals to any legal complaints they wrote for litigants.[74] Lawyers were not even allowed to work as legal consultants (*falu guwen*) at the county level.[75] Time and again the Shanghai Bar Association and other local bar associations petitioned the Ministry of Justice in Nanjing that lawyers be allowed to appear at the county judicial offices, but to no avail.

Not until early 1936 did the government make some changes. Nanjing enacted an ordinance on the establishment of a county judicial section (*xian sifa chu*), a new version of the county judicial office the Beiyang government had tried to establish.[76] During the next five months the government enacted two supplementary ordinances, by which lawyers were allowed for the first time to practice at county judicial sections.[77] Under the regulations, however, when a county magistrate did not appear as procurator at a trial presided over by a trial officer, lawyers were instructed not to attend either. The Nanjing government apparently accepted the thinking of the Beiyang government about not allowing a lawyer to act in trials without an equal opponent. That provision greatly curtailed the opportunity for lawyers to participate in the county judicial process. One writer of *Faling Zhoukan* (Weekly Review of Laws and Ordinances) commented that given the slothfulness to which county magistrates were prone, they would rarely appear at a trial and thus lawyers would have little chance to appear either.[78] It should also be noted that judicial sections were actually established in a limited number of counties. According to one account, nationwide there were more than fourteen hundred counties where magistrates exercised judicial powers.[79] Lawyers had no recognized role in those places.

The GMD Political Agenda in Judicial Reform

The GMD efforts at judicial reform and regulation of the legal profession were not politically impartial. In May 1927 Lu Xingyuan was

---

74. FZ, No.148 (1933: 5/3); Liu Zheng, *Lushi*, p.34.
75. *Shanghai Lushi Gonghui Huiyuan Yingxing Zhuyi Shixiang*, p.17; FZ, No.87–90 (1932: 3/23).
76. FZ, No.303 (1936: 4/22); *Xiandai Sifa* (Modern Judiciary), Vol.1, No.8 (1936), pp.179–81.
77. FZ, No.314 (1936: 7/8); No.329 (1936: 10/21); SnB, 1936: 12/4, p.10; 1937: 2/25, p.16.
78. FZ, No.331 (1936: 11/4).   79. FZ, No.295 (1936: 2/26).

appointed the president of the Provisional Court in the International Settlement. At his inaugural ceremony, Chen Dezheng, the head of the Propaganda Department of the MPH, delivered a speech, praising Lu in the following terms: Lu's attitude towards the GMD "has always been that of a faithful follower and a devoted disciple of our late president, Dr. Sun Yat-sen. Now that the government has appointed him to this important post, we have no doubt whatever in our minds but that he will do his utmost to uphold the doctrines and the traditions of the Kuomintang [GMD] in the administration of justice according to the law."[80] The political implications of these remarks did not escape the notice of the *North China Daily News*. Quoting Chen's speech, the editor observed: "We fail to see how Mr. Loo [Lu] can honestly use a law court to forward the interests of a party and at the same time administer what we call justice. We have no doubt that the Chinese see nothing incompatible in these two lines of endeavor."[81] Of course, upholding the GMD's cause in any line of endeavor was precisely what the party required of public officials and professionals.

Reversing the prohibition of judges from joining political parties in the Beiyang period, the GMD encouraged its party members to become judges and judges to join the GMD party. When the Ministry of Justice created a training institute for judges (*faguan yangcheng suo*) in early 1929, it readily announced that the two hundred positions were open only to the GMD party members with proper educational background.[82]

The same sort of thing was also seen in the legal profession. In December 1928 the Justice Ministry ordered all district courts to enforce the provision in the Regulations on Lawyers that barred lawyers from assuming paid public offices while practicing law.[83] However, to protect its party members and maintain the party's control over the profession, the GMD government made an exception to its own regulation. In December 1931 the Ministry of Justice instructed that the prohibition against lawyers taking paid public offices did not apply to officials of the GMD party headquarters (*dangbu*) at various levels who were paid "living allowances" (*shenghuo jintie*).[84] The exception was only part of the GMD drive to exert party dominance over the judicial system.[85]

80. *North China Daily News*, 1927: May 17, p.12.
81. *North China Daily News*, 1927: May 19, p.6.   82. SB, 1929: 2/23, p.4.
83. SB, 1928: 12/17, p.6.   84. SLGB, No.30 (Apr. 1932), p.146.
85. See Xiaoqun Xu, "The Fate of Judicial Independence," pp.9–16.

5

The Republican State and the Medical Profession

THE ROLE of the state in Chinese medical professionalization was a quite different story from its role in the legal professionalization. The Republican state paid much greater attention to the regulation of the legal profession and the judicial system, because modern state building required, and foreign powers demanded in exchange for their relinquishing extraterritoriality, the establishment of a modern Chinese judiciary. In contrast, the Republican state recognized the importance of medicine and public health as the domain for state action slowly and haphazardly.

Moreover, while traditional China did not have the legal profession (in spite of *songshi*) or an independent judicial system, native medicine did have a long and rich tradition. In the early twentieth century when Western medicine had been introduced into China for decades, native medicine continued to provide medical treatment for the majority of the Chinese population. When the state began to regulate medicine and the medical profession, it would immediately confront the question of whether medical professionalization and the development of medical science should entail the demise of native medicine. During the Beiyang period and much of the Nanjing Decade, an ambivalent attitude and an ambiguous policy toward native medicine on the part of the Republican state were important elements in the state's neglect of medicine and public health as a whole. To a large degree, societal forces in the conflict between native and Western medicine forced the issue and pushed the state to play an increasingly crucial role in the field of medicine and public health.

MEDICINE IN THE BEIYANG PERIOD

Native Medicine in Shanghai

For thousands of years native medicine was the only source of medical treatment for the Chinese. Within the tradition of native medicine stratification existed. Official physicians studied both Confucian classics and medical classics and served the imperial houses and high officials. Numerous independent practitioners from regular physicians to religious (Buddhist or Taoist) healers met the medical needs of the majority of the Chinese population. In the elite literary discourse and popular perception, native physicians fell into one of the following categories: Confucian-physicians (*ruyi*), enlightened or skilled physicians (*mingyi*), mediocre or unskilled physicians (*yongyi*), and shamanic physicians (*wuyi*).[1] Despite the diverse composition, the line between the categories was not clearly defined and often blurred. Independent practitioners, however categorized, were the backbone of native medicine.

From the mid-nineteenth century onward, the influence of Western medicine increased gradually, but its practitioners remained a small group in the vast Chinese population. In addition to the lack of resources required for its development, Western medicine encountered deep-seated suspicion and distrust from ordinary Chinese.[2] Nevertheless, Western medicine constituted not only an alternative but also a challenge to native medicine, especially in treaty ports such as Shanghai, where missionary and secular foreign medical institutions were most visible. More seriously, during the 1890s and the 1900s, a number of reform-minded intellectuals began to reexamine the national heritage in an effort to discover the secret of foreign powers' strength and the root of China's weakness. Informed by Social Darwinism, reformers from Kang Youwei, Liang Qichao, to Tan Sitong invariably found that medicine was a vital element contributing to national strength. They deplored the Chinese state's neglect of public health and the lack of progress in medical science in China. In their minds Western medicine, as one aspect

---

1. Ma Boying, *Zhongguo Yixue Wenhua Shi* (A history of medicine in Chinese culture) (Shanghai, 1994), pp.476–90; Paul U. Unschuld, *Medical Ethics in Imperial China* (Berkeley, 1979), pp.15–59. Unschuld's translation of *yongyi* into "regular physician" is incorrect.
2. S. H. Chuan, "Chinese Patients and Their Prejudices," *China Medical Journal*, 31,6 (Nov. 1917):504–10; James L. Maxwell, "A Century of Medical Missions in China," *China Medical Journal*, 39,7 (July 1925):636–50.

of Western science, was by definition superior to China's native medicine. Early critics of native medicine, however, did not suggest a total rejection of native medicine. Rather, they expressed a desire to realize the full potential of native medicine to strengthen the Chinese race and nation. In other words, it was considered not only desirable but also possible to develop Chinese native medicine through scientific research and in the light of Western medicine.[3]

Native medical practitioners felt enormous pressure from the criticism of their trade, criticism generated by a desire for China's modernization. They acknowledged certain defects in native medicine and some benefits of Western medicine. Attempts were made to combine the advantages of native and Western medicine. As early as 1904 Li Pingshu, a prominent Shanghai gentry-manager versed in native medicine, along with his friend Chen Lianfang, a native physician, founded a society to improve native medicine through research, though that society was short-lived.[4] One year later Li concluded a six-year contract with Zhang Zhujun, a female doctor trained by medical missionaries, to open a medical school for women where Li would teach native medicine and Zhang, Western medicine. In his autobiography Li Pingshu recalled his approach to medicine at that time. Having read some translated works on Western medicine, he was intrigued by the possibility of uniting native and Western medicine:

> Native medicine and Western medicine are on two different paths – one is based on the change of Qi and the other on the circulation of blood, obviously two different paths. Those who practiced Western medicine always regard [the theory of] Qi as absurdity because Qi is invisible. [They] do not know that invisible as it is, [the existence of] Qi is absolutely verified by various illness. But those who speak of the change of Qi get entangled in [the theory of] Yin-Yang and Five Elements. The more they speak, the more obscure it becomes, which leads to the criticism by Western medical practitioners. As for physiology, native medicine is less concrete than Western medicine. So I want to use Neijing, Nanjing, Shanghan Lun, and other [native medical] classics as the basis, and [the methods of] macro observation and micro analysis as references, to study

---

3. Ralph C. Croizier, *Traditional Medicine in Modern China: Science, Nationalism, and the Tensions of Cultural Change* (Cambridge, MA, 1968), pp.59–68.
4. Li Pingshu, *Qishi Zishu* (Autobiography at seventy) (Shanghai, 1924), p.51; Hu Daojing, "Shanghai de Xueyi Tuanti," *Shanghai Tongzhi Guan Qikan*, p.842.

physiology, the change of Qi, and the circulation of blood, decide the terminology of diseases, and collect the cures from all sources, hopefully to melt native and Western medicine in one pot.[5]

The efforts to merge native and Western medicine were carried on by others as well. In 1908, at the suggestion of Li Pingshu, a group of Shanghai gentry-merchants and gentry-managers financed the construction of a private Shanghai Hospital where both native and Western medicine would be applied. At the opening ceremony of the hospital Li gave a speech explaining the inevitability of the spread of Western medicine. Western learning that came into vogue after the opening of China to foreign trade had both harmed China and benefited China, said Li, and Western medicine was one thing that was benefiting China.[6]

Li Pingshu was able to provide an impartial evaluation of both forms of medical treatment because being a layperson he had no stake in the success of either native or Western medical practice. Moreover, in the first decade of the twentieth century, before the movement to adopt Western medicine began to threaten a demise of its Chinese native counterpart, even native physicians supported the use of Western methods to improve Chinese practice.

It was in such an environment that a number of native medical associations came on the scene in the wake of the founding of the Republic. On August 4, 1912, a group of more than seventy native physicians and pharmacists gathered in the home of Li Pingshu to found the Chinese Medical and Pharmaceutical Society (CMPS) (*zhonghua yiyao lianhe hui*). Yu Botao, a leading organizer, described the organization's mission: It would endeavor to preserve useful medical classics and expurgate false theories, to achieve unity of native medical practitioners, to study the nature and differences of various native drugs, and to improve the methods of preparing native drugs.[7] Thus the society had the dual purpose of improving native medicine and uniting its practitioners.

In early 1913, just a few months after the CMPS was founded, Yu Botao left the society for unknown reasons and established another native medical association. That association was called the Shenzhou Medical and Pharmaceutical General Association (SMPGA) (*shenzhou yiyao zonghui*).[8] It differed from the CMPS in that it claimed to be a

---

5. Li Pingshu, *Qishi*, p.52.   6. Li Pingshu, *Qishi*, pp.54–55.
7. SB, 1912: 8/6, p.6.   8. SB, 1913: 3/26, p.8.

national organization and set up branches in other cities and towns. By 1923 it was able to boast more than forty branches and over six thousand members in the country.[9]

A third major native medical association was the Shanghai Native Medical Society (SNMS) (*Shanghai zhongyi xuehui*), founded in 1921.[10] Its leaders were among the most renowned native physicians at the time, such as Ding Ganren, Ding Zhongying, and Xia Yingtang. It published a medical monthly, the *Journal of Native Medicine* (*Zhongyi zazhi*), held discussion sessions, and sometimes sponsored free medical treatment for the poor. In 1925 its membership rose to 676.[11]

Western-Style Doctors in Shanghai

The gradual expansion of Western medicine in Shanghai and the rest of the country led to the formation of Western medical associations. The earliest of such associations was the China Medical Missionary Association founded in 1886. Associations of Western-style Chinese doctors began to appear in Shanghai in 1915. The Medical and Pharmaceutical Society of the Chinese Republic (MPSCR) (*zhonghua minguo yiyao xuehui*) was established by doctors trained in Germany and Japan and joined by graduates from Chinese schools of Western medicine. The National Medical Association (NMA) (*zhonghua yixue hui*), on the other hand, was founded by a group of doctors trained in Europe and the United States or in American-managed medical schools in China. By 1919 the NMA had 450 members, of whom some 50 were trained abroad.[12] The NMA's *China Medical Journal* (*Zhonghua yixue zazhi*) was the most influential and prestigious medical journal in China. In 1916 the association formed the Health Education Committee and the Medical Terminology Evaluation Committee, both of which made considerable contributions to medical education and the unification of translated scientific terminology in China.[13] In 1925 the China Medical Missionary Association changed its name to the China Medical Association – in response to the rising Chinese nationalism of that

---

9. SB, 1923: 11/23, p.6.
10. *Shanghai Shi Guoyi Xuehui Shizhou Jinian Kan* (The tenth anniversary memorial journal of the Shanghai Native Medical Society) (1932), p.9; Hu Daojing, "Shanghai de Xueyi Tuanti," p.878.
11. *Shanghai Shi Guoyi Xuehui Shizhou Jinian Kan*, p.13.   12. NCH, 11/8/1919.
13. NCH, 8/19/1916, p.354; Shi Quansheng, *Zhonghua Minguo*, pp.420–21.

time – and eventually merged with the National Medical Association in 1932.[14]

The National Medical Association was a national organization, but most of its leaders practiced in Shanghai, which resulted in formation of the NMA Shanghai Branch in 1917.[15] Because the NMA functioned as a scholarly association and did not attend to the issue of professionalization, doctors of Western medicine had a need for an organizational vehicle to respond to issues affecting their professional interests. For that reason, on November 1, 1925, a new medical association was born – the Medical Practitioners' Association of Shanghai (MPAS) (*Shanghai yishi gonghui*).[16] The association limited its membership to doctors who graduated from foreign medical schools or Western-style medical schools in China. The bylaws of the MPAS stated its mission as follows: to promote scholarly progress, uphold medical ethics, promote and help local government with public health matters, protect members' professional rights, and foster a spirit of mutual assistance.[17] In April 1926 the MPAS had more than 100 members and by 1936 the number had grown to 354, of whom 34 (9.6%) were women and 122 (34.4%) were graduates from medical schools in the United States, Great Britain, Germany, France, or Japan.[18]

Another medical association of some importance was the Chinese Association of Western-style Medical Practitioners (CAWMP) (*zhonghua xiyi gonghui*). Founded in 1929, the CAWMP was open to practitioners of Western medicine who did not have formal training in medical schools and qualified to practice by virtue of learning the trade as private students or apprentices of Western-style doctors. Pang Jingzhou, the vice-president of the MPAS, indicated that the organization was a response to the policy of the MPAS to exclude medical practitioners without diplomas. With a condescending tone, Pang noted that CAWMP group of practitioners was good at the art of practicing (*kaiye shu*) and successful in winning over patients, but that none of the practitioners published anything on medical science or taught in any medical schools.[19] In other words, they were less than professional.

14. NCH, 10/5/1932, p.23; *Zhongguo Yijie Zhinan* (Directory of Chinese medical practitioners) (Zhonghua yixuehui, 1932), p.3.
15. SB, 1917: 4/4, p.5; 4/10, p.6.
16. SB, 1925: 10/29, p.5; 11/2, p.5; *Shanghaishi Nianjian* (1936), pp.T28–29.
17. "Shanghai Shi Yishi Gonghui Huizhang" (The bylaws of the Medical Practitioners' Association of Shanghai), in *Shanghai Shi Yishi Gonghui Huiyuanlu*.
18. SB, 1926: 4/25, p.5; *Shanghai Shi Yishi Gonghui Huiyuanlu*.
19. Pang Jingzhou, *Shanghaishi*, pp.50–51, 71–72.

The Beiyang Government and Medicine

The Beiyang government did not have formal policy toward medicine and public health. One major measure the Beiyang government took in the field of public health and medicine was the establishment of a Health Division (*weisheng si*) under the Ministry of the Interior in 1914. Another was the formation in 1919 of the National Epidemic Prevention Bureau, in the wake of the outbreak of plagues in Mongolia and north China two years earlier.[20]

But the neglect itself seemed disquieting to native physicians. In August 1912 a national conference on education in Beijing adopted a series of resolutions on educational issues, including the status of Western-style medical schools, without addressing the matter of native medical education. That action caused much uneasiness among native physicians. In March 1913 the newly founded SMPGA sent a telegram to Yuan Shikai, asking for the establishment of native medical schools. The SMPGA's request was referred to the Ministry of Education. When the Education Ministry took no action, the SMPGA sent delegates to Beijing to argue its case.[21] Nothing came out of the effort, but a native medical school was established in Shanghai on native physicians' own resources, with the blessing from the Greater Shanghai circuit administrator (*huhai daoyin*) and the Shanghai County magistrate.[22]

Chinese native physicians' efforts at such an early date at seeking government endorsement for native medical education were significant in light of professionalization in Western societies. In Western societies, formal education and credential recognition were the key for occupational groups to establish legitimacy and prestige as professionals. The difference between Anglo-American and the continental European models was seen in the state control over higher education, examination, and certification in Germany and France as opposed to professional groups controlling the credential recognition in the United States and Britain.[23] In China native medicine was traditionally taught in the

---

20. Ka-che Yip, *Health and National Reconstruction in Nationalist China* (Ann Arbor, 1995), pp.15–16.
21. SB, 1913: 3/31, p.8.
22. Longxi Buyi, "Shanghai Qige Zhongyi Xuexiao De Jiaocheng Ji Xiangwang" (The history and curriculum of seven native medical schools in Shanghai), YC, No.20 (Feb. 1928):1–2, No.21 (Mar. 1928):1–4.
23. Randall Collins, "Changing Conceptions in the Sociology of the Professions," in Rolf Torstendahl and Michael Burrage, eds., *The Formation of Professions*, pp.18–21; Magali

master-to-apprentice fashion and formal education was nonexistent and unimportant. Native physicians seeking official sanction for native medical education was a sign that native physicians had been influenced by the way Western medicine was taught and its legitimacy established, and was a concrete example of how some tradition-bound social groups in early-twentieth-century China were capable of adapting to the rush toward modernity.

In September 1913 Wang Daxie assumed the post of the minister of education and he soon began to talk about the abolition of native medicine and drugs – the first time that such a radical idea was officially suggested. Upon hearing the news, Yu Botao and Bao Shisheng of the SMPGA called on native medical associations across the country to uphold the cause of native medicine. In November 1914 a delegation representing native physicians from nineteen provinces went to Beijing to petition the State Council (*guowu yuan*) and the Ministry of Education. The delegation demanded that native medicine be included in the nation's education system as was Western medicine and that the policy to abolish native medicine be abandoned. In the end, no formal policy to abolish native medicine was instituted, but the government also brushed aside the demand for formalization and public funding of native medical education.[24]

In 1916 the SMPGA sent Bao Shisheng to the Ministry of Education in Beijing and again submitted a plan for integrating native medical education into the education system. The Education Ministry shelved the plan without action. In light of that second rejection, native medical practitioners established a few more native medical schools on their own resources. In 1917 Ding Ganren of the SNMS founded the Specialized School of Native Medicine (*zhongyi zhuanmen xuexiao*) in Nanshi. A year later Bao Shisheng established another native medical school. Two more native medical schools, including one for women, were founded in the mid-1920s.[25] The curriculum of those schools comprised a number of courses in Western medical science, showing the willingness of native

---

Sarfatti Larson, "In the Matter of Experts and Professionals," ibid., pp.29–30; Charles E. McClelland, *The German Experience*, pp.107–27; Eliot Freidson, *Professional Powers*, pp.34, 63–88; Bernard Barber, "Some Problems in the Sociology of the Professions," in Kenneth S. Lynn, ed., *The Professions in America* (Boston, 1965), pp.19–21.

24. Chen Bangxian, *Zhongguo Yixue Shi* (A history of Chinese medicine) (Shanghai, 1984), p.266; Shi Quansheng, *Zhonghua Minguo*, p.445; Ralph C. Croizier, *Traditional Medicine*, pp.68–69.

25. Longxi Buyi, "Shanghai Qige Zhongyi Xuexiao."

The Republican State and the Medical Profession

physicians to assimilate Western medicine to revitalize native medicine. The move to train female native physicians was another departure from the tradition for native medicine, probably prompted because women were being admitted into Western-style medical schools. During the same period private native medical schools appeared in other places as well.[26]

The issue of native medicine's status in the education system was once again thrust upon the national scene in 1925 when the Chinese Society for Improving Education (CSIE) (*zhonghua jiaoyu gaijin she*) passed a resolution at its annual meeting that native medicine be integrated into the education system. Three months later the National Federation of Educational Societies (NFES) (*quanguo jiaoyu lianhe hui*) passed a similar resolution at its annual meeting.[27] The CSIE and NFES were organizations led by intellectuals and gentry-managers of national reputation and influence. The CSIE's leaders included such well-known educators as Liang Qichao, Cai Yuanpei, and Huang Yanpei.[28] The NFES was an umbrella organization of provincial and local educational societies sanctioned and promoted by the government since the late Qing reform. The position of the CSIE and NFES on the issue lent considerable weight to the cause of native physicians who were greatly encouraged by the support. Yet, the government continued to display disinterest. The Ministry of Education repeatedly rejected the proposals for formalization of native medical education.

First Attempt at Medical Regulation

While the government refused to invest in native medical education, on recognition that native medicine was needed in the country, it made attempts to regulate native medicine. In May 1922 the Ministry of the Interior enacted a set of regulations that included examination and registration of both native physicians and Western-style doctors. The police departments at the provincial and municipal levels were to be responsible for administering the examination and registration.[29]

---

26. Shi Quansheng, *Zhonghua Minguo*, pp.440–41.
27. Yu Yunxiu, *Yixue Geming Lun Cuji* (On medical revolution, first volume) (Shanghai, 1928); Wang Qizhang, *Ershi Nianlai Zhongguo Yishi Zouyi* (Comments on China's medical work in recent twenty years) (Shanghai, 1935).
28. *Zhonghua Jiaoyu Gaijin She Gaiguan* (The Chinese Society for Improving Education at a Glance) (Shanghai, 1922), pp.6–8.
29. *Faling Daquan* (Complete collection of the laws and ordinances) (Shanghai, 1924), pp.530–34.

The government action was a response to the petitions of the National Medical Association in 1916 and 1922 demanding that Beijing start the registration of the medical profession.[30] When the government acted, however, Western-style doctors greeted the regulations with criticism. They insisted that it was not proper for the police to regulate the medical profession and proposed that the implementation of the regulations be postponed.[31]

That medicine came under administrative supervision by the police seemed odd, but it was understandable under the circumstances at that time. The Beiyang government never established a Ministry of Health. When the government decided to regulate medicine as a matter of social order, the Ministry of the Interior was called upon to do the job. It followed that the Interior Ministry's subordinate bureaucracies at the provincial and local levels – the police departments and bureaus – would be responsible for implementing the regulations. Because Western-style doctors knew about the situation when they proposed regulation, their criticism of police involvement in regulating medicine was less than genuine. The real opposition of Western-style doctors was to the recognition of native medicine as a separate but equal part of the medical profession under the regulations – recognition the Western-style doctors had not expected.

Ironically, native physicians opposed the regulations as well. They complained that the regulations did not provide practical methods for the examination of native physicians and that the registration fee was too high. Besides, they believed that under the regulations the treatment of Western-style doctors and native physicians was unequal, with the latter in an inferior status. Indeed they were suspicious that the government regulation was a first step in the direction of restricting and even abolishing native medicine – the examination of native physicians might well be a trick to outlaw their practice. At the time the majority of native physicians did not have formal training in native medical schools that had just recently been established. They became practitioners by virtue of practicing as apprentices first. Although they were trying to establish the legitimacy of native medicine, they did not want to risk abolition through overly stringent qualifications before the overall status of native medicine was clearly established as legitimate.

The three major native medical associations – the CMPS, the SMPGA,

30. NCH, 2/11/1922, p.377.   31. Shi Quansheng, *Zhonghua Minguo*, pp.432–33.

and the SNMS – publicly opposed the regulations.[32] They established a Jiangsu Provincial Federation of Native Medical Associations in July to lead the fight.[33] The federation sent a petition to the provincial government and met with the Shanghai police department chief to state its opposition to the regulations.[34] Partly because of the opposition of native physicians and partly because of Beijing's half-hearted interest in the matter, the regulations were not implemented.

The Shanghai Authorities and Medicine

Apart from the regulation attempt from the central government, the Shanghai authorities sometimes took actions aimed at medicine, but not necessarily for the purpose of medical professionalization. In June 1923 the Shanghai Bureau of Narcotic Regulation (*Shanghai weijing yaoping guanliju*) issued a public notice that all native drugstores register with the bureau. The fee for registration ranged from 50 yuan to 400 yuan, depending on the volume of a store's business. The measure set off a barrage of protests. The SMPGA immediately pointed out to the bureau that the narcotic controls were supposed to aim at cocaine and morphine, something that native drugstores never sold. The bureau replied that under the directives from the Ministry of the Interior, all drugs with anaesthetic properties should be banned and many of those drugs were sold in native drugstores. As far as the leaders of the SMPGA were concerned, however, the ban was too vague about what constituted a narcotic drug and the purpose of registration was to milk native pharmacies of fees. They contacted other public associations for joint action against the regulations. The SMPGA requested the Federation of Street Merchant Associations – one of the major merchant organizations in Shanghai – to call on its constituent associations and pharmacies to boycott the regulations. It even asked the Shanghai-Wusong administrator and Jiangsu provincial governor to present the association's position to the Ministry of the Interior.[35]

The SMPGA successfully turned the struggle into an issue of preserving native drug trade rather than an issue of registration. Thus informed, the trade associations of the herb industry (*yinpian tongye gonghui*) and of native drugs (*yaoye gonghui*) readily joined the SMPGA

32. SnB, 1922: 5/26, p.14.
33. SnB, 1922: 6/14, p.14; *Shanghai Shi Guoyi Xuehui Shizhou Jinian Kan*, p.10.
34. SnB, 1922: 6/26, p.14; 7/1, p.14.   35. SB, 1923: 7/1, p.5; 7/16 p.6; 7/28, p.6; 11/23, p.5.

to protest the bureau's regulations. The Shanghai General Chamber of Commerce too was involved, sending a petition to the Shanghai-Wusong administrator against the regulations.[36] With the backing of merchant organizations, the opposition of the native medical associations gained in strength and the regulations were eventually overturned. Through the battle the SMPGA emerged as the leading organization representing the interests of native medicine and native drug trade in Shanghai and beyond.

A Chinese municipal agency in charge of public health in Shanghai started in August 1926 when the warlord Sun Chuanfang was in control of Shanghai. It was called the Health Bureau of Shanghai-Wusong Commercial Port (*Songhu shangbu weisheng ju*) and the director was Dr. Hu Hongji, a public health expert trained at Johns Hopkins University. At the time of the bureau's establishment, Chinese practitioners of Western medicine in Shanghai already urged that the bureau begin the registration of medical practitioners in the city.[37]

In October 1926 the Health Bureau, upon the recommendation of its own Health Committee, issued regulations on the registration and examination of native physicians. Like the earlier measure tried by the Ministry of the Interior, government regulation was not necessarily a curse to native medicine, since it meant official recognition. The problem was that the Health Committee under the bureau consisted of Western-style doctors who would dominate the proposed examination committee. While hoping to receive official recognition, native physicians were concerned that the new measure could be another attempt to restrict native medicine. Not surprisingly, Western-style doctors who had opposed the Ministry of the Interior's regulations on the medical profession in 1922 now supported the regulations.[38] That support only deepened native physicians' suspicion that the regulations would give Western-style doctors some measure of control over native medicine.

The mixed messages in government action resulted in different responses from Shanghai native medical associations. The SNMS and the CMPS were more conciliatory toward the regulations. The former sent its membership roll for registration screening and the latter asked for the participation of native medical associations in examining native physicians without rejecting the bureau's measure out of hand.[39]

---

36. SB, 1923: 11/10, p.5; 11/12, p.5.
37. NCH, 8/28/1926, p.463.   38. SB, 1926: 10/26, p.4.
39. *Shanghai Shi Guoyi Xuehui Shizhou Jinian Kan*, pp.51–52; SB, 1926: 11/11, p.4.

The Republican State and the Medical Profession

The SMPGA, however, took a more confrontational stance toward the regulations. It denied their legitimacy altogether. In its view, the Health Committee of the bureau was not legally created and therefore the regulations written by the committee were null and void. It passed a resolution to oppose the examination and registration. It entertained journalists with a dinner party in order to explain its position: The regulations were not enacted by the central government but were based upon a few persons' opinions. The examination methods were inappropriate. Most importantly, Western-style doctors held four of the five posts as the examiners, showing the bias of the measure against native physicians.[40]

On November 11 a joint meeting of Shanghai native medical associations and institutions took place, with more than one thousand participants from twelve organizations. The meeting adopted a resolution drafted by the SMPGA – that the Health Bureau should reorganize the Health Committee and revise the regulations. A delegation was chosen to petition the bureau. Two days later another delegation was sent to Beijing to petition the Ministry of the Interior.[41]

But the negotiations with the bureau failed to persuade the bureau to accept either demand – to reorganize the Health Committee or to revise the regulations. The bureau's staunch position caused the division among the organizations of native physicians. On December 15 a second joint meeting of native physicians adopted new decisions to boycott the bureau, decisions the SMPGA had made. But the CMPS and the SNMS did not take part in the meeting. Both had proceeded to cooperate with the Health Bureau to participate in the examination process.[42] The separate actions of those two organizations undermined the SMPGA strategy to boycott the bureau. The SMPGA was forced to work with the bureau by late December.[43]

The incident provided an interesting example of how native medical associations interacted with each other while responding to the authorities. The different approaches of the three native medical organizations during the incident probably stemmed from their membership composition. The members of the CMPS and SNMS were mostly senior physicians with reputations; they were less worried about being disqualified by examinations. The SMPGA's membership was larger and much more

---

40. SB, 1926: 11/7, p.3; 11/10, p.3.   41. SB, 1926: 11/12, p.5; 11/15, p.5.
42. SB, 1926: 12/1, p.5; 12/21, p.6. *Shanghai Shi Guoyi Xuehui Shizhou Jinian Kan*, p.14.
43. SB, 1926: 12/22, p.7.

diverse, including less experienced practitioners more concerned about how the regulations were to be implemented. The internal division among native medical practitioners reminds one of the heterogeneity within various social groups in Republican Shanghai and resultant complex responses to state actions.

MEDICINE IN THE NANJING DECADE

The Regulation of Medicine

Clearly, during the Beiyang period the regulation of the medical profession was next to nonexistent and there was no national public health policy to speak of. By and large, medicine and public health were handled as a matter of maintaining social order to be taken care of by the local police. The woeful inadequacy in the national public health policy and in the regulation of the medical profession under the Beiyang government amounted, in the words of a critic, "to a national crime committed against the unfortunate men and women of China."[44] After the National Government was established, leading Chinese medical professionals urged Nanjing to rectify the situation and take up the important task in the national reconstruction.

Nanjing did regard medicine and public health as an important area for state action and exercised considerable regulatory power in the field. During the Nanjing Decade the government agency in charge of public health went through a number of changes. In April 1927 the National Government established the Ministry of Civil Affairs (*minzheng bu*), which included a Division of Health (*weisheng si*). After the Ministry of Civil Affairs became the Ministry of the Interior in April 1928, a separate Ministry of Health was established in November of that year, in addition to the Central Health Research Institute and the Central Health Committee. The development was hailed by the National Medical Association, the leading organization of Chinese practitioners of Western medicine, as a new beginning of the advancement of medicine and public health in China.[45] To the great disappointment of Chinese medical professionals, however, in November 1931 the Ministry of Health was dissolved as part of Nanjing's financial retrenchment, and was replaced by

---

44. Leo K. T. Yen, "Public Health under Nationalist Reconstruction," *The New China Edition*, CWR (10/10/1928):146.
45. Wu Lien-teh, "A Ministry of Health in China," CWR, 47,8 (1/19/1929):322.

the Health Administration (*weisheng shu*) five months later, again under the Ministry of the Interior.[46]

The frequent change in central health administrative agencies was accompanied by a series of sets of regulations on the medical profession. In December 1928 the Ministry of Health issued the Amended Provisional Regulations on Doctors and the Amended Provisional Regulations on Pharmacists, followed by the Regulations on Obstetricians in May 1929. Those documents stipulated qualifications, licensing procedures, disciplinary procedures, and obligations of those professions.[47] In May 1930, in an effort to separate Western medicine from native medicine, the government issued the Regulations on Practitioners of Western Medicine (*Xiyi tiaoli*). The regulations were similar to the Regulations on Doctors issued earlier and supposedly superseded the latter. The only major difference between the two documents was that the new regulations raised the age qualification for doctors from twenty to twenty-five.[48] In December 1930 the Examination Council (*kaoshi yuan*) issued the Regulations on Examination of Practitioners of Western Medicine (*Xiyi yishi kaoshi tiaoli*), but no examination was ever held in accordance with the regulations.[49] Finally in 1932 the Ministry of the Interior issued the Expedient Rules of Licensing Doctors (*Yishi biantong geizheng banfa*).[50] None of those regulations were seriously enforced. They were regarded as preposterous and ineffectual by leading practitioners of Western medicine in Shanghai.[51] The evaluation of dentists was not undertaken until 1936 under the Health Administration.[52]

Nanjing's policy toward native medicine was one of ambivalence and ambiguity. After enormous efforts made by native medical practitioners in the country and especially those in Shanghai, the Legislative Council (*lifa yuan*) adopted the Regulations on Native Physicians (*Zhongyi tiaoli*) in December 1933, but not until January 1936 were the regulations officially enacted (see Chapter 7).[53]

The Health Administration in Shanghai

Since the regulations issued from the central government were conflicting and confusing, the Shanghai Municipal Government tried to regulate

---

46. Shi Quansheng, *Zhonghua Minguo*, p.840; Ka-che Yip, *Health and National Reconstruction*, pp.47–51.
47. ZMXFD (1934), pp.1100–1105.   48. ZMXFD (1934), p.345.
49. Pang Jingzhou, *Shanghaishi*, p.81.   50. Ibid.
51. Ibid.; Wang Qizhang, *Ershi Nianlai*, pp.232–39.
52. SnB, 1936: 2/9, p.14.   53. SnB, 1936: 2/9, p.11.

the medical profession at the local level with more concrete measures. After the GMD took over Shanghai, the Shanghai Bureau of Health was reestablished as one of the ten bureaus of the new municipal government. Hu Hongji was reappointed the director of the bureau in July 1927. The bureau comprised three sections. The first section was in charge of city sanitation and street cleaning with a staff of 18 officers and 440 street cleaners. The second section was responsible for keeping vital statistics, carrying out meat inspection, and registering physicians, dentists, midwives, and pharmacists. The third section was to control contagious diseases, administer the vaccination against smallpox, and maintain a laboratory and more than thirty clinics in the city.[54]

In October 1927 the Shanghai Bureau of Health issued the Provisional Regulations on Practitioners of Native Medicine and the Provisional Regulations on Practitioners of Western Medicine. Those regulations required all medical practitioners to register with the bureau and submit their credentials for evaluation. The practitioners who failed to pass evaluation would have to take an examination. Western-style doctors and native physicians were to undergo separate evaluations supervised by the bureau.[55] At the same time the bureau issued the regulations on the registration of medical associations of all types, from native physicians' associations to Western-style doctors' associations, from professional associations to academic associations.[56]

The Bureau of Health's evenhanded approach to Western and native medicine won the cooperation and participation from both groups. The evaluation of medical practitioners duly started on November 16 and ended in January 1928. The evaluation committees certified 1,429 native doctors and 367 Western-style doctors. The doctors were all issued licenses by the Health Bureau.[57] The large number of native physicians required additional evaluations and examinations. By August 1931 six rounds of evaluation and examination had been administered and some 2,336 native physicians were certified on the last four occasions. In January 1930 the Health Bureau conducted a review of the credentials of native physicians certified in the first and second evaluations.[58]

In October 1927 the Shanghai Bureau of Health issued the Provisional Regulations on Midwives. Midwives were required to go through evalu-

---

54. NCH, 3/3/1928, p.353. 55. SB, 1927: 10/19, p.5; STSFH, pp.122–25.
56. STSFH, pp.125–26. 57. SB, 1928: 1/16, p.5; 1/27, p.5.
58. SB, 1930: 1/23, p.6; 5/4, p.6; 11/7, p.5; 1931: 8/12, p.6; *Shanghai Tebie Shi Di Sanci Dengji Zhongyi Minglu* (The third directory of registered native physicians in the Shanghai Special Municipality) (1929).

ation or take an examination before being eligible to register. Only those who registered could practice.[59] Within four months the bureau evaluated and certified eighty-two midwives. In November 1928 it further stipulated that graduates from obstetrical schools could practice as obstetricians and those who had some training in obstetrics without a diploma could practice only as midwives and should undergo a training course sponsored by the bureau. The training school for midwives was established in early 1930.[60] In the meantime the bureau enacted regulations on dental prosthetists in January 1928 and held examination for dentists in May 1929, before the evaluation of dentists was required by the central government.[61] In July 1930 the bureau administered registration for veterinarians for the first time.[62]

Government Regulation and Western-Style Doctors

The relationship between the state and Western-style doctors was an ambivalent one, just as that between the state and native medicine. In general, Western-style doctors supported government regulation because it tended to protect their professional privileges and put pressure on unqualified practitioners. Yet, when government regulation was deemed detrimental to their interests, Western-style doctors were quick to rise in opposition.

In 1929 the Shanghai Bureau of Health, at the suggestion of the Shanghai Municipal Party Headquarters (MPH), issued a notice setting a ceiling on the fees that Western-style doctors (*yishi*) could charge their patients. The MPH's interest and interference in medical affairs is a sign of the GMD party-state expanding its power in society. At the same time, the issue of doctors' fees reflected a pattern of the MPH criticizing and meddling in the business of the municipal government at the time.[63] The Bureau of Health was apparently accommodating such interference.

The measure met with strong opposition from Western-style doctors, however. In their view, doctors' fees were rewards for expertise, not ordinary commercial transactions or material exchanges. The government's interference in doctors' fees was both unwarranted and unnecessary, as fees were decided by social factors – the doctor's competence on the one

---

59. STSFH, p.121.   60. SB, 1928: 2/6, p.5; 11/14, p.6; 1930: 2/8, p.8.
61. SB, 1928: 1/27, p.5; 1929: 5/19, p.6.   62. SB, 1930: 7/20, p.5.
63. Christian Henriot, *Shanghai*, pp.37–52.

hand and living standards in a particular locale on the other. Doctors refused to treat their profession as charity. The problem of providing medical care for the poor was not to be solved by limiting doctors' fees but by social policies, because even if doctors reduced their fees, some poor would still not be able to afford medical care, while doctors would go bankrupt. Doctors were especially annoyed that the bureau did not try to put limits on medical practitioners of less competent sorts (*zayi*) but singled out doctors (*yishi*, lit. "medical master"). They refuted the argument that doctors would refuse to help patients because of a patient's inability to pay fees. Pang Jingzhou and Wang Qizhang, two leading members of the MPAS, argued that every doctor's fee was open to the public and patients knew the fee before going to any doctor. They categorically denied the existence of such cases as doctors refusing to see patients.[64]

In September 1929 the MPAS petitioned the Ministry of Health, with a concurrent copy to the Shanghai Municipal Government, demanding that it order the Shanghai Bureau of Health to revoke the regulations on doctors' fees.[65] The result was a compromise. The government did not relinquish its power to regulate, but accommodated doctors' demands to a degree. In October, with the approval of the MPH, the Shanghai Bureau of Health revised the scale for doctors' fees "in order not to cause difficulties for doctors." The new scale raised the ceiling of fees for special examinations, office visits, and house calls by 50 percent, 90 percent, and 100 percent, respectively.[66]

The regulations on doctors' fees were not enforced in any way, however. In the end they did not have much impact on how doctors conducted their business. Nevertheless, the episode is worth noting for two reasons. First, the suggestion from the MPH to limit doctors' fees was very much in line with its radical view of social classes in Shanghai. It may be taken as part of the conflict between the radical agenda of the MPH leadership and the modernization efforts of the Shanghai Municipal Government that Christian Henriot described.[67] Second, the concession made by the Shanghai Bureau of Health demonstrated both the effectiveness of the MPAS in protecting Western-style doctors' interests and the responsiveness of the government and the party-organ to the association's action. The Municipal Government and the MPH acted in

---

64. Wang Qizhang, *Ershi Nianlai*, pp.53–56; Pang Jingzhou, *Shanghaishi*, pp.16–17, 86–87.
65. SB, 1929: 9/24, p.6; 11/20, p.6.   66. SB, 1929: 10/15, p.7.
67. Christian Henriot, *Shanghai*, pp.37–47.

the public interest trying to bring down the cost of medical care and make it more affordable to average citizens. Yet their concern for the common people was apparently balanced by a consideration of doctors' interests. Therefore, the state was not always arbitrary, nor was the MPAS a passive recipient of government action. Even under the GMD party-state that was expanding its regulatory power in society, room for negotiations between the government and societal organizations still existed.

In January 1929 the Ministry of Health issued the Provisional Regulations on Doctors (*Yishi zanxing tiaoli*). The regulations disqualified those who did not graduate from medical schools and provided that the registration of doctors be conducted by police departments.[68] Unexpectedly, the MPAS, NMA, and MPSCR opposed the regulations, not because of the role envisioned for the police, but because of the exclusion of nongraduate practitioners – a sharp contrast with the Shanghai Bar Association that tried hard to exclude unqualified legal practitioners (see Chapter 8) and an interesting comparison with medical professionalization in Germany. Before the German unification in 1871, the Berlin Medical Society petitioned the Reichstag demanding, among other things, the abolition of sanctions against quackery (and of fixed fee schedules for medical services). Historians of the German medical profession interpreted the move as a demand for professional autonomy, which outweighed the consideration of monopoly over medical service, with an understanding that quackery would go on with or without laws against it.[69]

In the Chinese case, something other than professional autonomy was involved. The position the medical associations took was largely conditioned by the ongoing battle between Western medicine and native medicine. To Western-style doctors who graduated from medical schools, the difference between them and nongraduate practitioners was one of degree, but what divided Western-style doctors and native physicians was a difference in nature. Since the real advantage of native physicians lay in the social demand for their service, Western-style doctors did not want to weaken their force by excluding those practitioners who lacked formal training but were practicing Western medicine nonetheless. If practitioners without formal training were disqualified by government regulation, there would be more of a void to be filled by native physicians,

---

68. ZMXFD (1936), Vol.1, pp.1100–1101; Pang Jingzhou, *Shanghaishi*, pp.80–81.
69. Charles E. MacClelland, *The German Experience*, pp.78–79.

which would work against Western-style doctors' plan to restrict and abolish native medicine.

The NMA, MPSCR, and MPAS jointly petitioned the ministry for postponing the implementation of the regulations and making certain revisions. The MPAS telegraphed the ministry with three demands. First, the government should broaden the qualifications to allow most practicing Western-style doctors to register and devise as soon as possible appropriate outlets for those who did not qualify. Second, it should protect the medical profession and improve its living standard. Third, it should allow medical associations such as the MPAS to participate in making the Law on Medical Doctors (*Yishi fa*) that was being considered at the time.[70]

The Ministry of Health responded that the Ministry of the Interior would formulate the regulations and the National Government would approve them – the Health Ministry was only in a position to implement the regulations. It assured the MPAS that the protection of the medical profession would be clearly spelled out in the Law on Medical Doctors, but it reminded the MPAS that there was no legal basis to allow private associations (*siren tuanti*) such as the MPAS to participate in writing the law.[71]

The use of the term "private association" is noteworthy. It would appear that although the GMD state recognized the need to protect the medical profession in the public interest and included medical associations in the category of public associations or people's associations, the GMD would deny a role of any societal organization in writing laws. The way to do so was to identify the organizations as private. In other words, medical associations were recognized as public only in terms of their professional functions, but in the matter of making laws, only the state was public authority and represented the public, and societal institutions became private parties. The situation provides one more example of how such notions as public and private were contested in the state–society interaction at that time. Indeed, such a contestation itself was a form of the interaction.

For the moment, doctors were less concerned about their role in writing the law than the qualification of practitioners of Western medicine. On September 22, 1929, the autumn general meeting of the MPAS discussed the issue for several hours before arriving at the following decisions: First, MPAS members would not register under the current regu-

70. SB, 1929: 8/20, p.6.   71. Ibid.

lations but wait until the authorities came up with new measures. Second, the MPAS would make clear that the boycott of the regulations did not mean that the association opposed any regulatory measures by the government. Third, Zhu Minyi – the MPAS executive committee member who was also a member of the GMD Party Central Committee – would meet the minister of health to explain the MPAS's position.[72]

Although the MPAS was stalling the implementation of the regulations, the Shanghai Bureau of Health was rather conciliatory. On November 15 Hu Hongji issued a statement that the Bureau would allow doctors to practice under one of three conditions: They have (1) registered with the bureau, (2) received licenses from the Ministry of Health or Health Bureau, or (3) applied for licenses to the Health Ministry but have not received them.[73] In effect, all practicing Western-style doctors were allowed to continue their practices.

GMD Regulation of Medical Associations

In contrast to the legal profession, the regulations on the medical profession did not require the establishment of medical associations by doctors.[74] Nonetheless, wherever medical associations did exist, they fell under the GMD regulations on social and occupational associations. The party headquarters and government agencies exercised the supervisory authority over medical associations to enforce such regulations.

In October 1930, the Mass Training Committee of the MPH found fault with three major native medical associations in Shanghai – the Chinese Medical and Pharmaceutical Society, Shenzhou Medical and Pharmaceutical General Association, and Shanghai Native Medical Association (*zhongyi xiehui*). The committee ordered the organizations to dissolve and their members to join the Native Medical Society (*guoyi xuehui*). The reason for the action was that (1) the names and organizations of those associations did not conform to the regulations on people's associations and (2) only one native medical professional association was needed in Shanghai.

The three organizations resisted. They defended themselves on the ground that they were scholarly associations (*xueshu tuanti*) and had different functions from the professional association (*zhiye tuanti*) of

---

72. SB, 1929: 9/24, p.6.   73. SB, 1929: 11/16, p.6.
74. *Minguo Fagui Jikan* (A collection of the laws and regulations of the Republic) (Shanghai, 1929), Vol.3, pp.275–86.

native medicine. Eventually the three organizations were allowed to continue under the conditions that they reorganize and register with the Mass Training Committee and with the Bureau of Social Affairs and not interfere with professional issues in native medicine.[75] In reality, however, the CMPS, SMPGA, and SNMS would continue to be the leading vehicles not only in propagating the knowledge of native medicine but also in fighting for the professional status and legitimacy of native medicine.

In March 1931 the GMD Central Department of Mass Training issued a directive that merchants and workers in the drug trade should have separate trade associations (*tongye gonghui*) and separate labor unions (*gonghui*) in compliance with the related regulations. Similarly, doctors and pharmacists should belong to medical associations and pharmaceutical associations respectively to comply with the Amended Plan for Organizing People's Associations.[76] The Mass Training Committee of the MPH immediately challenged one of the Western-style doctors' associations in Shanghai, the Medical and Pharmaceutical Association of the Chinese Republic (*zhonghua minguo yiyao lianhe hui*) and ordered the organization to reorganize to separate doctors and pharmacists.[77] When a Dental Protection Society appeared in Shanghai in January 1935, the Bureau of Health and the Bureau of Social Affairs quickly put it out of business on the ground that its organization was incompatible with the regulations on social associations.[78]

The fate of the largest organization of native physicians in the country – the National Federation of Medical and Pharmaceutical Associations (NFMPA) – shows government supervision at the national level. The NFMPA led a successful struggle against Western-style doctors' attempt to abolish native medicine in 1929 (see Chapter 7). The success, however, brought the NFMPA's organizational anomaly to the attention of the government. As an umbrella organization, the NFMPA's constituent associations were of different sizes and geographical and functional orientations. Some were local societies with a few dozen members, others were associations of national scale, such as the SMPGA, and still others were provincial associations whose constituent associations also joined the NFMPA separately. When the NFMPA was established, it was supposed to overhaul its organizational duplication and supersede all the

---

75. SB, 1930: 11/22, p.6; *Shanghai Shi Guoyi Xuehui Shizhou Jinian Kan*, pp.17–18, 28–35.
76. *Renmin Tuanti Fagui Shili Huibian*, p.589.
77. SB, 1931: 3/12, p.5.   78. SnB, 1935: 1/30, p.11.

associations of national scale, resulting in a national organization with a single chain of command. But that did not happen because native physicians were unwilling to relinquish their old associations, even in such places as Shanghai.[79]

The organizational anomaly of the NFMPA was seized upon by the Ministry of Health, a stronghold of Western-style doctors, and became a liability. In October 1929 the Executive Council ordered the Ministry of Health that the NFMPA be allowed to be placed on file (*li'an*), which appeared to be a move in favor of the cause of native medicine made by a sympathetic Tan Yankai, the chairman of the council. In response, the Health Ministry sent back an opinion that the NFMPA should revise its bylaws and its name first. It raised three objections: First, the NFMPA was composed of only native physicians and native drug traders but was prefixed with the term "national" (*quanguo*). If organizations of Western-style doctors also called themselves national organizations to compete, it would be problematic for the Health Ministry. Second, several native medical associations also called themselves national associations, such as the SMPGA and MPSCR. It would create another problem if they were asked to file with the Health Ministry as separate national organizations. Third, the bylaws of the NFMPA stated that its national conference was the highest organ of power (*zuigao quanli jiguan*), but that expression was reserved for the GMD Party National Congress, as the GMD ruled the country through the party. A private association (*siren tuanti*) should not use that phrase. The organizational arrangement that the NFMPA bylaws described was an imitation of the GMD Party organization, which was inappropriate.[80]

While the first two of the three objections were reasonable, the last objection was farfetched. Such organizations as the NFMPA would normally be considered a public association, be it a social or occupational association, especially if it were filed with the government. The ministry deliberately referred to the NFMPA as a private association precisely to block it from establishing a public identity through filing with the ministry. Just as the ministry did when it denied the MPAS the right to participate in drafting the law on medicine, it tried to discredit the NFMPA by identifying it as a private association usurping the organizational structure and vocabulary of the public GMD party-state. Since the GMD always monopolized political vocabulary and reserved for itself the right to define the boundary between public and private, even Tan Yankai, who

79. QYTZHH, p.1. 80. QYTZHH, pp.21–22.

was sympathetic toward native medicine, did not seem to have politically correct reasons to disagree with the opinion. The Executive Council approved the ministry's message and on October 22 the ministry issued the message as a directive to the Shanghai Bureau of Health.[81] At a November meeting the NFMPA discussed the issue and decided to revise the bylaws of the association but keep its name.[82]

The NFMPA's resistance did not last long, however. After the GMD government enacted different sets of regulations on doctors and pharmacists in January 1931 and the GMD Party Central Department of Mass Training issued directives on separating pharmaceutical and medical professions in March 1931, the NFMPA lost any legal ground to exist. The NFMPA Standing Committee decided to comply with the regulations. On March 14, 1931, the delegates of the NFMPA from around the country voted to dissolve the organization and to establish two separate national federations of native medical associations and native drug trade associations.[83]

Chinese State and the Foreign Concessions

Despite the government efforts at regulation, self-styled medical practitioners abounded in Shanghai. Their presence, just as other illegal activities in the city, was spawned in large part by the divided jurisdictions among the Chinese municipality and the two foreign concessions. As the Chinese authorities instituted the registration of medical practitioners, those who did not qualify to practice simply moved from the Chinese areas to the foreign concessions. It would seem that during those years the Chinese authorities tried to exert control over the foreign concessions in Shanghai with some reason.[84] In 1928 the SMC of the International Settlement refused to cooperate with the Shanghai Bureau of Health in food inspection on the ground that Chinese inspection standards were inferior. In response Hu Hongji confronted the SMC with the evidence that quacks who had been driven out of the Chinese areas were operating freely in the International Settlement, including running dubious advertisements in newspapers published within the International Settlement.[85] The Shanghai Medical Society, an association of foreign medical professionals in the International Settlement,

---

81. QYTZHH, pp.21–22.   82. QYTZHH, p.49.   83. QYTZHH, pp.1, 30–31.
84. For the GMD efforts to control the foreign concessions, see Marie-Claire Bergère, *The Golden Age*, pp.279–80; Frederic Wakeman Jr., *Policing Shanghai*, pp.61–77.
85. CWR, 46,13 (11/24/1928):426–27.

opined that "conditions inside the settlement are little short of scandalous in that men whose qualifications are so poor that they cannot secure registration outside are now coming into the settlement to practice." The society urged the SMC to introduce compulsory registration without delay.[86]

Under the pressure of public opinion, the authorities of the French Concession moved one step ahead of the SMC to institute a registration system. Starting January 1, 1931, all doctors, surgeons, dentists, veterinary surgeons, and midwives who would practice in the French Concession were required to register with the Director of Public Health and Administration by presenting appropriate credentials and receive a license at a cost of 2 yuan. The penalty for failure to register was a fine of 20 yuan to 100 yuan; and for failure to get a license, 10 yuan to 50 yuan. The fines could be doubled for a second offense.[87]

The Shanghai Municipal Council had to follow suit. Due to the conflicting interests of nationals from various countries residing in the International Settlement, the final scheme instituted by the SMC in March 1931 was a compromise. Instead of compulsory registration, a voluntary registration system was set up and a Shanghai Medical Board was created to take care of the registration. The seven-member board included the commissioner of public health of the SMC and one representative each from the Shanghai Medical Society, the German Medical Society, the Russian Medical Society, the National Medical Association of China, the Shanghai Branch of the China Medical Association, and the SMC.[88] In 1933 there were voices demanding that the SMC adopt compulsory registration. The Shanghai Medical Board also recommended the measure. But it was never adopted.[89] By 1935 about 900 foreign and Chinese medical professionals had voluntarily registered with the SMC to practice in the International Settlement. By 1936 the number of registered medical practitioners reached 1,005 and among them were 676 Chinese doctors.[90] Yet, as Wu Liande, a leading Chinese doctor, conceded, "the authorities still have no power to discipline those who behave unprofessionally, as is the case in other countries."[91] "Unfortunately," deplored the *China Weekly Review*, "the average doctor's interest in his profession as a science after he leaves the medical school

---

86. NCH, 4/1/1930, p.14.   87. NCH, 12/16/1930, p.375.
88. NCH, 4/21/1931, p.88.   89. NCH, 2/8/1933, p.214.
90. "News and Notes," *China Medical Journal*, 50,4 (Apr. 1936):636.
91. NCH, 3/20/1935, p.456.

is in inverse proportion to his interest in making money out of an extended practice."[92]

Even less could be done about quacks, both foreign and Chinese. There were scattered reports about enforcement efforts made by the Shanghai Bureau of Health and about unregistered practitioners being fined by the authorities.[93] But those people could never be eliminated. In Pang Jingzhou's account, the medical profession in Shanghai remained a messy melange as of the 1930s. Many unqualified practitioners and outright quacks were making a living in the city at the expense of unsuspecting patients. Because those charlatans were practicing privately in thousands of patients' homes all over the metropolis, including the foreign concessions, there was practically no way to ban all those people from practicing.[94] Speaking of Chinese distrust of foreign doctors, the *China Weekly Review* noted that "China long has been victimized by Western 'quack' doctors who have plied their trade in the foreign settlements and thus have been exempt from Chinese law."[95]

But Chinese law hardly helped in the first place. From 1912 through 1937 the Criminal Code of the Republic had no articles prohibiting the practice of medicine by quacks. As Dr. J. H. Jordon, commissioner of the public health of the SMC, pointed out in 1937, the only criminal law under which quack practitioners could be prosecuted was Article 339 of the Criminal Code – offenses of fraud. In such cases, however, it was necessary but very difficult to prove that the quack practitioner had posed as a qualified doctor and accepted money for services rendered as a doctor, since patients often knew with whom they were dealing.[96] In 1935, for instance, a certain Zung Ping-wei was charged but acquitted at the First Special District Court of fraud for representing himself as a physician to practice. Only on the appeal by the SMC to the Second Branch of the Jiangsu High Court was Zung found guilty. The penalty: a fine of 200 yuan – about the income of one or two months for a medical practitioner in Shanghai.[97]

This state of affairs certainly cried out for effective government regulation and medical professionalization. But both fell rather short, in spite of the GMD state actions, which must in turn be evaluated in the context of this particular historical time and space – the semicolonial treaty port in prewar China.

92. CWR, 63,7 (1/14/1933):290.   93. SB, 1928: 9/6, p.6; 1929: 4/7, p.6.
94. Pang Jingzhou, *Shanghaishi*, pp.10–14.   95. CWR, 51,9 (2/1/1930):306.
96. CWR, 79,12 (2/20/1937):430.   97. NCH, 12/25/1935, p.534.

Conclusion to Part II

EVIDENTLY, the Republican state played an active role in promoting and regulating modern professions in the course of modern state building. For legal and medical practitioners, it is government regulations that activated professionalization. The purpose of the state was to promote modernization, fashion a modern state, and ensure sociopolitical control all at the same time. The state needed professionals to staff the state apparatus, including the judicial system, rationalize the appropriation of social resources, and generally expand state power in society. It tried to make sure that social organizations that were at least potentially subversive would remain politically neutral and harmless to the state. It also made efforts to supersede or restrict the public functions of societal institutions. Such efforts were most pronounced during the Nanjing Decade when the GMD regime reenforced the regulations on professions with a generic regulatory framework defining and confining all kinds of societal organizations.

Yet, in its efforts to dominate society, the state faced constraints and limitations, which are clearly seen in its dealing with professional associations. While hostile to popular activism and eager to control societal organizations and initiatives, both the Beiyang and the GMD governments held a certain respect for free professions, especially the legal profession, and both accepted the legitimacy of professional associations. The statist agenda had to be circumscribed or balanced because professions and professionals were indispensable for the modernizing projects of the state. Unlike other urban associations, the primary raison d'être of professional associations was professional and was so perceived by the state and society at large. That perception provided the basic political and social context in which professional associations operated.

But professionals were not passive objects to be regulated by the state and serve its purposes only. Rather, they too had their own agenda. First, they saw their professional associations as a necessary means to promote professionalism and look after their professional interests, that is, to bring about professionalization. Second, in due time and under certain circumstances, the organizational strength and the public status of the professional associations would serve as useful vehicles to articulate professionals' social and political concerns. Both the differences and the common ground between the scheme of the state and the purposes of professional groups constituted the dynamics of their interaction. How all this was played out in Republican Shanghai is the subject of Part III.

Part III

PROFESSIONALISM, NATIONALISM, AND POLITICS

As this study has shown, in a fundamental sense, Chinese professionals were products and beneficiaries of modernization, which entailed two related processes – (1) modern state building and (2) professionalization. Professionals distinguished themselves from other social groups in pursuing their interests and purposes particular to their status as practitioners of modern professions, while contributing, and claiming to contribute, to state building and the public good. The state also treated professions and professional associations primarily from this perspective. The process of professionalization thus fundamentally conditioned the relationship between professionals and the Republican state. That was the first element in the dynamics of interaction between the state and professions.

A second element in the dynamics was the rising nationalist sentiment and movement against foreign privileges or foreign aggression during the period under study. Nationalism, loosely defined, simply provided one more imperative for professionals to act in the public arena. Where foreign privileges affected their own interests, professionals conveniently utilized the nationalistic rhetoric to advance their cause and to enlist the support from and cooperated with the state. Where the state failed to act to resist foreign aggression, professionals joined the general public to demand the state to face its task. In so doing, professionals and their organizations inevitably became politicized. They carefully managed a balance between acting on political issues and maintaining professional identities. In either case they never failed to claim their publicness.

With the similar dynamics, however, each professional group faced a related, yet different problematic situation in their relations with the Republican state. Chinese journalists in Shanghai went through a transformation from "literary men" to professionals. Yet, the day that journalists came of age as a profession was the time they came into a profound clash with the state, as the hallmark of the profession – freedom of speech – was anathema to the Republican state, especially the GMD regime. The rise of the journalistic profession therefore was manifested in its challenge to the state authority in censorship and press control, and its professional and political maturity measured by its commitment to the principle that was essential to the profession and all citizens.

For the medical profession, the problem was a different sort. Although unqualified medical practitioners and outright quacks abounded in Shanghai, the overriding issue in medical professionalization was an intense conflict between native and Western medicine. As far as Western-style doctors were concerned, native medicine was the primary impediment to the advancement of their profession and Chinese medical science (to them these two were the same thing). From the perspective of native physicians, Western-style doctors were simply trying to drive them out of competition in the name of promoting medical science. Both camps sought to enlist the support of the state and swing the government policy toward medicine, since government leaders too were divided over what and how modernization in medicine or medical professionalization should entail. The conflict conditioned the overall relationship between the medical profession and the Republican state during the period under study.

The rise of the legal profession was a typical story of Chinese professionalization that involved constant interaction between the profession and the state on judicial issues and beyond. Although the legal profession was formally established by the state, lawyers frequently found that the state was not truly committed to the rule of law, judicial independence, and due process and that state policies were contradictory to their professional interests. While striving for their ideals and interests, lawyers had to cooperate with the state, not only for gaining legitimacy but also for fighting a battle against foreign lawyers' privileges. The Shanghai Bar Association skillfully combined lawyers' professional interests and nationalist goals. The SBA demanded that the state abide by the principles it accepted in theory on the ground that only in doing so could the state rightfully ask foreign powers to relinquish extraterritoriality. When the state failed to face up to the Japanese aggressions in the 1930s, the SBA openly voiced its dissent in the public arena.

The struggles added up to a composite picture of state–society interaction with "official initiatives and spontaneous social actions, public institutions and 'popular' organizations, and all the cooperation, compromise and conflict that obtains between the two sides."[1] An examination of the concrete cases of state–society interaction will demonstrate the richness and complexity of what this study calls a symbiotic dynamics in the state–society relationship.

1. Marie-Claire Bergère, *The Golden Age*, p.9.

6

From "Literary Men" to Professionals

Shanghai Journalists

IN EARLY-TWENTIETH-CENTURY China, journalists and writers were both born of the development of the modern press. A large number of journalists and writers clustered in Shanghai, the cosmopolitan treaty port. As Leo Ou-fan Lee described in his study of Chinese writers of the 1920s and 1930s, to a large extent literary writing as a vocation was heralded by literary journalism at the turn of the century and after.[1] Western-style and even traditional education prepared young people for practicing and consuming literary writing. The growth of the press and publishing industry in large cities such as Shanghai provided those people with the opportunity to pursue a new type of career. Lee used the term "literary journalism" because in the early twentieth century the line between literature and journalism was not clearly drawn and was easily crossed. Literary supplements of newspapers were one of the major outlets for the talent and aspirations of would-be writers. Many people wrote for both newspapers and literary publications and worked as both journalists and writers. Journalism and literary writing were almost indistinguishable, as reflected in the fact that both journalist and writer were considered "literary men" (*wenren*). In the words of a foreign observer in the mid-1920s, "most successful writers in all phases of literature today 'graduated' out of the ranks of newspaper editors and reporters."[2] From the early 1920s to the 1930s, however, a gap between those two kinds of endeavor was increasingly pronounced and widened, due to the gradual professionalization of journalism and journalists. Journalists identified themselves and were identified as professionals, an

---

1. Leo Ou-fan Lee, *The Romantic Generation of Modern Chinese Writers* (Cambridge, MA, 1973), pp.3–27.
2. *Chinese Recorder*, 56, 5 (May 1925):298.

identity that writers had yet to gain. What was significant is that the transformation of journalists from "literary men" to professionals was at the same time a process of journalists growing increasingly independent of and resistant to state control, as they began to struggle for freedom of press and speech. The story of Shanghai journalists shows a particular dimension and a different problematic situation for the state–society relationship in Republican China.

JOURNALISM AND JOURNALISTS IN SHANGHAI

Obstacles for Journalistic Professionalization

As noted in Chapter 1, the modern press in China was first developed by foreigners to disseminate the Christian message and circulate commercial information. From the 1890s onward Chinese newspapers and magazines proliferated mostly as organs of political propaganda for reform or revolution. Liang Qichao, for one, openly advocated and practiced the use of newspapers as factional organs (*dangbao*).[3] After the founding of the Republic, many newspapers continued to function as mouthpieces of political parties, factions, and individual politicians or warlords, engaging in political propaganda and character assassination, all of which was a far cry from true journalism. As Joan Judge's work demonstrated, well before the 1911 Revolution the editors of the Shi Bao – despite Liang Qichao's design – already regarded newspapers as an institution of public opinion exercising judgment on political issues in the interest of the people.[4] Yet such recognition did not directly and immediately lead to professionalism in the journalistic circle in Shanghai and elsewhere. One Japanese journalist observed in 1918 that the lack of education and hard work among Chinese journalists was the main reason for the inability of China's press to influence society. He held that the chief goal of Chinese journalists was to seek or maintain personal position and use that position to attack political opponents. Such activities disqualified Chinese journalists as journalists in the modern sense of that profession.[5]

Politicization of newspapers was not unique to China. In Japan modern newspapers were born of the political struggle between the Bakufu and

---

3. Joan Judge, "The Factional Function of Print: Liang Qichao, *Shibao*, and the Fissures in the Late Qing Reform Movement," *Late Imperial China*, 16,1 (June 1995):120–40.
4. Joan Judge, *Print and Politics*, pp.68–74.   5. DZ, 14,4:183–84 .

the Satsuma-Choshu coalition in 1868 and remained biased organs of different political factions and parties until the 1890s.[6] In the United States newspapers became weapons of political parties after the promulgation of the Constitution and the establishment of the party system. The role of the press was widely considered political and legitimately so until the 1830s when new concepts regarding the role of the press were articulated.[7] John B. Powell, the owner and editor of the *China Weekly Review*, observed in 1928: "Most of the [Chinese] papers are the organs of officials or cliques which use them for ulterior purposes. There is nothing peculiar about this situation for it is a state through which the press of every country has passed in its history."[8]

For newspapers to be politically biased did not necessarily mean the undoing of professionalism, but it did signify an early stage in the development of the journalistic profession. In early-twentieth-century China the political use of newspapers led to vulgarization. Publishing political newspapers involved little professionalism. In the 1920s, with a few hired hands and no reporters, one person acting as editor and writer at the same time could run such a political paper. With two hundred yuan a month, that kind of paper could produce one thousand copies a day.[9] "[M]any of the news agencies are political organs in disguise," commented one foreign observer in 1921, "others are blackmail organizations and a few are good.... Great men in China pay either a news agency or a syndicating reporter to puff them – which of course is done everywhere else."[10] The practice of paying newspapers for political purposes was so widespread that fraud in that business appeared. A journalist would promise a warlord or politician to publish a newspaper backing the warlord or politician, in return for a subsidy of five thousand yuan a month. The journalist would then go to a printer to produce five copies of the newspaper every day for a cost of thirty-five yuan to forty yuan a month. The journalist would send three copies to the sponsor to show the existence of the newspaper and pocket the rest of the funds. "This graft ran merrily along for some years, and still crops up,"

---

6. Jung Bock Lee, *The Political Character of the Japanese Press* (Seoul, 1985), pp.10–17.
7. Hazel Dicken-Garcia, *Journalistic Standards in Nineteenth-Century America* (Madison, 1989), pp.30–40.
8. CWR, 45,12 (8/18/1928):379.
9. Jiang Guozhen, *Zhongguo Xinwen Fada Shi* (A history of the development of Chinese journalism) (Shanghai, 1927), pp.53–54.
10. NCH, 11/19/1921, p.527.

reported Vernon McKenzie, Dean of School of Journalism at the University of Washington, in 1929.[11] One would find so-called newspapers that had no publishing office (*youbao wushe*) or newspapers that gathered news from other legitimate newspapers through cut and paste. Editors and reporters of news agencies and newspapers would fabricate special news.[12]

The lack of legal protection for freedom of the press contributed to the state of affairs. Because newspapers could be suppressed wholesale due to the displeasure of some officials, "no one of intelligence or reputation would invest good money in the publishing business under such conditions. The result is that most of the newspapers in the interior of the country are of the fly-by-night variety which are run by persons of no particular educational qualifications or professional ethics."[13] Quite a number of people engaged in that sort of journalism for the purpose of currying political favor and accumulating political capital.[14]

There were, however, well-known newspapers – such as the *Shen Bao*, the *Xinwen Bao*, and the *Shi Bao* – in Shanghai that were well-managed, professionalized publications with large circulations and good reputations. In fact it was through a resistance against political influence that those papers grew more professional and more popular. The insistence of the *Shi Bao*'s editors on managerial and editorial independence, for example, defeated Liang Qichao's design to use the paper solely as a factional organ.[15] A similar case has been made with the *Minguo Ribao* as a GMD party organ in the mid-1920s.[16]

Yet even in those newspaper offices, reporters and editors were often not adequately trained professionals. Journalism as a discipline began to appear in a few universities in Shanghai and elsewhere in the country in the 1920s and a number of Shanghai journalists were trained in the School of Journalism at the University of Missouri. But most journalists did not have college degrees and many had only primary or secondary education. According to Gu Zhizhong who worked for the *Xinwen Bao* at that time, before 1930 hardly any journalists graduated from a department or school of journalism, and few people cared about journalists'

11. CWR, 50,10 (11/9/1929):376.
12. Fang Hanqi, *Zhongguo Jindai Baokan Shi*, pp.728–31.
13. CWR, 47,6 (1/5/1929):225.   14. Fang Hanqi, *Zhongguo Jindai*, p.731.
15. Joan Judge, "The Factional Function."
16. John Fitszgerald, "The Origins of the Illiberal Party Newspapers: Print Journalism in China's Nationalist Revolution," *Republican China*, 21,2 (Apr. 1996):1–22.

From "Literary Men" to Professionals

educational background as long as they were equal to the job.[17] Gu himself was a middle school graduate.

It is a truism that the best journalists are not necessarily graduates from the best schools of journalism, just as the best novelists are rarely trained in literature. But apparently the lack of professional training did become a problem for many would-be journalists at that time. Although to be taken with a grain of salt, Lin Yutang laughed at the poor editing of such well-known newspapers as the *Shen Bao* and *Xinwen Bao* as late as 1937. The difference between those two big newspapers, said Lin, was that the former was poorly edited and the latter was not edited at all.[18]

A more serious problem than editorial skills, however, was a lack of professional ethics among journalists, as the establishment of professional ethics was a hallmark of professionalization. Writing in 1931, Zhang Jinglu noted that while Chinese journalists represented the interest of the public, their professional status was low because they worked hard but received meager pay.[19] On the other hand, he found the quality of journalists wanting:

> Of journalists employed by the average newspaper publishers and news agencies, most do not recognize their own [social] status and human dignity. There is a lot to be criticized in [their] words and deeds. Lacking knowledge of journalism, [they] make do perfunctorily with whatever they have and are incapable of creativity. When international disputes occur, near sighted and ignorant of the situation in the world, [they] are at a loss for what to say. These shortcomings have become almost commonplace among journalists. [They] have too high an opinion of themselves in the face of people below them and have an undue sense of inferiority before the powerful, so as to lose their human dignity and degrade their [social] status.[20]

Zhang Jinglu did not elaborate on what journalists had done to lose their human dignity and degrade their social status. Other sources, however, revealed that some journalists were open to bribes offered by influential figures and that many news reporters were friends or even members of

---

17. Gu Zhizhong, "Yisuo Bingbu Lixiang De Xinwen Xuexiao," p.33.
18. Yutang Lin, *A History of the Press and Public Opinion in China*, p.131.
19. Zhang Jinglu, *Zhongguo De Xinwen Jizhe Yu Xinwen Zhi* (Chinese journalists and Chinese newspapers) (Shanghai, 1932), pp.11–17.
20. Ibid., p.66.

the Shanghai underworld. Hang Shijun, later a member of the executive committee of the Shanghai Journalists Association, was said to be the first journalist to join the Green Gang. Other kinds of questionable behavior included distorting facts in exchange for bribes, threatening disclosure of scandals to blackmail, fabricating sensational social news (*shehui xinwen*) in emulation of tabloids, and using newspapers to settle personal scores.[21]

While some of those deeds might have been necessitated by circumstances for self-protection, such as using connections with the underworld, others can be seen only as outright unprofessional conduct. "Up to the present," observed the editor of the *China Weekly Review* in 1923, "the profession of journalism in China has been of low repute, the newspaperman being held in little higher regard than the mountebank, which he usually was." But, added the editor, "the Chinese editor will not always remain the slave of selfish interest, political or otherwise. He is already asserting his independence, which statement may be proved by reading the editorials of such papers as the *Shun Pao* [Shen Bao], *Sin Wan Pao* [Xinwen Bao], *Yi Shih Pao* [Yishi Bao] and others."[22] Another foreign observer, while acknowledging the "few brilliant exceptions among the Chinese-language newspapers," spoke of the Chinese newspaper world in which "blackmail competes with subsidy to the complete eclipse of advertising and subscription returns."[23] By all accounts, Shanghai journalists were a crop of people with diverse intellectual and social backgrounds. There was virtually no established code of professional conduct and no common professional goals among journalists. It was, therefore, rather difficult for Shanghai journalists to develop a sense of professional identity and community and act from that perspective. That state of affairs would explain the larger role of newspaper publishers and the low profile of Chinese journalists (reporters and editors) as a group in the early years of the Republic.

Publishers as the Vanguard of Journalistic Enterprise

The promoters of Chinese journalism were not journalists but publishers as entrepreneurs. Given their commercial concerns and the tradition

---

21. Lu Yi, interview with the author, January 12, 1992; Yu Jing, "Sanshi Nian Baojie Shixiao Lu" (Anecdotes from thirty years in the newspaper circle), WZX (Beijing, 1962), pp.92–101; Xu Zhucheng, *Baohai Jiuwen*, pp.235, 246; Zhu Zijia, *Huangpu Jiangde Zhuolang*, pp.181–82.
22. CWR, 26,1 (9/1/1923):3.   23. *Chinese Recorder*, 56,5 (May 1925):294, 296.

of elite urban associations, it is not surprising that newspaper owners and managers first recognized the advantage of having an organization for the purpose of promoting journalistic enterprise. On March 12, 1905, the *Shi Bao* published an editorial calling for the establishment of a national organization of journalists. The functions of such an organization would be to counter foreign newspapers' biased criticism of China, to resist government suppression, and to eliminate unhealthy behavior among journalists. The idea was supported by a number of newspapers including the *Shen Bao*, whose editorial the next day further elaborated on the benefits of such an organization.[24]

The proposed organization, however, did not appear until four years later. In 1909 the Shanghai Daily Newspapers Association (SDNA) (*Shanghai ribao gonghui*) was founded. It was an organization of owners and managers of Chinese newspapers in Shanghai, such as the *Shen Bao*, *Shi Bao*, *Shenzhou Ribao*, and *Xinwen Bao*. The stated mission of the SDNA was to cultivate mutual affection and seek the progress of newspapers. Interestingly, the association had a club for reporters (*jizhe julebu*) and a library open to reporters of member newspapers. The association's bylaws provided that the member newspapers share news information among themselves but carry no news items coming from nonmember newspapers.[25] That last provision indicated the SDNA's intention to provide benefits for member newspapers and exclude nonmember newspapers.

Clearly, the SDNA was not a professional association as defined in this study, but a trade association of newspaper owners and managers in the same category as the Shanghai Bankers Association (*Shanghai yinhang gonghui*) or the Shanghai Book Trade Association (*Shanghai shuye gongsuo*). The establishment of a club for reporters exhibited the paternalistic flavor that was characteristic of trade associations, just as the restriction on sharing news information was typical of trade associations that tended to draw a boundary between insiders and outsiders.

A similar creation was duplicated at the national level. In 1910 the National Newspapers Progress Association (NNPA) (*quanguo baojie jujin hui*) was founded. The membership of that association again consisted of newspapers represented by their owners and managers, not of individual journalists. In June 1912 the association held a special meeting

---

24. Ma Guangren, "Woguo Zaoqi De Xinwen Jie Tuanti" (Early journalistic associations in our country), XYZ, No.41 (Mar. 1988):61–62.
25. Ma, "Woguo Zaoqi," pp.62–63; Ge Gongzheng, *Zhongguo Baoxue Shi*, pp.297–300.

in Shanghai hosted by the SDNA. The meeting passed a number of resolutions. One of them opposed any press law and another proposed the establishment of a college of journalism and a journalists' club.[26] The association was too loosely structured to operate effectively, however. Its resolutions remained statements of intention rather than guidelines for action; no actions followed the resolutions. The organization simply faded from the scene in 1914 when Yuan Shikai began to impose restrictions on newspapers.

An effort to revive that national association was made in April 1919 when the National Newspapers Association of the Chinese Republic (NPACR) (*zhonghua minguo quanguo baojie lianhe hui*) was formed in Shanghai. The pronounced purposes of the association included protecting freedom of speech, facilitating business, and seeking the progress of journalism. From 1919 to 1921 the NPACR held three annual meetings and passed some twenty resolutions ranging from advocacy of freedom of speech to statements on the national situation. In 1921 the association fell apart due to internal divisions.[27] That was the end of any national organization among China's newspapers, while the SDNA remained an active public association in Shanghai.

Newspaper owners were the vanguard of association building among the newspaper personnel (*baoren*) because they ran newspapers as commercial enterprise and had business concerns similar to those of other industries. On the other hand, the print press as a modern invention had its particular cultural, social, and political functions not shared by other kinds of business. Joan Judge's study of the *Shi Bao* in the late Qing period (1904–1911) shows that editors and writers of the newspaper assigned to themselves a particular role in a middle realm to mediate between the state and the public.[28] During the Republican period, the rhetoric, if not the true vision, of publishers would describe newspapers as part of an emerging public sphere in which the public should participate or a public means (*gongqi*) by which the public good should be served. In concrete terms, newspapers should be free to publish any news and commentary. Freedom of speech was vital to a newspaper both for its commercial success and for its multifaceted public functions. Those two sides of the modern press could not be separated in the eyes of newspaper owners. It is out of those considerations that the SDNA

---

26. Ge Gongzheng, *Zhongguo*, pp.280–82; NCH, 6/15/1912, p.780.
27. Ma Guangren, "Woguo Zaoqi," pp.63–65; Ge Gongzheng, *Zhongguo*, pp.284–89.
28. Joan Judge, *Print and Politics*.

played a prominent role in Shanghai's public arena to defend freedom of speech. From the very beginning, therefore, newspaper owners claimed that their newspapers represented and reflected public opinion (*minyi*) and public voice (*gonglun*). They demanded freedom of speech as the most essential condition for the development of journalistic enterprise. Since the principle of freedom of speech worked not only to the advantage of newspaper owners but also to that of journalists who worked for newspapers, it was to become an important element in generating professional concerns and associational activities among Shanghai journalists.

FROM "LITERARY MEN" TO PROFESSIONALS

The Birth of the Shanghai Journalists Association

A true professional association of Chinese journalists in Shanghai did not appear until 1921, about the time that the National Newspapers Association disintegrated. Its appearance seemed almost accidental. In October of that year a joint national conference of provincial and local chambers of commerce and educational societies was held in Shanghai at the seat of the Shanghai General Chamber of Commerce. The agenda of the conference was to work out a plan for political reconstruction of the nation, which was part of the initiatives taken by Chinese bourgeoisie in Shanghai to play a major role in shaping the nation's political future.[29] The conference produced a statement on the national situation, but the conference organizers told news reporters not to publish the draft of the document because it needed to be voted on at the final session. However, the *Shang Bao* (Commercial News) – which was owned by Tang Jiezhi, a member of the Shanghai General Chamber of Commerce and a delegate to the conference – published the draft, stealing the show. All reporters covering the conference felt cheated by the conference organizers who appeared to have favored the *Shang Bao*. A wrangle broke out at the final session between the reporters and the organizers. A delegate from the Taiyuan Chamber of Commerce, "[being from] the interior, with the habit of despising reporters," shouted abuse at the reporters. Thus insulted, all reporters walked out of the conference. There was no coverage of the meeting in any newspapers the next day.

---

29. For the background of this event, see Marie-Claire Bergère, *The Goden Age*, pp.220–27.

According to Zhang Jinglu, who was a reporter at the time, that was the first time that Chinese journalists held a collective boycott. The anger of journalists was soothed only after Nie Yuntai, the president of the Shanghai General Chamber of Commerce, and Huang Yanpei, the president of the Jiangsu Provincial Educational Society, apologized to the journalists involved and to all newspapers and news agencies in Shanghai.[30]

The episode signified that Shanghai journalists had grown self-conscious of their professional role being different from that of mere "literary men," even though they had not been identified as *ziyou zhiye zhe* yet. They would not tolerate any more the abuse reserved for "immoral literary men" (*wude wenren*). It is in the wake of the incident that a group of reporters who had been involved felt strongly about the insult to journalists and decided that journalists needed an organization to promote their status and protect their reputation. On November 11 the Shanghai Journalists Association (SJA) (*Shanghai xinwen jizhe lianhuan hui*) was founded, with thirty-one members. Among the leaders of the association were Ge Gongzhen, Zhang Jinglu, Yan Duhe, and Pan Gongzhan.

Ge Gongzhen was a veteran journalist. He joined the *Shi Bao* in 1914 and worked his way up from proofreader to editor in chief. Leaving the *Shi Bao* in 1927 for a tour abroad, he attended an international conference on journalism in Switzerland. After returning to China at the end of 1928, he joined the *Shen Bao* in 1929 as the deputy chief of the designing department. In 1927 he published *The History of Chinese Journalism*, which is still an important source on the subject. Ge was widely recognized for his efforts to raise the standards of Chinese journalism and was an influential figure among journalists and intellectuals in Shanghai and beyond.[31]

Zhang Jinglu was better known as a publisher, but he began his career by contributing essays and fiction to newspapers while working as a bookkeeper in a restaurant. Thanks to his contribution, he was employed as an editor in 1916 by the *Gongmin Ribao* (Citizen's Daily) in Tianjin, a GMD organ, until the paper was shut down in 1917. In 1921 Zhang was already in the publishing business, but he was also working as a

---

30. Zhang Jinglu, *Zhongguo De Xinwen Jizhe* (Chinese journalists) (Shanghai, 1928), pp.76–78.
31. Hong Weijie, *Ge Gongzhen Nianpu* (A biographic chronicle of Ge Gongzhen) (Nanjing, 1990); MRD, p.114.

reporter for the National News Agency (*guowen she*). He later worked for the *Shang Bao* for a period of time. As a journalist and publisher, Zhang was intimately involved in the journalistic and literary circles in Shanghai.[32]

A journalist and writer, Yan Duhe was a native of Tongxiang, Zhejiang. He studied in the Shanghai Institute of Foreign Languages (*guangfang yuanguan*) and began to teach in elementary and middle schools at the age of nineteen. He worked as an editor in the China Book Incorporation for a year before entering the *Xinwen Bao* in 1914 to edit its literature supplements. Later he became the deputy editor in chief of the newspaper. Widely known for his fiction series published in various newspapers and counted among mandarin duck and butterfly writers, Yan was typical of those with an amphibious career between journalism and literary writing.[33]

Pan Gongzhan hailed from Wuxing, Zhejiang. While studying at St. Johns University in Shanghai, he was one of the leaders in the student movement of 1919. After graduation he taught at a private middle school and contributed to the *Shishi Xingbao* and the *Minguo Ribao*. He entered the *Shang Bao* as editor in 1921 and the *Shen Bao* in 1926. During those years he also taught at several colleges in Shanghai.[34] Because of his later affiliation with the GMD Party, he was to become an influential GMD official in Shanghai. In a way the careers of Ge, Zhang, Yan, and Pan represented the life experiences and the political spectrum of Shanghai journalists.

Under the SJA's initial bylaws, managers, editors in chief (*zong bianji*), and chief writers (*zhubi*) of newspapers were excluded from the organization, because they were deemed to have different interests from news reporters and editors. In 1922 the association revised its bylaws to accept editors in chief and chief writers, but still barred managers.[35] Newspaper managers' affiliation with the SDNA was probably a disqualifying factor. The discrimination in membership made the SJA an association of journalists as professionals, different from the SDNA. At its peak the SJA

---

32. Zhang Jinglu, *Zai Chubanjie Ershi Nian* (Twenty years in the publishing circle) (Shanghai, 1984), pp.49–57, 101–110; MRD, p.974.
33. *Yuanyang Hudie Pai Wenxue Ziliao* (Sources on mandarin duck and butterfly literature) (Fujian, 1984), pp.334–35; Hong Weijie, *Ge Gongzhen Nianpu*, p.15; Wang Zhongwei, "Wo yu Xinwen Bao de Guanxi," XYZ, No.12 (June 1982):127–50; MRD, p.1666.
34. MRD, pp.1466–67; Christian Henriot, *Shanghai, 1927–1937*, pp.54–58.
35. Zhang, *Zai Chubanjie*, pp.78–79.

had seventy-two members before it was superseded by its successor in 1927.[36]

Shanghai journalists did not seem sure what functions their association should have, however. According to its bylaws, the SJA was to "cultivate mutual affection and pursue scholarly study."[37] At the association's second annual meeting in November 1923 Ge Gongzhen further stated that the SJA's tasks were for members to study journalism and improve their skills, to achieve unity and promote the progress of journalism, to exchange views and arouse public opinion, and to associate with foreign journalists. The SJA did not address political issues, explained Ge, because journalists already had plenty of room to express their political views in newspapers.[38] Ge seems to have meant that the SJA would encourage journalists to arouse public opinion by expressing views on political issues in newspapers, but that the association itself was strictly professional and nonpolitical.

The SJA did not exactly focus on professional issues either. What the association did during the first few years of its existence was rather superficial and trivial. The association would meet once a month at a dinner gathering. It would ask members to donate money to hold a funeral for a deceased journalist or invite foreign journalists, returned students, and other academics to give speeches about journalism in the West and its prospects in China. For the most part it would organize entertainment for its members, as its name *lianhuanhui* (lit. "entertainment gathering") would imply.[39] The association once planned to establish a college of journalism with its own resources and to publish a periodical on journalism, but neither materialized.[40]

Even the murder of journalists by warlords did not galvanize professional spirit and associational activity within the SJA. In April 1926 Shao Piaoping, a well-known journalist who edited the *Jing Bao* (Capital News) in Beijing, was executed under the order of warlord Zhang Zongchang because Shao had attacked the Fengtian clique in the newspaper.[41] Just four months later another widely read journalist, Lin Baishui, suffered the same fate in Beijing. By some accounts, those two

---

36. Zhang Jinglu, *Zai Chubanjie*, pp.78–79.
37. Ge Gongzheng, *Zhongguo*, p.300.   38. SB, 1923: 11/18, p.5.
39. SB, 1922: 1/7, p.10; 1/9, p.10; 1923: 8/30, p.6; 9/19, p.6; 1924: 8/18, p.5; 9/29, p.4; 11/15, p.4; 1926: 3/8, p.3.
40. SB, 1924: 11/17, p.4; 12/29, p.4.
41. Xu Wen, *Shao Piaoping Zhuanlue* (A brief biography of Shao Piaoping) (Beijing, 1990); MRD, p.550.

men lived dissipated lives and used their newspapers to blackmail people, including political figures. When they failed to get a payoff, they would attack their targets in their papers. Their deaths were attributed to revenge against their questionable deeds.[42] The verity of this story is in doubt. Bao Tianxiao, a writer and one-time journalist who personally knew Shao Piaoping as a friend, did not buy this explanation but treated the reason for his death as a "mystery."[43] Even if the story were true, the killing of Shao and Lin for what they said in newspapers was sheer brutality and total disregard of the rule of law. Even foreign newspapers in China carried editorials denouncing the barbarity of Zhang Zongchang.[44] The SJA's autumn general meeting, after discussing the matter, decided to express condolences to the families of Shao and Lin and to "warn those who abused their power not to slay innocent people again." But it did not specify how the warning was to be given.[45] In fact the SJA took no concrete steps to advance the rights of journalists.

The SJA's Inaction toward Censorship

More striking was the SJA's noninvolvement in the campaign for freedom of speech. The issue presented itself soon after the founding of the Republic. Along with its clampdown on voluntary associations, the Yuan Shikai government enacted the Regulations on Newspapers (*Baozhi tiaoli*), in April 1914, which actually covered both newspapers and magazines. Under the regulations, a publisher should be thirty years old or above and apply for permission from the police, paying a deposit ranging from 100 yuan to 350 yuan. Each issue of the publication should carry the names and addresses of the publisher, editor, and printer, and be sent to the police for inspection. The press was forbidden to carry anything that would contradict the government system, disturb public order, harm social customs, divulge military and diplomatic secrets, and encourage criminal defendants. Personal attacks and reports about parliament meetings or lawsuits pending trial were prohibited. Violation of the Regulations on Newspapers was punishable by fine, banning of publication, and imprisonment.[46] In December 1914 the Publication Law (*Chuban fa*)

---

42. Lee-hsia Hsu Ting, *Government Control of the Press in Modern China, 1900–1949* (Cambridge, MA, 1974), pp.58–61.
43. Bao Tianxiao, *Chuanying Lou Huiyilu Xubian*, pp.71–78.
44. CWR, 37,12 (8/21/1926):289.   45. SB, 1926: 8/23, p.5.
46. ZMXFD (1924), pp.26–30.

was enacted. Its provisions were similar to the Regulations on Newspapers, but it covered all publications from newspapers and magazines to books.[47] The Regulations on Newspapers were annulled in July 1916. A number of newspapers and magazines were banned by the government even before the enactment of the Regulations on Newspapers and the Publication Law, and many more were banned thereafter.[48] Under the Yuan Shikai government, from April 1912 to June 1916, a total of seventy-three newspapers were shut down; forty-nine were prosecuted; nine newspaper offices were physically destroyed; and at least twenty-four journalists were killed and sixty went to jail.[49]

Shanghai was the center of the Chinese modern press because of the protection offered by the foreign concessions. Almost all the important Chinese newspapers in Shanghai were registered under foreigners' names or with foreign governments and operated in the foreign concessions.[50] Yet, the foreign concessions were not a free-for-all paradise. The authorities in the concessions also strove to control the Chinese press, though their methods were not as brutal as those of their Chinese counterparts. Even before the enactment of the Regulations on Newspapers and the Publication Law, the Municipal Police and the Mixed Court of the International Settlement were prepared to suppress any Chinese publications that were considered to be "calculated to destroy the peace of the country as a whole." They would see to it that "nothing is allowed inside the settlement which would not be tolerated outside."[51] Indeed, contemporary newspapers were punctuated with cases of Chinese publications including newspapers, magazines, and books being suppressed by the authorities in Shanghai's two foreign concessions.[52]

From 1914 onward the SMC prosecuted Chinese publishers and editors under the Regulations on Newspapers and the Publication Law of the Yuan Shikai government. At one point (January 1923) the Ministry of Justice was reported to have repealed the Publication Law.[53] But apparently the law was still in force thereafter. In 1925 A. Covey, a

---

47. ZMXFD (1924), pp.39–41.
48. See SB, 1913: 11/30, p.7; 12/16, p.8; 12/29, p.7; 1914: 2/15, p.7; 7/16, p.7; 8/30, p.7; 1915: 6/13, p.7.
49. Fang Hanqi, *Zhongguo Jindai*, p.720.
50. Jiang Guozhen, *Zhongguo Xinwen*, pp.69–71; NCH, 4/11/1914, p.86.
51. NCH, 8/30/1913, p.630.
52. Also see Lee-hsia Hsu Ting, *Government Control*, pp.67–78.
53. CWR, 23,10 (2/3/1923):379.

foreign lawyer defending the *Minguo Bao*, asked the International Mixed Court not to apply the Publication Law because it was not enforced in other parts of the country and because many public associations were demanding the annulment of the law. But the court decided that the law was desirable and should be applied before being officially repealed by the government in Beijing.[54]

As if the Chinese law was not enough for the SMC to rein in the Chinese press, from 1913 to 1925 the SMC repeatedly tried to institute a set of bylaws on printed matters. The gist of the set of bylaws was that "the Council should have full power of immediate action, without recourse to any other Authority, to prevent the publication of any printed matter of a character calculated to incite a breach of the peace."[55] The proposal was initially put forward in 1913 to 1915, a time when many Chinese publications were vehemently opposing Yuan Shikai's design to increase presidential powers and his monarchical ambition. But the ratepayers' meeting voted it down. The second attempt in 1916 also met with failure. In 1919 the SMC once again agitated for its passage amidst widespread opposition from not only the Chinese but also the foreign press and community in Shanghai. John B. Powell, the founder and editor of the *China Weekly Review*, argued against the measure. Citing freedom of press in many countries including Germany and the Ottoman Empire, he judged it dangerous to put such a "full power" to determine what was "calculated to cause a breach of the peace" in the hands of one person – the chief of the municipal police.[56] The measure passed at the ratepayers' meeting considering the measure because many people left early while all 138 Japanese ratepayers present voted yes (the Japanese were most annoyed by the criticism in the Chinese press of Japanese design on China). But the Diplomatic Body in Beijing vetoed it. The same proposal failed to be adopted in the subsequent ratepayers' meetings for lack of a quorum in 1920, 1921, 1922, and 1924. In April 1925 the SMC disguised the bylaws as an amendment to the 1858 Land Regulations, hoping to have the measure passed by the ratepayers' meeting. That move only invited even greater opposition from both the Chinese and foreign press in Shanghai and beyond.[57]

---

54. NCH, 4/25/1925, pp.158–59.   55. CWR, 9,5 (7/5/1919):174.
56. CWR, 9,5 (7/5/1919):172–74; for some of the Chinese responses, see CWR, 9,7 (7/19/1919):268–69.
57. Ma Guangren, "Shanghai Renmin Fandui Yinshua Fulü De Douzheng" (The Shanghai people's struggle against the printed matter regulations), XYZ, No.46 (June 1989):104–117.

In the movement of opposing censorship and demanding freedom of the press, it is such organizations as the Shanghai Daily Newspapers Association, the Book and Newspaper Association (*shubao lianhehui*), the Book Trade Merchants Association (*shuye shanghui*), and Book Trade Association (*shuye gongsuo*) that played a leading role. They spearheaded the movement to oppose the SMC bylaws on printed materials and the petition campaign to the Beijing government demanding an annulment of the Publication Law.[58] Not insignificantly, on both issues the Shanghai General Chamber of Commerce was firmly behind the four trade associations. The Chamber telegraphed Duan Qirui, the government head in Beijing at the time, the Legal System Council (*fazhi yuan*), and the Ministries of Interior and Justice, asking for the annulment of the Publication Law. It instructed Yu Qiaqing, the president of the chamber, who happened to be in Beijing at the time, to lobby the government for that goal. On the issue of regulations on printed materials proposed by the Municipal Council, the chamber wrote to the Commissioner of Foreign Affairs asking the commissioner to raise the issue with the SMC.[59] Those movements led by Shanghai bourgeois elite ended in victory: the Publication Law was annulled in January 1926 and the regulations on printed matter was again stillborn, and for good.[60] On both occasions, however, the SJA's glaring performance was its complete silence and inaction.

The SJA's neglecting of the issue of press freedom indicated the absence of a professional identity among journalists at that point. The lack of interest in the issue can be partly explained by the following situation: When the authorities of the foreign concessions in Shanghai found a newspaper or a publication offensive, they would prosecute, imprison, and fine the owner, manager, or editor in chief of the newspaper or the publishing house. Reporters and editors did not bear the brunt of suppression directly and were not personally affected unless and until the paper was shut down, which would mean the loss of jobs for journalists. The preceding situation also explains at least in part why trade associations of publishers adamantly opposed censorship and any restrictions on publications in the 1920s and why journalists did not. While invoking freedom of speech as a principle to oppose censorship, pub-

---

58. SB, 1925: 4/5, p.3; 4/12, p.3; 4/13, p.3; 4/15, p.3; Ma Guangren, "Shanghai Renmin."
59. SB, 1925: 4/9, p.3; 4/12, p.3; NCH, 4/18/1925, p.101.
60. Ma Guangren, "Shanghai Renmin"; Lee-hsia Hsu Ting, *Government Control*.

lishers and newspaper owners were certainly motivated by business concerns first and foremost. On the other hand, the fact that journalists were uninvolved in the issue serves as a telling index of the immaturity of Shanghai journalists as a professional community.

The Founding of the New SJA

The ineffectual existence of the SJA did not endear itself to journalists. Frustrated by its poor performance, some journalists sought to establish another organization. In early 1927, more than forty journalists decided to form a new association of journalists by first establishing two separate associations for newspaper reporters and news agency reporters.[61] On March 19, 1927, the Daily Newspaper Reporters Association (DNRA) (*ribao jizhe gonghui*) and the News Agency Reporters Association (NARA) (*tongxinshe jizhe gonghui*) were founded. Among the leaders of the DNRA were Shao Lizi, Chen Bulei, and Pan Gongzhan. Thus the DNRA superseded the SJA.[62]

The action of those journalists at that particular juncture was partly informed by the enthusiasm among Chinese residents in Shanghai for establishing public associations in false anticipation of a new political era with the arrival of the National Revolutionary Army (NRA) on the Northern Expedition. Shao Lizi of the *Minguo Ribao*, who was a GMD member, actually urged Shanghai journalists to visit the NRA that had arrived in Jiangxi Province, but few journalists were interested. In the end, only Chen Bulei and Pan Gongzhan both of the *Shang Bao* made the trip and thus established their revolutionary credentials with the GMD, paving the way for their later rise to political power.[63]

After the GMD took control of the city on March 23, the DNRA leaders made efforts to get on good terms with the new regime. The association participated in GMD-sponsored political rallies and its leaders paid a visit to the Political Department of the NRA Eastern Route Headquarters.[64] But political events overtook their efforts. During the political storms in March to April 1927 both the DNRA and the NARA were dissolved under circumstances that remain obscure.[65]

---

61. SB, 1927: 3/12, p.7; 3/14, p.5.   62. SB, 1927: 3/20, p.6; Zhu Zijia, *Huangpu*, p.5.
63. Zhu Zijia, *Huangpu*, p.5.   64. SB, 1927: 4/6, p.7.
65. Zhang Jinglu, *Zhongguo de Xinwen Jizhe Yu Xinwen Zhi*, pp.79–80. Zhang did not elaborate on what happened.

The desire among Shanghai journalists for a professional association did not wither away, however. On the heels of the demise of the DNRA and the NARA, a group of journalists came up with yet another journalists association. That organization was expected to be successful, because Chen Dezheng, the editor in chief of the *Minguo Ribao* since late March 1927 and the soon-to-be propaganda chief of the MPH, was among the organizers.[66] On April 29 a new Shanghai Journalists Association (*Shanghai xinwen jizhe lianhe hui*) was founded, with a membership of fifty-nine journalists from nine newspapers and four news agencies. Several leaders of the first SJA and of the DNRA held their posts on the executive committee of the new organization.[67] Though sources are silent on this point, the new association appears to have been a reorganization of the DNRA.

The new SJA took a few initiatives to promote professionalism and shape professional identity. In September 1927 the association decided to publish an annual periodical, to issue badges to its members, and to hold dinner gatherings once a month.[68] On November 3, 1928, it created a committee in charge of soliciting donations for building an association office. Among five members of the committee were Chen Dezheng, who had assumed the office in the MPH, and Chen Bulei, who had now become Chiang Kai-shek's secretary.[69] The SJA's executive committee also planned to publish a monthly. The editorial board of the publication again included Chen Dezheng and Chen Bulei, though the publication never appeared.[70]

Those actions of the SJA pointed to an intention to make use of the political connections enjoyed by people such as Chen Dezheng and Chen Bulei to advance the cause of journalism. Considering the official capacities of Chen Dezheng, Chen Bulei, and Pan Gongzhan in the GMD party and government, while being members of the SJA at least nominally, the formation of the new SJA must have had the blessing of the MPH from the beginning. During the remainder of the 1920s the SJA continued to operate with a low profile and outside politics, probably due to the tightened GMD control over societal organizations.

66. SB, 1927: 4/12, p.7. About the Minguo Ribao, see John Fitzgerald, "The Origins of the Illiberal Party Newspaper," and about Chen Dezheng's position in that paper, see Yuan Yiqin, "Shanghai Minguo Ribao Jianjie" (A brief sketch of the Republican Daily News of Shanghai), XYZ, No.45 (Mar. 1989):132–47.
67. SB, 1927: 4/30, p.6; Zhang Jinglu, *Zhongguo de Xinwen Jizhe*, pp.80–81.
68. SB, 1927: 9/12, p.5.   69. SB, 1928: 11/4, p.6.   70. SB, 1928: 11/11, p.6.

Toward Professionalization

Something of a turning point in the professional growth of Chinese journalists was reached in the early 1930s. Stephen MacKinnon has emphasized the importance of the 1930s in the history of the Chinese press. In the 1930s the Chinese press was characterized by newspaper and magazine publishing as a business, political patronage as an essential condition, a symbiotic relationship with the Western press circle, and subjection to censorship by the state.[71] As MacKinnon mentioned correctly, however, those characteristics existed well before the 1930s. A real and important departure from the past for the Chinese press in the 1930s was a newly found sense of professionalism and professional identity among journalists. Not insignificantly, that sense of professional identity emerged at least in part because the GMD party-state classified journalists into the category of *ziyou zhiye zhe* in 1929 to 1930.

In the 1930s journalists began to discuss professionalization (*zhiye hua*), specialization (*zhuanmen hua*), and objectivity (*keguan*). More institutions and journals of journalism were established in the late 1920s and the early 1930s. A new generation of journalists launched criticism of sensationalism and commercialism characteristic of old-style journalism. The criticism highlighted the importance of journalism in public life and heightened the sense of professional responsibility of journalists.[72]

In Shanghai that development was registered, both symbolically and substantively, in an effort to revitalize the Shanghai Journalists Association. On March 2, 1931, the SJA's general meeting revised its bylaws and redefined its mission as follows: "To develop the cause of journalism, to enhance the authority of public opinion, to uphold the interests of citizens, and to protect the livelihood of journalists."[73] Compared with the mission statement of the 1920s, the new goals were more directly related to the public and political functions of journalism and to the professional interests of journalists.

The movement toward professionalization continued thereafter. In September 1931 the general meeting of the SJA passed a resolution to

---

71. Stephen R. MacKinnon, "Toward a History of the Chinese Press in the Republican Period," *Modern China*, 23,1 (Jan. 1997):3–32.
72. Chang-tai Hung, *War and Popular Culture: Resistance in Modern China, 1937–1945* (Berkeley, 1994), pp.44–49.
73. Ma Guangren, "Woguo Zhaoqi," pp.66–67.

reorganize itself.[74] The reorganization was completed in June 1932, with more than two hundred members. The SJA changed its name to *Shanghai shi xinwen jizhe gonghui*.[75] The change in the association's name from *lianhuan hui* to *lianhe hui* to *gonghui* – with *gonghui* being a standard term for professional associations – reflected an increasingly conscious effort to highlight the publicness of the journalistic profession and its commonality with other professional groups. At the founding meeting of the reorganized SJA Yan Esheng – a well-known journalist and writer and an executive committee member of the SJA – announced that the tasks of the new organization were to promote the development of journalism and to elevate the status of journalists. The two tasks were closely related – without one, the other could not be accomplished.[76] The statement announced a new conception of journalists' role and captured their professional identity and public function. From that point onward the reorganized SJA assumed a much more assertive stance in performing professional and political functions.

The range of professional concerns of the SJA expanded considerably, as seen in the actions taken by the association's general meeting on May 2, 1937. The SJA decided to establish a library of journalism and to form teams of journalists to tour the country and go abroad. It demanded the central government to establish qualifications for journalists and order all GMD party and government agencies in the country to facilitate the journalist's job. It undertook the following four initiatives: (1) devise methods to prevent police detectives from passing themselves off as reporters, (2) review the qualifications of its members and expel inactive members, (3) protect its members and provide services for them, and (4) hire Western-style doctors and native physicians to provide journalists with free or half-rate medical care.[77] Evidently, by 1937 the Shanghai Journalists Association had traveled a long way to become a self-conscious professional association, signaling the transformation of journalists from "literary men" to professionals. One important sign of the professional maturity of the SJA in the 1930s was its assertive position on the issue of freedom of speech (*yanlun ziyou*), which made a sharp contrast with the SJA's behavior in the 1920s.

---

74. SnB, 1931: 11/15, p.15. 75. SnB, 1932: 6/15, p.10.
76. SnB, 1932: 6/26, p.13 77. SnB, 1937: 5/3, p.15.

FREEDOM OF SPEECH AND THE JOURNALISTIC PROFESSION

GMD Censorship

As early as 1927, when no laws and regulations on the press had been promulgated, the GMD authorities already began to use a postal ban as a means to suppress objectionable newspapers. In early June such a ban was imposed on the *Xinwen Bao* because the paper published a list of merchants and commercial firms from whom Chiang Kai-shek and the GMD wanted to borrow huge sums of money for the Northern Expedition.[78] By late 1928 and early 1929, as the country was nominally unified under the GMD government, Nanjing announced an end to censorship and the drafting of a publication law.[79]

Censorship was never ended but only institutionalized by law. The Publication Law (*Chuban fa*), enacted by the National Government on December 16, 1930, was more restrictive than the similar law under Yuan Shikai. Covering newspapers, magazines, books, and other printed materials, the law required registration of and application for permits by all publishers. Article 19 of the law prohibited publication of anything that would "undermine the GMD and the Three Principles of the People, subvert the government, harm the interests of the Republic, disturb the public order, and damage good social customs." No publication of anything about military and diplomatic activities was allowed.[80] Those provisions in effect allowed the authorities to ban any news and commentary on factional strife within the GMD, anti-Communist military campaigns, and government policy toward Japan – most important public issues during the Nanjing Decade.

The Implementing Specifics of the Publication Law (*Chuban fa shishi xize*) issued in October 1931 required that news publications had to be approved by the Ministry of the Interior and the GMD Central Headquarters.[81] Those regulations met with widespread opposition from the journalistic circles in the country. In early 1933, responding to the demands of journalists and publishers, Nanjing defined a few specific cat-

---

78. NCH, 6/4/1927, p.420.
79. NCH, 7/14/1928, p.51; 8/31/1929, p.321; CWR, 47, 6 (1/5/1929):225; 50,2 (9/4/1929): 108.
80. ZMXFD (1934), pp.406–8; CWR, 55,12 (2/21/1931):422–23.
81. ZMXFD (1934), pp.408–9.

egories of materials not to be published: those exposing foreign affairs secrets, relating to military and national defense plans, and detrimental to peace and order.[82]

In July 1935 Nanjing revised the Publication Law. It empowered local government agencies (county magistrate offices and bureaus of social affairs in municipalities) to shut down offensive publications and fine, detain, and imprison their publishers.[83] In the face of strong protest from the journalistic circles, the law was not enacted until July 1937.

Shanghai as a center of the Chinese press was also a center of government censorship. In addition to the Books and Journals Censorship Committee (*shubao jiancha weiyuan hui*), the Municipal Government and the Municipal Party Headquarters played a major role in controlling printed matter. Two former newspaper employees and now members of the standing committee of the MPH – Chen Dezheng, the chief of the Propaganda Department (1927–1930), and Pan Gongzhan, the director of the Bureaus of Social Affairs (1928–1932) and Education (1932–1937) – were key persons.[84] As former journalists who had once engaged in radical propaganda, Chen and Pan possessed a keen sense of what kind of message was subversive to the GMD regime; as GMD party and government officials, they suppressed such materials with zeal.

In examining the censorship role of the GMD state, it should be noted that besides aiming at political news and commentary in the press and other publications on political and ideological issues, the government censorship also targeted such nonpolitical materials as obscene tabloids and false advertisement in newspapers. In June 1927 the MPH's propaganda committee, the police, and the Shanghai District Court shut down an obscene tabloid, the *Pleasure World* (*Huahua shijie*).[85] In November 1929 the Shanghai Bureau of Education prohibited all mosquito papers from carrying advertisements for obscene drugs (*yinyao*) referring to aphrodisiacs. At the same time the GMD Central Department of Propaganda ordered a strict ban on reactionary mosquito papers (*fandong xiaobao*).[86] In 1933 the GMD Fourth Central Executive Committee Standing Committee adopted a resolution on banning indecent mosquito

---

82. NCH, 1/4/1933, p.2; 1/25/1933, p.124.   83. NCH, 7/17/1935, p.86.
84. Chen's political career was cut short in 1930 due to intraparty politics. See Chen Guanghui, "Guomindang Kongzhi Shanghai Jiaoyu de Chou'e Shouduan" (GMD's ugly means to control Shanghai's education), WZX (Shanghai, No.13, Sept. 1962), pp.139, 145–46; Christian Henriot, *Shanghai, 1927–1937*, pp.54–58.
85. SB, 1927: 6/17, p.7.   86. SB, 1929: 11/26, p.6; 11/27, p.6.

papers. Party and government offices, censorship offices, and postal inspection offices were charged with the responsibility of detecting, restricting, and banning such tabloids.[87] In June to July 1935 the Shanghai Bureaus of Public Security, Social Affairs, Education, and Health called a joint meeting. Attended by representatives from the SDNA and all newspaper publishers in Shanghai, the meeting laid down the rules of prohibiting false advertisement of medicine, especially that of aphrodisiacs and drugs for venereal diseases, in newspapers.[88] In early 1937 the Shanghai Bureau of Health issued regulations prohibiting any advertisement of drugs that was accompanied by written texts, photographs, or drawings of an immoral or obscene nature.[89] Those prohibitions were consistent with the intention of the GMD party-state to mold social morals, while eliminating political subversion, which underpinned the New Life Movement and the Cultural Reconstruction campaign (1934–1937).

Freedom of Speech as a Professional Concern

If Shanghai journalists were not vocal on the issue of press freedom before the 1930s, they were not unconcerned about it either. In April 1927, in the wake of Chiang Kai-shek's anti-Communist coup in Shanghai and a few days before the founding of the new SJA, the MPH held a dinner party at a hotel in honor of a group of local journalists. Huang Huiping, an official from the MPH, explained to the group why the anti-Communist purge had to be carried out, apparently hoping to get some good press about the turn of events. Speaking on behalf of the journalists present, Yan Shenyu, an editor of the *Minguo Ribao*, expressed support for Chiang's policy. He said that the Communism imported from Russia would never succeed in China since the conditions in the two countries were vastly different and that the Wuhan government was following a suicidal policy. Ironically, however, Yan criticized the Wuhan government in the following terms: "Though the Wu-han Government professed to permit freedom of speech and publication, it muzzled the press and censored everything and therefore its fall was certain."[90] Muzzling the press with censorship was exactly what the GMD was planning to do, though yet unknown to Yan. That which Yan stated may be taken

---

87. FZ, No.176 (1933: 11/15).
88. Shanghai Shi Jiaoyuju Dang'an, SMA, file number 235-1-91.
89. *CWR*, 80,9 (5/1/1937):328.   90. *North China Daily News*, 1927: Apr. 25, p.13.

as an early indication of the coming conflict between the professional interests of Shanghai journalists and the GMD agenda.

The tightened GMD censorship in the 1930s prompted the SJA to speak against the press control, and the SJA was not the only public association opposing the censorship. The Shanghai Daily Newspapers Association, the organization of newspaper publishers, continued to advocate press freedom. In December 1931 the MPH ordered a postal ban on all major newspapers in Shanghai amidst the indignant Chinese reaction to the Manchurian Incident. Consistent with its past record, the SDNA responded by calling an emergency meeting and publishing a declaration and sending petitions to the MPH, Municipal Government, Postal Administration, Ministry of Transportation and Communications, National Government, and GMD Party Center, strongly protesting the ban. The declaration stated that newspapers were the public means of the society (*shehui gongqi*) that recorded what the people should hear and see and expressed what the people wanted to say. Freedom of speech and press was a major article of civil rights contained in Sun Yat-sen's teaching and provided by the Provisional Constitution (*Linshi yuefa*). No governmental order could change it and no violence could destroy it.[91] Eloquent and forceful, that kind of public pronouncement no doubt lent a legitimizing force to and set the high moral ground for the SJA's fight for freedom of the press.

The first expression of the SJA's new stance on the issue came with the case of Liu Yusheng. In July 1932, Liu Yusheng, the editor in chief of the *Jiangsheng Bao* (Voice of Zhengjiang) in the city of Zhengjiang, was arrested on charges that he engaged in Communist propaganda, incited class struggle, and committed treason against the party-state (*dangguo*). The arrest was ordered by Gu Zhutong, chairperson of the Jiangsu Provincial Government. Liu was detained without trial for five months. The case became known to the Control Council (*jiancha yuan*) in Nanjing and the council intervened in December. A representative of the council arrived in Zhengjiang to investigate the case, but Gu refused to cooperate, even denying the investigator access to the files of the case. In response to Gu's intransigence, two council members proposed an impeachment against Gu on December 16. They charged Gu with violating the Provisional Constitution and human rights, sabotaging the control system (*jiancha zhidu*), disobeying government orders, and usurping the powers of the Ministry of the Interior (by shutting down

---

91. SnB, 1931: 12/12, p.3; SB, 1931: 12/12, p.5.

the newspaper).⁹² The council's intervention only irritated Gu. He simply ordered that Liu be shot. The execution was carried out on January 21, 1933.⁹³

The cold-blooded replay of the warlord slayings of Shao Piaoping and Lin Baishui instantly aroused public outrage in the country, especially among intellectuals and professionals. The National Bar Association and local bar associations issued statements to condemn the killing. The Chinese League for the Protection of Civil Rights (*zhongguo minquan baozhang tongmeng*), headed by Madam Sun Yat-sen and Cai Yuanpei, denounced the atrocity in a press conference in Shanghai.⁹⁴

For its part, the SJA's executive and supervisory committees called an emergency meeting and resolved to demand that the government prosecute Gu Zhutong.⁹⁵ In addition, the SJA formed a special committee on the case. Members of the committee went to Zhengjiang to collect all allegedly incriminating articles published in the *Jiangsheng Bao*. On February 8 the SJA executive committee sent a statement to the GMD Party Center and the National Government.⁹⁶ Citing the articles in the newspaper, the statement pointed out that the accusation of Communist propaganda was farfetched. The description of rural hardship and the laborer's life in the newspaper was hardly reactionary, as was confirmed in the Control Council's impeachment against Gu. Such callous disregard for human life and destruction of human rights as Gu brazenly committed was rare even during the warlord era. If Gu were not punished according to the law, there would be no way to advance the cause of journalism.⁹⁷

Under the pressure of public opinion, the National Government issued a directive on September 1 to the Ministries of the Interior and of Military Administration. It stated that the people had the freedom of expression that could not be restricted without due process of law and that journalists should be protected.⁹⁸ But in the end Gu was not prosecuted and only transferred from the post of the Jiangsu Provincial Government chairperson to another position.

If the deaths of Shao Piaoping and Lin Baishui in 1926 did not ignite much passion among Shanghai journalists for freedom of speech, the killing of Liu Yusheng in 1933 did. In the following years the SJA emerged a champion of freedom of speech, and its concern on the issue

---

92. SB, 1933: 1/25, p.5.   93. SB, 1933: 1/23, p.8; CWR, 63,10 (2/4/1933):420.
94. SB, 1933: 2/1, p.5.   95. SB, 1933: 2/1, p.5.   96. SB, 1933: 2/13, p.5.
97. Ibid.   98. Ma Guangren, "Woguo Zhaoqi," p.73.

often went beyond the protection of Shanghai journalists. In June 1934, for instance, the newspaper *Gongyan Bao* (Public Voice) in the city of Xuzhou was shut down and the owner arrested, because the paper offended a county magistrate for its editorial on corruption in the county administration. The SJA sent telegrams to the GMD Jiangsu Party Headquarters, the Jiangsu Provincial Government, and the Provincial Department of Civil Affairs, demanding that the violation of civil rights and the restriction of public opinion in the case be rectified.[99]

The suppressions of freedom of speech in various places were not isolated incidents, but the results of GMD policy. The SJA therefore kept its attention focused on Nanjing, pushing the GMD to loosen its grips on the people's voice. In early December 1934 the GMD was celebrating its success in driving the Red Army out of its base area in Jiangxi. The SJA executive-supervisory committees sent a telegram to the GMD Party Center to congratulate it on the victory. In the telegram, however, the SJA reminded the GMD that since the Communists were almost wiped out, all proposed programs should be put into practice. "Since domestic order is gradually stabilized, we especially hope that the protection of freedom of speech be seriously implemented so that journalists can augment their contribution [to the nation]."[100]

When the GMD government issued the revised Publication Law in 1935, the SJA was among the journalists' associations in the country that protested. While the opposition was directed at some practical problems the law would create for the press, the SJA kept focusing on the issue of press freedom.[101] In December 1935 the SJA general meeting once again sent telegrams to the GMD Central Executive Committee and the National Government demanding the removal of censorship and the protection of freedom of speech.[102]

As might be expected, all members of the SJA were not of one mind. Some journalists did not agree to or even care about what the press should be doing, nor as passionately concerned about freedom of speech as were others. The SJA's autumn general meeting in 1935 discussed a resolution on "struggle for freedom of speech and freedom of reporting (*jizai ziyou*) to restore the character of newspapers." Some members felt that although they wanted freedom of speech, they could really do

---

99. SnB, 1934: 6/10, p.10.   100. SnB, 1934: 12/11, p.12.
101. NCH, 7/31/1935, p.166; 8/7/1935, p.213; CWR, 73,10 (8/3/1935):332; 74,1 (9/7/1935):24.
102. SnB, 1935: 12/22, p.13; 12/23, p.8.

nothing about it if the government denied them the right. Others held that even in the absence of an official recognition of freedom of speech, they should express their desire for it, lest the public would not forgive the silence of journalists on the issue. In other words, some members of the SJA were aware that the public perceived journalists to be most concerned about freedom of speech. Yet, with a less than uniform commitment among SJA members, several concrete measures to seek freedom of speech were deleted from the resolution. Yun Yiqun, a reporter working for the *Li Bao* (Standing up) and a CCP member since 1926, criticized that when journalists themselves lacked confidence in fighting for freedom of speech, how could they possibly get it.[103]

In December of 1935, some journalists (not the SJA) joined to issue a Shanghai Journalists' Declaration on Struggle for Freedom of Speech. If the action was an effort to reach all Shanghai journalists beyond members of the SJA (since not all journalists joined the SJA) for the cause of freedom of speech, it proved to be a failure. Of nearly four hundred Chinese journalists in Shanghai at the time, only seventy-three journalists signed the declaration. Yun Yiqun attributed the failure to the ineffective efforts on the part of the organizers: more than two hundred journalists did not even know about the action. Pointing to inadequate actions of the SJA, Yun called for a united front for freedom of speech. Journalists should not only unite among themselves, but also bring newspaper owners and printing shop workers into the struggle.[104]

In July 1936 Yun Yiqun was probably speaking those words from the CCP policy of forming a united front. Having ignored professionals and intellectuals as petty bourgeoisie for fifteen years, however, the CCP was not in a position to capture or control journalists or any professional groups any more than the GMD was. A close examination of the SJA's leaders from 1921 to 1937 turns up not a single Communist among them, though left-leaning journalists could be found among SJA members.[105] A handful of Communists in the journalistic circle did join the clamor

---

103. *Shenghuo Ribao Xingqi Zengkan*, 1,8 (7/26/1936):93.   104. Ibid.
105. In all primary and secondary sources on the CCP history and the history of Chinese journalism I have come across, there is no reference to any Communist activities in the Shanghai Journalists Association. None of the journalists who were the leaders of the SJA has been identified as a Communist. Stranahan's study on the CCP organization in Shanghai during the Nanjing Decade corroborates my finding here. See Patricia Stranahan, *Underground: The Shanghai Communist Party and the Politics of Survival, 1927–1937* (Lanham, MD, 1998).

for freedom of speech, but it was nonpartisan journalists who started the struggle, in spite of, not because of, the CCP.

Moreover, the advocacy for freedom of speech and civil rights did not mean at all that journalists, or the SJA for that matter, were bent on undermining the existing government. If anything, the organization had strong connections with and was blessed by the GMD from the beginning. In the 1930s some leaders of the SJA still had close ties with the GMD. Indeed, some left-leaning journalists regarded the SJA as an outright GMD-sponsored organization.[106] Yet, just as in the case of the Shanghai Bar Association, which is shown in a later chapter, GMD connections and even GMD membership would not necessarily, and indeed did not, ensure a GMD agenda for the SJA. Journalists had their professional concerns that did not always coincide with the GMD agenda. Throughout the period under study, neither the GMD nor the CCP had successfully controlled or manipulated Shanghai journalists as a group.

The journey of Shanghai journalists from "literary men" to professionals provides an example of how the urban politics and state–society relations in Republican China were informed and mediated by the rising Chinese nationalism and the job-specific concerns of professionals. The arrival of Shanghai journalists at becoming a self-conscious profession was marked first by the formation of their professional association in the 1920s and second by their demand for freedom of speech in the 1930s. As far as the latter development was concerned, journalists were reacting to the increasingly tightened censorship imposed by the GMD in its coping with the rising national salvation movement. In the national crisis of the 1930s freedom of speech was a precious right for all Chinese citizens and especially for journalists. They wanted to speak out on the pressing issue of saving the nation. In that sense journalists as a group may be said to have become politicized. On the other hand, the awakened desire for press freedom may also be seen as a sign of their having become professionalized. By the 1930s the SJA had clearly evolved into a true professional organization with professional purposes. If newspaper owners demanded press freedom out of business concerns, now Shanghai journalists as a professional community held freedom of speech to be the necessary condition under which to carry out their professional duty as well as being a condition for national salvation. Ultimately the

---

106. Lu Yi, interview with the author, January 12, 1992.

SJA's cry against GMD censorship stemmed from a professional concern and reflected an awakened sense of professional identity among Shanghai journalists. And with that sense of identity they were able to voice their demands as a group even though all the while they were under the close surveillance of the GMD party-state.

7
National Essence versus Science
The Medical Profession in Conflict

THE MEDICAL profession in twentieth-century China comprised two major schools: native medicine and Western medicine. The difference between native and Western medicine in philosophy, theory, and technique made a conflict between the two schools almost inevitable, and the conflict was intensified during the Republican period when the professionalization process brought their differences into sharp focus. Chinese practitioners of Western medicine advocated national salvation through science and dismissed native medicine as superstitious, unscientific, and an impediment to the development of medical science in China. On the other hand, native medical practitioners insisted that what they learned and practiced was part of the national essence (*guocui*) and should be protected against the cultural invasion of imperialism (*diguo zhuyi wenhua qinlue*), including Western medicine. Both sides used such rhetoric to camouflage the business competition between them, but the rivalry and its implications did point to a cultural conflict between Chinese tradition and Western influence in China's modernization, as Ralph C. Croizier's study pointed out long ago. More recently, studies by Ruth Rogaski and Bridie J. Andrews show how Western medicine was adopted by the state (at the municipal level) as part of the modernization project and how it competed against and negotiated with native medicine in the Republican era.[1] This chapter will further illustrate that the problem of integrating or reconciling native medicine and Western medicine in early-twentieth-century China concerned a burning issue of

---

1. Ralph C. Croizier, *Traditional Medicine in Modern China*; Ruth Rogaski, "From Protecting Life to Defending the Nation: The Emergence of Public Health in Tianjin, 1859–1953," Ph.D. Dissertation, Yale University, 1996; Bridie J. Andrews, "Tuberculosis and the Assimilation of Germ Theory in China, 1895–1937," *Journal of the History of Medicine*, 52 (Jan. 1997):114–57.

the day: whether China's modernization meant Westernization or a modernization that would preserve what was regarded or claimed as national heritage. Equally significant is that since their professional status had to be conferred by the state, both native physicians and Western-style doctors tried to influence government policy toward medicine. It was amidst the passionate battle for legitimacy that practitioners of both kinds of medicine took collective action for group interests through their organizations. Thus the history of Shanghai medical associations constitutes another revealing dimension of state–society relationship in the Republican era that cannot be easily characterized in terms of either societal autonomy or state dominance.

NATIVE MEDICINE ON THE DEFENSIVE

The Assault on Native Medicine

As far as Western-style Chinese doctors were concerned, medical professionalization or the development of medical science in China should mean, as matter of course, the replacement of Western medicine for native medicine. By their education and training, practitioners of Western medicine instinctively looked down on native medicine. Most Western-style doctors were confident that given native medicine's backwardness, native medicine would die of natural causes with the inexorable advance of medical science. That was not to be the case, however. Tradition was on the side of native medicine and in the way of Western medicine. Most Chinese were accustomed to seeing native physicians when they became ill. Only after all else failed in the hands of native physicians would patients try Western medicine and foreign hospitals as the last resort.[2] As late as 1935 Wu Liande, a leading Chinese practitioner of Western medicine, estimated that out of every eight sick persons only one would approach a Western-style doctor.[3] Moreover, by the mid-1920s, Western-style doctors became alarmed by the increasing pressure that native medical practitioners brought to bear on the government through demands for a legitimate place in the nation's education system. For all these reasons, mere bias against native medicine was translated into an institutional agenda to eliminate it.

The Medical Practitioners' Association of Shanghai (MPAS) spearheaded the assault on native medicine. The founding of the association

---

2. NCH, 2/19/1916, p.433; 6/30/1916, p.736.   3. NCH, 3/20/1935, p.456.

in 1925 was in part a response to the native physicians' efforts at legitimation. It gave the elite among Western-style doctors in Shanghai an organizational vehicle to protect their privilege on the one hand and to rally their force against native medicine on the other.

Yu Yunxiu, the first president of the MPAS, was a staunch opponent of native medicine. He was credited by other Western-style doctors for firing the first wounding shot at native medicine as early as 1916 with a pamphlet denouncing native medicine as scientifically groundless. In 1925, after the Society for Promoting Education and the National Federation of Educational Societies endorsed the demands of native physicians for their inclusion in the education system, Yu Yunxiu published a long article refuting native physicians' justification for their demands. In February 1926 the National Medical Association's general meeting resolved to act in concert with the MPAS and the Medical and Pharmaceutical Society of the Chinese Republic (MPSCR) to oppose an integration of native medicine into the education system.[4] It was again Yu Yunxiu who, representing the three organizations, wrote a public letter to that effect to all provincial educational societies. He called native physicians' demand "ignorant of the scholarly development, contrary to the world's trend, and violating the law of nature."[5] The animosity between the two camps was heightened.

A dramatic turn of events in the conflict came in 1929. The Provisional Regulations on Doctors issued in January by the Ministry of Health was an ominous sign for native medicine because it covered only Western-style doctors without mentioning native medicine.[6] The intention of the ministry became clear in February when the Central Health Committee (CHC), appointed by the ministry, held a meeting in Nanjing. The health committee was composed of government health officials and leaders of Western medical associations around the country. An important agenda of the meeting was to decide how to deal with native medicine. Yu Yunxiu was a major voice in favor of its abolition. In his view, the theoretical basis of native medicine was fiction and its methods of diagnosis self-deception. Native medicine was incapable of preventing contagious diseases, and its theory on the cause of illness impeded the spread of scientific knowledge. "So long as the old medicine is not abolished, the people's thinking will not change; the cause of new medicine cannot advance; and the administration of health care cannot develop."[7]

4. SB, 1926: 2/23, p.3.   5. Yu Yunxiu, *Yixue Geming Lun Cuji*, p.129.
6. Ralph C. Croizier, *Traditional Medicine*, p.133.   7. QYTZHH, p.32

Yu further laid out a six-step plan to abolish native medicine. First, until the end of 1930, the Ministry of Health would allow native physicians to register and get licenses. Second, until the end of 1933, registered native physicians would receive health training to get certificates; and after 1933 no one would be allowed to practice native medicine without the certificate. Third, native physicians who were above fifty years of age and had practiced over twenty years would be exempted from the said health training and be given special licenses that would expire in fifteen years, but they could not treat contagious diseases and sign death certificates. Fourth, the future propagation of native medicine would be banned. Fifth, the mass media and publishing agencies would be forbidden to publicize unscientific medicine including advertisement in newspapers. Sixth, native medical schools would be banned. The six-step plan was a complete scheme to abolish native medicine gradually. To the shock and anger of native medical practitioners, the main points of Yu's proposal were adopted by the meeting. On February 23 the CHC passed a resolution that the registration of native physicians cease at the end of 1930 and that native medical schools and publications about native medicine be banned.[8]

Justifications for Abolishing Native Medicine

How did Western-style doctors justify their demand for abolishing native medicine? Their justifications centered on one key word – science. They asserted that Western medicine was based on scientific research and experiment, whereas native medicine was a thing of the past that was based on mysticism (*xuanxue*).[9]

Western-style doctors refused to accept the sanctity of native medicine on the ground that it was Chinese tradition and had a long history. If native medicine should be part of the education system just because it was inherited from ancient times, said Yu Yunxiu, then schools might as well be established for divination or astrology. He denied that native medicine had a theoretical basis. The so-called theory was nothing but Yin-Yang, Five Elements, Six Airs (*liuqi*), and Twelve Vital Channels (*shi'er mingmai*). As a description of natural phenomena, the theory was farther apart from today's scientific knowledge of nature than the earth

---

8. QYTZHH, pp.32–33; CWR, 48,2 (3/9/1929):64; Shi Quansheng, *Zhonghua Minguo*, p.856.
9. Pang Jingzhou, *Shanghaishi Jingshi Nianlai Yiyao Niaokan*, p.6.

was from heaven and was proven groundless by anatomy. As for experimentation, it was nonexistent in native medicine. Yu laughed at the argument that the Chinese body could be best cured by Chinese drugs. All drugs were produced on the earth and all human beings were conditioned by the same nature. Drugs that cure were blind to the difference between the West and the East.[10]

Western-style doctors were particularly irritated with the line drawn between *zhongyi* (Chinese medicine) and *xiyi* (Western medicine). They insisted that what separated native and Western medicine was not the difference between Chinese and Western, but between the old and unscientific and the new and scientific.[11] Yet, as Western-style doctors opposed people calling them *xiyi*, they persistently referred to native medicine and its practitioners as *jiuyi* (old medicine and its practitioners). Indeed, they asserted that native medicine did not even deserve the word medicine (*yi*) and that it should be more accurately called black magic (*wushu* or *xieshu*).[12]

The debate about name was by no means trivial. It symbolized the crux of the issue: whether Western medicine's triumph over native medicine would mean the imposition of Western influence upon Chinese national identity. Western-style doctors understood well the political and social implications of how they were perceived. They fervently opposed the connection between the modern and the Western and equated the modern with the new and scientific instead. They pointed out that Western medicine also had a history of evolving from an unscientific to a scientific stage. That Western medicine happened to have developed in the West did not mean it was exclusively Western: medical science was universal. For that reason, they criticized the *Xiyi tiaoli* (Regulations on Practitioners of Western Medicine) for its usage of the term *xiyi*.[13]

To argue that they were not the enemy of national heritage or national identity, Western-style doctors conceded that although native medicine was worthless, native drugs were potentially valuable to medical science.[14] The positive evaluation of native drugs on the part of Western-style doctors, or some of them, was not insincere. As early as 1917 Dr. Xu Shifang, a member of the NMA Shanghai Branch, urged his fellow

---

10. Yu Yunxiu, *Yixue Geming Lun Cuji*, pp.121–25.
11. Yu Yunxiu, *Yixue Geming*, p.127.
12. YP, No.14 (Feb. 1930):6, 9; No.44 (Apr. 1932):2–3.
13. Wang Qizhang, *Ershi Nianlai*, pp.234–35.   14. Pang Jingzhou, *Shanghaishi*, p.4.

doctors that they use the methods of Western medicine to do research on native drugs.[15] While recognizing the potential value of native drugs, however, Western-style doctors categorically rejected the role of native physicians in developing that potential. It was Western-style doctors, rather than native physicians, who were most qualified to research and develop native drugs, because developing and revitalizing native drugs would require knowledge of modern sciences, such as physiology, biology, chemistry, and physics. Only Western-style doctors were equipped with such knowledge.[16]

Western-style doctors earnestly denied that their opposition to native medicine was motivated by business competition. The old medicine was shaken by the new, said Pang Jingzhou, the vice-president of the MPAS, because of the rushing trend of science in the world, and the matter was not a sectarian fight for the livelihood of a small group of doctors.[17] Wang Qizhang, another leading member of the MPAS, participated in the 1922 National Educational Conference that rejected the demand for formalization of native medical education. He later defended his position by saying that he was just fulfilling his duty and obligation and not scrambling for power and profit at the expense of native physicians or trying to break the latter's rice bowl and starve them to death.[18] Yu Yunxiu claimed that he would be better off leaving native medicine alone or pretending to be good at both modern and native medicine. Only a concern about the future of China's medical science prompted him to criticize native medicine.[19] Moreover, Western-style doctors asserted that native medicine was doomed to perish anyway since it was incompatible with people's knowledge of the nature and the development of science.[20] It was the native physicians, they argued, who were out to defend their rice bowls. As Yu Yunxiu put it, irrational actions, such as native physicians' reactions to the CHC resolution, usually stemmed from private interests and concerns about the rice bowls.[21]

If the conflict between native medicine and Western medicine had remained a war of words about public and private interests or science and ignorance, it would have been of little consequence and importance to native physicians who had numerical superiority over Western-style

15. SB, 1917: 10/4, p.5. 16. Yu Yunxiu, *Yixue Geming*, pp.135–36.
17. Pang Jingzhou, *Shanghaishi*, pp.3–4.   18. Wang Qizhang, *Ershi Nianlai*, pp.151–52.
19. YP, No.106 (Nov. 1933):17.
20. Yu Yunxiu, "Preface" in Wang Qizhang, *Tutu Zai Yiyan*.
21. Yu Yunxiu, "Yisai Jiuyi Zi Judong" (So strange are old physicians' actions), YP, No.7 (July 1929):4–5.

doctors. The danger for native medicine, however, was that government agencies such as the Ministry of Education, Ministry of Health, and their corresponding bureaucracies at the provincial level and below were headed and staffed mostly by returned students or graduates from Western-style educational institutions in China. Those people were inclined to identify with the cause of science that Western-style doctors claimed to represent. They tended to view native medicine in a negative light, seeing it as part of the stale and backward tradition that blocked the way for China to advance to modernity.[22] That view accounted for the consistent refusal on the part of the Republican government to grant legitimacy to native medicine, especially within the education system. The Central Health Committee's resolution in February 1929 was only the latest assault on native medicine. But that time, instead of denying native medicine a legitimate status, it threatened to abolish native medicine altogether and thus created the most severe crisis that native physicians had ever faced. The challenge had to be answered if native medicine were to survive.

NATIONAL ESSENCE VERSUS SCIENCE

The Response of Native Medical Associations

Like a spark on a sea of oil, the publication of the CHC resolution in the *New Medicine and Society* (*xinyi yu shehui*), the MPAS's organ, triggered an instant flare of protests from native physicians and other groups across the country. Significantly, among the organizations first spurred into action was the Shanghai Merchants Association Drug Trade Branch (*Shanghai shi shangmin xiehui yaoye fenhui*).[23] The native drug trade felt threatened by the assault on native medicine because the well-being of the trade was dependent on prescriptions by native physicians, to say nothing of the nationalist sentiment involved in the whole conflict.

22. Although not a health or education official, Fu Sinian, a Western-educated professor of history and language and the managing director of the Academia Sinica, is typical of those modernists in their contempt for native medicine. As late as 1934 Fu called it the biggest shame that native medicine was still contending with Western medicine, as the former's uselessness was beyond question. He said that such words as "improving native medicine" were logically meaningless. See Fu Mengzheng, "Suowei Guoyi" (The so-called national medicine), *Duli Pinglun* (Independent Review), No.115 (Aug. 26, 1934):17–20; "Zailun Suowei Guoyi" (More on the so-called national medicine), ibid., No.118 (Sept. 16, 1934):3–5.
23. SB, 1929: 3/7, p.6.

Responding to the call by the Shanghai Native Medicine Association, more than forty associations of native medicine and the native drug trade convened a joint meeting in Shanghai on March 7, 1929, to map out a strategy for combating the CHC resolution. They founded the Shanghai Federation of Medical and Pharmaceutical Associations (SFMPA) (*Shanghai yiyao tuanti lianhe hui*) to lead the struggle.[24] The SFMPA decided that a national conference of native medical associations and native drug trade associations be held on March 17.

While determined to fight Western-style doctors head on, the SFMPA displayed some political sensitivity in that the leaders wanted no mass direct action that would inadvertently offend the authorities. At the SFMPA's meeting one delegate from a native drug trade union announced that unions in the nation's native drug trade had 4.3 million members who were willing to spearhead the resistance to the CHC. Encouraged but cautious, the meeting resolved that individuals from native medicine and native drug trade not deal with the outside on the issue and that the organization petition the central government.[25] Apparently, the leaders of the SFMPA placed emphasis on associational solidarity and on organized collective action to persuade the government to come to their side.

The cause of native medicine was a popular one. Within a few days other public associations came to the aid of native physicians and drug traders, issuing statements supporting the preservation of native medicine and drugs. The National Federation of Chambers of Commerce (*quanguo shanghui lianhe hui*), for example, telegraphed the National Government Office, Executive Council, and Ministries of Health, Finance, and Industry and Commerce demanding that native medicine and drugs be protected.[26] Public opinion, insofar as expressed in the press, was generally in favor of native medicine.

The CHC or the abolitionists in and out of the government were now put on the defensive. They had apparently underestimated the sensitivity of native physicians and the reaction from the public to the CHC action. Particularly they did not expect the native drug trade and the merchant community in general to rise with indignation and join native physicians to oppose the resolution. The MPAS, to which Yu Yunxiu belonged, tried to explain away the intention of Western-style doctors. The CHC resolution, announced the MPAS, did not intend to prohibit

---

24. SB, 1929: 3/8, p.6; 3/9, p.7.   25. SB, 1929: 3/9, p.7.
26. SB, 1929: 3/11, p.7; 3/2, p.6; NCH, 3/16/1929, p.442.

native physicians from practicing, and the association deeply regretted that native physicians and native drug traders should have misunderstood the resolution. The organization denied that Western-style doctors were motivated by business competition, which it called an insult.[27] Western-style doctors especially wanted people to believe that they criticized native medicine but not native drugs. They complained that native physicians manipulated the native drug trade and merchant organizations.[28]

Native physicians and native drug traders around the country enthusiastically supported the call for a national conference. After a two-day preliminary meeting, the national conference of native medical and pharmaceutical associations convened on March 17 at the seat of the Shanghai General Chamber of Commerce, which was indicative of the Chamber's support of native physicians' causes. Some 272 delegates representing 132 organizations from around the country attended.[29] On the first day the conference resolved that March 17 be the National Medicine Day (*guoyi jie*).[30]

Notably, the leaders of various Shanghai merchant organizations participated in the conference, including Feng Shaoshan of the National Federation of Chambers of Commerce, Lin Kanghou of the Shanghai General Chamber of Commerce, Wu Zhihao of the Federation of Street Merchant Associations, and Wang Xingyi of the Society for Supporting National Goods (*guohuo weichihui*). They delivered speeches supporting native medicine and drugs and their current struggle. Lin Kanghou's words best explained why the commercial community got involved: "To abolish native medicine inevitably leads to the destruction of native drugs and to promote Western medicine is no difference from promoting imperialism. Native medicine and native drugs should unite to resist economic invasion, and the General Chamber of Commerce will take unanimous action [with you]."[31] As the *China Weekly Review* put it, "the Chinese chambers of commerce have taken up the cudgels on behalf of the old-style doctors."[32]

27. SB, 1929: 3/25, p.6.
28. Pang Jingzhou, *Shanghaishi*, pp.78–79; Wang Qizhang, *Ershi Nianlai*, p.152; Zhou Mengbai, "Gao Zhongyaojia" (To native druggists), YP, No.11 (Nov. 1929):1–2.
29. *Quanguo Yiyao Tuanti Daibiao Dahui Tekan* (Special journal for the national congress of medical and pharmaceutical associations) (1929), p.3; according to another source, delegates numbered 281 representing 242 organizations from fifteen provinces. See QYTZHH, p.41.
30. *Quanguo Yiyao Tuanti Daibiao Dahui Tekan*, p.3.
31. QYTZHH, p.39.   32. CWR, 48,4 (3/23/1929):133.

National Essence versus Science

On the second day the conference passed a series of resolutions that defied the intentions of Western-style doctors and their supporters in the government.[33] On March 19, the last day of the conference, the National Federation of Medical and Pharmaceutical Associations (NFMPA) (*quanguo yiyao tuanti zong lianhe hui*) was established with a twenty-nine-member executive committee. The resolution of the meeting called on each native physician to donate at least one yuan and each native drugstore at least two yuan to finance the organization. Delegates were urged to unite with other public associations in their local areas to form support organizations for the cause. The conference ended with a statement that invoked the Three Principles of the People to justify the necessity of protecting native medicine and drugs.[34]

The conference and the founding of the NFMPA were a huge success for native medical practitioners in fighting for their cause. The perceived threat to their common interests united usually sectarian and individualistic native physicians and native drug traders. The leaders of the native medical associations in Shanghai were instrumental in bringing about an unprecedented unity of native physicians. Cai Jiping and Zhang Mei'an of the SMPGA; Ding Zhongying, Xia Yingtang, and Zhang Zanchen of the SNMS; and Xie Lihuan of the MPSCR were among the key figures in organizing the conference, establishing the NFMPA, and leading the struggle in general.

On March 20 the NFMPA made an important move – it sent a five-member delegation to Nanjing to lobby the government.[35] On March 21 the group first visited the GMD Third National Congress that was being held in Nanjing at the time. Ye Chucang, the deputy secretary of the Congress, met the delegates and expressed his sympathy with native medicine and drugs. The delegates then went to the Executive Council and got a sympathetic hearing from the Council Chairperson Tan Yankai, who also thought the abolition of native medicine inconceivable. The next day the delegates visited the homes of Zhang Jingjiang, Li Shizeng, and Chen Guofu – all members of the GMD Central Political Council and believers in native medicine. They all promised the delegates their support for the cause of native medicine.

Greatly encouraged by the meetings, on the following two days the group visited the Ministry of Health, Ministry of Industry and

---

33. QYTZHH, p.40; SB, 1929: 3/19, p.4.   34. QYTZHH, p.41; SB, 1929: 3/20, p.6.
35. QYTZHH, p.43; the report of the delegation's activity and the result appeared in pp.43–44 and in SB, 1929: 3/26, p.6, upon which the following narrative is based.

Commerce, Ministry of Education, and National Government Office. The delegates failed to meet the National Government Chairperson Chiang Kai-shek, minister of education, and minister of industry and commerce, because they were all attending the party congress. On March 23 the delegates were able to meet Hu Shuwei, the head of the Education Ministry's Division of Political Affairs. According to Hu, the CHC resolution was but a policy proposal and was unlikely to be adopted, because the ministry never intended to abolish native medicine. Hu further assured the delegates that the Western-style doctors only served a minority of urban bourgeoisie in big cities. The government's policy was to consider the welfare of the common people and the ministry would not work for the welfare of a small group of people. On the evening of March 24 the delegates were invited by Xue Dubi, the minister of education, to a dinner. Repeating what Hu had said, Xue promised that the ministry would not implement the CHC resolution. Feeling triumphant, the lobbying group returned to Shanghai on March 25.

The Advantages of Native Physicians

Native physicians were able to win this round of the fight thanks to several factors. First, within the GMD party and government there were conflicting opinions about how to treat native medicine. One may loosely classify GMD officials into two groups – the Westernizers and the cultural nationalists. Both were committed to modernization, but they were divided on the question of how to modernize. The fate of native medicine was part of that larger issue. The division of opinion accounted for a series of conflicting ordinances and regulations on medicine enacted by the government, which pleased neither Western-style doctors nor native physicians. It also offered opportunities for both camps to try to influence the government policy through their own sympathizers within the GMD regime. While the allies of Western-style doctors occupied various ministries and departments in government bureaucracy and tended to be returned students and graduates of modern schools in China, the supporters of native physicians were high officials in the GMD party organizations. It was no accident that the NFMPA's lobbying group visited Ye Chucang, Tan Yankai, Zhang Jingjiang, Li Shizeng, and Chen Guofu. Those officials were all committed cultural nationalists and strongly supported the protection of native medicine.[36] More impor-

---

36. Ralph C. Croizier, *Traditional Medicine*, pp.134–35.

tantly, they all had political influence or power. Although native physicians accused Western-style doctors of trying to destroy native medicine through political power, they themselves were not shy at all about pulling political strings. It was a measure of native medical leaders' political sophistication that they engaged in such lobbying activities. As this round of the fight and later developments demonstrated, their efforts to swing the government policy toward native medicine through their supporters within the GMD regime were crucial to the outcome of the contest.

Second, native physicians launched a propaganda campaign using political symbols. They understood that when China was struggling to modernize, they could not go against the banner of science. Their argument, not insincere at least for some of them, was that native physicians were willing and ready to move toward science but the abolitionists were denying native medicine the opportunity to become scientific (*kexue hua*). In answering Western-style doctors' attack on Yin-Yang and Five Elements as mystical theories, some native physicians would not regard the theory of Yin-Yang and Five Elements as something to be cast away, insisting that it was simply another philosophical system different from Western sciences, but by no means inferior.[37] More sophisticated arguments, however, ran along the following lines. (1) Yin-Yang and Five Elements were only part of native medical classics, not the whole. Native medical classics addressed three subjects: the cause, the symptom, and the cure of illness. Yin-Yang and Five Elements only concerned the cause of illness. Western-style doctors singled out this first part to attack but evaded the other two parts.[38] (2) Yin-Yang and Five Elements were but code names or substitutes for the medical concepts used in Western medicine to address the same phenomena. (3) Even native physicians themselves had long since advocated a reorganization (*zhengli*) of native medical theory. Very few native medical schools were still talking about Yin-Yang and Five Elements in analyzing the cause of disease.[39] (4) In the development of medicine, experience always came first and theory developed later to explain the experience. Although the theory of native medicine did not fit well with the concepts of Western medicine, the fact that native medicine cures illness could not be denied. Native medicine would be better explained and further developed

---

37. YC, No.25 (July 1927):1–2.
38. Lu Shi'e, *Guoyi Xingyu* (New talk on native medicine) (Shanghai, 1934), p.214.
39. SB, 1929: 3/19, p.4.

by applying scientific methods, but the abolition of native medicine would simply deprive it of the opportunity to inherit the past and develop the future.[40] Here native physicians were actually arguing for a version of modernization different from that which was conceived by Western-style doctors – a modernization that would preserve and renew Chinese cultural heritage.

Third, native physicians effectively utilized nationalistic discourse. By far the most powerful argument native physicians advanced was that native medicine was part of the national essence and that the fate of native medicine and drugs involved nationalism and the people's livelihood – two of the Three Principles of the People. The whole movement to oppose the CHC resolution in 1929 was organized around this central theme. The slogans at the national conference of native medical and drug trade associations summed it up: "Promote native medicine to prevent cultural invasion and promote native drugs to prevent economic invasion... to promote native medicine is to protect China's culture and economy, and to oppose the [CHC] resolution is to oppose imperialism."[41] Native physicians accused Western-style doctors of trying to ruin the Chinese nation by destroying its national heritage.

A new element – the people's livelihood – was added to the familiar theme of nationalism. Quoting Sun Yat-sen's words about the need to protect the inherited culture and to develop China's economy, native physicians made a strong case that the abolition of native medicine would endanger both. They portrayed Western-style doctors as selfish and mean-spirited persons who were motivated by a concern for their "rice bowl" or "bread problem" and an envy of native physicians' successful practice. Moreover, Western-style doctors were serving the interest of foreign drug companies by importing Western drugs worth millions of dollars. If the Western-style doctors' conspiracy for destroying native medicine and drugs were to succeed, it would result in China's total dependence on foreign drugs at a boundless cost.[42] On the other hand, since native physicians were ten times as many as Western-style doctors, the abolition of native medicine would leave sick people no recourse but to sit waiting to die. At the same time it would throw tens of millions of people in the native drug trade into unemployment.[43] Refuting Pang

---

40. QYTZHH, pp.42–43; YC, No.15 (Sept. 1927):1–3.   41. QYTZHH, pp.38, 39.
42. YC, No.13 (July 1927):5; No. 14 (Aug. 1927):1–3; No.15 (Sept. 1927):1–3; No.25 (Sept. 1928):1–2; No.26 (Oct. 1928):3–8; YCH (Aug. 1927), pp.181–82.
43. QYTZHH, p.42.

Jingzhou's assertion that opposing native medicine did not constitute a threat to the livelihood of people in the native drug trade, Lu Shi'e, a member of the Shanghai Native Medical Society, asked whether Western-style doctors would prescribe native drugs and who would frequent one hundred thousand native drugstores in the country if native physicians were banned. "The day native medicine dies is the day native drugs die."[44]

In manipulating political symbols, the play of words was extremely important. Just as Western-style doctors tried hard to equate Western medicine with science and the new, and native medicine with superstition and the old, native physicians spared no efforts to point out the foreign aspects of Western medicine and the Chinese aspects of native medicine. In a sarcastic style, Lu Shi'e observed that Western-style doctors called themselves *xinyi* and native physicians *jiuyi*, as if all the practices from foreign countries were new and should be promoted and China's own practices were old and should be thrown away. With that logic, continued Lu, within a few years China would surely become an old nation while foreign nations such as Teutonic, Slavic, and Japanese would be new nations and a thorough plan of genocide could be created.[45] Although hardly any Chinese would follow through such logic, it was effective in dramatizing the foreign aspects of Western-style doctors. As finding a fitting name for native medicine assumed an increased, if not an exaggerated importance for its proper perception and legitimacy, native physicians began, by 1929, to refer to native medicine as national medicine (*guoyi*) and to native drugs as national drugs (*guoyao*). In December 1929 an NFMPA emergency conference passed a resolution that all native medicine and drug establishments, such as associations, schools, and stores, call themselves *guoyi* and *guoyao* instead of *zhongyi* and *zhongyao*.[46] The use of political symbols proved effective in winning over public opinion and still more effective when combined with the lobbying of political figures.

Fourth, the most important element, however, was that the Western-style doctors' desire to eliminate native medicine contradicted the reality in China where resources in Western medicine were scarce and the vast population was dependent upon native medicine for health care. The retreat of the Ministry of Health in 1929 after the protest against the CHC resolution was telling. It is doubtful that the ministry did not

---

44. Lu Shi'e, *Guoyi Xingyu*, pp.213–14, 219–20.
45. Lu Shi'e, *Guoyi Xingyu*, pp.225–26.   46. QYTZHH, p.49.

discriminate against native medicine, but the ministry was apparently aware that native medicine was needed by the majority of the people and could not be abolished just by political fiat. The widespread and vehement opposition to the CHC resolution was a powerful reminder to the abolitionists of that reality.

TOWARD THE TRIUMPH OF NATIVE MEDICINE

A New Round in the Fight

The euphoria of victory among native physicians was short-lived, however. If the modernists in the government had given up the plan for abolishing native medicine in the near future, they had no intention to see it thrive. On April 29, 1929, the Ministry of Education issued a public notice ordering that all native medical schools change their names into tutoring institutes (*chuanxi suo*) that were not to be included in the education system and not to be placed on file (*li'an*) with the ministry. The justification for that measure was that in those schools "teaching and experimentation are not based on science and there are no unified standards for qualification and [educational] level of students."[47]

The new measure was a flat denial of the legitimacy of native medical education and by extension native medicine itself. Previously, the government did not grant native medical education official recognition, but did not interfere with those schools either, since they were established by native physicians with their own resources. The new measure, native physicians believed, was designed to explicitly reduce native medicine to an inferior status, the first step toward abolishing native medicine altogether.[48] What was more, the Ministry of Health also issued directives that native medical hospitals (*zhongyi yuan*) change their names into medical offices (*yishi*) and that native physicians not use the instruments and drugs of Western medicine. The actions of the two ministries added up to one single message: Western-style doctors and their allies in the government had not given up their design to de-legitimate native medicine after all. A new round in the fight had begun.

Native medical associations all around the country immediately responded.[49] The NFMPA sent three delegates to Nanjing on May 21. As the delegates failed to meet the minister of education, the NFMPA peti-

47. QYTZHH, p.65.   48. QYTZHH, p.68.   49. SB, 1929: 6/7, p.7.

tioned the Education Ministry in writing. The petition argued that the measure would reduce the quality of native medical schools and shut out the possibility for native medicine to become scientific. The petition also pointed out the problems the measure would create for graduates from the schools: while no national regulations on native physicians existed, local government regulations all required graduation from native medical schools (*zhongyi xuexiao*) as the qualification for new native physicians to practice[50] – which might have been the design of the ministry.

Ignoring the petition, the Education Ministry issued directives for provincial departments and municipal bureaus of education to enforce the measure. In late July the ministry ordered the Shanghai Bureau of Education to forbid two native medical schools in Shanghai to advertise in newspapers because they "falsely claimed to be colleges."[51]

The NFMPA tried desperately to stall the new measure. In July it convened a conference on native medical education that drafted a plan for a curriculum and unified admission standard (high school graduates) and created a committee to work on textbooks. Having thus positioned itself, on August 30 the NFMPA petitioned the Executive Council and the Ministries of Health and the Interior on the issue. But the petitions to the Executive Council got no response, while the two ministries replied that the issue was not their business.[52] The NFMPA considered the situation serious enough to convene an emergency conference from November 1 through 5. The conference decided to continue the fight and to send a new petition mission to Nanjing.[53]

The petition delegates arrived in Nanjing on December 17 and were greeted by the native medical associations and native drug trade associations in the capital.[54] On December 19 the delegates paid visits to a number of important figures in the party and the government. With the private lobbying done, the delegates started formal petition on December 20. Within two days they visited the National Government Office, Executive Council, Legislative Council, and GMD Party Central Headquarters. Their efforts paid off. On the night of December 23, a message from the National Government secretariat announced that Chiang Kai-shek, Chairperson of the National Government, had instructed the Exec-

50. QYTZHH, p.66.   51. SB, 1930: 8/1, p.8.   52. QYTZHH, p.69.
53. For the texts of the petitions, see QYTZHH, pp.52–54.
54. For the delegation's activities, see QYTZHH, pp.54–56.

utive Council to order the Ministries of Education and Health to revoke the measures in question.[55]

Within three months, however, the Ministries of Education and Health made a new move. In March 1930 they sent a joint message to the Executive Council to explain the problems they had tried to solve by the earlier measures. Under the Regulations on Hospital Management a medical establishment could not be called a hospital unless it met certain specified standards. The prohibition of native physicians from using the instruments and drugs of Western medicine had been a response to the Nanjing Bureau of Public Security's request for instructions on how to deal with quacks brandishing the stethoscope and syringe. The measure to change native medical schools into tutoring institutes was to address a practical problem. If the native medical school were designed for high school graduates, few would be willing to enroll in it. If it were for senior primary school graduates, the graduates would not have enough knowledge of sciences. If not specified, there would be no rules to regulate native medical schools. To improve native medicine, said the message, the ministries were planning to have institutions of native medical education organized as native medical societies (*zhongyi xueshe*) and regulated as academic associations by educational offices.[56]

In retrospect, the problem of regulating native medical schools appears to have been real. Even some native physicians, in warning the native medical community against complacency, openly admitted to the deficiencies in native medical schools: inadequate facilities, worse-than-mediocre faculty, and substandard students (the problems continued to exist as late as 1937).[57] On the other hand, the ministries obviously chose to minimize the institutional and conceptual profile of native medicine to restrict it rather than to enrich the substance of institutions to improve native medicine, because they did not believe it could be improved. Understandably, native physicians viewed such an approach as a move to de-legitimate native medicine.

Native medical associations rushed into action as soon as they heard of the new measure. To forestall the measure, the NFMPA telegraphed Chiang Kai-shek on March 15, 1930, to thank him belatedly for his order of December 23 and asked at which ministry native medical schools

---

55. QYTZHH, p.56; SB, 1929: 12/29, p.6.   56. QYTZHH, pp.70–72.
57. See Jiang Guangzhi, "Zhongyi Weihe Jiji Geming" (Why revolution is urgently needed in native medicine), YC, No.11 (May 1927):4–5; Lu Yuanlei, "Zhongyi Baoshang Zhixi" (The key to strengthening native medicine), ZXS, No.31 (June 1937):2–8.

should establish their files.⁵⁸ The purpose of the telegram was clear: It did not matter which ministry would administer native medical schools; if only Chiang would give a reply that did not negate the status of native medical schools, the reply would preempt the measure being put forward by the two ministries. Because the NFMPA had not immediately followed up on Chiang's earlier order, however, the NFMPA had already lost the initiative in the game of manipulating directives. Before the NFMPA got a response from Chiang, the National Government Office approved the two ministries' proposal.⁵⁹ The Ministry of Education immediately ordered native medical schools to change into medical societies.⁶⁰

The NFMPA responded as best as it could. In a petition sent to the Education Ministry on April 13, the NFMPA raised several questions: Since *xueshe* was defined as "academic association," could all medical associations, such as the NFMPA, admit students? Could the students, after graduation, be allowed to practice? Were there any standards for the training, examination, and evaluation of the students?⁶¹ Knowing that the Education Ministry had no plan and no taste for regulating native medical education, the NFMPA hoped that the petition would stall the ministry's measure. But the Education Ministry simply ignored the problems the NFMPA pointed out in its questions. The Education Ministry replied to the NFMPA that native medical societies (*zhongyi xueshe*) were free to admit students and hire teachers, but the training methods, the standards for evaluation, and the procedure for registration and practice were up to the Ministry of Health. The Health Ministry had stated that before regulations would be enacted by the central government, the NFMPA's issues would be taken care of according to local regulations.⁶² Yet, it was local regulations that required graduation from native medical schools (*zhongyi xuexiao*) as the qualification for new native physicians to practice. The Health Ministry's reply left the NFMPA where it had started – with unresolved issues. Then the NFMPA's request for the Health Ministry to postpone the implementation of the measure was rejected. Its petition to the Executive Council with the same argument received no response. Its earlier petition (March 15) to Chiang Kai-shek remained unanswered.⁶³

---

58. QYTZHH, p.70.
59. GZG, No.404 (1930: 3/4).   60. QYTZHH, p.73.
61. Ibid., pp.73–74.   62. Ibid., p.74.
63. Ibid., pp.74–75; SB, 1930: 5/16, p.6.

Native Physicians' New Strategy

The new round of fighting forced native physicians to reflect on their strategy and their future course of action. While the NFMPA was pushing for official recognition of native medical education, Jiang Wenfang, a member of the standing committee of the NFMPA, believed that even if native medical schools were integrated into the education system, they would soon die out. When native medical schools had the same right to be placed on file with the government as other schools, they would also have the obligation to abide by the same educational regulations. The regulations on private universities had strict provisions on the amount of funds and equipment in each institution. Native medical schools would have difficulty complying with such regulations. Jiang also noted other possible problems: Under the regulations of the Ministry of Education, a medical school could be established only as part of a university and there were specific rules on the qualifications of faculty and students. Because of those problems, Jiang Wenfang and Qiu Jisheng, an executive committee member of the NFMPA, came up with the idea to establish an institute of native medicine, after the model of the Institute of National Martial Arts (*guoshu guan*), which had been founded with government support.[64]

The NFMPA adopted the idea and speedily submitted a proposal for an Institute of National Medicine (*guoyi guan*) to the National Government chairperson, Chiang Kai-shek, and the Executive Council chairperson, Tan Yankai. In January 1930 Chiang Kai-shek ordered that the plan move ahead and the bylaws of the institute be submitted for approval. After the NFMPA sent the draft bylaws, however, the Ministry of Health demanded some revisions, and the matter was then buried in the bureaucratic procedures of the Health Ministry.[65]

At that juncture the cultural nationalists within the GMD power center played a pivotal role. In a session of the Central Political Council in May 1930, Tan Yankai, Hu Hanmin, Chen Lifu, Chen Chaoying, Shao Yuanchong, Jiao Yitang, and Zhu Peide put forward a separate proposal for an institute of native medicine. They managed to get the approval of the council.[66] On May 22 the National Government Office decreed that the Native Medical Institute be established.[67]

---

64. QYTZHH, p.86.   65. Ibid., p.86.
66. QYTZHH, p.86; Ralph C. Croizier, *Traditional Medicine*, p.134.
67. GZG, No.476 (1930: 5/23).

On March 17, 1931, the Day of National Medicine, the Institute of National Medicine (INM) (*guoyi guan*) was formally established in Nanjing with great fanfare, to the bitterness of Western-style doctors who accused native physicians of having played cunning tricks to bring about the INM.[68] With monthly funds of five thousand yuan provided by the government, the institute obtained a quasi-official status. Jiao Yitang, a veteran GMD official, was appointed the head of the institute. Other GMD high officials such as Shao Yuanchong, Shao Lizi, and Chen Lifu served on the board of directors of the institute. The honorary members of the board included such well-known figures as Wang Chonghui, Yu Youren, Dai Jitao, Chen Guofu, Lin Sen, Li Shizeng, Liu Zhi, Chen Mingshu, and Gu Zhenglun.[69] The preceding are but a partial list of the cultural nationalists within the GMD regime who supported the preservation of national essence including native medicine.

The Final Legitimation of Native Medicine

The establishment of the INM was a high point of the organized movement by native physicians, but it also marked the demise of the NFMPA (see Chapter 5). The establishment of the INM and the demise of the NFMPA ushered in a shift of the arena for the contention from the local level to the GMD party and government center. From 1931 onward both native physicians and Western-style doctors took little action in Shanghai, but the battle continued to be fought in Nanjing. At issue was the nature and function of the INM.

The official charge of the institution was to reorganize native medicine with scientific methods. Western-style doctors did not believe native medicine could be re-made by modern science and ridiculed the INM as an odd institution out of place. More importantly, they did not want to see the INM play any role in the country's health care system.[70] On the other hand, native physicians intended to make the institute an administrative organ in charge of native medicine so that native medicine would be beyond the regulation and discrimination of its detractors in the government.

At the June 1933 Central Political Council meeting, Shi Ying, the mayor of Nanjing, advanced a proposal seconded by twenty-nine council

---

68. YP, No.105 (Oct. 1933):16.
69. QYTZHH, p.104; Shi Quansheng, *Zhonghua Minguo*, pp.857–58.
70. YP, No.105 (Oct. 1933):17.

members including Ye Chucang, Chen Guofu, and Shao Lizi. The proposal contained a draft of the Regulations on Native Physicians (*Guoyi tiaoli*) that would entrust the administration of native medicine to the INM. The proposal failed to be adopted as such by the council, but was referred to the Legal System Committee (*fazhi weiyuanhui*) of the Legislative Council for further study.

That move by GMD officials on behalf of native medicine caused alarm among Western-style doctors who were bitter that native physicians managed to gain an upper hand through "corrupt key figures" in the GMD power center.[71] The Western-style doctors mounted a campaign to oppose the measure, arguing that to bestow administrative responsibility upon an academic institution, the INM, would disjoin the governmental system. In its petition to the Executive Council and Legislative Council, the National Association of Medical Doctors (*quanguo yishi lianhe hui*) accused native physicians of trying to usurp administrative privileges. The National Medical Association petitioned Sun Ke, chairperson of the Legislative Council, demanding that health administration should be unified and that the INM be abolished. Wang Qizhang went so far as to suggest that giving the INM administrative functions would be equal to setting up another government.[72]

While accusing native physicians of under-the-table dealings, Western-style doctors did not hesitate to use their political resources either. In early August 1933, Niu Huisheng and Yan Fuqing of the National Medical Association paid a private visit to Wang Jingwei – who had succeeded Tan Yankai in January 1932 as the chairperson of the Executive Council – to make their case, because Wang was a professed supporter of Western medicine. Following the visit, Wang wrote a letter to Sun Ke saying that granting native physicians administrative power would be no good to the country and asking that Sun devise ways to remedy the situation.[73] Sun apparently did his part. The Legal System Committee, chaired by Jiao Yitang, had adopted the draft of the Regulations on Native Physicians proposed by Shi Ying after substituting the term

---

71. Wang Qizhang, "Dule Zhongyi Tiaoli De Ganyan" (Reflections after reading the regulations on native medicine), YP, No.109 (Jan. 1934):4.
72. YP, No.104 (Sept. 1933):58–61; No.105 (Oct. 1933):1–181; No.106 (Nov. 1933):1–9.
73. Two years later *Yijie Chunqiu* somehow obtained Wang's letter and published its photocopy in the journal. See YC, No.105 (Sept. 1935), inside of the cover page. This disclosure invited sharp criticism of Wang from the native medical circle, see No.107 (Nov. 1935):1–11.

zhongyi for *guoyi* in an accommodation to the complaint of Western-style doctors[74] – but the regulations went no further.[75]

Western-style doctors were fighting a losing battle and only postponing the inevitable, however. At the GMD Fifth National Congress in November 1935, Feng Yuxiang and eighty other delegates proposed a resolution on equal treatment of native and Western medicine. It provided for (1) swift enactment of the adopted Regulations on Native Physicians, (2) employment of native physicians in government health agencies, and (3) establishment of native medical schools.[76] The proposal amounted to a total legitimation of native medicine. The resolution was passed by the party congress. Within two months, on January 22, 1936, the Regulations on Native Physicians (*Zhongyi tiaoli*) were finally enacted.[77] Under the Regulations on Native Physicians those who graduated from native medical schools, or practiced for over five years, or passed an examination or evaluation could be licensed to practice. Those native physicians who were already practicing were allowed to do so even before being evaluated – which in effect allowed all native physicians to practice legally, and all native physicians would eventually get licenses if they bothered to do so.

While native physicians received the news with joy, one more issue emerged: Who should be in charge of regulating native physicians? According to the Regulations on Native Physicians, the Ministry of the Interior was responsible for evaluating the qualifications of native physicians. However, the Health Administration – the successor to the Ministry of Health but now under the Ministry of the Interior – was a stronghold of Western-style doctors. Following the enactment of the regulations, the Health Administration issued the Rules on Evaluating Native Physicians (*Zhongyi shengcha guize*), which authorized local governments to carry out the evaluation. Native medicine was again rele-

---

74. At its annual meeting in October 1932, the National Medical Association adopted a resolution that the use of "*guoyi*" by native physicians, "implying as it does official connection with the State, is derogatory to the dignity of our country and misleading to the public" and that the NMA make immediate representation to the government to prohibit the improper use of the term. See NCH, 10/12/1932, p.65. For the Legal System Committee resolutions, see *Lifa Yuan Gongbao*, No.51, p.7; No.53, p.4; No.54, p.2; No.55, pp.2, 9–10.
75. Shi Quansheng, *Zhonghua Minguo*, p.858; Croizier, *Traditional Medicine*, pp.135–36.
76. YC, No.106 (Oct. 1935):1–2; *Mingri Yiyao* (Medicine of Tomorrow), No.1 (Jan. 1936):443–45.
77. SnB, 1936: 2/9, p.11; FZ, No.291 (1936: 1/29); GZG, No.2233 (1936: 12/21).

gated to an inferior status, because Western-style doctors were directly licensed by the Health Administration.

Native physicians were outraged. They found themselves still dealing with the same hostile government bureaucracy even after their legitimacy had been legally established. They argued that native medicine could not possibly get fair and equal treatment in the hands of Western-style doctors who occupied the Health Administration. Native medical associations and schools across the country launched a petition campaign demanding a separate agency either outside or within the Health Administration that would administer native medicine.[78] In response to the demand, a compromise was made in the Executive Council after heated debate: a Native Medicine Committee (*zhongyi weiyuan hui*) was to be established within the Health Administration.[79] In February 1937 nine well-known native physicians were invited to serve on the committee.[80]

The only remaining issue was the status of native medical schools. The Regulations on Native Physicians indirectly recognized native medical schools, but officially they were not part of the education system. In February 1937 the GMD Fifth Central Committee Third Plenum convened in Nanjing. Fifty-three GMD high officials put forward a motion calling for integrating native medical education into the nation's education system. Another motion for equal treatment of native and Western medicine proposed that native medical schools be integrated into the education system, that government health agencies employ both Western and native medical experts, that the government appropriate funds to establish native medical hospitals, and that schools and government agencies employ native physicians.[81] Meanwhile, delegates from more than fifty native medical organizations around the country arrived in Nanjing petitioning the conference for the same purposes.[82] As a result of the coordinated actions (one can imagine the organizational efforts and skills behind them), both motions were adopted by the plenum.[83]

Although the full-scale Japanese invasion in July 1937 and ensuing national efforts for the war of resistance precluded the implementation of the two measures, it is evident that by 1937 the issue of native medi-

78. ZXS, No.25 (Oct. 1936):2–8; No.26 (Nov. 1936):1–9; No.27 (Dec. 1936):2–3; YC, No.111 (Mar. 1936):32–34; No.118 (Oct. 1936):35–44.
79. ZXS, No.27 (Dec. 1936):67.   80. SnB, 1937: 2/6, p.16.
81. YC, No.120 (June 1937):1–4.   82. YC, No.120 (June 1937):41–42.
83. Shi Quansheng, *Zhonghua Minguo*, pp.859–60.

National Essence versus Science

cine had been settled and the legitimacy of native medicine was officially recognized. Native physicians won not only the battle but also the war through long years of organized struggle in which their professional associations proved to be indispensable.

The experience of medical professionalization in prewar China was unique due to the rivalry between modern and native medicine. Given the long history and widespread use of native medicine, Western medicine in China faced a great obstacle and a tough competitor in its effort to prevail in the country. Western-style doctors' priority was, therefore, to draw the line not between qualified doctors and unqualified practitioners but between Western medicine and native medicine. In their view, the advancement of medical science and the medical profession in China presupposed the demise of native medicine. Their assault on native medicine forced native physicians to defend by offense, screaming warnings against the cultural invasion of imperialism. Western-style doctors were thus easily depicted as unpatriotic Chinese. It is instructive to see that usually apolitical native physicians were so skilled in using the symbol of nationalism by identifying their trade with national essence. Such skillfulness can only be understood within the context of frequent public actions on the part of various social groups in Shanghai. The methods of mobilizing other social groups and organizations for support were also familiar. In other words, native physicians simply appropriated familiar practices from the collective political–social–cultural repertoire accumulated since the late Qing.

This conflict fought in the name of science and national essence points to a particular dimension of Chinese nationalism and an inherent tension between modernization and nationalism in modern China, showing how the tension was played out in the living experiences of different social groups. For native physicians and native drug traders, nationalism was not an abstraction but had concrete substance – it meant the preservation of their trade and livelihood. The struggle with Western-style doctors connected nationalism, an otherwise abstract concept, with the daily life of native physicians and native drug traders. By claiming that they represented national essence and national identity and that they were the agency of a Chinese modernization (to make native medicine scientific), native physicians both possessed or appropriated nationalism as a political weapon and endowed it with meaningful and tangible content.

Similarly, for Western-style doctors, modernization was also a concrete process – it meant the advancement of their profession at the expense of native medicine. Western-style doctors were comfortable in believing that their self-interest was identical to the interest of the nation and in arguing that they were fighting for the future of Chinese medical science. They clung to the word "science" and used it as a magic weapon against native medicine.

As both the discourse of nationalism and the discourse of modernization were potent in twentieth-century China, native physicians and Western-style doctors attempted to define the struggle between them in their own terms. Native physicians tried to define the struggle as a fight between the preservation of national essence and the invasion of Western imperialism. Western-style doctors tried to define the struggle as a fight between science and backwardness. The struggle, therefore, became a test to see on whose terms the battle would be fought, that is, which discourse would dominate the debate. Native physicians won the contest. While Western-style doctors contributed to the general criticism of Chinese tradition, they were in turn attacked as traitors to national identity long before those professionals with Western connections were so identified and thus marginalized by the Communists. The final legitimation of native medicine amply demonstrated the strength of cultural nationalism in the course of China's modernization.

8

Professionalism and Nationalism

The Shanghai Bar Association (I)

IN EARLY January 1912 a group of fourteen Chinese lawyers, upon learning that bar associations were being formed in Jiangsu and Zhejiang Provinces, decided to establish a lawyers' association in Shanghai. In a petition to Chen Qimei, the military governor of Shanghai at the time, they stated their purpose as follows:

> When it comes to legal disputes, the people's rights all rely upon the defense. Since to date the knowledge of law has not been widely shared, it is inevitable that honest people suffer injustice, cunning people get away with sharp tongue, magistrates try cases without getting to the truth, and the people's rights are not protected. Even if lawyers are hired, they are often foreigners who know little about Chinese customs and mores. Besides, while it is easy to find foreign lawyers in commercial cities and metropolises, they are not readily available in the interior. . . . Shanghai is a place of commerce where people clustered and lawsuits abound. Having been trained in law or served in the judicial system, we have [legal] knowledge and experience. Indignant that the foreign concessions have extraterritoriality, while our nation's sovereignty is incomplete, and that foreigners monopolized the lawsuits between the Chinese and foreigners, we plan to organize in the Shanghai area a lawyer's association of the Chinese Republic to protect the people's rights and to spread the spirit of the rule of law throughout the country.[1]

Explaining the raison d'être of a bar association in Shanghai, the statement foretold a pattern of associational actions of Chinese lawyers. It

---

1. SB, 1912: 1/7, p.5.

linked the fight for group interest – the advancement of professional status of lawyers – with larger national purposes and nationalist aspirations, from the rule of law and the protection of people's rights to resistance to foreign privileges in China. That kind of rhetoric was hardly new even in 1912. Nationalistic rhetoric, for instance, had been used to publicize and interpret local causes of native-place associations in Shanghai well before the 1911 Revolution.[2] The lawyers' statement may be seen as an indication that the use of such rhetoric or strategy had become commonplace in Shanghai's public arena.

To advance the position of Chinese lawyers as a profession was no easy task, however. In the face of the popular perception of lawyers as pettifoggers of low-life type, Chinese legal practitioners had to fight every step of the way to gain recognition as a legitimate profession by the state and society at large. Such fights entailed constant interaction with the government and the judicial system at both the central and local levels.

Moreover, the presence in Shanghai of the foreign concessions, the foreign-controlled Mixed Courts, and extraterritoriality greatly curtailed Chinese lawyers' professional opportunities and thus stimulated their nationalist sentiment in an occupation-specific fashion not shared by other social groups. Under such circumstances, the Shanghai Bar's efforts at professionalization were inevitably intertwined with, and ultimately benefited from, the rising Chinese nationalism in the 1920s and 1930s. At the same time, the Shanghai Bar's struggle enriched the content of Chinese nationalism.

THE ORGANIZATION OF THE SHANGHAI BAR

The Genesis

Within three weeks of receiving permission from Chen Qimei, the group of fourteen enterprising Chinese lawyers founded the General Bar Association of the Republic of China (GBARC) (*Zhonghua minguo lushi zong gonghui*), located in Nanshi.[3] The bylaws of the association claimed that its members could appear at all courts in the country. In other words, the GBARC was meant to be a national organization.[4] By the end of 1912 the association had over 170 members. Its membership overlapped with that of the Jiangsu General Bar Association, which had around two

---

2. Bryna Goodman, *Native Place, City, and Nation.*
3. NCH, 1/27/1912, p.235; SB, 1912: 1/29, p.5.   4. SB, 1912: 1/15, p.5.

hundred members, fifty to sixty of whom were practicing in Shanghai.⁵ Before the association had done any significant work, however, the Ministry of Justice enacted the Provisional Regulations on Lawyers on September 12, 1912. Under those regulations, the GBARC had to be reorganized to become a local bar association joined by qualified lawyers practicing in Shanghai only.

The Provisional Regulations on Lawyers had an immediate impact on individual lawyers who did not meet the educational qualifications set by the government. In early November 1912 the Jiangsu High Court notified lawyers that those who neither qualified nor were eligible for taking an examination should cease practicing by November 20.⁶ In late 1912 the GBARC was dissolved (so were, apparently, the general bar associations in Jiangsu and Zhejiang). With unqualified practitioners leaving the profession, qualified lawyers founded the Shanghai Bar Association (*Shanghai lushi gonghui*) in early 1913.⁷

By May 1913 the SBA had thirty-four members. Jin Minlan was elected president and Chen Zemin vice-president. Biographical information on Jin Minlan is unavailable, but Chen Zemin is a better-known figure in the history of the Shanghai Bar. Born in Wuxian, Jiangsu, in 1881, Chen studied law in Japan. A founding member of the Shanghai Bar, Chen was to play an important role in the organization. Active in national and local politics, he once served in the parliament in Beijing and later for a period of time was the president of the Federation of Street Merchants Association – an important merchant organization in Shanghai.⁸

Jin Minlan and Chen Zemin, plus seven councilors (*pingyi yuan*), all elected annually, served as the governing body of the Shanghai Bar. On May 25 the councilors' meeting resolved, among other things, that all lawyers practicing in Shanghai be licensed by the Ministry of Justice and join the association; wanting in either condition, one would not be recognized as a lawyer in Shanghai.⁹ That action signaled that qualified lawyers were eager to help enforce the government regulations and thus enhance their own professional stature and establish the Shanghai Bar as the sole legitimate body representing Shanghai lawyers.

The organizational form of the SBA remained unchanged until 1927 when reorganization took place under the GMD. On September 18, 1927,

---

5. SB, 1912: 11/22; 12/19, p.5.   6. SB, 1912: 11/13, p.5.
7. NCH, 4/19/1913, pp.181–82.   8. MRD, p.1037.
9. SB, 1913: 5/20, p.8; 5/27, p.7.

a total of 129 SBA members attended the first general meeting after the reorganization. An important change in the SBA's organization took place. With the approval of the Ministry of Justice, the SBA's presidential form of governance (*huizhang zhi*) was changed over to a committee system (*weiyuan zhi*), which was an exception to the Regulations on Lawyers of 1927. The SBA was to be governed by the joint meeting of a fifteen-member executive committee and a three-member supervisory committee. A three-member standing committee elected from the executive committee was to take care of day-to-day business. Both the executive and supervisory committees (ESC) were elected at the September meeting.[10]

On May 26, 1935, the Shanghai Bar's general meeting resolved to expand the three committees and elected thirty-seven members to the executive committee, eleven to the supervisory committee, and nine to the standing committee.[11] In April 1933 an ESC resolution had decided that the committees' alternate members attend the ESC joint meetings without voting privilege.[12] The committee system, the enlarged ESC, and the participation of alternate members in the ESC joint meetings all pointed to the efforts to democratize the Shanghai Bar's governance.

The joint meeting of the ESC would consider matters put forward by members of the Shanghai Bar and address issues raised by all possible parties – from the ministries and the GMD party organs in Nanjing, the Municipal Party Headquarters and the Municipal Government in Shanghai, the Jiangsu High Court and the district courts in Shanghai and their corresponding procuratorates, other urban associations, and ordinary citizens and litigants, to inmates in prisons. The joint meeting would vote to resolve most issues. Some essential matters would be left for the general meetings to decide, such as election of officers, plans to buy or build new association offices, and revisions of the bylaws. Judging from the record of the Shanghai Bar's activities, the bylaws and other rules were strictly followed and the internal workings of the Shanghai Bar were democratic and disciplined.

The Membership

The membership of the Shanghai Bar grew steadily. In April 1926 the membership of the Shanghai Bar was at 160, and by the end of 1929 it

---

10. SB, 1927: 9/19, p.6; FP, No.227 (1927: 11/6):13–14.
11. SLGB, No.33 (July 1935), pp.58–65.   12. SLGB, No.32 (June 1934), p.1.

had jumped to 475.[13] The number reached 595 in 1931; 1,108 in 1934; and 1,328 in 1937.[14] At the last general meeting of the prewar period, held on April 25, 1937, members numbered 1,340 – 415 attended the meeting.[15]

Where did these lawyers come from? Most of the lawyers who initiated the GBARC and founded the SBA were trained in Japan. A few were trained in the West or obtained the *juren* degree in law and government in the reformed civil service examination in the final years of the Qing dynasty. Some of them had served as judges or procurators in the post–1907 judicial system. After the founding of the Republic, schools of law and government mushroomed in the country. In 1914 Jiangsu Province alone had fifteen newly established schools of law, including five in Shanghai.[16] Some of those schools did not last long and were replaced by others. By the mid-1930s no less than eight institutions of higher education in Shanghai offered degree programs in law: Aurora University (founded in 1903), Fudan University (1905), China College of Shanghai (*zhongguo gongxue*) (1906), Law School of the Souchow University (1915), Shanghai College of Law (*Shanghai faxue yuan*) (1926), Shanghai College of Law and Political Science (*Shanghai fazhen xueyuan*) (1924), Chizhi College (1924), and Great China University (1924).[17] As Alison W. Conner has shown, in such Chinese law school as the Soochow Law School, curriculum was composed of Western law, both common law and continental law (the Chinese judicial system was based on continental law), though from the mid-1920s onward Chinese law courses were increasingly taught as well.[18]

Many members of the Shanghai Bar were graduates of those schools. Of 300 graduates of the Soochow University Law School during 1918 to 1933, for instance, 143 went into law practice.[19] Of 645 graduates of that school from 1918 through 1936, 228 practiced law in Shanghai (nine of them were women).[20] Some of the graduates went on to study abroad. Wu Jingxiong (John C. Wu), Chen Tingrui, Lu Dingkui, and He Shizhen,

---

13. SB, 1926: 4/26, p.3; SLGB, No.26 (Jan. 1930), pp.37–72.
14. *Shanghai Lushi Gonghui Huiyuanlu*, 1931, 1934, 1937.
15. SnB, 1937: 4/26, p.11.   16. DZ, 9,12 (Feb. 1914):18–19.
17. W. Y. Chyne, *Handbook of Cultural Institutions in China* (Shanghai, 1936), pp.34–35, 57, 59, 97–98, 104–6, 238, 250–51.
18. Alison W. Conner, "Legal Education during the Republican Period," p.88.
19. *Sili Dongwu Daxue Falu Xueyuan Yilan* (Soochow University Law School annual announcement) (1933), p.102.
20. *Dongwu Daxue Faxue Yuan Tongxue Lu* (Alumini directory of Soochow University Law School) (1936).

all graduates from the Soochow Law School, earned doctoral degrees in law at the University of Michigan and joined the Shanghai Bar. Three of them served as judicial officials at different times. To what degree the experience of receiving legal training in the West and in Western-style Chinese law schools shaped or impacted those lawyers' behavior can only be speculated. It seems reasonable to assume, however, that they had a better understanding of and a stronger commitment to the rule of law and due process as well as legal professionalization. They were to have some conflicts with the Republican state when they entered law practice and began to deal with the judicial system that had yet to be fully established in accordance with the principles of the rule of law and judicial independence.

Growing Pains

Although the Shanghai Bar Association would prove to be the best-organized professional association in Shanghai, it was not immune to organizational problems. In its first few years the SBA operated rather smoothly. In May 1914 Xu Erjin was elected president and Huang Zhenpan vice-president. In March 1915 Chen Zemin was elected president and Xu Qian vice-president.[21] No elections were reported in 1916 and 1917, though they seemed to have taken place.

Trouble began to show in 1918. Under the government regulations at that time, if lawyers in a locality were fewer than twenty, they were allowed to join the bar association of a neighboring district.[22] For that reason lawyers from places around Shanghai, such as Suzhou, Nantong, and Changshu, entered the SBA, thus swelling its membership to more than two hundred within a few years. At the general meeting on April 2, 1918, election of new officers was scheduled to take place. It was reported that Cai Nipei, the president, wanted to keep the job, with the support from lawyers practicing in Shanghai. On the other hand, lawyers practicing in Suzhou preferred Chen Zemin, who was a native of Wuxian, a county adjacent to Suzhou. Before a vote could be taken to resolve the issue, Yang Jingbing proposed that only the votes of those who were present, and not mail-in votes, should be counted. Disagreement on the

---

21. SB, 1914: 5/19, p.7; 1915: 5/30, p.8.
22. Yu-Chuan Chang, "The Bar Association in China," CSPSR, 23,3 (Oct.–Dec. 1938): 238.

procedure caused the election to be postponed. Another issue that was debated and unresolved was where to build a new office of the association. Shanghai lawyers wanted the new office to be built in Shanghai, but lawyers practicing in Suzhou preferred somewhere outside Shanghai (and thus very likely in Suzhou). The debate was so heated that the meeting broke off without results.[23]

The 1918 episode is noteworthy for important reasons. At a first glance, it seems that intra-association solidarity and division could still be defined by geography even in a professional organization such as the SBA. At a closer look, however, the conflict was not exactly one based on native-place ties, since the division was between lawyers practicing, but not necessarily born, in Shanghai and those practicing in Suzhou. Suzhou lawyers seem to have had concerns about whether (or to what extent) the Shanghai Bar would take care of their interests if the president was a lawyer practicing in Shanghai and the association was headquartered in Shanghai. Their concerns were new, predicated on the very nature of the SBA as a professional association that Suzhou lawyers had to join in order to practice. Their concerns provided evidence that the Shanghai Bar was more than a formality and was important to member lawyers. At the very least, lawyers intended to make the association work for them.

From December 1918 through November 1919 three consecutive general meetings were aborted because not enough people showed up to secure a quorum.[24] Not until December 28, 1919, was a quorum finally achieved in a dubious fashion. Fifty-eight people actually attended the meeting, carrying the proxies of 116 members who were not present and thus providing 174 votes. Cai Nipei was reelected president and Lu Bingzhang was elected vice-president, along with eight managing officers (*ganshi yuan*).[25]

Disgruntled members soon challenged the legality of the election procedure to the Jiangsu High Court responsible for supervising and disciplining bar associations in the province. The court instructed the Shanghai District Procuratorate to look into the matter. Under the pressure, the president, vice-president, and eight managing officers decided to resign. At the same time, they requested the Ministry of Justice to

23. SB, 1918: 4/3, p.5.
24. SB, 1918: 12/16, p.5; 1919: 4/28, p.5; 12/1, p.5; NCH, 5/3/1919, p.271.
25. SB, 1919: 12/29, p.5.

clarify whether the procedures at the previous general meeting were permissible.[26] The answer was negative.[27]

Due to the repeated failure to secure a quorum at general meetings, however, a new election was not held; Cai Nipei and Zhang Jiazhen remained the president and vice-president until March 1922. By then lawyers from outside Shanghai had left the SBA to form local bar associations in their own districts. A quorum was achieved by discounting lawyers who had not paid membership fees for four months (under the bylaws such members should be expelled). Zhang Yipeng and Zhang Jiazhen were elected president and vice-president.[28] Zhang Yipeng's background was almost identical to Chen Zemin's background. A native of Wuxian, Jiangsu, Zhang Yipeng obtained the *juren* degree in 1893 and then studied law in Japan. Before starting a law practice in Shanghai in the early 1920s, he had served in several judicial posts including acting minister of justice in Beijing at one point. He was to play an important role in the Shanghai Bar before 1927.[29]

The quorum problem seemed to suggest that most SBA members joined the Shanghai Bar because the membership was mandatory. They joined as free riders who enjoyed the benefit of being part of the Shanghai Bar but did not care enough to fight for the cause of the profession, let alone issues other than professional issues. On the other hand, active members as a minority was not uncommon in professional associations, or any voluntary associations, in China or elsewhere. The bar associations in the United States, for example, had a similar experience during the period of intensive association building and government lobbying in the late nineteenth and early twentieth centuries.[30] In 1920 less than 10 percent of lawyers joined the American Bar Association.[31] The fact that only a minority of SBA members were active by no means diminishes the significance of the Shanghai Bar as an important player in the public arena.

26. SB, 1920: 1/26, p.5; 2/4, p.5.
27. SB, 1920: 7/27, p.5. In the directive the Ministry indicated that similar incidents had occurred in other bar associations in Hubei and Hunan Provinces.
28. The membership at the time was 200 and those attending the meeting numbered 83. The quorum was secured by discounting 47 members who owed membership fees for four consecutive months. One member protested such a proceeding but was overruled by a majority vote. See SnB, 1922: 3/20, p.14.
29. MRD, p.899.
30. Richard L. Abel. *American Lawyers* (London, 1989), pp.44–47.
31. Samuel Haber, *The Quest for Authority and Honor in the American Professions, 1750–1900*, p.230.

THE EFFORTS AT PROFESSIONALIZATION

The Status of the Shanghai Bar

The first and foremost task of the Shanghai Bar was to establish its authority as the sole legitimate body representing the legal profession in Shanghai. Under the Regulations on Lawyers (Article 22 of the 1912 Provisional Regulations on Lawyers and Article 24 of the 1927 Regulations on Lawyers), only members of a local bar association could practice in a given area under the jurisdiction of a district court. But judges often neglected the provision, failing to check the identity of lawyers who appeared in courts. From the mid-1920s onward the SBA tackled the problem in an aggressive manner.

In June 1926 Wang Kaijiang, a councilor of the SBA, proposed that the Shanghai Bar publish the names of its members every three months and that members display their membership certificates in their law offices or indicate their membership status on the signboards of their firms. The councilors' meeting adopted the proposal. In September the Shanghai Bar published in newspapers for the first time the list of its members who numbered 173.[32] That practice does not seem to have continued, however.

In the summer of 1928 the Shanghai Bar's general meeting decided to issue badges to members. The ESC required members to wear the badge when performing their duties, not to lend it to anyone, and to return it when ceasing practice in Shanghai. The Shanghai Bar informed the Provisional Court and other public associations in Shanghai of the new practice and received positive responses.[33] Only the *North China Herald* criticized the SBA for trying to monopolize law practice in Shanghai, which was indeed the intention of the Shanghai Bar.[34]

The SBA was most frustrated by the Mixed Courts where nonmember or one-time-member lawyers routinely appeared at trials. The root of the problem was that theoretically the Shanghai Bar's authority only covered the Chinese areas of the city over which the Shanghai District Court had jurisdiction. Chinese lawyers practicing within the International Settlement and French Concession had never joined the SBA and only registered with the Mixed Courts. According to the rules of the International Mixed Court, Chinese lawyers who applied for practice at

---

32. SB, 1926: 6/9, p.5; 9/20, p.4.   33. SLGB, No.24 (Dec. 1928), pp.4–5, 9–10.
34. NCH, 10/27/1928, p.146.

the court should have licenses issued by the Ministry of Justice.[35] But the Shanghai Bar asserted that some of those lawyers admitted to the court did not even have such licenses.

The Shanghai Bar was powerless in that situation until such time as the rendition of the Mixed Court took place. Within three weeks after the Provisional Court was established, the SBA submitted a list of its 198 members to the Office of the Shanghai Commissioner of Foreign Affairs (*Shanghai jiaoshe gongshu*) to make those lawyers eligible to appear at the court.[36] Zhang Yipeng, the president of the Shanghai Bar, petitioned the Jiangsu provincial governor, expounding the advantages of allowing nobody but SBA members to appear at the Provisional Court. Individual bar members also petitioned the governor, asking for a strict evaluation of the qualifications of lawyers to appear at the Provisional Court.[37]

A strategic move on the part of the SBA was to prevent a separate bar association from emerging in the International Settlement. It succeeded in dissuading Xu Weizhen, the newly appointed president of the Provisional Court, from endorsing another bar association in Shanghai. In late December 1926, when Xu had just arrived in Shanghai to oversee the rendition of the Mixed Court, the Shanghai Bar entertained him with a dinner party, at which Xu promised that there would be no new bar association in Shanghai. In February 1927, after the court had been reorganized into the Provisional Court, Xu once again announced that lawyers would be eligible to appear at the court by joining the Shanghai Bar and that forming another bar association was out of the question.[38]

After the GMD government appointed Lu Xingyuan the president of the Provisional Court in May 1927, Nanjing never considered a new bar association in the foreign concessions either. That might be expected, since the Shanghai Bar was reorganized under the direction of the MPH and the PCSB (see Chapter 4) and since the GMD wished to revise unequal treaties and recover foreign concessions in China. Apparently failing to appreciate the politics of the GMD, some non-SBA-member lawyers tried to form a separate bar association in the International Settlement in order to practice at the Provisional Court without joining the SBA. In December 1928 the Shanghai Bar petitioned Nanjing to

---

35. Kotenev, *Shanghai: Its Mixed Court and Council*, pp.205–6.
36. SB, 1927: 1/20, p.6.   37. SB, 1927: 1/25, p.5; 3/3, p.5.
38. SB, 1926: 12/31, p.6; 1927: 2/16, p.5.

prohibit such a move. On January 21, 1929, the Ministry of Justice officially issued an order to the Jiangsu Provincial Government saying that no bar associations could be established in Shanghai's foreign concessions.[39]

The announcement of government policies did not suffice for the SBA to achieve its goals. Lu Xingyuan, the president of the Provisional Court, as well as judges in the court continued to allow nonmember lawyers to appear at the court. The Shanghai Bar had to act locally to help enforce the policy. In September 1928 the Shanghai Bar ordered its members not to proceed with their cases in court when faced with any nonmember lawyer representing the other party.[40] The Shanghai Bar also sent all members a list of nonmember lawyers so that the nonmembers could be identified.[41] Pressed by the Shanghai Bar, the Provisional Court referred the matter to the Ministry of Justice in Nanjing in October 1928. The Shanghai Bar sent Li Shirui, a member of the executive committee, to Nanjing to argue its case. In November the Justice Ministry came down on the side of the SBA, telling the Provisional Court to enforce Article 24 of the Regulations on Lawyers.[42] The Shanghai Bar immediately notified all its members of the Justice Ministry's directive, asking its members to help enforce the provision rigorously by refusing to deal with any nonmember lawyer in court. At the same time the ESC invited nonmember lawyers to join the Shanghai Bar.[43]

The persistent efforts of the SBA paid off. After 1928 there was dramatic growth in the SBA membership. Lawyers who had always practiced in the two concessions but had not joined the SBA signed up out of necessity. Although those lawyers' presence in the Shanghai Bar increased the number of nonactive members and contributed to the quorum problem, the status of the Shanghai Bar was assured as the sole legitimate body representing the legal profession in Shanghai.

Protection of Professional Rights

A concrete issue with regard to professional autonomy that the SBA strove to protect was the right of its members in discharging their pro-

---

39. FP, No.239–240:14; Guo Wei and Zhou Dingmei, *Lushi Banshi Shouxu Chengshi Huishu*, p.30.
40. SLGB, No.24, p.10.   41. SLGB, No.24, p.14.
42. The directive was repeated in January 1929. Both directives appeared in *Lushi Banshi Shouxu Chengshi Huishu*, pp.31–31. Also see NCH, 12/15/1928, p.412.
43. SLGB, No.24, pp.18–19; SB, 1928: 12/11, p.8. In July 1931, after the French Mixed

fessional duties. The issue was important and necessary because the rule of law and due process were still new concepts in China and because the popular perception of a lawyer remained largely that of a traditional pettifogger. More importantly, when attacks on lawyers came from the government itself, whether the Shanghai Bar was able to withstand the pressure would be an ultimate test of its viability as a professional association.

A typical test came with the assassination of Song Jiaoren in the spring of 1913. Song was a prominent leader of the GMD party founded in August 1912. Respected as the best and most articulate of leading GMD figures, Song advocated a party-majority cabinet after the GMD had won the parliament election in late 1912. Hoping to check the power of Yuan Shikai and pursue his own political agenda with a GMD-dominated cabinet, Song became the bête noire of Yuan Shikai. Acting on Yuan's behalf, Zhao Bingjun, the prime minister in the Yuan Shikai government, and Hong Shuzu, the secretary of the cabinet, conspired to murder Song. They contracted Ying Guixin, a political misfit, to do the job. Ying in turn hired Wu Shiying, an unemployed former soldier, to carry out the hit. On March 20 Song was shot at close range by Wu at Shanghai Railway Station and died in a hospital two days later. Within two weeks Ying Guixin and Wu Shiying were apprehended by the police of the International Settlement.

The two suspects, Ying Guixin and Wu Shiying, were in the custody of the police of the International Settlement and preliminary hearings were held at the Mixed Court. After repeated requests by the Chinese government and the Chinese press, the two men were turned over to the Chinese authorities in Shanghai to be tried at the Shanghai District Court. The families of the two men hired two lawyers, but were told by Cheng Dequan, the governor of Jiangsu, that with such overwhelming evidence, neither party needed a lawyer.[44] Within a few days Wu Shiying died mysteriously in the barracks where the two men were detained.

Yet, Yang Jingbing, a member of the SBA, agreed to take up the case of Ying Guixin anyway. Song Jiaoren's assassination was a public outrage. Popular emotion ran high regarding the case itself and its impli-

Court was changed into the Second Special District Court and the Jiangsu High Court Third Branch, the SBA quickly sent the two courts a list of its members and demanded that the practice of nonmember lawyers appearing at the court cease. SLGB, No.30, p.3.

44. SB, 1913: 4/20, p.7.

cations for the nation's political future. It took great courage for Yang to represent the accused who was vilified daily in the press. In spite of being attacked in the press by people who thought a heinous murderer such as Ying did not deserve a legal defense, Yang handled the case in a professional manner as a defense lawyer. In the capacity as a defense lawyer, he protested the practice of Mu Xiangyao, the police commissioner, who detained Ying without proper procedure.[45] Yang wrote to Governor Cheng Dequan asking for assurance that Ying would not die under detention like Wu Shiying.[46] In a telegram to the Ministry of Justice, Yang said that in order to maintain the independence of the judicial system, Ying should be tried at the Shanghai District Court instead of at a special court that was being proposed at the time.[47] He asked the Justice Ministry to make efforts to have another key conspirator, Hong Shuzu, extradited from the German Concession in Qingdao where Hong was hiding.[48]

Due to the outbreak of the Second Revolution in July 1913, Ying escaped from detention during the fighting around Shanghai and his trial never took place.[49] Yet the trouble for Yang Jingbing had just begun. He was charged with the offense of insulting judges while representing Ying and was suspended from practice by the Ministry of Justice. Pleading innocent, Yang went to Beijing to argue his own case. At that juncture, the Shanghai Bar Association, which had been established for only six months, came forward to stand by Yang, as did the bar associations in Wuxian, Huating, and Wuxi.[50] Those bars adopted resolutions that if the Lawyers' Disciplinary Committee of the Jiangsu High Court were to try Yang, they would send lawyers to defend him.[51] The resolutions were a tremendous moral support for Yang. In the end, the charge against Yang

45. SB, 1913: 5/13, p.8; 5/23, p.8.
46. *Song Jiaoren Xue'an* (The bloody case of Song Jiaoren's [murder]) (Changsha, 1986), pp.368–69.
47. *Song Jiaoren Xue'an*, pp.369–70.
48. SB, 1913: 5/12, p.7.
49. Ying went to Beijing to ask Yuan Shikai for reward and boasted to anyone who would listen about his "contribution" to the Yuan's cause, while Yuan was denying his involvement in the assassination. He effectively made himself such a nuisance to Yuan that the latter had his henchmen murder Ying on board a train. See *Song Jiaoren Xue'an*, p.466; NCH, 1/24/1914, p.275.
50. As mentioned previously, lawyers in the three counties joined the Shanghai Bar Association for lack of enough members. It seems that at this point bar associations existed in these places but would soon be dissolved, probably demanded by the judicial authorities in accordance with the Provisional Regulations on Lawyers.
51. SB, 1913: 2/2, p.7; 7/9, p.7.

proved to have no substance. In early February 1914 the Ministry of Justice reinstated Yang and six other Shanghai lawyers who had been suspended for political reasons – allegedly joining the rebels in the Second Revolution.[52]

The Yang episode shows that although the Shanghai people were familiar with the idea of due process and legal defense, there was a deep-seated assumption among many including those working in the judicial system that the accused was guilty until proven innocent and that the guilty deserved no legal protection. It is within this context that the position of the SBA was significant. Individual lawyers, including Yang, might have had their own political judgment on what Song's murder meant. Yet, they did not sacrifice the principles of the rule of law and due process for political and emotional reasons. Facing both popular and government pressure, Yang Jingbing and the Shanghai Bar had stood firm in defense of these principles. In so doing, they also defended the professional rights of lawyers.

The attack on lawyers for representing accused criminals proved to be a perennial problem throughout the period under study. As late as the 1930s, police, court clerks, and even judges often harassed lawyers who represented defendants. On August 2, 1930, for instance, lawyer Zhang Xingyuan arrived at the Jiangsu High Court Second Branch in the French Concession, representing a certain Wu Suzhong who was accused of being a Communist. An investigator from the Shanghai-Wusong Garrison Headquarters scolded Zhang for defending a Communist. As a lawyer, replied Zhang, he had to perform his duty according to the law. If he did not take the case, the defendant would find another lawyer or the court would have to appoint a lawyer for the defendant. At that response, the investigator shouted at Zhang and punched him several times. In response to the incident, the SBA sent a protest letter to the Garrison Headquarters. Pointing out that it was part of the legal procedure for a lawyer to represent any defendant, the Shanghai Bar's letter stressed the danger of employing investigators so ignorant of the law and the harm such behavior inflicted on the movement to abolish extraterritoriality.[53] In fact just a few months earlier a similar incident had occurred and the Shanghai Bar had protested then too. Such incidents and protests seem to have been part of the life for Shanghai lawyers and the Shanghai Bar.

52. SB, 1913: 9/4, p.7; 1914: 2/2, p.7.   53. SLGB, No.28 (Jan. 1931), pp.9, 92–94.

THE SHANGHAI BAR AND THE RENDITION OF
THE MIXED COURTS

The statement of the lawyers who founded the General Bar Association of the Chinese Republic in 1912 had already expressed resentment against foreign lawyers' monopoly of litigation in Shanghai. One of the actions that the GBARC took in its short life-span was agitation against foreign lawyers appearing in Chinese courts.[54] By the mid-1920s Chinese lawyers in Shanghai had established themselves as a profession; a stronger desire had risen to expand their scope of practice and exclude or at least limit foreign lawyers' practice. For those Chinese lawyers, nationalism and imperialism were not abstract concepts, but were concrete issues about their professional careers and opportunities. The coincidence of nationalist purposes and lawyers' professional interests explains to a large extent the SBA's active involvement in the movement for the rendition of the Mixed Courts and for the abolition of extraterritoriality. Equally striking was the responsiveness of the government to the Shanghai Bar's opinions.

The Issue of the Mixed Courts

The Mixed Courts in Shanghai's foreign concessions were a legal anomaly born of special historical circumstances. Under the Agreement on Establishing the Mixed Court (*Yangjing bang sheguan huishen zhangcheng*) signed in 1868, foreigners in Shanghai enjoyed extraterritoriality, but criminal and civil cases involving Chinese and nontreaty foreigners that occurred in the foreign concessions were tried at the Mixed Court in the International Settlement. The court was under Chinese jurisdiction, but when cases involved foreigners, foreign assessors were to sit with Chinese magistrates and try the cases together. The punishment of criminals and the enforcement of decisions in civil cases had to be carried out by the Chinese authorities. Because the Chinese judicial and administrative procedures were clumsy and full of opportunities for abuses and corruption, foreigners in Shanghai's International Settlement were dissatisfied with the state of affairs.

During the 1911 Revolution, the Chinese officials in charge of the Mixed Court in the International Settlement fled and the court ceased to function. The foreign Consular Body in Shanghai and the SMC seized

---

54. NCH, 4/26/1913, p.238.

the opportunity to take over the court in the name of keeping law and order. The Consular Body simply arrogated to itself the power to appoint Chinese judges to the court. The SMC would pay the salary of Chinese judges and clerks of the court. The municipal police of the International Settlement assumed court-related duties and took charge of the court prison. Thus the International Mixed Court was turned into a judicial arm of the SMC, totally independent of the Chinese authorities and the Chinese judicial system. The court also expanded its authority well beyond what the 1868 agreement originally prescribed for it. Notably, now foreign assessors would sit and try all cases, criminal and civil, together with Chinese judges, even if the cases involved Chinese only. The conviction and sentence at the court was final and no formal appeal was instituted. The French Mixed Court evolved in a more or less similar fashion.[55]

The Chinese authorities never officially accepted foreign seizure of the Mixed Courts. After the founding of the Republic, the Beiyang government repeatedly sent official notes to the American and British ministers in Beijing, demanding the return (called "rendition" at the time) of the court in the International Settlement to the Chinese authorities. The British and American ministers always responded with counterproposals that asked for an expansion of the International Settlement.[56] The obstinate American and British position was largely shaped by the American and British negative view of the Chinese judicial system and American and British commercial interests in China that would supposedly suffer under the Chinese system. In 1914 the *North China Herald* opposed the rendition of the Mixed Court, saying that the court was of great importance to the commercial interests of foreigners in Shanghai and that "the courts presided over by Chinese officials cannot be trusted to do justice impartially."[57]

55. For the detail of the evolution of the Mixed Courts, see A. M. Kotenev, *Shanghai*; George W. Keeton, *The Development of Extraterritoriality in China*, Vol.1 (Shanghai, 1928), pp.344–404; Thomas B. Stephens, *Order and Discipline in China: The Shanghai Mixed Court, 1911–1927* (Seattle, 1992), pp.44–65; "Evolution of a Court: Story of the Gradual Growth of the French Concession Tribunal," NCH, 8/11/1931, p.212. For the Chinese perspective, see "Shanghai Lingshi Tuan Zhanguan Gongxie Zhi Jingguo" (The course of the foreign Consular Body taking over the Mixed Courts), FP, No.119 (1925: 10/11):20–21, No.120 (1925: 10/18):16–23; "Waiguo Qinhai Zhongguo Sifa Zhi Shishi" (The facts of foreign powers' encroachment upon China's judiciary), FP, No.150 (1926: 5/16):20–34; Fei Chengkang, *Zhongguo Zujie Shi* (A history of foreign concessions in China) (Shanghai, 1991), pp.134–50.
56. A. M. Kotenev, *Shanghai*, p.273; Fei Chengkang, *Zhongguo*, pp.150–51.
57. NCH, 1/24/1914, p.235.

The Shanghai Bar in Action

During 1912 to 1930 the Shanghai Bar consistently stood behind the government's efforts to reclaim the Mixed Courts and abolish extraterritoriality. In December 1918 at Chen Zemin's suggestion, an SBA general meeting formed a committee to provide well-researched plans to assist the government in effecting the abolition of extraterritoriality at the Paris Peace Conference.[58] The Chinese efforts at the Paris Peace Conference ended in failure; the issue of extraterritoriality was not even on the table.

During March to May 1922, a number of bar associations in the country urged the Shanghai Bar to take the lead to organize a national judicial conference in Shanghai. The Shanghai Bar obliged. Nineteen bar associations and three schools of law and government around the country decided to participate.[59] When the conference took place in September to October 1922, the SBA presented a resolution that the bar associations demand the government to take steps to reclaim the Mixed Court in the International Settlement.[60]

In 1924 the Beijing government once again initiated negotiations to reclaim the International Mixed Court. The British and Americans insisted on an expansion of the International Settlement as one of the conditions for returning the court.[61] The SBA sent a telegram to Prime Minister Sun Baoqi, Foreign Minister Gu Weijun, and Justice Minister Wang Chonghui, advising them that the rendition of the court not be linked with other issues and that the government plan carefully and act promptly. The Shanghai Bar also sent one of its councilors, Li Zuyu, to Beijing to consult with the government.[62]

The Shanghai Bar was not the only public association in Shanghai that acted for the cause. The author of the history of the Mixed Court published in 1925, A. M. Kotenev, acceded that the Chinese government's efforts at the rendition of the Mixed Court were supported by a certain part of the Chinese population headed by the Chinese General Chamber of Commerce and the Shanghai Bar. "These two bodies at their meetings passed strong resolutions in favour of the restoration of the Mixed Court to the Chinese authorities and sent their representatives to Peking

---

58. SB, 1918: 12/16, p.5.
59. SnB, 1922: 3/12, p.14; 3/18, p.14; 3/31, p.14; 4/24, p.13; 4/24, p.13; 5/1, p.14; 5/6, p.13; 5/9, p.14.
60. SnB, 1922: 9/19, p.13; NCH, 9/30/1922, p.954.
61. NCH, 4/19/1924, p.81.   62. SB, 1924: 5/5, p.5.

to urge the Government to take speedy measures to effect an unconditional surrender of the Mixed Court on the part of the Consular Body."[63] The Shanghai Federation of Street Merchants Associations also played a part. While the Chamber of Commerce sent a delegate along with Li Zuyu of the SBA to Beijing, the Federation of Street Merchant Associations telegraphed Gu Weijun, asking him not to agree to the expansion of the International Settlement.[64] Because of the strong opposition of the Chinese to the British and American conditions, the negotiations led nowhere.

It was the high tide of Chinese nationalism during the May Thirtieth Movement that finally pushed the British and Americans to seek a settlement on the issue through serious negotiations with the Chinese. Even the *North China Herald* had come around to state that "[t]here is no question but that the Mixed Court must be handed back."[65] The talks were resumed in early 1926, but deadlocked again. During the negotiations the issue of expanding the International Settlement was dropped. It was the issue of foreign assessors trying Chinese criminal cases that divided the two sides. The Chinese government insisted that Chinese judges should try all Chinese cases in the to-be-reorganized court. The Diplomatic Body disagreed.

At that juncture, the Shanghai Bar played a pivotal role. At the suggestion of lawyers Song Shixiang and Chao Kun, an SBA general meeting on April 25, 1926, resolved that the goal of the rendition should be the removal of the worst of all evils. The resolution stated that foreigners' right to try Chinese civil cases and the foreign consuls' right to sign subpoenas and arrest warrants should be abolished so as to restore the court to the pre-1911 status. The Shanghai Bar also decided to ask the Jiangsu provincial government to negotiate with foreign consuls in Shanghai to settle the issue locally. Li Zuyu and Wang Kaijiang were elected the delegates to Nanjing for that mission.[66]

The Shanghai Bar, along with the Shanghai General Chamber of Commerce, suggested to Chen Taoyi, the Jiangsu governor, and Sun Chuanfang, the warlord in control of Jiangsu and Zhejiang at the time, that the Jiangsu provincial government assume the negotiations with the foreign consuls in Shanghai to settle the issue. Another professional association, the Institute of Chartered Accountants of Shanghai (ICAS) (*Shanghai*

---

63. A. M. Kotenev, *Shanghai*, p.278.
64. SB, 1918: 5/30, p.5; FP, No.49 (1924: 6/1):11–12.
65. NCH, 7/17/1926, p.100.   66. SB, 1926: 4/26, p.3.

kuaijishi gonghui), also sent a telegram to the central government and the Jiangsu provincial government in support of the proposed local negotiations. The ICAS specifically pointed out that it was in agreement with the SBA and other organizations on this issue.[67]

Sun Chuanfang and Chen Daoyi agreed to take action. Ding Wenjiang, the administrator of Shanghai-Wusong (*Songhu duban*) at the time, and Xu Yuan, the Jiangsu commissioner of foreign affairs, were assigned to lead the negotiations. The Consular Body accepted the proposal with the blessing of the Diplomatic Body in Beijing.[68] The Beiyang government was reluctant to let the negotiations move out of its hands to Shanghai, but it had no better alternatives, given the deadlock in Beijing. The Ministries of Justice and Foreign Affairs advised Ding Wenjiang, however, that the key Chinese position be the denial of foreigners' right to try Chinese criminal cases and the abolition of the procurator at the court. On their part, following the instructions from the Diplomatic Body in Beijing, the British, American, and Japanese consuls who participated in the negotiations refused to give up the right to try all Chinese cases. The talks stalled.[69]

In early June, Zhang Yipeng, the president of the SBA, sent the Jiangsu provincial government a proposal based on the Shanghai Bar's April 25 resolution that the priority be the removal of foreigners' right to try Chinese civil cases. Sun Chuanfang accepted the idea for compromise. He advised Ding Wenjiang to heed the "local opinion" (in defiance of Beijing's guidelines) and make necessary concessions to reach a provisional agreement as soon as possible. Under those instructions, the negotiations were resumed on June 21, and by early July a draft agreement had been reached.[70]

The draft agreement did not specify the status of foreign lawyers in the to-be-reorganized court. Feeling their jobs threatened, foreign lawyers in Shanghai launched a campaign to oppose the agreement. They sent telegrams to the Diplomatic Body and dispatched five delegates to Beijing to make their case.[71] On July 17, in the name of the American Far East Bar Association, American lawyers in Shanghai published a statement denouncing the agreement. The statement denigrated the

---

67. SB, 1926: 5/21, p.3; *Shanghai Zhonghua Minguo Kuaiji Shi Gonghui Nianbao* (1928), p.56.
68. Fei Chengkang, *Zhongguo*, pp.151–52; A. M. Kotenev, *Shanghai*, pp.178–79.
69. Fei Chengkang, *Zhongguo*, p.152.
70. Fei Chengkang, *Zhongguo*, pp.151–52; NCH, 5/1/1926, p.202; 5/22/1926, p.346.
71. A. M. Kotenev, *Shanghai*, pp.179–80.

Chinese judicial system, pointed a finger at Chinese official corruption, and held the draft agreement invalid because Sun Chuanfang, as a local warlord, did not represent the Chinese government.[72]

The Shanghai Bar swiftly struck back with its own statement the next day. The statement refuted the foreign lawyers' attack on the Chinese judicial system. Just as one should not, went the statement, cite the lynching of blacks or the corruption under Prohibition to say that the United States is a lawless country, so should one not harshly judge China. Furthermore, the problems within the Chinese judicial system had nothing to do with the rendition of the Mixed Court – a separate issue from the abolition of extraterritoriality, because foreign powers usually cited the defects of the Chinese judicial system to justify extraterritoriality. The statement also rejected the claims that the presence of foreign lawyers at the Mixed Court improved its operation and charged that brokers or touts hired by foreign lawyers were worse than the runners of Chinese yamen.[73] The Shanghai Bar opposed the right of foreign lawyers to practice after the rendition of the court on several grounds stressing Chinese sovereignty and court efficiency.[74]

The SBA sent telegrams to foreign ministers in Beijing as well. In the letter to the American minister, the Shanghai Bar protested against the American lawyers' insult to China's government, judiciary, and legal profession. With a legal mind, the Shanghai Bar pointed out that American lawyers' comments about Sun Chuanfang's administrative status bordered on instigating China's internal rebellion.[75] The SBA urged the Jiangsu provincial government to lodge an official protest to foreign ministers on the issue.[76]

The ICAS again joined the SBA in the campaign, proving the solidarity and common interests of Chinese lawyers and accountants.[77] It published a public rebuttal against the statement of the American Far Eastern Bar Association on July 21.[78] It also asked the associations of

---

72. SB, 1926: 7/14, p.3; NCH, 7/17/1926, p.108.
73. For the problem of Chinese brokers employed by foreign lawyers, see A. M. Kotenev, *Shanghai*, pp.210–12.
74. SB, 1926: 7/18, p.3; NCH, 7/24/1926, p.159.
75. SB, 1926: 7/22, p.3.   76. SB, 1926: 7/21, p.3.
77. Chinese accountants in Shanghai also sought to exclude foreign accountants from Chinese business establishments and especially wanted to perform the duty of court accountants in civil cases at the Mixed Court, which at the time was monopolized by a British accounting firm with a handsome profit. See A. M. Kotenev, *Shanghai*, pp.258–60.
78. SB, 1926: 7/21, p.3.

accountants in Beijing and Tianjin to make their views known to the Diplomatic Body and help assure the signing of the agreement.[79] On July 29 the ICAS sent a telegram to the State Council and the Ministry of Foreign Affairs urging the government to protest foreign lawyers' interference with China's domestic politics, echoing the view of the SBA.[80]

Problems after the Rendition of the Mixed Court

The Provisional Regulations on the Rendition of the Shanghai Mixed Court (*Shouhui Shanghai huishen gongxie zanxing zhangcheng*) known as the Rendition Agreement was signed on August 31, 1926.[81] The document did not mention the status of foreign lawyers at the Provisional Court that would replace the Mixed Court. But the supplementary notes to the agreement provided that foreign lawyers could appear at the court for either party where (1) a consular official sat with a Chinese judge; (2) the Shanghai Municipal Council was plaintiff; and (3) a foreigner with extraterritorial rights sued a foreigner without extraterritorial rights.[82] Thus the SBA managed to win what it wanted most: the rendition excluded foreign lawyers from Chinese civil cases. As noted earlier, another important gain for the Shanghai Bar was the extension of its authority into the International Settlement and over all Chinese lawyers appearing at the Provisional Court.

The rendition agreement did not completely remove the foreign control over the court. Under the agreement, the Jiangsu provincial government would appoint the president and the judges of the Provisional Court. It would also approve the court sentences ranging from imprisonment of ten years and above to the death penalty. In Chinese cases relating to the order and the regulations of the International Settlement or involving any Chinese hired by foreigners with extraterritorial rights, foreign consuls were to appoint a deputy to the court, who could not question defendants and witnesses without a Chinese judge's consent and could not interfere with sentences. On the other hand, the chief clerk

---

79. Ibid.
80. *Shanghai Zhonghua Minguo Kuaiji Shi Gonghui Nianbao* (1928), p.58.
81. NCH, 10/2/1926, p.18; A. M. Kotenev, *Shanghai*, pp.181–83; George W. Keeton, *The Development*, Vol.1, pp.393–95. For the Chinese version of the agreement, see SB, 1926: 9/28, p.3; FP, No.171 (1926: 10/10):16–18.
82. *North China Daily News*, 1927: Jan. 1, p.13; A. M. Kotenev, *Shanghai*, pp.184–86; George W. Keeton, *The Development*, Vol.1, p.396.

of the court was to be recommended, and the clerk's replacement approved, by the consular leader. The court police and the court prison remained under the control of the SMC Police Commission. The rendition turned out to be a partial one.

The continued ambiguity as to who was the ultimate authority at the Provisional Court was bound to create problems for the operation of the court and proved to be a source of concern and frustration for all parties concerned. On the one hand, the foreign deputies sitting in the court frequently complained about the interference in cases tried at the court from the Chinese military and civilian authorities and protested against the rulings made by Chinese judges, especially after the GMD took over Shanghai in the spring of 1927.[83] On the other hand, the court police provided by the SMC would fail to carry out a Chinese judge's order or injunction, the court prison guards would refuse to allow Chinese lawyers to meet with defendants in detention, and a foreign deputy would interfere in court proceedings without a Chinese judge's consent.[84]

A typical incident took place in the spring of 1929. During a trial on February 23, a Chinese lawyer failed to follow a Chinese judge's order. Before the judge made further move, Van den Berg, a Dutch diplomat appointed by the Consular Body as a deputy to the court, suspended the lawyer from practicing and had the lawyer removed from the courtroom by the court police. That action had no legal ground under either the 1926 rendition agreement or the 1868 agreement by which the Mixed Court was originally established. After Chinese protests, Van den Berg rescinded his suspension order but insisted on bringing formal charges against the lawyer in question for his misconduct outside the court that day. The SMC duly pressed charges against the lawyer, but a Chinese judge simply dismissed the case after the first hearing.

He Shizhen, the president of the Provisional Court since August 1928, lodged a protest to the Consular Body, demanding that Van den Berg be replaced, that the deputies to the court respect the authority of Chinese judges, and that no such incident occur in the future. On his part, Edwin Cunningham, American consul general serving as the leader of the Consular Body, defended Van den Berg and refused to replace him. In the meantime, under He's instruction, Chinese judges announced a boycott

---

83. NCH, 12/21/1928, p.366; 1/26/1929, p.164; 2/2/1929, p.191; 2/16/1929, p.274; 3/9/1929, p.410; 11/2/1929, p.185; 11/16/1929, p.256; 12/14/1929, p.436; 12/31/1929; 1/14/1930, p.61; George W. Keeton, *The Development*, Vol.1, pp.396–400.
84. SLGB, No.24, pp.16, 17; No.26, pp.4, 6, 11, 12, 16, 17, 33; NCH, 12/28/1929, p.511.

against Van den Berg. Judge Gu adjourned all cases that would otherwise have been tried with Van den Berg sitting in the court.⁸⁵

The SBA acted vigorously to demand a redress of the violation of the rendition agreement by Van den Berg. While contacting other public associations in Shanghai to take concerted action, the Shanghai Bar communicated its position to the Consular Body, Provisional Court, Ministry of Justice, provincial government, and SBA members. It demanded that Van den Berg be removed as a deputy to the court and that foreign consuls promise to prevent similar incidents in the future. All SBA members were advised that should they ever encounter foreign consuls usurping the authority of Chinese courts, they should refuse to proceed until the situation was rectified.⁸⁶

In the end, in order to allow the court to operate normally, He Shizhen and Edwin Cunningham reached an agreement that the matter would be settled by talks between the Chinese commissioner of foreign affairs and Cunningham. The boycott against Van den Berg ceased in early April.⁸⁷ The general problem from which the incident resulted remained, however. Incidents of a foreign deputy interfering with a Chinese judge's ruling continued to occur frequently at the court.⁸⁸

Further Recovery of Judicial Rights

Three years of experience proved that the Provisional Court could not function properly as a judicial organ. As the rendition agreement approached expiration at the end of 1929, the SBA advocated a complete integration of the court into the Chinese judicial system. The Shanghai Bar organized a Judicial Rights Recovery Committee and urged the national government to effect the integration of the courts in Shanghai's foreign concessions.

Nanjing was not unconcerned with the matter. More nationalistic in its outlook than the Beiyang regimes it replaced, the GMD government was determined to assert China's sovereignty, though it lacked adequate means to achieve the goal. On May 8, 1929, the Ministry of Foreign Affairs notified the ministers of the United States, Great Britain, France, Netherlands, Norway, and Brazil that China intended to reorganize the

---

85. NCH, 3/9/1929, p.410; 3/16/1929, p.441; 3/23/1929, p.486; 3/30/1929, p.527.
86. SLGB, No.25 (July 1929), pp.9–12; NCH, 5/11/1929, p.230; Frank Ching, *Ancestors*, pp.422–24.
87. NCH, 4/6/1929, p.17.   88. NCH, 4/6/1929, p.17; 12/28/1929, p.511.

Provisional Court that was out of place in the national system. In June the Shanghai commissioner of foreign affairs formally informed the foreign consuls that the Chinese government deemed it inappropriate to renew the rendition agreement. The negotiations over the issue started on December 9, 1929.[89]

The SBA once again engaged the government to influence the negotiations. On December 5 the Shanghai Bar sent a message to the Ministries of Justice and of Foreign Affairs proposing unilateral reorganization of the Provisional Court at the expiration of the rendition agreement. The Shanghai Bar put forward eight goals the reorganization should achieve. Tan Yigong and Li Shirui, two of the SBA executive committee members, traveled to Nanjing to sell their plan to the two ministers.[90]

One week later, while the negotiations were under way, the Shanghai Bar made another proposal to the Foreign Affairs and Justice Ministries. The government might make concessions on the issue of a foreign deputy's observation in a trial involving foreign interests or foreigners, but it should never allow foreign consuls or the SMC to interfere with the administrative and appointive power of the court. At the same time, the ESC decided that in public the Shanghai Bar would continue to insist on its earlier position.[91] On December 25 the SBA followed up with a third message to the two ministries. In the past three years, it said, the judicial system suffered most from the foreign deputy's usurpation of court authority and the refusal of the SMC-controlled court police and court prison to execute the court's orders. Those two biggest obstacles should be removed by all means. And the French Mixed Court should be reclaimed at the same time.[92]

How the opinions of the SBA influenced the government position is unknown, but the result of the negotiations appears to have satisfied some of the SBA's demands. After relatively speedy negotiations between Nanjing and the foreign ministers, the Agreement on the Chinese Court in Shanghai's International Settlement was signed on February 17, 1930, and became effective on April 1, 1930.[93] Under the

89. NCH, 4/29/1929, p.144; 5/25/1929, p.307; 7/20/1929, p.93; 12/21/1929, p.467; 12/31/1929, p.546; Fei Chengkang, *Zhongguo*, pp.154–55.
90. SLGB, No.26 (Jan. 1930), pp.84–86, 91–93.
91. SLGB, No.26, pp.31–32.   92. SLGB, No.26, pp.86–88.
93. NCH, 2/25/1930, p.301; for Chinese version of the agreement, see SB, 1930: 2/19, p.6; GZG, No.408 (1930: 5/1), pp.6–8; ZMXFD (1934), pp.1128–29.

agreement, the Provisional Court became the First Special District Court where Chinese laws were fully applied. A new Jiangsu High Court Second Branch (in the same building) was established as its appellate court. All judges and court officials were to be appointed by the Chinese judicial authorities. The practice of foreign deputies sitting in the court was abolished. But the officers and members of judicial police for the court were to be appointed by the president of the branch high court "upon the recommendation of the Municipal Council" and subject to dismissal by the president "at the request of the Municipal Council."[94]

The Shanghai Bar lost no time to push the government to recover the French Mixed Court.[95] Probably to forestall the Chinese government action, on January 25, 1930, the French Consul-General Edgar Koechlin initiated a reorganization of the French Mixed Court that would allow the Chinese magistrate to try Chinese criminal cases without an assessor sitting in the court.[96] But such a measure was no longer enough to please the Chinese. Nanjing made it clear to the French that the Mixed Court in the French Concession had to be abolished and replaced by a Chinese court.[97] Realizing the time had come, the French did not try to resist. On July 28, 1931, the agreement on the French Mixed Court was signed. The court was changed into the Second Special District Court and the Jiangsu High Court Third Branch. Judges and court officials of both courts were to be appointed by the Chinese authorities. Like the courts in the International Settlement, however, the officers of the judicial police and the court personnel were to be appointed by the Branch High Court upon the recommendation of the authority of the French Concession.[98]

As for the status of foreign lawyers, both the agreement on the courts in the International Settlement and that on the courts in the French Concession provided that foreign lawyers could practice in the courts in cases involving foreigners or foreign interests. But they were subject to the evaluation, licensing, supervision, and disciplinary procedures administered by the Ministry of Justice just as were their Chinese counterparts.

---

94. NCH, 2/25/1930, p.301.
95. SLGB, No.29 (Aug. 1931), pp.27, 30, 133–34; NCH, 3/4/1930, p.345.
96. NCH, 2/11/1930, p.219.   97. NCH, 3/25/1930, p.476; 6/2/1930, p.298.
98. NCH, 8/4/1930, p.148; for the Chinese version of the agreement, see SB, 1931: 7/30, p.5; ZMXFD (1934), pp.1130–31.

By April 1930 eleven foreign lawyers had been licensed – including Flora Rosemberg from France, the first foreign female lawyer licensed to practice in the Chinese courts in the International Settlement.[99] In September 1930, at the suggestion of Xu Weizhen – who was appointed the president of the Jiangsu High Court Second Branch – the Ministry of Justice ordered that a lawyers' disciplinary committee be created in the Second Branch to oversee foreign and Chinese lawyers practicing in the International Settlement. Thus the Chinese regulation of foreign lawyers was finally institutionalized.[100]

Although the rendition of the courts was still a bit less than complete in view of the concession authorities' role in the appointment of judicial police, the overall outcome was an unqualified victory for the Shanghai Bar. Foreign lawyers lost many of their privileges and were limited to practicing in cases involving foreigners only. The Shanghai Bar had successfully extended its professional authority in the foreign concessions. Fittingly, in anticipation of the expansion of its authority and operation, the Shanghai Bar bought a building at 572 Rue de Admiral Bayle (*Huangpi nanlu*) in the French Concession as its headquarters and moved into the new offices in October 1929.[101]

The professionalization of Chinese lawyers was a complex process in which the evolution of Chinese judicial and legal practices and the presence of Western dominance in Shanghai intersected. The Shanghai Bar's role in the movement to reclaim the Mixed Court shows that the self-interest of a particular social group in Chinese society was intertwined with the nationalist cause and that such a group was motivated by both to engage in what is called the "nationalist movement." During the movement to reclaim the Mixed Court, the government at both the national and provincial levels was quite receptive and responsive to the opinions of the Shanghai Bar and other urban associations and did not reject the active role of the SBA in the matter. This was actually a recognition of the publicness of the Shanghai Bar, delineating an area where the state and societal institutions could and did work together for nationalist purposes, even though such purposes served the professional interests of lawyers as well. Lawyers were able to play an important role in the matter of the Mixed Court, partly because the issue concerned the judi-

---

99. CWR, 52,9 (4/26/1930):326.
100. SB, 1930: 9/5, p.5; Guo Wei and Zhou Dingmei, *Lushi Banshi Shouxu*, pp.38–39.
101. SLGB, No.26, p.18.

cial system and thus was considered within the purview of the legal profession. When the Shanghai Bar began to assert a public role beyond legal and judicial issues, a different dynamics took place, which is the topic of Chapter 9.

9

Professionalism and Politics

The Shanghai Bar Association (II)

THE Shanghai Bar Association was a professional organization sanctioned by the Republican government from the beginning, and thus a legally established association (*fatuan*) or public association (*gongtuan*). The status of professional association was essential for the legitimacy of the organization, especially during the Nanjing Decade, as the government strictly regulated social associations and relentlessly suppressed real or perceived subversive organizations in society. The Shanghai Bar Association did start out for professional purposes, as shown in Chapter 8. Since the Regulations on Lawyers of 1912 and 1927 prohibited bar associations from undertaking matters beyond judicial affairs, the Shanghai Bar's activities mostly aimed at the professionalization of lawyers, the recovery of the nation's judicial rights, and the establishment of the rule of law and judicial independence in the country. Yet, if professionalization per se was an apolitical goal, the demand for the rule of law and judicial independence often challenged the practices of the authorities and thus assumed political meanings. Furthermore, if the demand for the rule of law and judicial independence could be defended as judicial issues and therefore professional concerns for lawyers, the same could not be said of the actions directed at national politics and the government's foreign policies. It is these two areas, however, that the Shanghai Bar Association found itself being drawn into in the 1920s and 1930s. Why was the bar compelled to play a political role? How did it justify its actions on political issues in the public arena? What strategies and tactics were used? How did the government respond and how did the association adjust to the responses? In answering these questions, this chapter points to a concrete form and a specific avenue that a social group chose to interact with the state – political action through professional association.

BETWEEN PROFESSIONALISM AND POLITICS

Professional Purpose over Political Impulse

Article 30 of the 1912 Provisional Regulations on Lawyers and Article 32 of the 1927 Regulations on Lawyers explicitly forbade bar associations to take action on matters other than those relating to the judicial system. Bar associations, therefore, were not supposed to concern themselves with political issues. For the most part the Shanghai Bar complied with those provisions, but did so not without some difficulties as Shanghai repeatedly proved to be the center of political agitation and movement.

The May Fourth Movement of 1919 was the first political movement during which the Shanghai Bar was taken to the task of making a public stand. The movement was precipitated by the failure of the Chinese delegation at the Paris Peace Conference to reclaim the former German leasehold in Shandong Province from the Japanese. On May 4, 1919, indignant college and middle school students in Beijing started demonstrations and sacked the house of a government official who was held responsible for China's diplomatic failure. As a result, some students were arrested, but more demonstrations and anti-Japanese boycotts were organized in cities across the country. Shanghai became one of the important scenes where demonstrations were held and boycotts carried out.[1]

Amidst the political excitement that permeated most public associations in Shanghai, the SBA was discreet. On May 7, 1919, the Shanghai Bar telegraphed the Ministry of Justice asking for a fair trial of the students arrested in Beijing. It also requested that the Beijing Bar Association help defend the students in court.[2] Apart from those two telegrams, the SBA did nothing. While individual lawyers might have shared the nationalist sentiment and expressed their views as citizens, the Shanghai Bar as a professional association was clearly not prepared to jump into the political water. The opinions it offered to the government were safely within the limits of judicial matters. The cautiousness that the Shanghai Bar exercised may be understood as necessary self-protection.

The Shanghai Bar exercised similar caution on other occasions. In 1922 the Hangxian Bar Association proposed to the SBA that they together

---

1. Joseph Chen, *The May Fourth Movement in Shanghai* (Leiden, 1971).
2. SB, 1919: 5/7, p.5.

initiate a conference to be attended by delegates from several provinces for a discussion of the political situation in the country. The SBA's councilors resolved, however, that there was no lack of political organizations in the country and that it was not appropriate for bar associations to initiate political actions.[3] In contrast, when the Hangxian Bar suggested an alternative – a national judicial conference – and when the idea was supported by other bar associations in the country, the SBA did not shy away from organizing such a conference (see Chapter 8).

In early 1925 the Shanghai Daily Newspapers Association and three other publishing trade associations launched a campaign against the censorship regulations on printed matter proposed by the SMC (see Chapter 6). They called upon all major public associations in Shanghai to show solidarity with them. The SBA once again struggled between its willingness to support the campaign and its overriding concern to comply with the Regulations on Lawyers. Finally, the Shanghai Bar resolved to send a councilor to the four organizations to explain that as prohibited by the Regulations on Lawyers, the SBA could not send telegrams to the central government on the issue, but that individuals in the association supported their cause and were willing to help.[4]

A greater challenge to the Shanghai Bar was presented by the May Thirtieth Movement of 1925. In the wake of the shooting death of eleven Chinese students by the municipal police of the International Settlement on May 30, 1925, Shanghai was turned into the primary scene of the nationalist movement that spread to the rest of the country. In the midst of antiimperialist statements, manifestos, rallies, demonstrations, and boycotts sponsored by various public associations in Shanghai, the Shanghai Bar was conspicuously silent. The silence did not go unnoticed. A certain Wang Juwei wrote twice to the editor of the *Shi Bao* on June 5 and 8. Wang asked why the SBA should have remained reticent at a time when all social groups ought to be demonstrating national solidarity. Wang urged the Shanghai Bar to take a stand and help the victims of the incident.[5]

Perhaps in response to such criticisms, Wang Kaijiang, a councilor of the SBA, acted. On June 6 and 7 Wang put forward a proposal on the course of action the Shanghai Bar should take. "Although this association should obey the law [of being nonpolitical], at the time of such extraordinary events, it is duty-bound to offer assistance." In his view, the Shanghai Bar could do the following: collect the evidence needed to help

3. SLGB, No.6 (1922), p.3.   4. SB, 1925: 5/4, p.4.   5. SB, 1925: 6/5, p.4; 6/8, p.4.

the government seek a legal settlement; start a movement to reclaim judicial rights in the International Settlement; and offer volunteer legal defense to arrested Chinese.[6]

On June 9, after Wang Juwei's second letter to the *Shi Bao*, the SBA came up with a public telegram sent to the central government, the provincial government, and the Shanghai municipal government. The telegram was not nearly as inflammatory as other public discourses among the Chinese at the time. Instead it contained a legal argument that the May Thirtieth Incident was not to be explained away as a self-defense on the part of the municipal police.[7] That the telegram was published at all was probably a public gesture of the Shanghai Bar in support of the Shanghai people rather than an effort to advise the government. It turned out to be the only public expression of the SBA's position during the movement. In all the preceding examples, the Shanghai Bar apparently behaved with a keen sense of what it could do legitimately as a professional organization and what it could not.

Political Actions through a Surrogate

The stance of the Shanghai Bar during the May Thirtieth Movement demonstrated the dilemma faced by the association when intense nationalist fervor in the country demanded that it take a public stand. Whether the SBA was overly cautious is difficult to say, but some of its members grew increasingly uncomfortable and impatient with their inability to play a political role. In the early 1920s the political disintegration of the country caused by strife among warlords and political factions disappointed the educated elite and the general public. Some Shanghai lawyers felt an urge to step into the political arena somehow, if not for other reasons, simply because they believed that as legal experts they were most qualified to find a formula to end the political chaos in the country.

At a meeting on July 15, 1923, a group of SBA members came to the conclusion that under the Regulations on Lawyers, the Shanghai Bar was in no position to influence the political scene and that a new organization was needed for lawyers to make a contribution in the political area. At the meeting Zhang Yipeng, the president of the SBA, gave a speech on the political problems in the country and possible solutions. People

---

6. SB, 1925: 6/6, p.4; 6/7, p.3.   7. SB, 1925: 6/9, p.3.

should, said Zhang, leave aside the political disorder at the national level and concentrate instead on solving the problems at the provincial level by making provincial constitutions. "When every province has its own constitution, even if the central [government] is in disorder, it will have no impact on provinces. If the Provisional Constitution is overthrown, the whole country will sink into a lawless situation. But if it is to be upheld, there are many difficulties in implementing it. If each province makes its own constitution, it does not violate the Provisional Constitution and will have swift and proper result."[8] Zhang's speech laid down the agenda for the proposed new organization.

Three days later the Society for Promoting the Rule of Law (SPRL) (*fazhi xiejin hui*) was founded by sixteen politically active SBA members. The bylaws of the society stated that its mission was to discuss political issues and promote the rule of law and that its membership was limited to lawyers only.[9]

The relationship between the SBA and the SPRL was a close one. The leaders of the two organizations were actually the same group of lawyers. Zhang Yipeng and Zhang Jiazhen were the president and vice-president of the SBA. Xi Yuchang, Wang Kaijiang, Tang Yingsong, Qin Liankui, Cai Nipei, and a few others were current or past or future councilors of the SBA. All these people served as directors (*lishi*) of the SPRL. Wang Kaijiang was its most active member and was responsible for a number of proposals adopted by the organization. For all practical purposes, the SPRL was a surrogate of the SBA and its task was to do what the lawyers could not in the name of the Shanghai Bar. The lawyers in the SPRL were both politically active and innovative, trying to influence the nation's political future by acting through a surrogate. The political culture that had developed in Shanghai made the task relatively easy – an association with professed public purpose such as promoting the rule of law could legitimately act on political issues in the public arena. By channeling their political initiatives through the SPRL, the lawyers avoided endangering their professional association.

The formation of the new organization gave lawyers much liberty to speak out their views on social and political matters. In 1923 to 1924 the SPRL published its opinions on a number of issues. The SPRL denied the legitimacy of the parliament in Beijing that voted to prolong its own tenure; it proposed more reforms in the judicial system; and it advocated

---

8. SB, 1923: 7/16, p.5.   9. SB, 1925: 7/19, p.5.

universal education on ethics in educational institutions across the country.[10] By far the most prominent, however, was the society's stand on the issue of making a provincial constitution. Established in the name of promoting the rule of law, the SPRL centered its work on a provincial constitution, which fit lawyers' professional concerns and expertise. In September 1923 Wang Kaijiang submitted the following proposal:

> The parliament's tenure has now expired; a president has not been chosen; the chief executive [*zhizheng*, the title of Duan Qirui] was not legitimate and his tenure has expired too. Legally, there is no central government to speak of. This is the best opportunity for the people to remake the nation. We citizens ought to rise to the occasion and change the course [of our history]. With the spirit of a democratic state system, all citizens, upon whom sovereignty rests, [ought to] on their own initiative put an end to the disorderly situation and make plans for long-term peace and stability. For expediency, it is better to address facts than to talk about law. The starting point is that this society unites other associations to form a joint conference, which lays down a plan for a multiprovincial congress, and convenes the congress according to the plan to make a multiprovincial constitution.... Before that constitution is made, each province should make its own provincial constitution. Such seems to be the way to achieve the goal of fundamental reconstruction.[11]

At Wang's suggestion, the society decided to work immediately on the scheme of bringing about a Jiangsu provincial constitution and contact other public associations for initiating a congress to draft a provincial constitution. The organizations to be contacted included the Shanghai General Chamber of Commerce, Jiangsu Provincial Assembly, Jiangsu Educational Society, Jiangsu Agricultural Society, all county chambers of commerce, county educational societies, county agricultural societies, labor unions, and local bar associations in Jiangsu Province.[12] This was but one example of communications and connections among public associations in and beyond Shanghai and their concerted political actions in the public arena.

The Shanghai Bar received correspondence from the SPRL as well, though the leaders of the two organizations were the same people. On

---

10. SB, 1923: 10/8, p.6; 1924: 2/25, p.5; 4/7, p.5.   11. SB, 1923: 9/16, p.5.
12. SB, 1923: 7/22, p.5; 7/30, p.5; 8/13, p.5.

August 26 the SBA councilors unanimously passed a resolution to support the SPRL's initiative. The SBA also received a letter from another organization called the Jiangsu Society (*su she*) addressing the same issue.[13] The SBA gave a very supportive response to the Jiangsu Society. Under the Provisional Constitution, went the SBA's letter, the sovereignty rested with the people. It was therefore not incumbent upon the provincial assembly alone to make a provincial constitution. The SBA wholeheartedly supported the initiative of other public associations in advocating a provincial constitution at a time of national crisis.[14]

The idea of a provincial constitution was part of the movement for provincial autonomy and a federal republic at that time.[15] But it did not prove viable. In any case, it was soon overshadowed by the rising tide of a nationalist movement in the wake of the May Thirtieth Incident. In early 1926 there were sporadic activities to revive the provincial constitution movement and the SBA even elected its delegates to a constitution-making convention.[16] But with the advent in the summer of 1926 of the Northern Expedition aiming to unify the country under a single national government, the movement for a provincial constitution fizzled out quietly. The SPRL disappeared with the issue.

The experience of Shanghai lawyers in the movement of a provincial constitution is historically important. Besides the organizational innovation that allowed the Shanghai Bar members to play a political role, note how these lawyers commented on the country's political situation from a legal point of view and employed such notions as "democratic state system" and "sovereign rests with citizens." All this served to push the

---

13. The Su She was an organization of Jiangsu gentry-merchants and gentry-managers. Its agenda was to lobby the government to pursue certain policies and carry out certain reforms concerning the Jiangsu Province. See SnB, 1921: 6/16, p.10; 9/22, p.14.
14. SB, 1923: 8/27, p.6.
15. For the currency of this idea at the time, see "Provincial Home Rule in China," NCH, 11/6/1920, pp.387–88; "Federated States of China," NCH, 12/11/1920; Rodney Gilbert, "China's Search for Peace," NCH, 1/26/1924, pp.150–51; Upton Close (G. W. Hall), "Reunification Awaits Peking's Acceptance of Provincial Autonomy," CWR, 21,5 (7/1/1922):167; "Self-Government for the Provinces of China," CWR, 21,13 (8/26/1922):481–82; J. J. Heeren, "The Drift toward Federalism: A Step toward China's National Unity," CWR, 22,10 (11/4/1922):331–32. Also see Ernest P. Young, *The Presidency of Yuan Shih-k'ai*, pp.19–25; Prasenjit Duara, "Provincial Narratives of the Nation: Centralism and Federalism in Republican China," in Harmi Befu, ed., *Cultural Nationalism in East Asia: Representation and Identity* (Berkeley, 1993), pp.9–35; Edward McCord, *The Power of the Gun*.
16. SB, 1926: 6/28, p.4.

idea of a provincial constitution as the best solution to the country's political problem. These lawyers expected themselves to play a large role as legal experts in the making of a provincial constitution. More significantly, these lawyers complied with the regulations from Beijing on the legal profession to maintain their professional status, thus helping to maintain the legitimacy of the central government. At the same time they perceived the disappearance of the state as such and were actually helping render Beijing irrelevant. A provincial constitution and a resultant provincial constitutional government would provide a new authority or state power from which the legal profession would obtain recognition. This was how social actors would help define the authority of the state and the reach of state power.

Professional Autonomy and Political Control

From the viewpoint of Shanghai lawyers, legal professionalization should not only entail the establishment of the profession's privilege in society, but its bar association should also be independent of the political control of the state. To be sure, the Shanghai Bar was never entirely independent since the legal profession was licensed by the government and was intricately involved in the judicial system that was part of the state apparatus. Yet this unique but ill-defined position of the legal profession in judicial process gave the SBA certain leverage to resist some forms of control imposed by the state. During the Beiyang period the SBA enjoyed a wider functional space, because the regulatory framework set by the Provisional Regulations on Lawyers and directives from the Ministry of Justice was of professional nature. In contrast, the GMD was bent on imposing systematic control over all societal organizations, including professional associations. The regulatory framework was not only professionally but also politically defined.

As noted in Chapter 3, during the Nanjing Decade, all societal organizations in Shanghai were required to register with a GMD party organ and with the Bureau of Education or the Bureau of Social Affairs. In October 1930 the Mass Training Committee of the MPH sent the SBA a notice saying that the association was a "correct and healthy" one, but that it had failed to apply for the permission from and register with the committee, in accordance with the regulations on social associations.[17] It asked the Shanghai Bar to comply immediately. In response, the SBA

---

17. For the regulations, see Chapter 3.

wrote to the committee, arguing that the Shanghai Bar was different in nature from other social associations:

> The legal profession is established according to the organic law of courts, and as one of the three professions within the judicial system, it is different from other ordinary legitimate occupations in society. Lawyers' qualification to practice is recognized through the evaluation and licensing by the Ministry of Justice Selection Committee, by the registration with the high court, and by the admission into the bar association. The agencies that supervise it are the Ministry of Justice and the Lawyer's Disciplinary Committee. In performing its duty the profession is subject to no direction or supervision of any superior offices, so as to maintain its spirit of professional independence and allow lawyers to protect human rights according to the law, in the same way as parliament members in session are subject to no outside interference. The bar association organized on such basis, therefore, is on a different legal footing from other social associations organized in an ordinary way.... Before the national government changes the Regulations on Lawyers or instructs it to do so, it is not proper for this association to apply for the permission.[18]

Illustrative of the relationship between the GMD party and the government, the Ministry of Justice ruled that although different from other voluntary associations, bar associations were subject to the direction of the party headquarters in the matter of carrying out the party doctrine.[19] In the end, the SBA registered wtih the Shanghai County Party Headquarters in 1931, thus complying with the GMD regulations but deliberately slighting the MPH.

Furthermore, the preceding correspondence from the Shanghai Bar is an important document. For one thing, it demonstrates the Shanghai Bar's understanding and defense of its professional autonomy. It went beyond the question of getting permission from the MPH, which the Shanghai Bar would have no problem doing successfully. Instead, it articulated the legitimacy of the legal profession and of the Shanghai Bar and it argued for lawyers' freedom from the control of the GMD party machine in such broad terms as professional independence and protection of human rights. The use of such language was of no

---

18. SLGB, No.28 (Jan. 1930), pp.132–33.
19. Guo Wei and Zhou Dingmei, *Lushi Banshi Shouxu*, p.33.

small significance in the Chinese context of that time. More importantly, the Shanghai Bar's argument underscores the unique but ill-defined position of the legal profession and bar associations vis-à-vis both the state and society. The Shanghai Bar clearly claimed to be part of the judicial system and thus part of the state apparatus, which was arguably true at least to some extent. Yet it made this claim to ward off a certain form of control coming from the GMD party that was even more indistinguishable from the state. At the same time, the Shanghai Bar often assumed the stance of representing society at large against government policy and action.

After the SBA was reorganized in 1927, the *North China Herald* reported that the executive committee members of the new association were all GMD members, implying that the SBA was controlled by the GMD.[20] Relying on the *Herald*, Alison W. Conner has referred to this as the "capture" of the Shanghai Bar by the GMD party.[21] Yet, the historical scene was more complex than that. Although the group that took over the SBA's leadership in 1927 was backed by the MPH and the PCSB, those people, most of whom would dominate the ESC for years to come, were not necessarily following the political will of the MPH. They might as well have utilized the MPH to serve their own purpose in the 1927 takeover. The resistance in 1930 to the MPH and other instances discussed in this chapter show the limits of the GMD control over the association. In other words, the SBA's role should be defined not only by whether the MPH supervised it, but also by whether the SBA could and would act against the will of the GMD party-state even under that supervision.

Professional Concerns and Political Implications

Judicial issues often had political implications. For the Shanghai Bar to insist on the rule of law and due process would inevitably confront the state that did not practice those principles it accepted in rhetoric. To minimize the political risk involved when it spoke against government practices in the judicial process, the Shanghai Bar advocated its views on judicial issues by appealing to nationalist goals. Since after the rendition of the Mixed Courts in 1927 and 1930, the Nanjing government contin-

---

20. NCH, 8/25/1928, pp.329–30.
21. Alison W. Connor, "Lawyers and the Legal Profession during the Republican Period," p.244.

ued to seek the abolition of extraterritoriality, the SBA used that goal to justify the necessity of practicing the rule of law and judicial independence. The Shanghai Bar frequently petitioned the GMD government for justice on behalf of political prisoners who were mistreated by prison guards, or on behalf of ordinary people who were executed without trial by the military for allegedly being Communists. As far as the Shanghai Bar was concerned, however, nothing was more objectionable than the Emergency Law on Crimes against the Republic.

Enacted on January 31, 1931, the Emergency Law on Crimes against the Republic was an instrument for the GMD party-state to eliminate political enemies. It provided the death penalty and heavy prison terms (fifteen years to life) for anyone who would disturb public order or instigate others to do so and for anyone who would organize assemblies or associations or publicize ideology incompatible with the Three Principles of the People to harm the Republic. Under the emergency law, the military apparatus in martial law areas and the special courts made up of county magistrates and county trial officers in "bandit-suppressing" areas were authorized to try those accused.[22]

The arbitrary nature of the law invited strong opposition from lawyers. Within four months of the enactment of the law, the SBA called for an amendment of it. In the SBA's view, the emergency law broke apart judicial authority, destroyed the hierarchical structure of the trial system, and left the heaviest sentence in the hands of county magistrates and county trial officers who had no legal training. The Shanghai Bar proposed to amend the law in the following five terms: (1) Except under special circumstances, trials under the emergency law would be public; (2) except in war zones, such trials would allow legal defense for defendants; (3) all sentences would be reported to and approved by a superior court or office; (4) defendants in such cases would be allowed to appeal; and (5) an expiration date would be set for the law.[23] Obviously, the SBA opposed the emergency law from a narrow legal point of view. In such political environment as the Shanghai Bar found itself, it was in no position to argue whether political activity was criminal in the first place. What it tried to do was to restore some semblance of due process even in cases prosecuted under the emergency law and to provide legal protection for the defendants as much as possible.

22. ZMXFD (1936), p.5549; FZ, No.32 (1931: 2/11).
23. SLGB, No.29 (Aug. 1931), pp.32–33, 55–56.

In December 1931 the executive committee of the Shanghai Bar sent a telegram to the GMD Fourth Central Committee First Plenum demanding that a national judicial conference be convened, the emergency law annulled, trial organs other than courts of law dissolved, and all defendants except soldiers tried by civilian courts only.[24] Thus the Shanghai Bar stepped up its demand from amending the law to annulling it. The National Bar Association (*quanguo lushi xiehui*) – founded in 1929 – took up the demand and addressed it to the Ministry of Justice in 1932.[25] In early 1935 the GMD government enacted a new criminal code. The SBA took the opportunity to intensify its drive for the annulment of the emergency law. In February 1935 the SBA contacted other bar associations in the country to take joint action.[26] They sent the Ministry of Justice a petition asking that the central government annul all special criminal laws, including the emergency law, because the new criminal code was in force. The Justice Ministry passed the petition on to the GMD Central Political Council and that was the end of the matter. The emergency law was never annulled. Contrary to the lawyers' demand, in September 1937, after the Japanese invasion had started, the GMD amended the emergency law to impose more severe punishment for the offenses under the law.[27]

Although the SBA's drive to annul the emergency law failed to achieve its goal, the drive shows the possibility of the legal profession protesting against government action on legal and judicial issues in a rather restricted public arena. The political implications of opposing the emergency law were obvious. For ordinary citizens, the opposition itself could be readily accused of harming the Republic under the very law being questioned. The Shanghai Bar's bold calls for amending and repealing the law testified to its commitment to judicial independence and due process. On the other hand, the fact that it suffered no reprisal from the government demonstrates that the legal profession and bar associations could say and do what other social organizations could not do. The SBA fully utilized its position of legitimacy to advocate the principle of the rule of law on every occasion. In that situation the professional interests of lawyers were a less important factor.

---

24. SLGB, No.30 (April 1932), p.34.
25. SB, 1932: 1/19, p.4; SLGB, No.31 (June 1933), pp.23–24.
26. SLGB, No.33 (July 1935), pp.45, 49; SnB, 1935: 3/11, p.10.
27. SnB, 1937: 9/5, p.2.

INTO THE POLITICS OF NATIONAL SALVATION

A Turning Point for the SBA

The Shanghai Bar Association was able to create a surrogate – the SPRL – to carry out its political agenda in the 1920s, because the Beiyang government did not have systematic regulations on public associations. Under the GMD rule, however, neither government regulations nor party surveillance would have allowed an SPRL to survive. Shanghai lawyers knew the situation well and they did not attempt to form such an organization. In the first three years of the Nanjing decade, the reorganized SBA displayed little interest in political issues, while concentrating on judicial issues even though some of those issues (for example, the emergency law) also had political implications.

It is the Manchurian Incident of 1931 and the feeble response of the government that gave rise to a new upsurge of the Chinese nationalist movement that engulfed the SBA and other social groups. The Manchurian Incident was the culmination of a long-planned scheme of aggression on the part of the Japanese military forces – the Kwantung Army – in Manchuria. On the night of September 18, 1931, the Japanese blew up a piece of rail track of the Japanese-owned Southern Manchurian Railway. Blaming Chinese troops for the explosion, the Kwantung Army launched an attack on the city of Mukden. Helped by the nonresistance policy of Nanjing and the ineffectual action of the League of Nations, Japanese forces completed the occupation of all Manchuria by January 1932. In that month the Japanese spread the hostilities to Shanghai. In part to retaliate for the anti-Japanese activities of the Shanghai people and in part to share the glory of the Japanese army's feat in Manchuria, on January 28, 1932, the Japanese marines began the offensive against Chinese troops in Shanghai. To the surprise of the Japanese, the Chinese Nineteenth Route Army offered fierce resistance. While receiving enthusiastic support from the Shanghai people, the Chinese troops were not backed by Nanjing. After three months of bloody fighting and the nearly total destruction of the Chinese areas of the city by Japanese bombardment, a cease-fire was arranged in March and a truce was signed in early May through the good office of Western diplomats in Shanghai.[28]

---

28. For details of the Manchurian Incident and the Shanghai hostilities, see Sara M. Smith, *The Manchurian Crisis, 1931–1932* (New York, 1948); Sadako N. Ogata, *Defiance in Manchuria: The Making of Japanese Foreign Policy* (Berkeley, 1964).

Professionalism and Politics

Compared with the nationalist movement of the 1920s, the anti-Japanese national salvation movement of the 1930s carried with it an unusual sense of crisis and urgency. While the earlier movement went against foreign privileges in China dating back to the mid-nineteenth century, the anti-Japanese movement was to save the very national entity of China. The Japanese aggression set off a tidal wave of nationalist fervor among the Chinese. All social groups in the country were spurred into action. From September 18 to December 30, 1931, over one hundred national salvation organizations were formed in all walks of life in Shanghai. During the same period, public associations and newly founded national salvation societies in Shanghai held no less than 138 public rallies and issued at least 532 declarations and circular telegrams, publicly expressing disapproval of Nanjing's Japan policy and demanding resistance against Japanese aggression. Of those statements and telegrams, 217 were from the industrial and commercial sectors, 94 from students, 61 from workers, 40 from educators, and 18 from the cultural circle.[29] Even the GMD party organizations in Shanghai, including the MPH, published circular telegrams to the Party Center urging the unity of the party and government and the recovery of lost territory in Manchuria.[30]

The Shanghai Bar was among the most vocal participants in the national salvation movement. On September 25, six days after the Japanese attack on Mukden, the ESC called an emergency meeting. Li Shirui was elected to chair the meeting. Although the Shanghai Bar was not supposed to discuss issues beyond judicial ones, said Li, the Japanese occupation of the Northeastern Provinces was an extraordinary development to which the association had to respond. Keenly aware of the risky nature of the decision to leap into the political water, Cai Nipei suggested that notes of the discussion not be kept. Tang Yingsong disagreed: The Japanese occupation of the Northeastern Provinces was a grave matter and people had been surprised by the silence of the SBA.

At the time the Anti-Japanese National Salvation Society (NSS) (*kangri jiuguo hui*) had been founded in Shanghai and it comprised representatives from various public associations. The organization was

---

29. *Jiuyiba-Yierba Shanghai Junmin Kangri Yundong Shiliao* (Sources on the anti-Japanese resistance movement of the Shanghai military and civilians from September 18 [1931] to January 28 [1932]), pp.112–38.
30. *Jiuyiba-Yierba*, pp.171–73.

trying to work out some collective responses to the Japanese aggression. According to Tang Yingsong, the SBA's delegate to the NSS was handicapped at the NSS meetings because the Shanghai Bar did not have a public stand yet. It was high time, said Tang, for SBA members to come up with sound suggestions to support the government and make a contribution to the nation's cause. The Shanghai Bar did not need to follow the routine rules. Tang's words prevailed. The meeting resolved to convey its position to the government by telegram, to send condolences to refugees from the Northeastern Provinces, to answer the National Bar Association's call for national solidarity, to ask other local bar associations to convene special meetings and address the matter, and to summon all bar members to a special general meeting to discuss further actions.[31] The SBA had crossed a political threshold.

The special general meeting held on September 30 decided on four areas of action for the Shanghai Bar: (1) to do research on the policy toward Japan for the government to consider; (2) to implement an anti-Japanese economic boycott; (3) to organize military volunteers; and (4) to collect and distribute information about the atrocities committed by the Japanese. Four committees were formed – one to deal with each task.[32]

In the following months, the SBA played a visible role in the anti-Japanese nationalist movement. It sent telegrams to the government and the Minister of Foreign Affairs, calling for a hard line at the League of Nations; it published a manifesto on the nation's situation. It telegraphed the Heilongjiang provincial government chairperson, Ma Zhanshan, urging him to fight the Japanese; it asked the Ministry of Foreign Affairs to distribute copies of all international agreements and treaties regarding the Northeastern Provinces for lawyers to study. It prepared and published materials in Chinese and English about the Japanese encroachment upon China. It donated three thousand yuan, and urged its members to donate individually, to the Nineteenth Route Army resisting the Japanese attack in Shanghai. It lodged protests against the Shanghai Municipal Council for prosecuting Chinese who enforced the anti-Japanese boycott and for allowing the Japanese to use the International Settlement for military operations.[33]

What the SBA had done was part of a general outpouring of popular

---

31. SLGB, No.30, pp.9–11.   32. SLGB, No.30, pp.11–16.
33. SLGB, No.30, pp.25, 32, 39, 40.

activism triggered by a sense of national crisis, not a display of antagonism against the state. But as Nanjing continued to appear unresponsive to the public opinion, the Shanghai Bar came to take a critical view of the government. At their meetings SBA leaders began to criticize Nanjing for lack of a consistent foreign policy and for its reluctance to mobilize the people to resist Japan. On December 16 the ESC made a decision to publish a manifesto laying out the SBA's view on the national crisis. Li Shirui was assigned to write the document.[34] Published on December 29, 1931, the manifesto was not just a criticism of Nanjing's policy toward Japan per se, which was no longer uncommon, but a general indictment of the GMD's record during five years of its rule:

> The authorities held the national power in the name of the Guomindang and of the GMD's political doctrine for five years now. As we see it, less than one percent of the GMD's political doctrine has been put into practice. What society has reaped are the disaster of wars, the scourge of bandits, the prevalence of corruption, the failure of all policies, and [now] the deluge – the invasion by a brutal outlaw. The society's [attitude] toward the authorities turned from skepticism to disappointment, from disappointment to grievance and resentment. Today disturbances exist all over the country and all the time. . . . The members of this association, for fear of speaking from an improper position, have never wished to comment on the nation's major policies. But [now the nation is like] a leaking boat in a storm and a collapsing house. Even the perfect man who always keeps his mouth shut cannot escape disaster. Therefore with the sense [that the nation's fate is] everyone's duty, we point out here the fourteen most painful things that the people feel in their hearts. First, the civil war has been going on for years and the people can bear it no more. Second, the people's rights have been denied and the people's opinions cannot be expressed. Third, national territory has been lost and the country broken up. Fourth, clumsy diplomacy has led to international isolation. Fifth, the military system has not been reformed and the national defense has been lax. Sixth, finances have been in disorder and accounting messy: Seventh, measures have been lacking to defuse class struggle. Eighth, no plans have been made to relieve disaster-stricken areas. In addition, we have stagnant

---

34. SLGB, No.30, pp.31–32.

education, a backward economy, a broken judiciary, corrupt officials, clogged transportation, and nonexistent reclamation [of agricultural land]. All these are scourges to the country and the nation.

The manifesto further made other points. The country was called a republic (*minguo*) and the party name was for the citizens (*guomindang*, lit. "citizens' party"), but the people were not allowed to question anything. The government concentrated on civil wars, paying little attention to foreign affairs, which led to international isolation. The government's policy toward workers and peasants only led to the deepening of citizens' suffering. The inequality in life resulted in a class struggle that an anti-Communist campaign was unable to eliminate. The manifesto proposed that Nanjing should allow more input from a wide range of experts to make policy more carefully.[35]

To evaluate the significance of the manifesto, the historical circumstances need to be noted. When the SBA was publishing the document, the politics within the GMD regime had gone through a series of turbulences. In May 1931 the factional strife led to the establishment of a separate GMD government in Guangzhou by an anti–Chiang Kai-shek faction. From late October to early November, under the pressure of popular demand that the party and the government unite to resist Japan, representatives from both governments attended a so-called conference for peace and unity held in Shanghai. They agreed that two separate GMD national congresses would be held in Nanjing and Guangzhou and that two central committees elected thereby would merge and convene the Fourth Central Committee First Plenum to settle all issues. But the congress held in Guangzhou was further split and a splinter group of GMD officials went to Shanghai to hold yet another national congress. After the three congresses ended, the Nanjing government called the other two factions to join the First Plenum, but the Guangzhou faction insisted that Chiang Kai-shek had to step down. On December 15 Chiang resigned from his offices to effect unity. The government without Chiang, however, did not fare better. Friction among Wang Jingwei, Sun Ke, and Hu Hanmin surfaced. Wang decided to make an alliance with Chiang. In late January 1932 Chiang Kai-shek returned from retirement to become the chairperson of the Military Commission, while Wang Jingwei assumed the post of the chairperson of the Executive Council. In March 1932 the GMD Fourth Central Committee Second Plenum confirmed

---

35. SLGB, No.30, pp.96–100; SnB, 1931: 12/29, p.10.

that political arrangement.[36] Those political maneuvers made it easier for the SBA to issue its manifesto in late December when Chiang was in retirement, presumably blaming him for the past failures and calling on the new government to revitalize itself.

Even under such circumstances, however, the manifesto was nothing less than a sweeping attack on the GMD regime. Its appearance suggested three developments. First, by late 1931 such social elements as lawyers came to the conclusion that the GMD state had failed in its duty and deserved open criticism. Second, the fervent nationalist sentiment inflamed by the Japanese aggression created a political environment in which SBA leaders believed they could get away with an attack on the government in the name of national salvation. They did not even worry about Article 32 of the Regulations on Lawyers, which seemed altogether irrelevant at the time of national crisis. Third, although the national crisis provided the impetus for open political action, the Shanghai Bar apparently had wider concerns about internal social and political problems in the country. Its call for more input from professional groups – experts – to make public policy showed their desire to see a more liberal or even democratic form of government that would be more effective in defending national sovereignty.

From then on the SBA assumed the role of a public pressure group pushing Nanjing to adopt a resistance policy toward Japan. It launched a campaign of telegrams to the GMD party, government, and individual officials, calling on Nanjing to stop internal strife and strengthen resistance to the Japanese advance.[37] The telegrams often contain harsh words criticizing the government.[38] The public telegrams to the government represented open dissent from Nanjing's policy. Although the actions did not produce immediate results, they contributed to the mobilization of public opinion, which grew increasingly critical of the government and which would eventually help force Chiang Kai-shek to change his Japan policy.

Professional Duty and Political Alienation

The Shanghai Bar's actions at the time may be better understood when viewed in the context of its alienation from the GMD party-state, which

---

36. Ji Hongsheng, *Zhongguo Guomindang Shigang* (An outline history of the Chinese Nationalist Party) (Shanghai, 1990), pp.121–27.
37. SLGB, No.30, pp.101, 110–111; SnB, 1932: 1/15, p.14.   38. SLGB, No.30, pp.108–9.

can be traced at least back to 1929. In the spring of that year, Wu Mai, a delegate of the SBA to the first conference of the National Bar Association (NBA), put forward several proposals. One of them was to require that lawyers study the GMD party doctrine (*dangyi*) and participate in national revolution (*guomin geming*). When the ESC in Shanghai learned of the proposals, Tan Yigong, an executive committee member and a GMD party member, observed that such things as participating in the revolution and studying the party doctrine were the obligations of ordinary citizens and should not be advocated by a bar association. The ESC resolved to notify the NBA that Wu was not authorized to make the proposals and that those were his personal opinions, not the SBA's. It asked Wu to retire from the conference.[39]

At the SBA general meeting on January 25, 1931, Wu Mai again proposed that the Shanghai Bar establish an institute for studying party doctrine. Tang Yingsong, another executive committee member, objected. Since the SBA was under the supervision of the MPH and some bar members were GMD party members, and since many bar members studied the party doctrine on their own, it was unnecessary to make studying the party doctrine a particular task of the Shanghai Bar. When Wu's proposal was put to a vote, it was rejected.[40]

On the surface the Shanghai Bar's position on the two occasions could be explained as an effort to keep itself nonpolitical and strictly professional. At the same time, however, the position did reflect a feeling of discontent with the GMD. It is not known how many Shanghai lawyers were GMD party members or how many lawyers really cared about the party doctrine, despite the *North China Herald* report that all members of the ESC of the Shanghai Bar were GMD party members.[41] In any case, leaders such as Tang Yingsong, Tan Yigong, and Li Shirui were not interested in the GMD party ideology at all and rejected the idea of turning the Shanghai Bar into a political cheering team for the GMD party, while their party membership provided a degree of protection. Quite clearly, there was resistance to receiving political indoctrination and performing political conformity under the GMD.

As Nanjing failed to adopt a resistance policy toward Japan after the Manchurian Incident, other signs of political alienation among Shanghai lawyers appeared. Since the GMD took over Shanghai, it had been a routine practice for the SBA to read Sun Yat-sen's will and bow to the

---

39. SLGB, No.25 (July 1929), p.14.   40. SLGB, No.29, p.9.
41. NCH, 8/25/1928, p.329.

GMD party flag at the opening of its general meetings and at the initiation of new ESC members – which was a routine ritual exercised by all public institutions and organizations at the time. On March 20, 1932, Lu Jiading, an executive committee member, proposed that at the coming spring general meeting the ritual of reading Sun's will and the practice of inviting the MPH representative be abolished and the soldiers who died fighting the Japanese be honored instead. The ESC adopted the proposal and carried it out at the general meeting on March 27. When the ESC members elected by the general meeting took office on April 10, they also did away with the ritual, giving as their reason that in the national emergency all ceremonies should be simple.[42] The contempt for the GMD-ordered political exercise was hardly concealed.

The SBA's relations with the authorities became strained in another respect. The Shanghai Bureau of Public Security (BPS) always resented the fact that lawyers, that is, SBA members, appeared in court to defend people charged by the bureau as Communists. On the other hand, lawyers regarded the bureau as a major violator of the rule of law and due process. Because of the SBA's visible role in the anti-Japanese nationalist movement, animosity between the bureau and the Shanghai Bar intensified and led to a direct confrontation in late 1931.

On December 9, 1931, in support of students arrested for demonstrations in Nanjing a few days earlier, thousands of Shanghai college students attended a rally to listen to the report on student petitions in Nanjing given by two student representatives from Beijing University and the Central University in Nanjing. The BPS and the MPH chose to use violence against students. The two student representatives were beaten and one of them was kidnapped by hired thugs.[43] The incident invited loud protests from various public associations in Shanghai.[44] The Shanghai University Faculty Anti-Japanese National Salvation Society (*Shanghai daxue jiaoyuan kangri jiuguo hui*) asked the SBA to provide moral and legal assistance.[45]

In the wake of the incident, lawyer Wu Mai went with a few teachers and students to the BPS, trying to effect the release of some students arrested earlier. Instead of getting the students released, Wu himself was badly beaten by the guards under the order of the bureau chief. He was

---

42. SLGB, No.29, p.47; No.31, pp.1–3, 5.
43. *Jiuyiba-Yierba*, pp.66–71; Jeffrey N. Wasserstrom, *Student Protests in Twentieth-Century China: The View from Shanghai* (Stanford, 1991), pp.184–88; Christian Henriot, *Shanghai, 1927–1937*, pp.74–76.
44. *Shen Bao*, 1931: 12/8, p.14, 12/11, p.14; 12/13, p.14.   45. SLGB, No.30, p.31.

then arrested and taken to Nanjing where he spent seven days in jail. That blatant injustice was something that the SBA could not tolerate. Although SBA leaders might not have been fond of Wu Mai, as instances cited earlier would suggest, they quickly assured Wu that action would be taken to get redress. With widespread support from other public associations, including local bar associations around the country, the SBA lodged protests to the BPS, Ministry of Justice, Control Council, and Executive Council in Nanjing demanding the prosecution of the persons responsible for the crime. Charges against the BPS chief were filed. The case was eventually brought to the Jiangning District Court (in Nanjing) in May. At the same time the SBA secured the promise from the Jiangning Bar Association that it would render legal assistance in the case.[46]

In all those instances, the Shanghai Bar insisted on its professional autonomy and duty, and opposed interference from the GMD party-state apparatus. At the same time, however, those instances were unmistakable manifestations of alienation from and resistance to the practices of the regime, which were by no means apolitical.

The GMD Response

How did the GMD party-state deal with the fact that the SBA was moving away from its control and even becoming a vocal dissenting voice in the public arena? While the call for effective resistance against the Japanese was common among all public associations in the country, the scathing indictment in December 1931 of the GMD party and government per se was an unprecedented affront. It is noteworthy that the GMD regime never invoked Article 32 of the Regulations on Lawyers to discipline the SBA for its political activities during those months, which indicated how the national crisis had changed the political culture in the country. But the lack of discipline did not mean the GMD would tolerate criticism that called into question its very legitimacy.

In January 1933 a GMD party branch, to which Li Shirui belonged, notified him that he was expelled from the party for advocating the abolition of reading Sun's will and bowing to the party flag and inciting reactionaries to publish the December 1931 manifesto smearing the party and the government. The party branch asked the Party Center and

---

46. SLGB, No. 31, pp.11, 12, 13, 27.

the Ministry of Justice to revoke Li's license to practice law. It also sent a letter to the SBA to verify whether it was Li who proposed to do away with the aforementioned rituals. Thus disciplined by the party, Li wisely sent the Shanghai Bar his resignation from the executive committee to disassociate his actions from the organization.[47] It is not clear whether the party branch's move was locally initiated or engineered from the Party Center (apparently the party branch did not have accurate information about who did what at the ESC meetings). Judging from Li's reaction, however, he seemed to have felt that, one way or the other, he was in a dangerous situation – his antiparty and government action had been brought to the attention of the GMD party center.

The SBA's handling of the matter was swift and skillful. First, it replied to the GMD party branch that at the meeting in question, indignant over Japanese atrocity, someone proposed to honor anti-Japanese martyrs instead of performing the rituals, but the person was not Li Shirui. Second, it asked Li to stay on the job while the association argued on his behalf with the Ministry of Justice – an assurance that the Shanghai Bar was not running way from him in the time of trouble. Third, it telegraphed the Justice Ministry, insisting that although it was not the Shanghai Bar's business to say whether Li deserved the party disciplinary action, the association was of the opinion that to revoke Li's license would clearly be a violation of the Regulations on Lawyers.[48]

A few days later a rumor surfaced that Li was about to be secretly arrested. The SBA quickly sent a telegram to the GMD Party Center and the National Government Office. It described Li as a discreet lawyer who had never violated the Regulations on Lawyers and the SBA's bylaws in his seventeen years of practice. It praised Li for his devotion to the anti-Japanese movement and expressed doubts about the accusation that Li organized a secret party and embezzled funds collected by the Federation of the Shanghai National Salvation Societies (*Shanghai gejie jiuguo lianhe hui*). If Li were guilty of wrongdoing, there should be a public trial according to the law. To do otherwise would encourage

---

47. SLGB, No.31, pp.196–97.
48. SLGB, No.31, pp.54, 196–98. The party branch's demand that Li's license be revoked could have been based on the GMD regulations on the people's associations, which provided that persons who were expelled from the GMD party could not join occupational associations (see Chapter 3). On the other hand, under the Regulations on Lawyers, revoking a lawyer's license would require a "trial and conviction" by the Lawyers' Disciplinary Committee of a provincial high court. The Shanghai Bar was arguing that there was no cause to disbar Li Shirui.

slander and cause resentment against the government, which would do harm to the nation.[49] By such actions the SBA argued for Li's innocence and warned against possible secret arrest and trial. In the end, Li was not prosecuted, nor disbarred, but he never resumed his post in the SBA executive committee. He chose to keep a low profile and stay out of trouble. When he died of illness in March 1936, the ESC held a special meeting to discuss how to take care of his two children.[50]

The SBA Adjustment

If the purpose of the GMD party machine in disciplining Li was to send a message to the SBA, the message appears to have been received. After the Li episode, the SBA tried to stay with the mainstream. Starting in the spring of 1934, the representative of the MPH again attended the SBA general meetings. In that year, after the Shanghai County Party Headquarters moved out of the municipal boundary, the SBA applied for being put on file (*bei'an*) with the MPH.[51] The ritual of reading Sun's will and bowing to the party flag was resumed in 1935.[52] When the GMD trumpeted its victory in crushing the Communists (the Red Army was forced to abandon its base area in Jiangxi and started the Long March) in late 1934, the SBA participated in the celebration sponsored by the MPH. It sent a telegram to Chiang Kai-shek, congratulating him on his success and urging him to wipe out the remnant Communists.[53] The Shanghai Bar also took part in and donated money for the celebration of Chiang Kai-shek's fiftieth birthday in 1937.[54] Apparently, despite its dissatisfaction with Nanjing, the SBA regarded the GMD government as legitimate and did not perceive the Communists as a desirable or viable alternative.

On the other hand, while the Shanghai Bar became more careful about what it would say in public, it did not relinquish its involvement in the politics of national salvation. What had changed was its style. The SBA consciously adopted the tactics of joining other public associations for political action to avoid being conspicuous and looking radical. At the ESC meeting on February 5, 1936, a question was brought up as to whether the Shanghai Bar should join the Federation of National

---

49. SLGB, No.31, pp.59, 198–99.   50. SnB, 1936: 3/20, p.12.
51. SLGB, No.32 (June 1934), pp.227–28; No.33 (July 1935), p.1.
52. SLGB, No.33, p.61.   53. SLGB, No.33, pp.33–34, 152–53.
54. SLGB, No.34 (July 1936), pp.69, 85.

Salvation Societies. The committees decided that individual bar members might join that organization in the name of the legal profession (*lushi jie*) but not in the name of the SBA.[55] That resolution pointed to the delicate relationship between political actions of individual lawyers and the SBA's identity as a professional association.

The Shanghai Bar Association was not a monolithic body; it was composed of individual lawyers who did not necessarily share the same view on all issues and who did not behave exactly the same way with regard to political matters. As earlier discussion suggests, while the leadership of the Shanghai Bar as a whole was both politically active and cautious, there was a spectrum of possible political behavior among individual lawyers. As far as the national salvation movement was concerned, some Shanghai lawyers were more active than others and joined issue-oriented political organizations.

Four of the Seven Gentlemen arrested by the GMD government in November 1936 – Shen Junru, Shi Liang, Sha Qianli, and Wang Zhaoshi – were SBA members. For their activities in the national salvation movement, especially in the Shanghai Cultural Circle National Salvation Society, the Seven Gentlemen were prosecuted under the emergency law, the very law that the SBA had fought in vain to abolish. Their trials started in June 1937 amidst widespread opposition from the public, but before the court had a chance to convict the defendants, the full-scale Sino–Japanese War broke out in July 1937. Under popular pressure for unity and resistance, the authorities released the seven defendants on bail on July 31, 1937.[56]

During the whole course of that highly publicized event, the SBA kept a low profile – the SBA never spoke publicly about the matter, while twenty-one of its members, all well-known lawyers, formed the strongest defense team ever in the history of Shanghai to represent the Seven Gentlemen in court.[57] While the lawyers in the defense team took up the case as a pro bono job, all of the lawyers were not necessarily politically

---

55. SLGB, No.34, p.51.
56. For the Seven Gentlemen's case, see Hu Yuzhi, "Wei Quanmin Kangzhan Benzou Huhao" (Run and cry for an all-people resistance), WZX (Beijing, No.106, July 1986), pp.16–25; Xie Jusan, "Shanghai Jiuguohui Qi Junzi Beibu An Yiwen" (Anecdotes about the case of the Seven Gentlemen of the Shanghai National Salvation Society), WZX (Shanghai, No.5, 1980), pp.63–74; Parks M. Coble Jr., "Chiang Kai-shek and the Anti-Japanese Movement in China: Zou Tao-fen and the National Salvation Association, 1931–1937," *Journal of Asian Studies*, 44,2 (Feb. 1985):293–310.
57. Xie Jusan, "Shanghai Jiuguohui."

motivated. Wang Baoji, who represented Sha Qianli, for instance, did so because like Sha, he was a native of Wuxian, Jiangsu, and Sha's family asked him to render assistance. Wang was there to help a friend in any way he could, not to make a political stand one way or the other.[58] On the other hand, the political attitude of the SBA leadership was reflected in that, as known political activists, both Shen Junru and Shi Liang had served on the SBA's executive committee since 1932 and 1933 respectively. With their arrest, no suggestion was made and no action taken to relieve them of their posts in the SBA. On the contrary, after the Seven Gentlemen were released, the executive committee passed a resolution that the Shanghai Bar hold a dinner party for its four members of the Seven Gentleman to extend condolences.[59] The sympathy of the Shanghai Bar with national salvation activists was evident, but the Shanghai Bar's leaders behaved with sufficient caution to maintain their organization's viability as a professional association.

The experience of the Shanghai Bar illustrates some important patterns of state–society interaction in the Republican era. As a professional group, Shanghai lawyers no doubt pursued their group interests. They wanted to widen the scope of their practice and assert their professional privilege and autonomy, taking advantage of the legitimate status the state granted. Representing the legal profession, the Shanghai Bar Association constantly acted to advance lawyers' interests. Shanghai lawyers would argue that their goals were identical with the interests of society at large, such as the realization of the rule of law and judicial independence.

Besides judicial issues, the impulse for political (public) action beyond group interests always existed among lawyers. The organizational form they would choose for collective action depended on political circumstances and the issues involved. In the early 1920s the issue of finding a political formula for the nation was important enough to spur Shanghai lawyers into political action, but they did so through a surrogate so as to comply with the government regulations. Under the GMD rule, acting through a surrogate was impossible and joining political organizations was dangerous. As a result, Shanghai lawyers as a group either would not take collective political action, or would act through their professional association when warranted by the importance of the issue. The

---

58. Wang Baoji, interview with the author, July 31, 1994.
59. SnB, 1937: 8/3, p.12.

national salvation against the Japanese aggression was exactly an issue of such importance and the SBA (and other public associations) acted accordingly.

During the Nanjing Decade political dissent in the name of national salvation seemed to be the only legitimate dissent, but even that alone was not always sufficient to protect one from government suppression. The nationalist dissent had to be expressed by otherwise nonpolitical organizations. Specifically issue-oriented organizations such as the Shanghai Cultural Circle National Salvation Society were not tolerated by the GMD regime. In other words, the legitimacy of public associations in general and such professional associations as the SBA in particular helped lawyers' professional associations to avoid being regarded and targeted as subversive political organizations that the GMD would be anxious to suppress. The SBA carefully walked the fine line between playing a political role in the public arena and being viewed as politically subversive.

Conclusion to Part III

CHAPTERS 6 through 9 amply demonstrate that under government regulation and even with the GMD party supervision, professional associations were still able to act in the public arena on a wide range of professional, social, and political issues. Professional associations did so in no small part because a political culture of urban elite associations playing a public role had been formed by the Republican era. As government sanction endowed them with publicness, professional associations were among the most legitimate urban associations in a position to challenge state policies and practices.

Professionals also appropriated to their own advantage the political rhetorics issuing from the state. The GMD regulations specified conformity to the Three Principles and party policies as a precondition for the government sanction of any public association. Yet, professional associations (and other public organizations too) could and did always oppose government actions by turning the GMD's provision on its own head, that is, by accusing the GMD's policy of violating the Three Principles and Sun Yat-sen's legacy. All the professional groups examined earlier employed these tactics in their struggles of different kinds.

The assumed publicness not only shielded professional groups from state pressure but also protected their particular group interests. Representing the legal profession, the Shanghai Bar acted to advance lawyers' professional interests while arguing that lawyers' goals were identical with the interests of society at large, such as the realization of the rule of law and judicial independence. Journalists demanded freedom of speech and press because they regarded this freedom as a necessary condition under which to carry out their professional duty and pursue their professional career, as well as a condition for national salvation. Similarly, both Western and native medicine and the social groups they embodied actively sought recognition and support from the state for their claims to professional status in society at large. They invited government action to serve their self-interests and would criticize the government particularly when it failed to act on their behalf.

The role of professional associations in the public arena need not be exaggerated. Professional associations often had to oppose government policies in the name of nationalist goals. Such opposition points to the limits of their sociopolitical role in the public arena. Furthermore, while using their professional associations for political purposes, professionals took pains to maintain the professional character of their associations in order to distinguish them from political organizations and keep them viable as such. These organizations were thus able to continue to serve the professional purposes when they had difficulty pursuing a political agenda or when they were faced with internal divisions on political issues. These aspects of associational behavior of Chinese professionals may also be taken as cool-headed strategies to negotiate their social and functional space in a particular historical context.

All these cases show that the ways in which the state and society interacted in the Republican era were far richer, and the motives and dynamics far more complex, than the notion of societal autonomy, embedded in the civil society framework, would allow one to fully comprehend and appreciate.

Conclusion

SYMBIOTIC DYNAMICS IN THE STATE–SOCIETY RELATIONSHIP

This book has argued for an understanding of state–society interaction in Republican China as a symbiotic dynamics that grew out of the modernization process. The formulation in this book may not be a revelation; but, the notion of an evolving process in which both the state and society struggle to define themselves in relation to each other with overlapping and shifting boundaries captures the essence of that which transpired between the Chinese state and urban society in the Republican era.

As the history of Chinese professionals in Republican Shanghai shows, during that period, the state and society were mutually dependent and interpenetrated: Legitimacy and authority on either side were often contingent and contested; private, group, and public interests and crosspurposes overlapped and negotiated. For professional groups, a total autonomy from the state was inherently impossible, due to the government's power to license the professions and due to the professionals' role in modern state building – especially the lawyers' role in the judicial system. The professional functions of *ziyou zhiye zhe* and the process of professionalization entailed both government sanction and government regulation. The difference between the Beiyang period and the Nanjing Decade in government regulation and supervision of societal institutions may be considered in degree – effectiveness and capability – rather than in nature – intention and purpose. State intervention in society was motivated by social considerations and political purposes – as seen in the government regulation of the legal and medical professions or the prohibition of dubious and false advertisement in the press. State intervention was a sign of modern state building – the state assuming increasing public responsibilities and expanding state power in society as public authority for the purpose of the public good.

In the Republican era, modern state building or state formation was far from completion. The nature, form, legitimacy, authority, and boundaries of the state had yet to be properly defined, which had to happen in the state's actual interaction with society. During the Republican era, especially between 1916 and 1928, the state was not a monolithic, static entity, but often a fluid, shifting, and multiple entity – an entity that could be defined separately, negotiated with simultaneously, and ignored partially or temporarily by societal actors at different times. Very often it is societal institutions' actions that help define the legitimacy and reach of state power – such as professional groups asking for state recognition and accepting government regulation.

Society was not a static entity with fixed boundaries either, nor an entity passively acted upon by the state. Urban society in the Republican era was evolving and growing into a more complex formation in flux. The rise of professionals as a social category or class was only one aspect of the increasing heterogeneity of urban society and it represented a particular kind of social class formation brought forth by modernization. The resultant complexity of urban society presented a formidable task for the state. The modernizing state actually contributed to the rise of professionals by promoting and regulating professions, yet it never had complete control over the outcome of its own actions or the actions of social actors. The lack of complete autonomy from or the close identification with the state on the part of professional groups did not prevent the professional groups from taking public actions. Government regulation imposed restrictions and conferred legitimacy at the same time. Considerable social or functional space was therefore available for professional groups to act in the public arena under different circumstances and they constantly tried to push the boundaries farther of such a space. Professional groups would resist state intervention in society at some times and invite intervention at other times – depending on whether such intervention would serve their interests and the public good.

Some scholars conceptualize civil society as a public sphere between the state and society. Professional associations, and the Shanghai Bar Association in particular, were indeed situated between the state and society and on behalf of the state and society at the same time. Yet this in-between position was not defined by institutionalized autonomy, but by the lack of autonomy from and identification with the state on the one hand, and the possibility of acting on behalf of society and in the

Conclusion

interests of the general public on the other hand. In areas where the divide between the state and society became blurred, such as in the judicial system and the legal profession, government regulations could be regarded as aiming at the state apparatus as well as at societal institutions and social groups.

These aspects of the state–society interaction underscored the constant contestation between the two sides about the publicness of urban voluntary associations, and contributed to the multiple and shifting meanings of publicness as defined and interpreted by both the state and social actors under changing historical conditions. Most critically, such contestation did not lead to the complete success of social groups and organizations in claiming to represent the public and obtaining institutionalized autonomy vis-à-vis the state, nor did it result in a total conquest by the state over the urban society or any of its component segments.

Earlier studies on the Nanjing Decade often discussed state corporatism to explain the GMD policies in dealing with the social groups in Shanghai.[1] Such analysis is well taken and shared by this study. But state corporatism only accounts for the motive on the part of the GMD state. It did not speak to the initiatives and strategies on the part of social actors, nor to the behavior of the Beiyang regimes that lacked any articulated ideology. This study has shown that both proactive and reactive behavior of social actors was as important as that of the state. As a way to conceptualize these complex relationships and processes, the notion of symbiotic dynamics emphasizes the motives, initiatives, and strategies on both sides.

SYNTHESIS OF URBAN SOCIETY AND ITS RELATIONSHIP WITH THE STATE

How does the case made from the experience of Chinese professionals fit into the scholarship on Republican China? Does this study revise the current understanding of Chinese urban society in the Republican era? It will be obvious to China specialists that while based on original research, this study has benefited from a growing body of scholarship on Republican Shanghai that has been built up in recent years. To situate the relationship of professional groups with the state in a broad histori-

---

1. Joseph Fewsmith, *Party, State, and Local Elites in Republican China*, pp.159–66; Brian G. Martin, *The Shanghai Green Gang*, pp.161–63.

cal context, this Conclusion features a synthesis of previous studies on Republican Shanghai in light of this study. It also presents the argument that the symbiotic dynamics in the relationship between Chinese professionals and the Republican state was not an isolated phenomenon, but was generally characteristic of the relations between the state and other social segments in Republican Shanghai.

First of all, one may contextualize the case of Chinese professionals by taking a look at the relationship between the state and other social groups and organizations. The most important social segment in Shanghai since the late Qing was of course the bourgeoisie that enjoyed economic dominance and political and social influence in the late Qing and the early Republic. Their important role in the city's economic, social, and political life in that transitional period was well documented. But what was their role in the Nanjing Decade? Several scholars have discussed the demise of the political and economic power of this class under the GMD rule, but with different interpretations.[2] Parks M. Coble Jr. agreed with Lloyd Eastman in defining the nature of the GMD regime as autonomous, not responsible and responsive to any social groups but itself. Joseph Fewsmith made a distinction between the GMD party and the GMD state, both of which constituted the GMD regime. He saw the demise of the party's authority along with more militant middle-class merchants and the rising dominance of the state through a conditioned alliance with the merchant elite in a scheme of state corporatism. In the same vein and with more nuance, Marie-Claire Bergère and Christian Henriot allowed more room for the bourgeoisie or a part of it to negotiate with the state for a role to play in developing and managing the modernizing economy in Shanghai and beyond. Bergère used such terms as "symbiosis" and "intermediation" in discussing the relationship between the Shanghai bourgeoisie and the GMD state. In spite of the divergent perspectives of these analyses, symbiotic dynamics is at work.

A second important social segment in Shanghai was the working class. Alain Roux's studies and Elizabeth J. Perry's studies on Shanghai workers have corrected some simplistic assumptions about the Chinese

---

2. Parks M. Coble Jr., *The Shanghai Capitalists and the Nationalist Government, 1927–1937*; Joseph Fewsmith, *Party, State, and Local Elites in Republican China*; Marie-Claire Bergère, *The Golden Age of the Chinese Bourgeoisie, 1911–1937*; Christian Henriot, *Shanghai, 1927–1937*.

working class in Republican China.³ Their studies have convincingly established that Shanghai workers were not a united, homogeneous class. Workers were divided and their politics defined by native origins, cultural traditions, job skills, daily experiences, and the efforts of outside organizers. The heterogeneity therefore seemed to be a common trait for any social class or category in Chinese urban society that one wishes to define. Perry's analysis of how job-specific experience was a factor in shaping workers' different responses to labor unrest is a relevant point to compare with the case made about different professional groups in this study. Beyond this, Perry made another important point that to a considerable degree the workers' politics shaped the policies and directions of the Chinese state throughout the twentieth century. In her analysis, workers' actions, even when they failed in immediate outcome, would help condition or modify the behavior of the state and its policies. Negotiations that involved bargaining and deal making between workers (their leaders) and political parties or states were practices taken for granted by both sides. In contrast to the characterization of the Chinese state as despotic, bureaucratic, autonomous, or totalitarian, Perry's study "emphasizes the dynamic influence of local society, divided though it was, on state transformation."⁴ Using symbiotic dynamics to characterize the relationship between Shanghai workers and the Republican state would not seem far off the mark.

Speaking of Shanghai workers' politics, one must mention the complex and often contradictory role of the Green Gang, the notorious underworld in Republican Shanghai. An important dimension of the symbiotic dynamics between Shanghai's working class and the GMD state was revealed in the intricate relationship between the Green Gang and the leaders of the GMD regime and thus its mediation between workers and the regime.⁵ As noted earlier, a key feature in the symbiotic dynamics was a contestation over the publicness of societal institutions. The Green Gang was not a public association, but an underworld organization. Officially, it did not even exist. Yet, every informed person in Shanghai knew of or felt its presence. Because its leaders had a hold on many

---

3. Alain Roux, *Le Shanghai Ouvrier des Années Trente*; Elizabeth J. Perry, *Shanghai on Strike*.
4. Elizabeth J. Perry, *Shanghai on Strike*, p.8.
5. See Elizabeth J. Perry, *Shanghai on Strike*; Frederic Wakeman Jr., *Policing Shanghai*; Nicholas R. Clifford, *Spoilt Children of Empire*; and especially Bryan G. Martin, *The Shanghai Green Gang*.

workers and other social elements that routinely escaped the reach of the state, it was relied upon by and developed important ties with the authorities (not only the Chinese state but also the administrations of the two foreign concessions in Shanghai). To transform this power into public forms and to legitimate his relationship with the state, or rather the state's relationship with him, Du Yuesheng became a public figure serving in a variety of public capacities, including being the vice chairperson and then chairperson of the Shanghai Civic Association. In addition, he created the Endurance Club, a surrogate, in a way that was not much different from the way the leaders of the Shanghai Bar Association begot the Society for Promoting the Rule of Law in 1923.[6] All the while, his primary power base remained to be the Green Gang – a supposedly covert but virtually public organization. Indeed, at times when the Green Gang was mediating between workers and factory owners or the authorities, it was arguably playing a public role. Here again can be seen the contest over and the mixture of the public and the private, a characteristic in the symbiotic relationship between social actors and the Republican state.

Across social classes was the proliferation of student organizations studied by Jeffrey N. Wasserstrom and native-place associations studied by Bryna Goodman. Wasserstrom was interested in the cultural repertoire (especially the theatrics) that students drew on in playing a public role in radical movements, and Goodman explored the transition of native-place organizations from traditional forms and content to modern ones. But many strategies and tactics, actions and reactions, concessions and gains that transpired between the state and students or native-place associations were familiar, that is, similar to those seen between the state and other social groups and organizations. The contestation over publicness was also an important part of their stories. The notion of a symbiotic dynamics would encompass the cases Wasserstrom and Goodman have made.

The case of Chinese professionals may be contextualized further by reviewing the relationship between professionals and other social groups. A salient feature in the relationship between professionals and other social groups was their mutual support and cooperation in times of confronting local and national issues. The Shanghai General Chamber of Commerce exhibited a great deal of public-mindedness and frequently appeared as a heavyweight supporter in the struggle led by professional

---

6. Bryan G. Martin, *The Shanghai Green Gang*, pp.172–78, 180–82.

Conclusion

groups, though to a lesser extent after its reorganization under the GMD. The Shanghai Bar Association, Institute of Chartered Accountants of Shanghai, and organizations of native physicians all received significant support from the General Chamber of Commerce in their battles against foreign interests or state policies. Similarly, the Shanghai Daily Newspapers Association stood side by side with the Shanghai Journalists Association in demanding freedom of speech and press. The SDNA had actually begun this fight long before the SJA did. An alliance was forged between the Shanghai bourgeoisie and the middle-class professionals. The affinity between these two social categories or classes was largely fostered by their common concerns or interests, and the concerns in turn defined by their superior positions in society in all dimensions – economic, social, cultural, and political – compared to the lower classes. It would also seem that the Shanghai bourgeoisie recognized and appreciated the increasing importance of professionals in urban society.

In contrast, there were few, if any, concerted actions between professional associations and organizations of Shanghai workers, except that workers and apprentices in the native drug trade may have been involved in the native physicians' fight for legitimacy. Individual professionals may have supported workers' strikes, but such actions should not be confused with the kind of organizational cooperation that existed between professional associations and bourgeoisie organizations. There were no working-class initiatives to join the struggles of professionals, or for that matter, the Shanghai bourgeoisie. This should not be surprising if one considers that, unlike skilled workers, unskilled workers were less involved in labor unions and union-organized strikes because they had less to gain in the outcome.[7] In other words, people who were situated at a lower rung of the social hierarchy had less commitment to the betterment of their social environment since they had less stake in it and felt powerless about it. Issues such as judicial independence or freedom of speech, for example, had little to do with working-class people's daily struggles for survival. But these issues, to say nothing of the national salvation movement, were ultimately important to any and all citizens including workers. It is in this sense that professionals could and did claim that they represented the public.

For professionals, the forms of interaction with the state and strategies adopted in the process did not arise from a void. These forms and strategies were part and parcel of the social actors' repertoire accumulated at

---

7. Elizabeth J. Perry, *Shanghai on Strike*.

least since the late Qing, long predating the rise of professions. While the way professional associations interacted with the state was not radically different from that of other urban associations, their professional concerns constituted a unique and important dimension of the changing social configuration in Republican Shanghai and the changing meanings of publicness. As noted earlier in this study, the emergence of professions in the course of modernization was a new phenomenon and professional groups bore some new characteristics. One of these was their closer identification with the state and their larger public role at the same time. In such a position, the professionals and their associations effectively utilized the repertoire for interacting with the state, while significantly contributing to the repertoire. As a result, their relationship with the state turned out to be the best example of the symbiotic dynamics, but by no means an exception. The symbiotic relationship between Chinese professionals and the Republican state was an integral part of the larger process of modern state building, a new social configuration, and interaction between the state and urban society that were evolving and defining themselves.

FROM REPUBLICAN CHINA TO POST-MAO CHINA

The case of Chinese professionals in Republican China has intimate relevance to an observation of post-Mao China. In a more than superficial sense, the changes taking place in China since the late 1970s have amounted to a return to the Republican era, and parallels between the two periods are numerous. One of these, and one of the important developments in post-Mao China, has been the reemergence of professions after the forced de-professionalization during the Maoist era. In August 1980 the Chinese government promulgated the Provisional Regulations for Lawyers of the People's Republic of China, marking the re-recognition by the state of lawyers as a necessary and legitimate profession.[8] Although today's Chinese lawyers have yet to gain the status that the legal profession had enjoyed during the Republican era, the trend toward more autonomy of the legal profession has been under way. In June 1993 the Ministry of Justice decided to further reforms in the legal

---

8. For the details of the regulations and lawyers' qualifications and operations under them, see James V. Feinerman, "Law and Legal Profession in the People's Republic of China," in Merle Goldman, et al., eds., *China's Intellectuals and the State* (Cambridge, MA, 1987), pp.107–27.

Conclusion

profession and to encourage the development of a financially self-reliant and professionally self-regulating legal profession.[9] The government encouragement has led to a rapid growth of the legal profession. In Shanghai 65 law firms with about 2,000 lawyers were operating in 1992.[10] In Guangdong Province there were 345 law firms with more than 5,000 lawyers in 1993.[11] By 1998 lawyers numbered 110,000 nationwide and the government plans to raise the number to 150,000 by the year 2000.[12] A comparable development took place in accountancy. In 1992 there were 42 accounting firms with 460 certified accountants in Shanghai.[13] As a result of these developments the Shanghai Bar Association and the Shanghai Certified Accountant Institute were reestablished. The government especially encouraged the rebirth and growth of these two professions because it regards this as movement toward keeping on a par with international norms and as improvement of the environment for foreign investment. The full implications of the reemergence of professions for China's sociopolitical and economic developments have yet to be studied.

The growth of professions and professionalization is only one aspect of post-Mao social and political changes. Another related phenomenon is the rise of voluntary associations in the country, both rural and urban. Those organizations are of a wide variety, more complex in their composition and functions than the social associations in the Republican era – and they have appeared in larger numbers. According to the China News Agency (*zhongguo xinwen she*), as of April 1993 there were 180,000 registered voluntary associations in the country. Among them 1,399 were national organizations, over 19,000 were provincial level ones, and the rest were local.[14] No doubt voluntary associations, both legitimate and illicit, have continued to proliferate since then.

It is these developments, among other things, which accompanied or resulted from the post-Mao reforms that have caught the attention of China scholars in social sciences. As mentioned at the beginning of this book, a key concern for them is whether these phenomena constitute a reemergence of civil society in China at long last. Initially, most social scientists tend to find such a reemergence, but often with a qualified definition.

---

9. *Renmin Ribao Haiwaiban* (The People's Daily Overseas Edition), June 28, 1993, p.3.
10. *Qiao Bao* (China Press), Sept. 14, 1992, p.5.   11. *Qiao Bao*, July 1, 1993, p.5.
12. *Renmin Ribao Haiwaiban*, Oct. 12, 1998, p.4.
13. *Qiao Bao*, September 14, 1992, p.5.   14. *Qiao Bao*, May 6, 1993, p.5.

Conclusion

David Strand discussed the public (mass) participation in local politics and related this to civil society.[15] He allowed that if Gramsci's distinction between the private institutions of civil society and the public institutions of the state did not apply to traditional China, it did have relevance for twentieth-century China.[16] He traced the continuity of civil society in China from 1919 through 1989.[17]

Martin K. Whyte also observed the existence of civil society in late imperial and Republican China and its reemergence in post-Mao China. Whyte defines civil society as "the existence of institutionalized autonomy for social relationships and associational life, autonomy vis-à-vis the state." He notes that in real life civil society is not to be understood in either-or terms but in terms of degree. A minimal civil society involves only a modest amount of autonomous social life, whereas a fully developed civil society contains much broader social networks with free communication and a rich variety of autonomous secondary groups. "[T]he existence of a well-formed civil society involves clear limits on the state's ability to control society and its constituent individuals" and an explicit "recognition by the state of the right and ability of the activities and organizations of civil society to proceed without substantial state interference or control." With such a definition, Whyte found that a de facto civil society existed in late imperial China, but he qualified that it was a "nascent civil society," not well institutionalized.[18]

Similarly, Mayfair Mei-hui Yang defined civil society both as "the realm of nongovernmental private economic activities and sectional economic interests" and as "the realm of political society, that of public and voluntary associations such as religious and cultural organizations, independent newspapers, occupational and professional societies, and local self-government." She argued that "[a] distinct premodern civil society existed in the form of corporate groups and voluntary associa-

---

15. David Strand, *Ricksha Beijing*, pp.168ff.
16. David Strand, "Mediation, Representation, and Repression: Local Elites in the 1920s Beijing," in Mary B. Rankin and Joseph W. Esherick, eds., *Chinese Local Elites and Patterns of Dominance*, p.225.
17. David Strand, "Civil Society and Public Sphere in Modern Chinese History," in Roger V. Des Forges, et al., eds., *Chinese Democracy and the Crisis of 1989* (Ithaca, 1992); "Protest in Beijing: Civil Society and Public Sphere in China," *Problems of Communism*, 34,3 (May–June 1990):1–19.
18. Martin K. Whyte, "Urban China: A Civil Society in the Making?", in Arthur L. Rosenbaum, ed., *State and Society in China: The Consequences of Reform* (Boulder, CO, 1992), pp.77, 78, 82.

Conclusion

tions" that "were formed and managed outside of or independent of the state."[19]

The strain in applying the notion of societal autonomy embedded in the civil society concept to China forced some scholars to modify the concept. Gordon White's case study of Xiaoshan City in Zhejiang Province, for example, found that the proliferation of voluntary associations resulted from two imperatives. On the one hand, there was a spontaneous response on the part of members of society to the impersonal market force ushered in by the reforms. On the other hand, there was an effort on the part of the state to facilitate policy implementation and socioeconomic regulation in the changing environment through co-opting or sponsoring such associations. He preferred an understanding of civil society in post-Mao China as intermediate social associations (something of a bourgeois society). He stressed a close relationship between socioeconomic changes set in motion by the reforms and the rise of new forms of social organizations based on voluntary participation and with some autonomy from the state.[20]

Later Gordon White applied a sociological definition of civil society to post-Mao China, by which he referred to "social organizations which demonstrate characteristics of spontaneity, voluntariness, and autonomy in their constitution and activities." He cautioned, however, that unlike the ideal type, in reality civil society and the state overlap and interpenetrate to varying degree.[21] The similar approach of redefining civil society to explain the developments in contemporary China is also seen in another volume on the subject.[22]

The shifting views regarding the usefulness of the civil society concept in studying China were clearly reflected in a recent volume of collected essays.[23] Describing the urban scene in contemporary China, several

---

19. Mayfair Mei-hui Yang, "Between State and Society: The Construction of Corporateness in a Chinese Socialist Factory," *Australian Journal of Chinese Affairs*, No.22 (July 1989), pp.35–36. For defining civil society as voluntary associations, see John Kean, "Despotism and Democracy," in John Kean, ed., *Civil Society and the State: New European Perspectives* (London, 1988), pp.35–71; John Kean, *Democracy and Civil Society* (London, 1988), pp.3, 58.
20. Gordon White, "Prospects for Civil Society in China: A Case Study of Xiaoshan City," *Australian Journal of Chinese Affairs*, No.29 (Jan. 1993):63–87.
21. Gordon White, "The Dynamics of Civil Society in Post-Mao China," in Brian Hook, ed., *The Individual and the State in China* (Oxford, 1996), pp.196–221; also see Gordon White, Jude Howell, and Shang Xiaoyuan, *In Search of Civil Society* (Oxford, 1996).
22. Timothy Brook and Michael Frolic, eds., *Civil Society in China* (New York, 1997).
23. Deborah Davis et al., eds., *Urban Spaces in Contemporary China* (Cambridge, 1995).

scholars expressed discomfort with using the civil society framework to analyze the changes in post-Mao China. Jeffrey N. Wasserstrom and Gordon White called for more attention to "the variations in civil societies and public spheres of differing cultures and differing time periods." They were dissatisfied with the assumptions that often make a direct connection between civil society and democracy and posit an incompatibility between civil and state organizations, between public and private spheres.[24] Similarly, commenting on a complex mixture of private, public, and state initiatives and involvement in the expansion of urban associations in post-Mao China, Elizabeth J. Perry noted that "a conventional view of civil society is of limited assistance" in making sense of the phenomenon. Viewing the state–society relationship as a zero-sum game "does not shed much light on a China where private ties, public associations, and state agents are so thoroughly intertwined."[25]

Xue Liang Ding's study on the political changes in post-Mao China represented a major exception among social scientists studying the same developments.[26] He proposed the notion of "institutional parasitism" as an alternative to the scheme of "civil society versus the state." The notion described the phenomenon that "the party-state set up institutions for its own use and then these institutions were gradually co-opted by critical forces that used them for counterpurposes, all the while keeping up the front that these were still party-state institutions."[27] This model is insightful, but it also has limitations when applied to societal institutions that are not initiated by the state.

This brief review highlights the deficiency of the civil society concept in explaining sociopolitical changes in post-Mao China and Republican China. A similar difficulty stems from the very continuity between the two periods that was interrupted by the Maoist era. In this light one may consider the Maoist efforts as the most ambitious, and failed, attempt among Communist experiments in the twentieth century to break away from the pattern of modernization seen first in the West. At the same time the continuity suggests the powerful, persistent naturalizing effect of native environment and tradition on the pattern and the resulting

---

24. Jeffrey Wasserstrom and Liu Xinyong, "Student Associations and Mass Movements," in Deborah Davis et al. eds., *Urban Spaces in Contemporary China*, p.375; Gordon White, "The Dynamics of Civil Society in Post-Mao China," pp.198–99.
25. Elizabeth J. Perry, "Introduction" to "Part III: Urban Associations," in Deborah S. Davis et al., eds., *Urban Spaces in Contemporary China*, pp.300–301.
26. Xue Liang Ting, *The Decline of Communism in China* (Cambridge, 1994).
27. Ibid., p.27.

Conclusion

complexities that defy an analytical framework derived from the Western experience. For this reason this study proposes the notion of symbiotic dynamics for studying state–society relations in both periods. This formulation is broad enough to encompass all different kinds of motives, strategies, relationships, and processes in state–society interaction. More importantly, it captures the essence of the relationship between the two sides, even in its most varied form, by stressing a multidimensional, more symbiotic, and interactive nature of the social dynamics in twentieth-century China.

Glossary

aiguo xueshe 愛國學社
bangshen yuan 幫審員
Bao Shisheng 包識聲
Bao Tianxiao 包天笑
baoren 報人
Baozhi tiaoli 報紙條例
bei'an 備案
bianji 編輯
bianji zhuren 編輯主任
buzhang 部長
Cai Jiping 蔡濟平
Cai Nipei 蔡倪培
Cai Yuanpei 蔡元培
chahui 茶會
Chao Kun 巢堃
chaozhou huiguan 潮州會館
Chen Bulei 陳布雷
Chen Chaoying 陳紹英
Chen Dezheng 陳德徵
Chen Guofu 陳果夫
Chen Leng 陳冷
Chen Lifu 陳立夫
Chen Mingshu 陳銘樞
Chen Qimei 陳其美
Chen Taoyi 陳陶遺
Chen Tingrui 陳霆銳
Chen Zemin 陳則民
Cheng Dequan 程德全

Chuban fa 出版法
Chuban fa shishi xize 出版法實施細則
chuxu hui 儲蓄會
chuzhang 處長
chuzhen 出診
chuanxi suo 傳習所
Dagong Bao 大公報
Dai Jitao 戴季陶
daliyuan 大理院
dangbao 黨報
dangbu 黨部
dangguo 黨國
dangren 黨人
dangwu yu minzhong xunlian weiyuanhui 黨務與民眾訓練委員會
dangyi 黨義
dangzhi 黨治
daoyin 道尹
Daqing lüli 大清律例
Daqing xianxing xinglü 大清現行刑律
Daxin Jie 大興街
Di Chuqing 狄楚青
difang zizhi 地方自治
diguo zhuyi wenhua qinlue 帝國主義文化侵略
Ding Ganren 丁甘仁
Ding Wenjiang 丁文江
Ding Zhongying 丁仲英
Du Yuesheng 杜月笙
faguan yangcheng suo 法官養成所
falü 法律
falü guwen 法律顧問
fandong fenzi 反動分子
fandong xiaobao 反動小報
fatuan 法團
Fayuan bianzhifa 法院編制法
fazheng 法政
fazhi jiuguo 法治救國
fazhi weiyuanhui 法制委員會
fazhi xiejin hui 法治協進會
fazhi yuan 法制院
fei 匪

Glossary

Feng Shaoshan 馮少山
Feng Yuxiang 馮玉祥
fengshui 風水
Fengyang lu 鳳陽路
fu buzhang 副部長
fuxian 賦閑
Fuzhou lu 福州路
gaizu guiyue 改組規約
ganshi yuan 干事員
gaodeng youmin 高等游民
Ge Gongzhen 戈公振
Geji shenpanting shiban zhangcheng 各級審判廳試辦章程
gong 公
gong fatuan 公法團
gongfei 公費
gonggu ju 公估局
gonghe dang 共和黨
gonghui 公會
gonghui 工會
gonghui tongyi weiyuanhui 工會統一委員會
gonglun 公論
gongmin hui 公民會
Gongmin Ribao 公民日報
gongqi 公器
gongquan 公權
gongshang tuanti 工商團體
gongsuo 公所
gongtuan 公團
Gongyan Bao 公言報
gongyi tuanti 公益團體
Gu Weijun 顧維鈞
Gu Zhenglun 谷正倫
Gu Zhutong 顧祝同
guandu shangban 官督商辦
guangfang yuanguan 廣方言館
guocui 國粹
guohuo weichihui 國貨維持會
guojia 國家
guomin dahui 國民大會
guomin geming 國民革命

guomin zhengfu 國民政府
guomindang 國民黨
guoshu guan 國術館
guowen she 國聞社
guowu yuan 國務院
guoyao 國藥
guoyi 國醫
guoyi guan 國醫館
guoyi jie 國醫節
Guoyi tiaoli 國醫條例
guoyi xuehui 國醫學會
He Shizhen 何世楨
Hu Bang'an 胡邦安
Hu Hanmin 胡漢民
Hu Hongji 胡鴻基
Hu Shuwei 胡樹威
huaan hequn renshou baoxian gongsi 華安合群人壽保險公司
huahua shijie 花花世界
Huang Yanpei 黃炎培
Huang Yaomian 黃藥眠
Huang Zhenpan 黃鎮磐
Huangpi nanlu 黃陂南路
huashang 華商
huayang caipan suo 華洋裁判所
Hubei lu 湖北路
hubu yinhang 戶部銀行
huhai daoyin 滬海道尹
huhai daoyin gongshu 滬海道尹公署
hui 會
huiguan 會館
huining huiguan 徽寧會館
huizhang zhi 會長制
huxue hui 滬學會
jiancha yuan 監察院
jiancha zhidu 監察制度
Jiang Wenfang 蔣文芳
Jiangsheng Bao 江聲報
Jiao Yitang 焦易堂
jiaoyu jiuguo 教育救國
jiaoyu ting 教育廳

jiaoyu yanjiu hui 教育研究會
Jin Minlan 金泯瀾
Jin Xiongbai 金雄白
Jing Bao 京報
jinye gongsuo 金業公所
jiuyi 舊醫
jizai ziyou 記載自由
jizhe julebu 記者俱樂部
jizhe lianhuan hui 記者聯歡會
jucan hui 聚餐會
juewu 覺悟
junzheng 軍政
juren 舉人
juzhang 局長
kaiye shu 開業術
Kang Youwei 康有為
kangri jiuguo hui 抗日救國會
kaoshi yuan 考試院
keguan 客觀
kexue hua 科學化
kexue jiuguo 科學救國
keyuan 科員
kezhang 科長
kuaijishi gonghui 會計師公會
Li Bao 立報
Li Haoran 李浩然
Li Pingshu 李平書
Li Shirui 李時蕊
Li Shizeng 李石曾
Li Yuanhong 黎元洪
Li Zuyu 李祖虞
li'an 立案
lifa yuan 立法院
lishi 理事
liyi 吏役
lianhe hui 聯合會
lianhuanhui 聯歡會
lianxi jizhe 練習記者
Liang Qichao 梁啟超
Lin Baishui 林白水

Lin Kanghou 林康侯
Lin Sen 林森
Linshi Yuefa 臨時約法
liuqi 六氣
Liu Yusheng 劉煜生
Liu Zhi 劉峙
Lu Bingzhang 陸秉章
Lu Dingkui 陸鼎逵
Lu Jiading 陸家鼎
Lu Shangtong 盧尚同
Lu Shi'e 陸士諤
Lu Xingyuan 盧興原
Lu Yi 陸怡
Lü Yuequan 呂月泉
Lüshi denglu zhangcheng 律師登錄章程
lüshi gonghui 律師公會
lüshi jie 律師界
Lüshi zanxing zhangcheng 律師暫行章程
Lüshi zhangcheng 律師章程
luandang 亂黨
Ma Zhanshan 馬占山
maiban 買辦
menzhen 門診
mimi jieshe 秘密結社
mishu 秘書
mishuzhang 秘書長
minguo 民國
Minguo Ribao 民國日報
Minhu Bao 民呼報
minquan 民權
minsheng 民生
minzheng bu 民政部
minzheng zhang 民政長
minzhong tuanti 民眾團體
minzhong tuanti dengji tiaoli 民眾團體登記條例
minzhong yundong zhidao weiyuanhui 民眾運動指導委員會
minzhu 民主
mingyi 民意
mu 畝
Mu Xiangyao 穆湘瑤

nanqu gongmin hui 南區公民會
Neijing 內經
Niu Huisheng 牛惠生
nonghui 農會
Pan Gongzhan 潘公展
Pang Jingzhou 龐京周
pingyi yuan 評議員
Qi 氣
qianzhuang 錢莊
qiangxue hui 強學會
Qin Liankui 秦聯奎
qingdang 清黨
Qiu Jisheng 裘吉生
Qu Qiubai 瞿秋白
quanguo 全國
quanguo baojie jujin hui 全國報界俱進會
quanguo gongmin hui 全國公民會
quanguo jiaoyu lianhe hui 全國教育聯合會
quanguo lüshi xiehui 全國律師協會
quanguo shanghui lianhe hui 全國商會聯合會
quanguo yishi lianhe hui 全國醫師聯合會
quanguo yiyao tuanti zong lianhe hui 全國醫藥總聯合會
quanzhang huiguan 泉漳會館
renmin tuanti 人民團體
Renmin tuanti sheli chengxu an 人民團體設立程序案
ribao jizhe gonghui 日報記者公會
ruyi 儒醫
sanmin zhuyi 三民主義
sanshen zhi 三審制
Sha Qianli 沙千里
shachuan 沙船
shanhou dajiekuan 善后大借款
Shang Bao 商報
shangchuan huiguan 商船會館
Shanghai daxue jiaoyuan kangri jiuguo hui 上海大學教員抗日救國會
Shanghai faxue yuan 上海法學院
Shanghai fazheng xueyuan 上海法政學院
Shanghai funü xiehui 上海婦女協會
Shanghai gejie jiuguo lianhe hui 上海各界救國聯合會
Shanghai geming tongzhi hui 上海革命同志會

Shanghai gupiao shangye gonghui 上海股票商業公會
Shanghai huashang zhengjuan jiaoyisuo 上海華商證卷交易所
Shanghai jiaoshe gongshu 上海交涉公署
Shanghai jinye jiaoyisuo 上海金業交易所
Shanghai kuaijishi gonghui 上海會計師公會
Shanghai lüshi gonghui 上海律師公會
Shanghai pingzhun gupiao gongsi 上海平準股票公司
Shanghai quyin suo 上海取引所
Shanghai ribao gonghui 上海日報公會
Shanghai shangtuan 上海商團
Shanghai shangwu zonghui 上海商務總會
Shanghai shangye huiyi gongsuo 上海商業會議公所
Shanghai shi guoyi xuehui 上海市國醫學會
Shanghai shi shangmin xiehui yaoye fenhui 上海市商民協會藥業分會
Shanghai shi xinwen jizhe gonghui 上海市新聞記者公會
Shanghai shi yishi gonghui 上海市醫師公會
Shanghai shuye gongsuo 上海書業公所
Shanghai tebieshi zhengfu 上海特別市政府
Shanghai weijin yaoping guanli ju 上海違禁藥品管理局
Shanghai xian jiaoyuhui 上海縣教育會
Shanghai xinwen jizhe lianhe hui 上海新聞記者聯合會
Shanghai xinwen jizhe lianhuan hui 上海新聞記者聯歡會
Shanghai yiyao tuanti lianhe hui 上海醫藥團體聯合會
Shanghai yinhang gonghui 上海銀行公會
Shanghai zaliang youping jiaoyisuo 上海雜糧油品交易所
Shanghai zhengjuan wuping jiaoyisuo 上海證卷物品交易所
Shanghai zhongyi xiehui 上海中醫協會
Shanghai zhongyi xuehui 上海中醫學會
Shanghai zong shanghui 上海總商會
Shanghan Lun 傷寒論
Shao Lizi 邵力子
Shao Piaoping 邵飄萍
Shao Yuanchong 邵元沖
shehui gongqi 社會公器
shehui tuanti 社會團體
shehui xinwen 社會新聞
Shen Bao 申報
Shen Enfu 沈恩郛
Shen Junru 沈君儒
shenpan yuan 審判員

Shenzhou Ribao 神州日報
shenzhou yiyao zonghui 神州醫藥總會
sheng sifa choubei chu 省司法籌備處
shenghuo jintie 生活津貼
Shi Bao 時報
Shi Liang 史良
Shi Liangcai 史量才
Shi Ying 石英
shibo fensi 市舶分司
shi'er mingmai 十二命脈
Shishi Xingbao 時事新報
shiye jiuguo 實業救國
Shouhui Shanghai huishen gongxie zanxing zhangcheng 收回上海匯審公廨暫行章程
shubao jiancha weiyuan hui 書報檢查委員會
shubao lianhehui 書報聯合會
shuju 書局
shuye gongsuo 書業公所
shuye shanghui 書業商會
shuzhang 署長
Sichuan 四川
sidang 私黨
sifa jianxi suo 司法見習所
sifa yuan 司法院
sili tuanti 私立團體
siren tuanti 私人團體
sizhang 司長
Song Jiaoren 宋教仁
Song Shixiang 宋士鑲
Songhu duban 淞滬督辦
songhu jingbei silingbu 淞滬警備司令部
songhu shangbu weisheng ju 淞滬商埠衛生局
songshi 訟師
Su Bao 蘇報
su she 蘇社
Sun Baoqi 孫寶琦
Sun Chuanfang 孫傳芳
Sun Ke 孫科
taiping baoxian gongsi 太平保險公司
Taixing lu 泰興路

Tan Sitong 譚嗣同
Tan Yankai 譚延闓
Tan Yigong 譚毅公
Tang Jiezhi 湯介之
Tang Yingsong 湯應嵩
tezhen 特診
tianhou shengmu 天后聖母
tongmeng hui 同盟會
tongqian 銅錢
Tongren lu 同仁路
tongshi 通事
tongye gonghui 同業公會
tongxiang hui 同鄉會
tongxinshe jizhe gonghui 通信社記者公會
Wang Baoji 汪寶楫
Wang Chonghui 王寵惠
Wang Daxie 汪大燮
Wang Jingwei 汪精衛
Wang Kaijiang 王開疆
Wang Qizhang 汪企張
Wang Xingyi 汪星一
Wang Zhaoshi 王照時
Wang Zhongfang 汪仲芳
Wei Daoming 魏道明
Weihai minguo jinji zhizui fa 危害民國緊急治罪法
weisheng shu 衛生署
weisheng si 衛生司
weiyuan zhi 委員制
Wenhua tuanti zuzhi dagang shishi xize 文化團體組織大綱實施細則
wenren 文人
wentan 文壇
Wu Jingheng 吳敬衡
Wu Jingxiong 吳經熊
Wu Kaisheng 吳凱聲
Wu Mai 吳邁
Wu Shiying 武士英
Wu Xin 吳馨
Wu Zhihao 鄔志豪
wude wenren 無德文人
wushu 巫術

wuyi 巫醫
Xi Yuchang 席裕昌
Xia Yingtang 夏應棠
xiyi 西醫
Xiyi tiaoli 西醫條例
Xiyi yishi kaoshi tiaoli 西醫醫師考試條例
xian sifa chu 縣司法處
xian sifa gongshu 縣司法公署
Xian sifa gongshu zuzhi zhangcheng 縣司法公署組織章程
xian zhishi 縣知事
Xian zhishi jianli sifa shiwu zanxing tiaoli 縣知事兼理司法暫行條例
Xian zhishi shenli susong zanxing zhangcheng 縣知事審理訴訟暫行章程
xianrou ye gongsuo 鮮肉業公所
xianzheng 憲政
xianzheng yanjiu hui 憲政研究會
xiaobao 小報
Xie Lihuan 謝利桓
xiejin 謝金
xiehui 協會
xieshu 邪術
xintuo gongsi 信托公司
Xinwen Bao 新聞報
xinwen gongzuo zhe 新聞工作者
xinwen jizhe 新聞記者
xinwen jizhe gonghui 新聞記者公會
xinyi yu shehui 新醫與社會
xingzheng yuan 行政院
Xiuzheng renmin tuanti zuzhi fang'an 修正人民團體組織方案
Xu Eryin 徐爾金
Xu Maoyong 徐懋庸
Xu Qian 徐謙
Xu Shiying 許世英
Xu Weizhen 徐維震
Xu Yuan 許源
Xu Zhucheng 徐鑄成
xuanxue 玄學
Xue Dubi 薛篤弼
xuehui 學會
xueshu tuanti 學術團體
Xunhuan Ribao 循環日報

xunzheng 訓政
Yan Duhe 嚴獨鶴
Yan Esheng 嚴諤聲
Yan Fuqing 顏福慶
Yan Shenyu 嚴慎予
Yan'an donglu 延安東路
yanlun ziyou 言論自由
Yang Jingbing 楊景斌
yanghang 洋行
Yangjing bang sheguan huishen zhangcheng 洋涇洪設官會審章程
yangzhuang 洋莊
yaoye gongsuo 藥業公所
yaoye gonghui 藥業公會
Ye Chucang 葉楚滄
yi 醫
yichuan 驛傳
yidang zhiguo 以黨治國
yishi 醫師
yishi 醫士
yishi 醫室
Yishi biantong geizheng banfa 醫師變通給證辦法
Yishi fa 醫師法
yishi gonghui 醫師公會
Yishi zanxing tiaoli 醫師暫行條例
yin gongsi 銀公司
yinhao 銀號
yinliang 銀兩
yinlu 銀爐
yinpian tongye gonghui 飲片同業公會
yinyang 陰陽
yinyao 淫藥
yinyuan 銀元
Ying Guixin 應桂馨
yongyi 庸醫
youbao wushe 有報無社
Yu Botao 余伯陶
Yu Youren 于佑仁
Yu Yunxiu 余雲岫
Yuan datou 袁大頭
Yuan Shikai 袁世凱

Yuan Xitao 袁希濤
yubei lixian gonghui 預備立憲公會
yulun 輿論
Yun Yiqun 惲逸群
zabei gongmin hui 閘北公民會
zayi 雜醫
zai'an 在案
Zhang Binglin 章丙麟
Zhang Guotao 張國燾
Zhang Jiazhen 張家鎮
Zhang Jingjiang 張靜江
Zhang Jinglu 張靜廬
Zhang Mei'an 張梅庵
Zhang Shizhao 章士釗
Zhang Xun 張勛
Zhang Yipeng 張一鵬
Zhang Zanchen 張贊臣
Zhang Zhujun 張竹君
Zhang Zijun 張子君
Zhang Zongchang 張宗昌
zhening huiguan 浙寧會館
Zhenba lüshi weiyuanhui zhangcheng 甄拔律師委員會章程
zhenshou shi 鎮守使
Zheng Rucheng 鄭汝成
Zheng Yuxiu 鄭毓秀
zhengli 整理
zhengwen she 政聞社
zhishi fenzi 知識分子
zhishi jieji 知識階級
zhixing dangyi 執行黨義
zhiye 職業
zhiye hua 職業化
zhiye tuanti 職業團體
zhizheng 執政
zhongguo baoxue shi 中國報學史
zhongguo gongxue 中國公學
zhongguo minquan baozhang tongmeng 中國民權保障同盟
zhongguo tongshang yinhang 中國通商銀行
zhonghua jiaoyu gaijin she 中華教育改進社
zhonghua minguo lüshi zong gonghui 中華民國律師總公會

zhonghua minguo quanguo baojie lianhe hui 中華民國全國報界聯合會
zhonghua minguo yiyao xuehui 中華民國醫藥學會
zhonghua minguo yiyao lianhe hui 中華民國醫藥聯合會
zhonghua xiyi gonghui 中華西醫公會
zhonghua yixue hui 中華醫學會
zhonghua yiyao lianhe hui 中華醫藥聯合會
Zhongwai Xinbao 中外新報
zhongyang minzhong xunlian bu 中央民眾運動訓練部
zhongyao 中藥
zhongyi 中醫
Zhongyi shengcha guize 中醫審查規則
Zhongyi tiaoli 中醫條例
zhongyi weiyuan hui 中醫委員會
zhongyi xiehui 中醫協會
zhongyi xueshe 中醫學社
zhongyi xuexiao 中醫學校
zhongyi yuan 中醫院
Zhongyi zazhi 中醫雜志
zhongyi zhiye tuanti 中醫職業團體
zhongyi zhuanmen xuexiao 中醫專門學校
Zhu Jianxia 朱劍霞
Zhu Kewen 朱克文
Zhu Peide 朱培德
Zhu Minyi 諸民誼
zhubi 主筆
zhuanke xuexiao 專科學校
zhuanmen hua 專門化
zhuangzhi 狀紙
zili hui 自立會
ziyou zhiye tuanti 自由職業團體
ziyou zhiye zhe 自由職業者
zong bianji 總編輯
zuigao quanli jiguan 最高權力機關
zuojia 作家
zuotanhui 座談會

Bibliography

INTERVIEWS

Lu Yi (b. 1910), journalist, January 12, 1992.
Qin Sou'ou (b. 1902), writer, January 5, 1992.
Wang Baoji (b. 1908), lawyer, July 31, 1994.
Wu Kaisheng (b. 1900), lawyer, December 30, 1991.
Xu Jie (b. 1901), professor and writer, January 13, 1992.
Zhang Zanchen (b. 1903), native physician, December 25, 1991.
Zhu Kewen (b. 1907), Western-style doctor, December 18, 1991.

ARCHIVAL MATERIALS

Shanghai Shi Jiaoyuju Dang'an (The archives of the Shanghai Municipal Bureau of Education), 1929–1937. The Shanghai Municipal Archives (SMA).

CHINESE NEWSPAPERS AND JOURNALS

Chen Bao Fujuan (Morning News Supplement). 1921–1928.
Dongfang Zazhi (DZ) (East Miscellany). 1912–1937.
Duli Pinglun (Independent Review). 1932–1937.
Faling Zhoukan (FZ) (Weekly Review of Laws and Ordinances). 1932–1937.
Falü Pinglun (FP) (Law Review). 1923–1935.
Faxue Zazhi (Law Journal). 1928–1939.
Guowen Zhoubao (National News Weekly). 1916–1937.
Kuaiji Zazhi (Journal of Accounting). 1933–1935.
Lixin Kuaiji Jikan (Lixin Quarterly of Accounting). 1935.
Mingri Yiyao (Medicine of Tomorrow). 1936–1937.
Qiao Bao (China Press). 1992–1993.
Renmin Ribao Haiwaiban (The People's Daily Overseas Edition). 1993, 1998.
Shehui Yibao (Social Journal of Medicine). 1930–1937.
Shehui Yiyao (Medicine for Society). 1934–1937.
Shen Bao (SnB) (Shanghai News). 1921–1922, 1931–1937.
Shenghuo Ribao (Life Daily). 1936.

Shenghuo Ribao Xingqi Zengkan (Sunday Supplement to Life Daily). 1936.
Shi Bao (SB) (Eastern Times). 1912–1932.
Xiandai Sifa (Modern Judiciary). 1935–1937.
Xiangdao (Guide). 1922–1927.
Yijie Chunqiu (YC) (Spring and Autumn, Medical Circle). 1927–1937.
Yishi Gonglun (Public Review of Medical Affairs). 1933–1937.
Yiyao Pinglun (YP) (Medical Review). 1928–1937.
Zhonghua Faxue Zazhi (China Law Journal). 1930–1937.
Zhongyi Xin Shengming (ZXS) (New Life of Chinese Medicine). 1934–1937.
Zhongxi Yiyao (Chinese and Western Medicine). 1935–1937.

CHINESE GOVERNMENT DOCUMENTS

Guomin Zhengfu Gongbao (GZG) (National Government Bulletin). 1927–1937.
Lifa Yuan Gongbao (Bulletin of Legislative Council). 1928–1929.
Sifa Gongbao (Judicial Bulletin). 1929–1932, 1934–1937.
Sifa Yuan Gongbao (Bulletin of Judicial Council). 1932–1934.
Zhengfu Gongbao (ZG) (Government Bulletin). 1912–1927.
Zhengfu Gongbao Fenlei Huibian (ZGFH) (A compilation of the Government Bulletin by subject). 1915.

CHINESE YEARBOOKS AND SOURCE COLLECTIONS

Bayisan Kangzhan Shiliao Xuanbian (Selected sources on the resistance battle of August 13 [1937]). Shanghai: Shanghai renmin chubanshe, 1986.
Ershi Shiji Shanghai Da Bolan (A chronicle of twentieth-century Shanghai). Shanghai: Shanghai renmin chubanshe, 1995.
Jiefang Qian Shanghai De Xuexiao: Shanghai Wenshi Ziliao Xuanji (Shanghai's schools [and universities] before the liberation: Selected sources on Shanghai's culture and history). Shanghai: Shanghai renmin chubanshe, 1988.
Jiu Shanghai De Jinrong Jie: Shanghai Wenshi Ziliao Xuanji (The financial world of old Shanghai: Selected sources on Shanghai's culture and history). Shanghai: Shanghai renmin chubanshe, 1988.
Jiu Shanghai De Waishang Yu Maiban: Shanghai Wenshi Ziliao Xuanji (Foreign merchants and compradors in old Shanghai: Selected sources on Shanghai's culture and history). Shanghai: Shanghai renmin chubanshe, 1987.
Jiuyiba-Yi'erba Shanghai Junmin Kangri Yundong Shiliao (Sources on the anti-Japanese resistance movement of the Shanghai military and civilians from September 18 [1931] to January 28 [1932]). Shanghai: Shanghai shehui kexueyuan chubanshe, 1986.
Shanghai Beike Ziliao Xuan (Selected sources from inscriptions about Shanghai). Shanghai: Shanghai renmin chubanshe, 1980.
Shanghai Yanjiu Ziliao (SYZ) (Sources for Shanghai study). Shanghai: Shanghai tongshe, 1936; Shanghai shudian, 1984.
Shanghai Yanjiu Ziliao Xuji (SYZX) (A sequel to sources for Shanghai study). Shanghai: Shanghai tongshe, 1939; Shanghai shudian, 1984.

Bibliography

Shanghaishi Nianjian (Shanghai municipal yearbook). 1935–1937.
Shenbao Nianjian (Shenbao yearbook). 1933–1935.
Wenshi Ziliao Xuanji (Selected sources on culture and history). Shanghai, 1960–1991.
Wenshi Ziliao Xuanji (Selected sources on culture and history). Beijing, 1954–1991.
Xin Wenxue Shiliao (Sources on the history of new literature). Beijing: Renmin wenxue chubanshe, 1979–1991.
Xinwen Yanjiu Ziliao (XYZ) (Sources for research on journalism). Beijing: Zhongguo shehui kexueyuan xinwen yanjiusuo, 1980–1991.
Yi'erjiu Yihou Shanghai Jiuguohui Shiliao Xuanji (Selected sources on the national salvation societies in Shanghai after December 12 [1935]). Shanghai: Shanghai shehui kexueyuan chubanshe, 1987.
Yijie Chunqiu Huibian (YCH) (A collection of essays from Spring and Autumn Medical Circle). Shanghai: Yijie chunqiu she, 1935.
Yuanyang Hudie Pai Wenxue Ziliao (Sources on mandarin duck and butterfly literature). Fuzhou: Fujian renmin chubanshe, 1984.

DOCUMENTS AND BOOKS IN CHINESE AND JAPANESE

An Guanying, et al., eds. *Zhonghua Bainian Lao Yaopu* (Century-old drugstores in China). Beijing: Zhongguo wenshi chubanshe, 1993.
Bao Tianxiao. *Chuanying Lou Huiyi Lu* (A memoir from the mansion of bracelet shadow). Hong Kong: Dahua chubanshe, 1971.
    Chuanying Lou Huiyi Lu Xubian (A sequel to the memoir from the mansion of bracelet shadow). Hong Kong: Dahua chubanshe, 1973.
Chao Juren. *Wo Yu Wode Shijie* (I and my world). Taibei: Longwen chubanshe, 1990.
Chen Bangxian. *Zhongguo Yixue Shi* (A history of Chinese medicine). Shanghai: Shangwu yinshuguan, 1937; Shanghai shudian, 1984.
Chen Chujun and Yu Xingmo. *Tegong Miwen: Juntong Huodong Jishi* (Secret information on special agents: A record of the activities of the Military Commission's Bureau of Investigation and Statistics). Beijing: Zhongguo wenshi chubanshe, 1990.
Dongwu Daxue Faxue Yuan Tongxue Lu (The alumni directory of Soochow University Law School). 1936.
Du Xucheng. *Minzu Ziben Zhuyi Yu Jiu Zhongguo Zhengfu, 1840–1937* (Nationalist capitalism and the government of old China, 1840–1937). Shanghai: Shanghai shehui kexueyuan chubanshe, 1991.
Faguang Tekan (A special book on lights of law). Shanghai: Da ribao guan, 1935.
Faling Daquan (A complete collection of the laws and ordinances). Shanghai: Shangwu yinshuguan, 1924.
Fang Hanqi. *Zhongguo Jindai Baokan Shi* (A history of newspapers and magazines in modern China). Taiyuan: Shanxi jiaoye chubanshe, 1981.
Fei Chengkang. *Zhongguo Zujie Shi* (A history of foreign concessions in China). Shanghai: Shanghai shehui kexueyuan chubanshe, 1991.

Bibliography

Feng Yingzhi. *Baohai Yijiu* (Reminiscences of newspapers). Taiyuan: Shuhai chubanshe, 1991

Fu Weikang. *Zhongyao Xueshi* (A history of Chinese native drugs). Chengdu: Bashu shushe, 1993.

Gao Changhong. *Zhoudao Chuban Jie* (Walk into the publishing world). Shanghai: Taidong tushuju, 1929; Shanghai shudian, 1985.

Ge Gongzheng. *Zhongguo Baoxue Shi* (A history of Chinese journalism). Shanghai: Shangwu yinshuguan, 1927. Beijing: Sanlian shudian, 1955.

Ge Yuanxu. *Huyou Zaji* (Random notes of the tour in Shanghai). 1876; Shanghai: Shanghai guji chubanshe, 1989.

Gu Yuezhong. *Diguo Zhuyi Zai Shanghai De Jiaoyu Qinlue Huodong Ziliao Jianbian* (A brief compilation of sources on imperialist activities in Shanghai's education). Shanghai: Shanghai jiaoyu chubanshe, 1982.

Guo Bingwen. *Zhongguo Jiaoyu Zhidu Yange Shi* (A history of evolution of the Chinese educational system). Shanghai: Shangwu yinshuguan, 1922.

Guo Wei and Zhou Dingmei. *Lüshi Banshi Shouxu Chengshi Huishu* (An annotated compilation of the procedures for lawyers' practice). Shanghai: Faxue bianyishe, 1937.

Guo Weidong and Liu Yigao, eds. *Jindai Waiguo Zaihua Wenhua Jigou Zonglu* (A comprehensive listing of foreign cultural institutions in modern China). Shanghai: Shanghai renmin chubanshe, 1993.

Guoyi Minglu (The directory of native physicians). Shanghai: Shanghai shi guoyi xuehui zuzhibu, 1932.

Hong Weijie. *Ge Gongzhen Nianpu* (A biographic chronicle of Ge Gongzhen). Nanjing: Jiangsu renmin chubanshe, 1990.

Hu Bang'an. *Guoyi Kaiye Shu* (The art of practicing native medicine). Shanghai: Hushi yishi, 1933.

Hu Daojing. "Shanghai De Xueyi Tuanti" (Academic and artistic associations in Shanghai), *Shanghai Tongzhi Guan Qikan* (Journal of the Shanghai General History Institute), 1929:823–946.

Hu Xianghan. *Shanghai Xiaozhi* (Miscellaneous notes on Shanghai). Shanghai: Chuanjing dang shudian, 1930; Shanghai: Shanghai guji chubanshe, 1989.

Huang Shiquan. *Songnan Mengying Lu* (A record of shadowy dreams of southern Shanghai). Shanghai, 1883; Shanghai: Shanghai guji chubanshe, 1989.

Huang Tianpeng. *Zhongguo Xinwen Shiye* (China's journalistic enterprise). Shanghai: Lianhe shudian, 1930.

Ji Hongsheng. *Zhongguo Guomindang Shigang* (An outline history of the Chinese Nationalist Party). Shanghai: Baijia chubanshe, 1990.

Jiang Guozhen. *Zhongguo Xinwen Fada Shi* (A history of the development of Chinese journalism). Shanghai: Shijie shuju, 1927.

Jiaoyu Bu. *Jaoyu Faling Huibian* (A collection of laws and regulations on education). Nanjing, 1933.

Jin Liren and He Shiyou. *Yang Xianjiang Zhuanji* (A biography of Yang Xiangjiang). Nanjing: Jiangsu jiaoyu chubanshe, 1990.

Jiu Shanghai De Zhengjuan Jiaoyisuo (Stock exchanges in old Shanghai). Shanghai: Shanghai guji chubanshe, 1992.

Bibliography

Lai Guanglin. *Zhongguo Jindai Baoren Yu Baoye* (Journalists and newspapers in modern China). Taiwan: Shangwu yinshu guan, 1980.

Lai Xinxia. *Beiyang Junfa Shigao* (A draft history of Beiyang warlords). Wuhan: Hubei renmin chubanshe, 1983.

Li Pingshu. *Qishi Zishu* (Autobiography at seventy). Shanghai, 1924; Shanghai guji chubanshe, 1989.

Li Weiqing. *Shanghai Xiangtu Zhi* (Notes on Shanghai's environment and products). Shanghai, 1907; Shanghai guji chubanshe, 1989.

Liu Huiwu. *Shanghai Jindai Shi* (A history of modern Shanghai). Shanghai: Huadong shifan daxue chubanshe, 1989.

Liu Shaotang. *Minguo Dashi Rizhi* (A chronicle of important events of the Republic of China). Taibei: Zhuanji wenxue chubanshe, 1978.

Liu Zheng. *Lushi Daode Lun* (On the ethics of lawyers). Shanghai: Shangwu yinshuguan, 1934.

Lixing Kuaiji Shiwu Suo Gaikuang (Lixing accounting firm at a glance). Shanghai: Lixing kuaiji shiwu suo, 1932.

Lu Shi'e. *Guoyi Xinyu* (New talks about native medicine). Shanghai: Daxin shuju, 1934.

Lüshi Shiwusuo Suode Sui Ji Kuaiji Shang Yingxing Zhuyi Shixiang (A reminder of regulations on law firms' income tax and accounting). Shanghai: Shanghai lüshi gonghui, 1937.

Ma Boying. *Zhongguo Yixue Wenhua Shi* (A history of medicine in Chinese culture). Shanghai: Shanghai renmin chubanshe, 1994.

Ma Min and Zhu Ying. *Chuantong Yu Jindai De Erchong Bianzhou: Wanqing Suzhou Shanghui Ge'an Yanjiu* (Dual variations of tradition and modernity: A case study of the Suzhou Chamber of Commerce in late Qing). Chengdu: Bashu shushe, 1993.

Ma Xuexin, et al., eds. *Shanghai Wenhua Yuanliu Cidian* (A dictionary of the origins and flows of the Shanghai culture). Shanghai: Shanghai shehui kexueyuan chubanshe, 1992.

Minguo Fagui Jikan (A collection of the laws and regulations of the Republic). Shanghai: Minzhi shuju, 1929.

Minguo Renwu Dacidian (MRD) (A comprehensive who's who of the Republic of China). Shijia zhuang: Hebei renmin chubanshe, 1991.

Minguo Renwu Zhuan (Biographies of the Republic of China). Vols.1–7, Beijing: Zhounghua shuju, 1978–1993.

Minguo Shanghai Xianzhi (MSX) (Gazetteer of Shanghai County in the Republic). 1935.

Minguo Yiyao Weisheng Fagui Xuanbian, 1912–1948 (Selected compilation of laws and regulations concerning medicine and health in the Republic of China, 1912–1948). Jinan: Shangdong daxue chubanshe, 1990.

Minguo Yuannian Zhongyang Jiaoyu Huiyi Jueyi An (Resolutions of the central education conference in the first year of the Republic). Shanghai: Zhonghua shuju, 1912.

Pan Nianzhi. *Zhongguo Jindai Falu Sixiang Shi* (A history of legal thought in modern China). 2 Vols. Shanghai: Shanghai shehui kexueyuan chubanshe, 1992–1993.

Bibliography

Pang Jingzhou. *Shanghai Shi Jinshi Nianlai Yiyao Niaokan* (An overview of Shanghai's medicine in the recent ten years). Shanghai: Zhongguo kexue gongsi, 1933.

Qian Jiaju and Guo Yangang. *Zhongguo Huobi Shi Gangyao* (An outline history of Chinese currencies). Shanghai: Shanghai renmin chubanshe, 1986.

Qian Shipu. *Beiyang Zhengfu Zhiguan Nianbiao* (A chronicle of Beiyang government officials). Shanghai: Huadong shifan daxue chubanshe, 1991.

Beiyang Zhengfu Shiqi De Zhengzhi Zhidu (The political system during the Beiyang period). Beijing: Zhonghua shuju, 1984.

Qin Shaode. *Shanghai Jindai Baokan Shilun* (On the history of newspapers and periodicals in modern Shanghai). Shanghai: Fudan daxue chubanshe, 1993.

Quanguo Dengji Yishi Minlu (A national directory of registered doctors). Nanjing: Zhongyang weisheng shu, 1942.

Quanguo Minzhong Yundong Gaikuang (A national overview of mass movement). Nanjing: Zhongguo guomindang zhongyang zhixing weiyuanhui minzhong yundong zhidao weiyuanhui, 1934.

Quangguo Wenhua Jiguan Yilan (An overview of cultural institutions in the country). Nanjing: Jiaoyubu, 1934.

Quanguo Yiyao Tuanti Zonglianhehui Huiwu Huibian (QYTZHH) (A compilation of the proceedings of the national federation of medical and pharmaceutical associations). Shanghai, 1931.

Ren Jianshu, ed. *Xiandai Shanghai Dashi Ji* (A chronicle of modern Shanghai [1919–1949]). Shanghai: Cishu chubanshe, 1996.

Renmin Tuanti Fagui Huibian (A compilation of the laws and regulations on people's associations). Wuxian: Wuxian dangwu zhengli weiyuanhui, 1930.

Renmin Tuanti Fagui Shili Huibian (A compilation of the interpretations of the laws and regulations on people's associations). Nanjing: Zhongyang minzhong xunlian bu, 1937.

Shanghai Fangzhi Gongren Yundong Shi (A history of Shanghai textile workers' movement). Beijing: Zhonggong dangshi chubanshe, 1991.

Shanghai Geming Wenhua Dashiji, 1937–1949 (A chronicle of revolutionary culture in Shanghai, 1937–1949). Shanghai: Shanghai fanyi chuban gongsi, 1991.

Shanghai Gonggong Zujie Nasui Huaren Hui Zhongyao Wenjian (Important documents of the Chinese Ratepayers Association of the Shanghai International Settlement). 1937.

Shanghai Jinrong Jiguan Yilan (Shanghai's financial institutions at a glance). Shanghai: Shanghai yinhang zhoubao she, 1920.

Shanghai Lüshi Gonghui Baogaoshu (SLGB) (The report of the Shanghai Bar Association). 1921–1922, 1924, 1928–1936.

Shanghai Lüshi Gonghui Huiyuan Yingxing Zhuyi Shixiang (A handbook of guidelines for members of the Shanghai Bar Association). 1936.

Shanghai Lüshi Gonghui Huiyuanlu (The membership directory of the Shanghai Bar Association). 1931, 1933–1937.

Shanghai Lüshi Gonghui Zhanxing Huizhe (The provisional bylaws of the Shanghai Bar Association). 1928.

Bibliography

Shanghai shehui kexueyuan jingji yanjiusuo. *Shanghai Duiwai Maoyi* (Shanghai's foreign trade). 2 Vols. Shanghai: Shanghai shehui kexueyuan chubanshe, 1989.
Shanghai Shi Guoyi Gonghui Huiyuanlu (The directory of the Shanghai Native Medical Association). 1936.
Shanghai Shi Guoyi Xuehui Shizhou Jinian Kan (The tenth anniversary memorial journal of the Shanghai Native Medical Society). 1932.
Shanghai Shi Shehui Tongji Gaiyao (A summary of the social survey in Shanghai). Shanghai: Shanghai shi shehuiju, 1935.
Shanghai Shi Tongji Bucong Cailiao (Supplementary to the Shanghai survey). Shanghai: Shanghai difang xiehui, 1935.
Shanghai Shi Xinwen Jizhe Gonghui Huiyuanlu (Fu Zhiyuan Lu Ji Zhangcheng) (The directory of the Shanghai Journalists Association, with directory of officers and the bylaws attached). 1934.
Shanghai Shi Yanjiu (The Shanghai history studies), No.2. Shanghai: Xuelin chubanshe, 1988.
Shanghai Shi Yishi Gonghui Huiyuanlu (fu Huizhang) (The directory of the Medical Practitioners' Association of Shanghai, with the bylaws attached). 1936.
Shanghai Shi Yishi Gonghui Zhangcheng (The bylaws of the Shanghai [native] Medical Practitioners Association). 1927.
Shanghai Shudian Diaocha (A survey of Shanghai's bookstores). Shanghai: Shanghai shi jiaoyu ju, 1935.
Shanghai Tebieshi Di Sanci Dengji Zhongyi Minglu (The third list of registered native physicians in the Shanghai Special Municipality). Shanghai: Shanghai tebieshi wei sheng ju, 1929.
Shanghai Tebieshi Shizheng Fagui Huibian (STSFH) (A compilation of the municipal ordinances and regulations of the Shanghai Special Municipality). Shanghai: Shanghai tebieshi zhengfu mishuchu, 1928.
Shanghai Zhonghua Minguo Kuaijishi Gonghui Nianbao (The annual report of the Institute of Chartered Accountants in Shanghai of the Chinese Republic). 1926, 1928.
Shi Quansheng. *Zhonghua Minguo Wenhua Shi* (A cultural history of the Republic of China). Changchun: Jilin wenshi chubanshe, 1990.
Sili Dongwu Daxue Falu Xueyuan Yilan (Soochow University Law School annual announcement). Shanghai, 1933.
Song Guobing. *Yisong Anjian Huichao* (A collection of medical malpractice lawsuits). Shanghai: Zhonghua yixuehui, 1935.
Song Jiaoren Xue'an (The bloody case of Song Jiaoren's [murder]). Changsha: Yuelu shushe, 1986.
Su Zhiliang and Chen Feili. *Jindai Shanghai Hei Shehui Yanjiu* (A study on modern Shanghai's underworld). Hangzhou: Zhejiang renmin chubanshe, 1991.
Takahaku Kikuchi. *Chugoku Daisan Shili Shiron* (A historical treatise on the third force in China). Tokyo: Kyuko Shoin Co. Ltd., 1987.
Tang Hai. *Zhongguo Laodong Wenti* (The problem of Chinese labor). Shanghai: Guanghua shuju, 1927.

Bibliography

Tang Zhenchang. *Shanghai Shi* (A history of Shanghai). Shanghai: Shanghai renmin chubanshe, 1989.

Tang Zhijun, ed. *Jindai Shanghai Dashi Ji* (A chronicle of modern Shanghai [1840–1919]). Shanghai: Shanghai cishu chubanshe, 1989.

Tao Xingzhi. *Zhongguo Jiaoyu Gaizhao* (The reform of Chinese education). Shanghai: Yadong tushu guan, 1928.

Wang Huilin and Zhu Hanguo, eds. *Zhongguo Baokan Cidian (1918–1949)* (A dictionary of Chinese newspapers and periodicals, 1815–1949). Taiyuan: Shuhai chubanshe, 1992.

Wang Jinwu. *Zhongguo Xiandai Zichan Jieji Minzhu Yundong Shi* (A history of bourgeois democratic movement in modern China). Changchun: Jilin wenshi chubanshe, 1985.

Wang Qizhang. *Ershi Nianlai Zhongguo Yishi Zouyi* (Comments on China's medical work in the recent twenty years). Shanghai: Zhengliao yibao she, 1935.

Wang Tao. *Yingxu Zazhi* (Random notes about Shanghai). Guangzhou, 1875; Shanghai: Shanghai guji chubanshe, 1989.

Wang Zhiyi, et al., eds. *Bianji Jizhe Yibairen* (One hundred editors and reporters), Shanghai: Xuelin chubanshe, 1985.

Wu Lilan and Lin Qi. *Wu Kaisheng Boshi Zhuanji* (A biography of Dr. Wu Kaisheng). Hong Kong: Dadi yinshua chuban gongsi, 1993.

Xinyi Yu Shehui Huikan (A collection of articles from *New Medicine and Society*). Vol.1 (Shanghai, 1928); Vol.2 (Shanghai, 1934).

Xu Dingxin and Qian Xiaoming. *Shanghai Zong Shanghui Shi, 1902–1929* (A history of the Shanghai General Chamber of Commerce, 1902–1929). Shanghai: Shanghai shehui kexueyuan chubanshe, 1991.

Xu Mao. *Zhonghua Minguo Zhengzhi Zhidu Shi* (A history of the political institutions in Republic China). Shanghai: Shanghai renmin chubanshe, 1992.

Xu Maoyong. *Xu Maoyong Huiyi Lu* (Memoir of Xu Maoyong). Beijing: Renmin wenxue chubanshe, 1982.

Xu Wancheng. *Quanguo Baokan She Diaocha Lu* (A national survey on publishers of newspapers and magazines). Shanghai: Longwen shudian, 1936.

Quanguo Tushu Guan Diaocha Lu (A national survey on libraries). Shanghai: Longwen shudian, 1935.

Shanghai Dazhongxiao Xuexiao Diaocha Lu (A survey on Shanghai's universities, middle schools, and primary schools). Shanghai: Longwen shudian, 1935.

Xu Wen. *Shao Piaoping Zhuanlue* (A brief biography of Shao Piaoping). Beijing: Beijing shifan xueyuan chubanshe, 1990.

Xu Zhucheng. *Baohai Jiuwen* (Reminiscences of old newspapers). Shanghai: Shanghai renmin chubanshe, 1981.

Yang Honglie. *Zhongguo Falü Fada Shi* (A history of the development of Chinese laws). Shanghai: Shangwu yinshuguan, 1930; Shanghai shudian, 1990.

Yao Gonghe. *Shanghai Xianhua* (Leisured talk about Shanghai). Shanghai: Shangwu yinshuguan, 1917; Shanghai guji chubanshe, 1989.

Yu Yunxiu. *Yixue Geming Lun Cuji* (On medical revolution, first volume). Shanghai: Yushi yanjiu shi, 1928.
Zhang Jinglu. *Zai Chubanjie Ershi Nian* (Twenty years in the publishing circle). Shanghai: Shanghai zazhi gongsi, 1938; Shanghai shudian, 1984.
  Zhongguo De Xinwen Jizhe (Chinese journalists). Shanghai: Guanghua shuju, 1928.
  Zhongguo De Xinwen Jizhe Yu Xinwen Zhi (Chinese journalists and Chinese newspapers). Shanghai: Xiandai shuju, 1932.
Zhang Zhongli. *Jindai Shanghai Chenghsi Yanjiu* (An urban study of modern Shanghai). Shanghai: Shanghai renmin chubanshe, 1990.
Zhonggong Shanghai Shiwei Dangshi Yanjiu Shi. *Zhongguo Gongchandang Zai Shanghai, 1921–1991* (The Chinese Communist Party in Shanghai, 1921–1991). Shanghai: Shanghai renmin chubanshe, 1991.
Zhongguo Fazhi Xiandai Huade Jincheng (The modernization process in Chinese legal system). Beijing: Zhongguo renmin gong'an daxue chubanshe, 1991.
Zhongguo guomindang zhongyang zhixing weiyaunhui minzhong yundong zhidao weiyuanhui. *Quanguo Minzhong Yundong Gaikuang* (A national overview of people's movements). Nanjing, 1934.
Zhongguo Shehui Kexue Yuan Jindai Shi Yanjiu Suo Fanyi Shi. *Jiadai Laihua Waiguo Renming Cidian* (A dictionary of foreigners in modern China). Beijing: Zhongguo shehui kexue chubanshe, 1981.
Zhongguo Yijie Zhinan (The directory of Chinese medical practitioners). Zhonghua yixuehui, 1932.
Zhonghua Jiaoyu Gaijin She Gaikuang (The Chinese Society for Improving Education at a glance). Shanghai, 1922.
Zhonghua Minguo Faling Daquan (The complete collection of the laws and ordinances of the Republic of China). Shanghai: Shangwu yinshuguan, 1915.
Zhonghua Minguo Huobi Shi Ziliao Di'er Ji, 1924–1949 (The second volume of sources on the history of currencies in the Republic of China, 1924–1949). Shanghai: Shanghai renmin chubanshe, 1991.
Zhonghua Minguo Lüshi Xiehui Diliu Jie Daibiao Dahui Tekan (The special journal of the sixth conference of the Bar Association of the Republic of China). 1934.
Zhonghua Minguo Lüshi Xiehui Diwu Jie Daibiao Dahui Tekan (The special journal of the fifth conference of the Bar Association of the Republic of China). 1933.
Zhonghua Minguo Xianxing Fagui Daquan (ZMXFD) (The complete collection of the current laws and regulations of the Republic of China). Shanghai: Shangwu yinshuguan, 1934, 1936.
Zhonghua Yixue Hui Huiwu Baogao (The report on the work of the Chinese Medical Association). 1934.
Zhou Yumin and Shao Yong, *Zhongguo Banhui Shi* (A history of Chinese secret societies). Shanghai: Shanghai renmin chubanshe, 1993.
Zhu Lianbao. *Jindai Shanghai Chuban Ye Yinxiang Ji* (An impression of the publishing trade in modern Shanghai). Shanghai: Xuelin chubanshe, 1993.

Zhu Zijia (Jin Xiongbai). *Huangpu Jiangde Zhuolang* (The muddy wave of the Huangpu River). Hong Kong: Wuxing ji shubao she, 1964.

Zhuo Zunhong, et al., eds. *Kangzhan Qian Shinian Huobi Shi Ziliao* (Sources on the history of currencies in the decade prior to the war of resistance). Taipei: Zhongyang wenwu gongyingshe, 1987.

Zou Yiren. *Jiu Shanghai Renkou Bianqian De Yanjiu* (A study of population changes in old Shanghai). Shanghai: Shanghai renmin chubanshe, 1980.

YEARBOOKS, NEWSPAPERS, AND JOURNALS IN ENGLISH

China Medical Journal, 1912–1937.
China Weekly Review (CWR), 1922–1938.
China Yearbook, 1913–1935.
Chinese Recorder, 1920–1928.
Chinese Social and Political Science Review (CSPSR), 1917–1938.
Millard's Review, 1917–1922.
North China Daily News, 1912–1914, 1926–1927.
North China Herald (NCH), 1912–1937.

WORKS IN ENGLISH AND FRENCH

Abel, Richard L. *American Lawyers*. London: Oxford University Press, 1989.

All About Shanghai and Environs: A Standard Guide Book. Shanghai: The University Press, 1935.

Anderson, Benedict. *Imagined Communities: Reflection on the Origin and Spread of Nationalism*. London: Verso, 1991.

Andrews, Bridie J. "Tuberculosis and the Assimilation of Germ Theory in China, 1895–1937," *Journal of the History of Medicine*, 52 (Jan. 1997):114–57.

Bastid, Marianne. *Educational Reform in Early-Twentieth-Century China*. Ann Arbor: Center for Chinese Studies, the University of Michigan, 1988.

Baudelot, Christian, et al., eds. *La Petite Bourgeoisie en France*. Paris: Francois Maspero, 1975.

Beckhofer, Frank, and Brian Elliott, eds. *The Petite Bourgeoisie*. New York: St. Martin's Press, 1981.

Bedeski, Robert E. *State Building in Modern China: The Kuomintang in the Prewar Period*. Center for Chinese Studies, University of California, Berkeley, 1981.

Bendix, Rainhard, John Bendix, and Norman Furniss. "Reflections on Modern Western States and Civil Societies," in R. G. Braungart and M. M. Braungart, eds., *The Political Sociology of the State*. Greenwich, CT: Jai Press, 1990.

Bergère, Marie-Claire. *The Golden Age of the Chinese Bourgeoisie, 1911–1937*. Cambridge: Cambridge University Press, 1989.

"Les Capitalistes Shanghaiens et la Période de Transition entre le Régime Guomindang et le Communisme (1948–1952)," *Etudes Chinoises*, 8,2 (Autumn 1989):7–30.

Bibliography

"'The Other China': Shanghai from 1919 to 1949," in Christopher Howe, ed., *Shanghai: Revolution and Development in an Asian Metropolis*. Cambridge: Cambridge University Press, 1981.

Bernhardt, Kathryn, and Philip Huang, eds. *Civil Law in Qing and Republican China*. Stanford: Stanford University Press, 1994.

Borthwick, Sally. *Education and Social Change in China*. Stanford: Hoover Institute Press, 1983.

Britton, Roswell S. *The Chinese Periodical Press, 1800–1912*. Shanghai: Kelly and Walsh, 1933.

Broman, Thomas. "Rethinking Professionalization: Theory, Practice, and Professional Ideology in Eighteenth-Century German Medicine," *The Journal of Modern History*, 67 (Dec. 1995):835–72.

Cameron, Meribeth E. *The Reform Movement in China, 1898–1912*. Stanford: Stanford University Press, 1931.

Chamberlain, Heath B. "On the Search for Civil Society in China," *Modern China*, 19,2 (Apr. 1993):199–215.

"Civil Society with Chinese Characteristics," *China Journal*, 39 (Jan. 1998).

Chang, Yao-tseng. "The Present Conditions of the Chinese Judiciary and its Future," *The Chinese Social and Political Science Review*, 10,1 (Jan. 1926):170–75.

Chang, Yu-chuan. "The Legal Practitioner in China," *The Chinese Social and Political Science Review*, 22,2 (July–Sept. 1938):147–84.

"The Bar Association in China," *The Chinese Social and Political Science Review*, 22,3 (Oct.–Dec. 1938):235–81.

Chauncey, Helen R. *Schoolhouse Politicians: Locality and State during the Chinese Republic*. Honolulu: University of Hawaii Press, 1992.

Chen, Joseph. *The May Fourth Movement in Shanghai*. Leiden: Brill, 1971.

Cheng, Ying-wan. *Postal Communication in China and Its Modernization, 1860–1896*. Cambridge, MA: Harvard University Press, 1970.

Chesneaux, Jean. *The Chinese Labor Movement, 1919–1927*. Stanford: Stanford University Press, 1968.

ed. *Popular Movements and Secret Societies in China, 1840–1950*. Stanford: Stanford University Press, 1972.

Chevrier, Yves. "La Question de la Société Civile, la Chine et le Chat du Cheshire," *Etudes Chinoises*, 14,3 (Autumn 1995):153–251.

Ch'i, Hsi-sheng. *Warlord Politics in China, 1916–1928*. Stanford: Stanford University Press, 1976.

Ching, Frank. *Ancestors: 900 Years in the Life of a Chinese Family*. New York: William Morrow, 1988.

Choa, G. H. *"Heal the Sick" Was Their Motto: The Protestant Medical Missionaries in China*. Hong Kong: The Chinese University Press, 1990.

Chow, Tse-tsung. *The May Fourth Movement: Intellectual Revolution in China*. Stanford: Stanford University Press, 1960.

Chyne, W. Y. *Handbook of Cultural Institutions in China*. Shanghai: Chinese National Committee on Intellectual Cooperation, 1936.

Clifford, Nicholas R. *Shanghai: 1925 Urban Nationalism and the Defense of*

Foreign Privilege. Ann Arbor: The University of Michigan Center for Chinese Studies, 1979.

Spoilt Children of Empire: Westerners in Shanghai and the Chinese Revolution of the 1920s. Hanover, NH: Middlebury College Press, 1991.

Coble Jr., Parks M. *The Shanghai Capitalists and the Nationalist Government, 1927–1937*. Cambridge, MA: Harvard University Press, 1980.

"Chiang Kai-shek and the Anti-Japanese Movement in China: Zou Tao-fen and the National Salvation Association, 1931–1937," *Journal of Asian Studies*, 44,2 (Feb. 1985):293–310.

Facing Japan: Chinese Politics and Japanese Imperialism, 1931–1937. Cambridge, MA: Harvard University Press, 1991.

Cochran, Sherman. *Big Business in China*. Cambridge, MA: Harvard University Press, 1980.

Cocks, Geoffrey, and Konrad H. Jarausch, eds. *German Professions, 1800–1950*. Oxford: Oxford University Press, 1990.

Cole, James H. *Shaohsing: Competition and Cooperation in Nineteenth-Century China*. Tucson: University of Arizona Press, 1986.

Conner, Alison W. "Lawyers and the Legal Profession during the Republican Period," in Kathryn Bernhardt and Philip Huang, eds., *Civil Law in Qing and Republican China*. Stanford: Stanford University Press, 1994, pp.215–48.

"Legal Education during the Republican Period: Soochow Univerity Law School," *Republican China*, 19,1 (Nov. 1993):85–112.

Croizier, Ralph C. *Traditional Medicine in Modern China: Science, Nationalism, and the Tensions of Cultural Change*. Cambridge, MA: Harvard University Press, 1968.

Curran, Thomas D. "Education and Society in Republican China," Ph.D. dissertation, Columbia University, 1986.

Darwent, C. E. *Shanghai: A Handbook for Travelers and Residents to Chief Objects of Interest in and around the Foreign Settlements and Native City*. Shanghai: Kelly and Walsh, 1920.

Davis, Deborah, and Ezra F. Vogel, eds. *Chinese Society on the Eve of Tiananmen: The Impact of Reform*. Cambridge, MA: Harvard University Press, 1990.

Davis, Deborah S., et al., eds. *Urban Spaces in Contemporary China*. Cambridge: Cambridge University Press, 1995.

Des Forges, Roger V., et al., eds. *Chinese Democracy and the Crisis of 1989*. Albany, NY: State University of New York Press, 1992.

Dicken-Garcia, Hazel. *Journalistic Standards in Nineteenth-Century America*. Madison: The University of Wisconsin Press, 1989.

Ding, Xue Liang. *The Decline of Communism in China*. Cambridge: Cambridge University Press, 1994.

Dingwall, Robert, and Philip Lewis, eds. *The Sociology of the Professions: Lawyers, Doctors, and Others*. London: The Macmillan Press, 1983.

Dirlik, Arif. "The Ideological Foundations of the New Life Movement: A Study in Counterrevolution," *Journal of Asian Studies*, 34,4 (Aug. 1975):945–80.

Bibliography

Duara, Prasenjit. *Culture, Power, and the State: Rural North China, 1900–1942*. Stanford: Stanford University Press, 1988.

Rescuing History from the Nation. Chicago: University of Chicago Press, 1995.

"Provincial Narratives of the Nation: Centralism and Federalism in Republican China," in Harmi Befu, ed., *Cultural Nationalism in East Asia: Representation and Identity*. Berkeley: University of California Institute of East Asian Studies, 1993. pp.9–35.

Eastman, Lloyd. *The Abortive Revolution: China under Nationalist Rule, 1927–1937*. Cambridge, MA: Harvard University Press, 1974.

"Fascism in Kuomintang China: The Blue Shirts," *China Quarterly*, 49 (1972):1–31.

"The Kuomintang in the 1930s," in Charlotte Forth, ed., *The Limits of Change: Essays on Conservative Alternatives in Republican China*. Cambridge, MA: Harvard University Press, 1976.

Elman, Benjamin A. *From Philosophy to Philology: Intellectual and Social Aspects of Change in Late Imperial China*. Cambridge, MA: Harvard University Press, 1990.

Elvin, Mark. "The Gentry Democracy in Chinese Shanghai, 1905–1914," in Jack Gray, ed., *Modern China's Search for a Political Form*. Oxford: Oxford University Press, 1969.

Elvin, Mark, and G. W. Skinner, eds. *The Chinese City between Two Worlds*. Stanford: Stanford University Press, 1974.

Esherick, Joseph W. *Reform and Revolution in China*. Berkeley: University of California Press, 1976.

Feuerwerker, Albert. *The Chinese Economy, 1870–1949*. Ann Arbor: The University of Michigan Center for Chinese Studies, 1995.

Fewsmith, Joseph. *Party, State, and Local Elites in Republican China: Merchant Organizations and Politics in Shanghai, 1890–1930*. Honolulu. University of Hawaii Press. 1985.

Fitzgerald, John. *Awakening China: Politics, Culture, and Class in the Nationalist Revolution*. Stanford: Stanford University Press, 1996.

"The Origins of the Illiberal Party Newspapers: Print Journalism in China's Nationalist Revolution," *Republican China*, 21,2 (Nov. 1996):1–22.

Freidson, Eliot. *Professional Powers*. Chicago: University of Chicago Press, 1986.

Gamewell, M. N. *The Gateway to China: Pictures of Shanghai*. New York: Fleming H. Revell, 1916.

Gaster, Michael. *Chinese Intellectuals and the Revolution of 1911*. Seattle: University of Washington Press, 1969.

Goldman, Merle, et al., eds. *China's Intellectuals and the State*. Cambridge, MA: Harvard University Press, 1987.

Goodman, Bryna. "New Culture, Old Habits: Native-Place Organization and the May Fourth Movement," in Frederick Wakeman and Wen-hsin Yeh, eds., *Shanghai Sojourners*. Berkeley: University of California Center for Chinese Studies, 1992, pp.76–107.

Native Place, City, and Nation: Regional Networks and Identities in Shanghai, 1853–1937. Berkeley: University of California Press, 1995.

"Locality as Microcosm of the Nation? Native-Place Networks and Early Urban Nationalism in China," *Modern China*, 21,4 (1995):387–419.

Greenwood, Ernest. "Attributes of a Profession: Revisited," in Sheo K. Lal, et al., eds. *Readings in the Sociology of the Professions*. Delhi: Gain Publishing House, 1988.

Grieder, Jerome B. *Intellectuals and the State in Modern China*. New York: Free Press, 1981.

Gulick, Edward V. *Peter Parker and the Opening of China*. Cambridge, MA: Harvard University Press, 1973.

Haber, Samuel. *The Quest for Authority and Honor in the American Professions, 1750–1900*. Chicago: The University of Chicago Press, 1991.

Habermas, Jürgen. *The Structural Transformation of the Public Sphere: An Inquiry into a Category of Bourgeois Society*. Tr. by Thomas Burger. Cambridge, MA: The MIT Press, 1989.

Hamrin, Carol L., and Timothy Cheek, eds. *China's Establishment Intellectuals*. Armonk, NY: M. E. Sharpe, 1986.

Hargrove, Erwin C. *Professional Roles in Society and Government: The English Case*. London: Sage Publications, 1972.

Henriot, Christian. *Shanghai, 1927–1937: Municipal Power, Locality, and Modernization*. Berkeley: University of California Press, 1993.

Honig, Emily. *Sisters and Strangers: Women in the Shanghai Cotton Mills, 1919–1949*. Stanford: Stanford University Press, 1986.

Chinese Ethnicity. New Haven: Yale University Press, 1994.

"Invisible Inequalities: The Status of Subei People in Contemporary Shanghai," *China Quarterly*, 122 (1990):273–92.

Howe, Christopher, ed. *Shanghai: Revolution and Development in an Asian Metropolis*. Cambridge: Cambridge University Press, 1981.

Hsia, Ching-lin. *The Status of Shanghai: A Historical Review of the International Settlement*. Shanghai: Kelly and Walsh, Ltd., 1929.

Huang, Philip C. C. "The Paradigmatic Crisis in Chinese Studies," *Modern China*, 17,3 (1991):299–341.

"'Public Sphere'/'Civil Society' in China," *Modern China*, 19,2 (1993):216–40.

Civil Justice in China: Representation and Practice in the Qing. Stanford: Stanford University Press, 1996.

Hung, Chang-tai. *War and Popular Culture: Resistance in Modern China, 1937–1945*. Berkeley: University of California Press, 1994.

Inglehart, Ronald. *Modernization and Postmodernization: Cultural, Economic, and Political Changes in 43 Societies*. Princeton: Princeton University Press, 1997.

Isaacs, Harold R. *The Tragedy of the Chinese Revolution*. Stanford: Stanford University Press, 1961.

Israel, John. *Student Nationalism in China, 1927–1937*. Stanford: Stanford University Press, 1966.

Jarausch, Konrad H. *The Unfree Professions: German Lawyers, Teachers, and Engineers, 1900–1950*. Oxford: Oxford University Press, 1990.

Jeans, Roger B., ed. *Roads Not Taken: The Struggle of Opposition Parties in Twentieth-Century China*. Boulder, CO: Westview Press, 1992.

Johnson, Chalmers A. *Peasant Nationalism and Communist Power: The Emergence of Revolutionary China, 1937–1945*. Stanford: Stanford University Press, 1962.

Johnson, Linda C. *Shanghai: From Market Town to Treaty Port, 1074–1858*. Stanford: Stanford University Press, 1995.

"Shanghai: An Emerging Jiangnan Port, 1683–1840," in Linda C. Johnson, ed. *Cities of Jiangnan in Late Imperial China*. Albany: State University of New York Press, 1993.

Johnson, Terence J. *Professions and Power*. Hong Kong: Macmillan Education Ltd., 1972.

Jones, Susan Mann. "The Ningpo *Pang* and Financial Power at Shanghai," in Mark Elvin and G. William Skinner, eds., *The Chinese City between Two Worlds*. Stanford: Stanford University Press, 1974, pp.73–96.

Judge, Joan. *Print and Politics: "Shibao" and the Culture of Reform in Late Qing China*. Stanford: Stanford University Press, 1996.

"The Factional Function of Print: Liang Qichao, *Shibao*, and the Fissures in the Late Qing Reform Movement," *Late Imperial China*, 16,1 (June 1995):120–40.

Kann, Eduard. *The Currencies of China: An Investigation of Gold and Silver Transactions Affecting China, with a Section on Copper*. Shanghai: Kelly and Walsh, 1927.

Kean, John. *Democracy and Civil Society*. London: Verso, 1988.

Kean, John, ed. *Civil Society and the State: New European Perspectives*. London: Verso, 1988.

Keeton, George W. *The Development of Extraterritoriality in China*. Shanghai: Kelley and Walsh, 1928.

Kirby, William C. *Germany and Republican China*. Stanford: Stanford University Press, 1984.

Kocka, Jurgen, and Allan Mitchell, eds. *Bourgeois Society in Nineteenth-Century Europe*. Oxford: Berg Publisher, 1993.

Kotenev, A. M. *Shanghai: Its Municipality and the Chinese*. Shanghai: North China Daily News and North China Herald, 1927.

Krause, Elliot A. *The Sociology of Occupations*. Boston: Little, Brown, and Company, 1971.

Lanning, G., and S. Couling. *The History of Shanghai*. Shanghai: Kelly and Walsh, Ltd., 1921.

Larson, Magali Sarfatti. *The Rise of Professionalism: A Sociological Analysis*. Berkeley: University of California Press, 1977.

Lavau, Georges, Gerard Grunberg, and Nonna Mayer, eds. *L'Univers Politique des Classes Moyennes*. Paris: Presses de la Fondation Nationale des Sciences Politiques, 1983.

Lee, Frederic E. *Currency, Banking, and Finance in China*. Washington, DC: Government Printing Office, 1926. New York: Garland Publishing, reprint, 1982.

Lee, Jung Bock. *The Political Character of the Japanese Press*. Seoul: National University Press, 1985.

Lee, Leo Ou-fan. *The Romantic Generation of Modern Chinese Writers*. Cambridge, MA: Harvard University Press, 1973.

Lee, Leo Ou-fan, and Andrew J. Nathan. "The Beginnings of Mass Culture: Journalism and Fiction in the Late Ch'ing and Beyond," in David Johnson, Andrew Nathan, and Evelyn Rawski, eds., *Popular Culture in Late Imperial China*. Berkeley: University of California Press, 1985.

Lei, Guang. "Elusive Democracy: Conceptual Change and the Chinese Democracy Movement, 1978-79 to 1989," *Modern China*, 22,4 (Oct. 1996):417–47.

Lewis, Roy, and Angus Maude. *Professional People*. London: Phoenix House, 1952.

Lieberthal, Kenneth, et al., eds. *Perspectives on Modern China: Four Anniversaries*. Armonk, NY: M. E. Sharpe, 1991.

Lin Yutang, *A History of the Press and Public Opinion in China*. Shanghai: Kelly and Walsh, 1936.

Link, E. Perry. *Mandarin Ducks and Butterflies: Popular Fiction in Early-Twentieth-Century Chinese Cities*. Berkeley: University of California Press, 1981.

Lu, Hanchao. "Away from Nanking Road: Small Stores and Neighborhood Life in Modern Shanghai," *Journal of Asian Studies*, 54,1 (1995):93–123.

"Creating Urban Outcasts: Shantytowns in Shanghai, 1920–1950," *Journal of Urban History*, 21,5 (1995):563–96.

"Arrested Development: Cotton and Cotton Markets in Shanghai, 1350–1843," *Modern China*, 8,4 (1992):486–99.

Lynn, Kenneth S., ed. *The Professions in America*. Boston: Houghton Mifflin, 1965.

Macauley, Melissa. *Social Power and Legal Culture: Litigation Masters in Late Imperial China*. Stanford: Stanford University Press, 1998.

McClelland, Charles E. *The German Experience of Professionalization*. Cambridge: Cambridge University Press, 1991.

McCord, Edward A. *The Power of the Gun: The Emergence of Modern Chinese Warlordism*. Berkeley: University of California Press, 1993.

McElderry, Andrea L. *Shanghai Old Style Banks (ch'ien chuang), 1800–1935*. Ann Arbor: The University of Michigan Center for Chinese Studies, 1976.

MacKinnon, Stephen R. "Toward a History of the Chinese Press in the Republican Period," *Modern China*, 23,1 (1997):3–32.

MacPherson, Kerrie L. *A Wilderness of Marshes: The Origins of Public Health in Shanghai, 1843–1893*. Oxford: Oxford University Press, 1987.

Mann, Susan. *Local Merchants and the Chinese Bureaucracy, 1750–1950*. Stanford: Stanford University Press, 1987.

Martin, Bryan G. *The Shanghai Green Gang: Politics and Organized Crime, 1919–1937*. Berkeley: University of California Press, 1996.

Meijer, Marinus J. *The Introduction of Modern Criminal Law in China*. Arlington, VA: University Publications of America, Inc., 1976.

Misra, B. B. *The Indian Middle Classes*. Oxford: Oxford University Press, 1961.

Murphey, Rhoads. *Shanghai: Key to Modern China*. Cambridge, MA: Harvard University Press, 1953.

Bibliography

Nathan, Andrew J. *Peking Politics: 1918–1923*. Berkeley: University of California Press, 1976.

Chinese Democracy. Berkeley: University of California Press, 1985.

National Institute of Social and Economic Research. *Growth of Middle Class in Pakistan*. Karachi, 1971.

Ogata, Sadako N. *Defiance in Manchuria: The Making of Japanese Foreign Policy*. Berkeley: University of California, 1964.

Pavalko, Ronald M. *Sociology of Occupations and Professions*. Itasca, IL: F. E. Peacock Publishers, 1988.

Perkin, Harold. *The Rise of Professional Society: England since 1880*. London: Routledge, 1989.

Perry, Elizabeth J. *Shanghai on Strike: The Politics of Chinese Labor*. Stanford: Stanford University Press, 1993.

Pilbeam, Pamela M. *The Middle Class in Europe, 1789–1914: France, Germany, Italy, and Russia*. Chicago: Lyceum Books. 1990.

Prasad, Bhagwan. *Socioeconomic Study of Urban Middle Classes*. Delhi: Sterling Publishers. 1971.

Pye, Lucian W. "How China's Nationalism Was Shanghaied," *Australian Journal of Chinese Affairs*, 29 (1993):107–33.

Rankin, Mary B. *Elite Activism and Political Transformation in China: Zhejiang Province, 1865–1911*. Stanford: Stanford University Press, 1986.

"The Origins of a Chinese Public Sphere," *Etudes Chinoises*, 9,2 (Autumn 1990):13–60.

"Some Observations on a Chinese Public Sphere," *Modern China*, 19,2 (1993):158–82.

Rankin, Mary B., and Joseph W. Esherick, eds. *Chinese Local Elites and Patterns of Dominance*. Berkeley: University of California Press, 1990.

Rawski, Evelyn S. *Education and Popular Literacy in Ch'ing China*. Ann Arbor: University of Michigan Press, 1979.

Rawski, Thomas G. *Economic Growth in Prewar China*. Berkeley: University of California Press, 1989.

Raynor, John. *The Middle Class*. London: Longmans, Green, 1969.

Reader, W. J. *Professional Men: The Rise of the Professional Classes in Nineteenth-Century England*. New York: Basic Books, 1966.

Reed, Bradly W. "Money and Justice: Clerks, Runners, and the Magistrate's Court in Late Imperial Sichuan," *Modern China*, 21,3 (1995):345–82.

Reed, Christopher A. 1995. "Sooty Sons of Vulcan: Shanghai's Printing Machine Manufacturers, 1895–1932," *Republican China*, 20,2 (Apr. 1995):9–54.

Reynolds, Douglas R. *China, 1898–1912: The Xinzheng Revolution and Japan*. Cambridge, MA: Harvard University Press, 1993.

Rogaski, Ruth. "From Protecting Life to Defending the Nation: The Emergence of Public Health in Tianjin, 1859–1953," Ph.D. Dissertation, Yale University, 1996.

Rosenbaum, Arthur L., ed. *State and Society in China: The Consequences of Reform*. Boulder: Westview Press, 1992.

Roux, Alain. *Le Shanghai Ouvrier des Années Trente: Coolies, Gangsters et Syndicalistes*. Paris: L'Harmattan, 1993.

Bibliography

Rowe, William T. *Hankow: Commerce and Society in a Chinese City, 1796–1889.* Stanford: Stanford University Press, 1985.
  Hankow: Conflict and Community in a Chinese City, 1796–1895. Stanford: Stanford University Press, 1989.
  "Public Sphere in Modern China," *Modern China*, 16,3 (July 1990):309–29.
  "The Problem of 'Civil Society' in Late Imperial China," *Modern China*, 19,2 (Apr. 1993):139–57.
Schoppa, R. Keith. *Chinese Elites and Political Change: Zhejiang Province in the Early Twentieth Century.* Cambridge, MA: Harvard University Press, 1982.
Schwarcz, Vera. *The Chinese Enlightenment: Intellectuals and the Legacy of the May Fourth Movement of 1919.* Berkeley: University of California Press, 1986.
Schwartz, Benjamin. *In Search of Wealth and Power.* Cambridge, MA: Harvard University Press, 1964.
Shanghai Municipal Council (SMC). *Report for the Year 1935 and Budget for the Year 1936.* Shanghai: North China Daily News & Herald, Ltd., 1936.
Sheridan, James E. *China in Disintegration: The Republican Era in Chinese History, 1912–1949.* New York: Free Press, 1975.
Sheng Jun. *The Index of Living Cost in Shanghai.* Shanghai: The National Tariff Commission, 1930.
Smith, Sara R. *The Manchurian Crisis, 1931–1932: A Tragedy in International Relations.* Westport, CT: Greenwood Press, 1970.
Stapleton, Kristin. "Urban Politics in an Age of 'Secret Societies': The Cases of Shanghai and Chengdu," *Republican China*, 22,1 (Nov. 1996):23–64.
Stephens, Thomas B. *Order and Discipline in China: The Shanghai Mixed Court, 1911–1927.* Seattle: University of Washington Press, 1992.
Stranahan, Patricia. "Stranger Bedfellows: The Communist Party and Shanghai's Elite in the National Salvation Movement," *The China Quarterly*, 129 (March 1992):26–51.
  Underground: The Shanghai Communist Party and the Politics of Survival, 1927–1937. Lanham, MD: Rowman & Littlefield Publisher, Inc., 1998.
Strand, David. *Rickshaw Beijing: City People and Politics in the 1920s.* Berkeley: University of California Press, 1989.
Szymanski, Albert. *Class Structure: A Critical Perspective.* New York: Praeger Publishers, 1983.
Tao, L. K. "Unemployment among Intellectual Workers in China," *The Chinese Social and Political Science Review*, 13,3 (July 1929):251–61.
Thomson Jr., James C. *While China Faced West: American Reformers in Nationalist China, 1928–1937.* Cambridge, MA: Harvard University Press, 1969.
Ting, Lee-hsia Hsu. *Government Control of the Press in Modern China, 1900–1949.* Cambridge, MA: Harvard University Press, 1974.
Torstendahl, Rolf, and Michael Burrage, eds. *The Formation of Professions: Knowledge, State, and Strategy.* London: Sage Publications, 1990.
Tsai, Wen-hui. *Patterns of Political Elite Mobility in Modern China, 1912–1949.* Hong Kong: Chinese Materials Center, 1983.
Unger, Jonathan, ed. *Chinese Nationalism.* Armonk, NY: M. E. Sharpe. 1996.

Bibliography

Unschuld, Paul U. *Medical Ethics in Imperial China*. Berkeley: University of California Press, 1979.

Wacquant, Loic J. D. "Making Class: The Middle Class(es) in Social Theory and Social Structure," in Scott G. McNall et al., eds., *Bringing Class Back In: Contemporary and Historical Perspectives*. Boulder: Westview Press, 1991.

Wagner, Rudolf G. "The Role of the Foreign Community in the Chinese Public Sphere," *China Quarterly*, 142 (1995):423–43.

Wakeman Jr., Frederic. "The Price of Autonomy: Intellectuals in Ming and Ch'ing Politics," in S. N. Eisenstadt and S. R. Graubard, eds., *Intellectuals and Tradition*. New York: Humanities Press, 1973.

"Civil Society and Public Sphere Debate," *Modern China*, 19,2 (1993):108–38.

Policing Shanghai, 1927–1937. Berkeley: University of California Press, 1995.

Wakeman Jr., Frederic, and Wen-hsin Yeh, eds. *Shanghai Sojourners*. Berkeley: University of California Center for Chinese Studies, 1992.

Waldron, Arthur. *From War to Nationalism: China's Turning Point, 1924–1925*. Cambridge: Cambridge University Press, 1995.

Wang, L. Sophia. "The Independent Press and Authoritarian Regimes: The Case of the *Dagong Bao* in Republican China," *Pacific Affairs*, 67,2 (1994):216–41.

Wang, Y. C. *Chinese Intellectuals and the West*. Chapel Hill: University of North Carolina Press, 1966.

Wang, Y. P. *The Rise of the Native Press in China*. New York: Columbia University, 1924.

Wasserstrom, Jeffrey N. *Student Protests in Twentieth-Century China: The View from Shanghai*. Stanford: Stanford University Press, 1991.

White, Gordon. "Prospects for Civil Society in China: A Case Study of Xiaoshan City," *Australian Journal of Chinese Affairs*, 29 (Jan. 1993).63–87.

"The Dynamics of Civil Society in Post-Mao China," in Brian Hook, ed., *The Individual and the State in China*. Oxford: Clarendon Press, 1996.

White, Gordon, Jude Howell, and Shang Xiaoyuan. *In Search of Civil Society: Market Reform and Social Change in Contemporary China*. Oxford: Clarendon Press, 1996.

White III, Lynn T. "Nongovernmentalism in the Historical Development of Modern Shanghai," in Lawrence J. C. Ma and Edward W. Hanten, eds., *Urban Development in Modern China*. Boulder, CO: Westview Press, 1981.

Whyte, Martin K., "Urban China: A Civil Society in the Making?" in Arthur L. Rosenbau, ed., *State and Society in China: The Consequence of Reform*. Boulder, CO: Westview Press, 1992.

Wong, R. Bin. *China Transformed: Historical Change and the Limits of European Experience*. Ithaca: Cornell University Press, 1997.

Wu, John C. H. *Beyond East and West*. New York: Sheed and Ward, 1951.

Xu, Xiaoqun. "The Making of Chinese Communists, 1921–1935: A Biographic Study," *Chinese Historians*, 4,1 (1990):34–63.

"The Fate of Judicial Independence in Republican China, 1912–1937," *China Quarterly*, 149 (March 1997):1–28.

Yang, Mayfair Mei-hui. "Between State and Society: The Construction of Corporateness in a Chinese Socialist Factory," *Australian Journal of Chinese Affairs*, 22 (July 1989):31–60.

Ye, Xiaoqing. "Shanghai Before Nationalism," *East Asian History*, 3 (1992):33–52.

Yeh, Wen-hsin. *The Alienated Academy: Culture and Politics in Republican China, 1919–1937*. Cambridge, MA: Harvard University Press, 1990.

"Corporate Space, Communal Time: Everyday Life in Shanghai's Bank of China," *American Historical Review*, 100,1 (Feb. 1995):97–122.

Yip, Ka-che. *Health and National Reconstruction in Nationalist China: The Development of Modern Health Services, 1928–1937*. Ann Arbor: Associations for Asian Studies, Inc., 1995.

Young, Ernest P. *The Presidency of Yuan Shih-k'ai: Liberalism and Dictatorship in Early Republican China*. Ann Arbor: University of Michigan Press, 1977.

"The Hung-hsien Emperor as a Modernizing Conservative," in Charlotte Forth, ed., *The Limits of Change*. Cambridge, MA: Harvard University Press, 1976.

Index

Agreement on Establishing the Mixed Court, 229
Agreement on the Chinese Court in Shanghai's International Settlement, 238
Amended Plan for Organizing People's Associations, 150
Amended Procedures for Organizing People's Associations, 99–100
Amended Provisional Regulations on Doctors, 143
Amended Provisional Regulations on Pharmacists, 143
American Bar Association, 222
American Bar Far East Association, 233, 234
Anti-Japanese National Salvation Society, 255
Association for Preparing a Constitution, 86
Aurora University, 219

Bank of China, 29
Bank of Communications, 29
Bank of the Board of Revenue, 29
banking and credit service institutions, 30
Bao Shisheng, 136
Bao Tianxiao, 173
Beiyang Army, 68
Berlin Medical Society, 147
Book and Newspaper Association, 176

"book bureau," 47
Book Trade Association, 167, 176
Book Trade Merchants Association, 176
Books and Journals Censorship Committee, 182
Bureau of Education, 104, 182, 183, 249
Bureau of Health, 144, 149, 150, 152, 154, 183; regulating doctors' fees, 54, 145–6
Bureau of Social Affairs, 96, 103, 104, 150, 183, 249
Bureau of Public Security, 103, 183, 261–2

Cai Jiping, 199
Cai Nipei, 220, 221, 222, 246, 255
Cai Yuanpei, 86, 87, 137, 185
Central Health Committee (CHC), 142, 192–3
Central Health Research Institute, 142
Central Political Council, 199, 208, 209
Chao Kun, 232
Chaozhou Native Association, 84
Chen Bao, 73
Chen Bulei, 177, 178
Chen Dezheng, 71, 128, 178, 182
Chen Guofu, 199, 200, 209, 210
Chen Leng, 86
Chen Lifu, 208, 209

319

Index

Chen Minshu, 209
Chen Qimei, 215, 216
Chen Shaoying, 208
Chen Taoyi, 232, 233
Chen Tingrui, 219
Chen Zemin, 217, 220, 222
Cheng Dequan, 90, 91, 226
Chiang Kai-shek, 96, 97, 122, 181, 200, 205, 207, 208, 258–9, 264
China College of Shanghai, 219
China Medical Association, 133–4; Shanghai branch of, 153
China Medical Journal, 133
China Medical Missionary Association, 133
China Merchant Steam Navigation Company, 26, 32
China Weekly Review, 64, 153, 154, 163, 166, 175, 198
Chinese and Foreign Court, 119
Chinese Association of Western-Style Medical Practitioners, 134
Chinese Commercial Bank, 29
Chinese Communist Party (CCP), 76, 85, 96, 105
Chinese currency, 50–1
Chinese League for Protection of Civil Rights, 76, 185
Chinese Maritime Customs, 35
Chinese Medical and Pharmaceutical Society (CMPS), 132, 149
Chinese nationalism, 16–17, 133, 188, 213, 216, 232; *see also* nationalism
Chinese Safety United Life Insurance Company, 33
Chinese Society for Improving Education (CSIE), 137, 192
Chizhi College, 219
civil society, 13–15, 17, 269, 272, 279–82
class formation, 3, 6–7, 21, 38, 72; and modernization, 272
Committee on Directing Mass Movement, 101
Committee on Party Affairs and Mass Training, 102
Consular Body, 229–30, 233, 236, 237

Control Council, 184–5, 262
county magistrates, performing judicial functions, 113–15
Criminal Code of Great Qing, 39
cultural nationalists, 200, 208, 209
Cunningham, Edwin, 236, 237
Currently Applied Criminal Code of Great Qing, 39

Dagong Bao, 56, 57
Dai Jitao, 209
Daily Newspaper Reporters Association, 177
Department of Mass Training, Guomindang (GMD) Party Central, 104, 152
Di Chuqing, 86
Ding Ganren, 133, 136
Ding Wenjiang, 233
Ding Zhongying, 133, 199
Diplomatic Body, 175, 232, 233, 235
Drug Trade Guild, 84
Du Yuesheng, 66, 276
Du Zhongyuan, 77
due process, 158, 220, 226, 228, 251, 253

Endurance Club, 276
emergency law, 252–3, 254, 265
Emergency Law on Crimes against the Republic, 102, 252; *see also* emergency law
Examination Council, 143
Executive Council, 104, 151, 197, 205–6, 210, 212, 262
Expedient Rules of Licensing Doctors, 143
extraterritoriality, 39, 116, 158, 215, 216, 228, 229, 231, 234, 252

fatuan, 94; defined by the Judicial Council, 100–1; *see also* legally established associations
Federation of Shanghai National Salvation Societies, 263
Federation of Street Merchant Associations, 97, 198, 217, 232

Index

Federation of Universities in Shanghai, 96
Feng Shaoshan, 198
Feng Yuxiang, 211
First Special District Court, 40, 154, 239
France, 134, 135, 237
freedom of speech, 17, 58, 168–9, 173, 176, 180, 187, 188–9, 268, 277
French Concession, 8, 41, 44, 49, 64, 153, 223, 225, 228, 230, 239
French Mixed Court, 40, 238, 239; *see also* Mixed Court(s)
Fresh Meat Trade Association, 84
Fudan University, 219

Ge Gongzhen, 56, 170, 172
General Bar Association of the Republic of China (GBACR), 51, 108, 109, 216, 217, 229
gentry-merchant organizations, 4, 14, 83
German Medical Society, 153
Germany, 43, 109, 134, 135; medical professionalization in, 147
Gold Trade Association, 31, 32
gong fatuan, defined by Judicial Council, 100–1
gongfei, 13
Gongmin Ribao, 170
gongtuan, 94; *see also* public associations
Gongyan Bao, 186
Great Britain, 43, 134, 237
Great Peace Insurance Company, 33
Green Gang, 66, 85, 96, 166, 275–6
Gu Weijun, 231, 232
Gu Zhenglun, 209
Gu Zhizhong, 56, 164, 184
Guangxi High Court, 117

Hangxian Bar Association, 243
Hart, Robert, 35
He Shizhen, 71, 219, 236–7
Health Administration, 143, 211, 212
Health Bureau of Shanghai-Wusong Commercial Port, 140–1

Health Education Committee, 133
Heaven and Earth Society, 85
Hong Kong and Shanghai Banking Corporation, 28, 29
Hong Shuzu, 226, 227
Hu Bang'an, 55
Hu Hanmin, 208, 258
Hu Hongji, 140, 144, 149, 152
Hu Mei'an, 31
Hu Shuwei, 200
Huang Yanpei, 8, 77, 87, 137, 170
Huang Yaomian, 67
Huang Zhenpan, 220
Huizhou-Ningguo Native Association, 84
human rights, 184, 250

imagined community, 16, 17
Implementing Specifics of the Publication Law, 181
Institute of Chartered Accountants in Shanghai, 74, 232, 234–5
Institute of Chartered Accountants of the Chinese Republic, 74
Institute of National Martial Arts, 208
Institute of Native Medicine, 209–11
intellectual class, 72–3
International Mixed Court, 40, 223, 230, 231; *see also* Mixed Court(s)
International Settlement, 28, 35, 40, 41, 43, 44, 64, 223, 225, 230, 239, 240, 244; Chinese professionals living in, 48–9; Mixed Court in, 229–30; occupations of the Chinese in, 37–8; quacks in, 152, 154

Japan, 24, 34, 92, 93, 109, 134; newspapers in, 162–3
Jiang Wenfang, 208
Jiangning Bar Association, 262
Jiangning District Court, 262
Jiangsheng Bao, 85
Jiangsu Agricultural Society, 247
Jiangsu Department of Justice, 124
Jiangsu Educational Society, 170, 247

Index

Jiangsu General Bar Association, 216
Jiangsu High Court, 116, 218, 221, 227; enforcing regulations on lawyers, 110–11, 217; located in Suzhou, 40; registration of lawyers with, 109; Second Branch of, 40, 154, 228, 239, 240; Third Branch of, 40, 239
Jiangsu Provincial Assembly, 247
Jiangsu Provincial Federation of Native Medical Associations, 139
Jiangsu Society, 248
Jiao Yitang, 208, 209, 210
Jin Minlan, 217
Jin Xiongbai, 71
Jing Bao, 172
Jordon, J. H., 154
journalistic profession, 158, 163
Judicial Council, 100, 101
judicial independence, 17, 19, 158, 242, 252, 253, 266, 268, 277
jury trial, experiment of, 41

Kang Youwei, 130
Koechlin, Edgar, 239
Korea, 24
Kotenev, A. M., 231
Kwantung Army, 254

Labor Union Unification Committee, 96
labor unions, 1, 85, 103, 106, 150
Land Regulations, 175
Law on Medical Doctors, 148
Law on Stock Exchanges, 32
Lawyers' Disciplinary Committee, 227, 250, 263
Leaf, Earl H. 69
League of Nations, 254, 256
legal profession, 40, 108, 109, 121, 129, 149, 158, 225, 241, 250, 251, 253, 265, 268, 273; under the Guomindang (GMD), 124; in post-Mao China, 278–9; providing volunteer service, 112–13; regulation of, 110–13
Legal System Committee, 121, 210

legally established associations, 13; disuse of the term, 100–1
Legislative Council, 143, 205, 210
Li Bao, 187
Li Haoran, 56
Li Shirui, 225, 238, 255, 257, 262–4
Li Shizeng, 199, 200, 209
Li Shuping, 131–2
Li Yuanhong, 91
Li Zuyu, 231, 232
Liang Qichao, 73, 86, 130, 137; and factional organs, 162–4; as Minister of Justice, 117
Lin Baishui, 172, 185
Lin Kanghou, 198
Lin Sen, 209
"literary men," 18, 48, 71, 157, 161, 162, 170, 188
Liu Yusheng, 184–5
Liu Zhi, 209
Lockhart, William, 43
Long March, 264
Lu Bingzhang, 221
Lu Dingkui, 219
Lu Jiading, 261
Lu Shangtong, 111
Lu Shi'e, 203
Lu Xingyuan, 71, 127, 224, 225
Lu Yi, 56, 64
Lü Yuequan, 33

Ma Zhanshan, 256
Major, Ernest, 46
Manchuria, Japanese occupation of, 254; *see also* Northeastern Provinces
Manchurian Incident, 184, 260; Shanghai Bar Association aroused by, 254–9
Mao Dun, 32
Mass Training Committee, of Municipal Party Headquarters, 149, 150, 249–50
May Fourth Movement, 93, 94; and Shanghai Bar Association, 243
May Thirtieth Movement, 93, 94, 232;

322

Index

and Shanghai Bar Association, 244–5
McKenzie, Vernon, 164
Medical and Pharmaceutical Society of the Chinese Republic (MPSCR), 133, 150, 192
Medical Practitioners' Association of Shanghai (MPAS), 19, 134; attacking native medicine, 191–2
medical profession, 129, 148, 149, 158
Medical Terminology Evaluation Committee, 133
Merchant Ship Association, 84
middle class, 18, 23, 38, 77; and professional identity, 72; professionals as, 6–7, 21; stratification within, 67–8
Minguo Bao, 175
Minguo Ribao, 164, 177, 178
Minhu Bao, 87
Ministry of Agriculture and Forestry, 90
Ministry of Civil Affairs, 142
Ministry of Education, 92, 98, 104, 196, 200; restricting native medical education, 135–7, 204–7
Ministry of Foreign Affairs, 233, 235, 237, 238, 256
Ministry of Health, 142–3, 146–7, 149, 151, 192, 196, 199, 203, 208; restricting native medicine, 204–7
Ministry of Industry and Commerce, 199–200
Ministry of Justice, 40, 124, 125–6, 127, 217, 218, 221, 224, 225, 227, 233, 237, 238, 243, 249, 250, 253, 262, 263; banning legal practice at county level, 114–16, 126–7; demands on judges by, 118–19; favoring Guomindang (GMD) party members, 128; licensing foreign lawyers, 239–40; of the PRC, 278; regulating lawyers, 110–16
Ministry of the Interior, 90, 120, 141, 142, 184, 185, 205, 211; and censorship, 181; Health Division of, 135; and native medicine, 137–9
Ministry of Transportation and Communications, 184
missionaries, and Western medicine, 43; and Chinese journalism, 45
Mixed Court(s), 40, 41, 93, 216, 223, 224, 240, 251; Chinese lawyers practicing at, 42; enforcing regulations on lawyers, 111; rendition of, 113, 230–5, 237–9; suppressing Chinese publications, 174–5
modern state building, 16, 83, 129, 271, 272, 278; *see also* state building
modernization, 2, 3, 4, 202, 271, 272, 278, 282; China's, 78, 190–1; and class formation, 49; and nationalism, 16–17, 213–14; and native medicine, 131; of postal service, 35–6; and professionalization, 12; and professions, 21–2; of Shanghai, 26; and white-collar workers, 36–7
mosquito papers, 46, 182–3
Mu Xiangyao, 90, 91, 227
Municipal Party Headquarters (MPH), 96, 102, 104, 218; and censorship, 182; and medical regulation, 145–6; and reorganization of Shanghai Bar Association, 122–4

National Association of Medical Doctors, 210
National Bar Association (NBA), 185, 253, 256, 260
National Citizens' Association, 91–2
National Epidemic Prevention Bureau, 135
National Federation of Chambers of Commerce, 197, 198
National Federation of Educational Societies, 137, 192
National Federation of Medical and Pharmaceutical Associations

323

Index

(NFMPA): demise of, 150–2, 209; fighting for native medicine, 199–200, 204–8; founding of, 199
National Government Office, 200, 205, 208, 263
National Medical Association (NMA), 138, 142, 153, 192, 210; founding of, 133; Shanghai Branch of, 134
National Medicine Day, 198, 209
National News Agency, 56, 171
National Newspapers Association of the Chinese Republic, 168
National Newspapers Progress Association, 167
National Revolutionary Army, 68, 95, 177
nationalism, 94, 202, 229; modernization and, 18; and professionals, 157; *see also* Chinese nationalism
native banks, 25–6
native drug trade, 277; supporting native medicine, 139–40, 196–9
native medical education, 135–7
native medicine, 44, 158; arguments for, 201–3; attack on, 191–5; called national medicine, 203; government policy toward, 129; legitimized, 213; and Shanghai authorities, 139–42; stratification within, 130; and Western medicine, 131–2
Native Medicine Committee, 212
native-place associations, 1, 4, 5, 83, 103, 106, 216, 276; called *gongsuo*, 13; Guomindang (GMD) policy toward, 101–2
New Life Movement, 183
New Medicine and Society, 196
New Policy reform, 39, 68, 80, 94; and transformation of knowledge structure, 4–5
News Agency Reporters Association, 177
1911 Revolution, 87, 90
Nineteenth Route Army, 254, 256

Ningbo Native Association, 84
Niu Huisheng, 210
North China Daily News, 45, 128
North China Herald, 36, 45, 52; on rendition of Mixed Court, 230, 232; on Shanghai Bar Association, 53, 223, 251, 260
Northeastern Provinces, 255, 256; *see also* Manchuria
Northern Expedition, 94, 95, 177, 181, 248

occupational associations, 98, 99, 121, 149
Organic Law of Judicial Courts, 39; barring judges from party affiliation, 117
Organizational Regulations of County Judicial Offices, 114
Oriental Banking Corporation, 28

Pan Gongzhan, 71, 171, 177, 178, 182
Pang Jingzhou, 44, 54, 55, 134, 146, 154, 195
Paris Peace Conference, 231
Parker, Peter, 43
parliament, 90, 217, 247
Patriotic Study Society, 86
Paulum, E. H., 44
people's associations, 80, 98, 100, 125; medical associations as, 148
people's rights, 215, 216, 257
political culture, 16, 17, 87, 268
Political Information Society, 86
Powell, John B., 163, 175
price of rice, in Shanghai, 61–2
private associations, 89, 101, 148, 151
Procedures for Establishing People's Associations, 98
professional associations, 1, 83, 106, 249; agenda of, 155–6; characteristics of, 5–6; and foreign presence, 16; maintaining professional character, 269; nature of, 14; and other urban associations, 15; and professionalization, 10–11, 12–13;

and the state, 15–17, 79, 278; between state and society, 272–3
professional class, 38; differentiation within, 7
professional community, 7, 76, 177; journalists as, 188; in Shanghai, 8, 18, 45; size of, 48–9
professional employment, 19; and education, 68–71
professional income, 51–7; compared to other social groups, 57–60
professional identity, 75, 76, 166, 178; of journalists, 176, 179, 180, 189
professionalization, 3, 9–13, 18, 57, 179, 216, 240, 242, 271; and government regulation, 15, 155; of journalism, 161; legal, 129, 220; medical, 17, 42, 129, 158; in post-Mao China, 279; and professional ethics, 165; and professionals, 7; and social differentiation, 71–2; and state building, 18; in Western societies, 135
provincial constitution, 247–9
Provisional Constitution, 91, 94, 184, 246, 248
Provisional Court, 113, 128, 223, 224, 225, 237, 239; problems at, 235–7; reorganization of, 40, 238–40; replacing International Mixed Court, 235
Provisional Regulations on: County Magistrates' Disposal of Lawsuits, 114; County Magistrates' Management of Judicial Affairs, 114; High and Lower Courts, 39; on Midwives, 144; Practitioners of Native Medicine, 144; Practitioners of Western Medicine, 144
Provisional Regulations on Doctors, 192; doctors opposing, 147–9
Provisional Regulations on Lawyers, 40, 51, 114, 123, 217, 223, 249; on lawyers' qualifications, 108–9; of the People's Republic of China, 278

public associations, 13, 15, 105–6, 124, 223; disuse of the term, 100–1; legitimacy of, 267; medical associations as, 148; MPH survey of, 104–5; after 1911 Revolution, 87–9; Shanghai Bar and other, 264; supporting Shanghai Bar, 262
public means, 168, 184
public sphere, 13–15, 272
Publication Law: of 1914, 93, 173, 174; of 1930, 181, 182
publicness, 95, 100, 157, 278; contention over, 80–1, 275; of journalistic profession, 180; of professional associations, 12–13, 107, 268; and professionalization, 12–13; of Shanghai Bar, 240; shifting meanings of, 273

Qin Liankui, 66, 246
Qiu Jisheng, 208
Qu Qiubai, 72, 74
quacks, 158, 206
Quanzhou-Zhangzhou Native Association, 84

Railroad Rights Movement, 30
reading audience, in Shanghai, 47–8
Red Gang, 85
Regulations on: Examination of Practitioners of Western Medicine, 143; Hospital Management, 206; Lawyers' Selection Committee, 125; Native Physicians, 143, 210, 211–12; Newspapers, 173; Obstetricians, 143; Practitioners of Western Medicine, 194; Registration of Lawyers, 125; Registration of Mass Associations, 102
Regulations on Lawyers, 223, 250; of 1927, 125, 218, 225, 258, 262
rendition agreement, 235, 236, 237, 238
rent for housing, in Shanghai, 62–3
reorganization loan, 91

Research Society for Constitutional Government, 86
Revolutionary Alliance, 87
rule of avoidance, 112; under Guomindang (GMD), 126
rule of law, 6, 17, 19, 41, 118, 158, 216, 220, 226, 228, 240, 251, 252, 261, 263, 266, 268
Rules on Evaluating Native Physicians, 211
Russian Medical Society, 153

sandship, 24
scholarly associations, 98, 104
Second Revolution, 90, 91, 227
Second Special District Court, 40, 239
secret societies, 1, 4, 83, 85, 95, 106
Self-Reliance Society, 87
Self-Strengthening Movement, 26
Seven Gentlemen, 265
Sha Qianli, 265, 266
Shang Bao, 169, 171, 177
Shanghai Bankers' Association, 5, 167
Shanghai Bar Association (SBA), 19, 51, 109, 110, 116, 127, 158, 240, 242, 266, 272; alienation from Guomindang (GMD), 259–61; complying with regulations, 244–5; defending Yang Jingbing, 227; founding of, 217; internal problems of, 220–2; membership of, 42, 218–19; organization of, 217–18; in post-Mao China, 279; preventing nonmembers from practicing, 223–5; and rendition of Mixed Courts, 231–40; reorganization of, 123–4
Shanghai Bureau of Narcotic Regulation, 139
Shanghai Certified Accountants Institute, in post-Mao China, 279
Shanghai Chinese Merchant Cotton Goods Exchange, 32
Shanghai Chinese Merchants Stock Exchange (SCMSE), 31–2
Shanghai College of Law, 219
Shanghai College of Law and Political Science, 219
Shanghai Commercial Consultative Association, 84
Shanghai County Educational Society, 86
Shanghai County Party Headquarters, 250, 264
Shanghai Cultural Circle National Salvation Society, 265, 267
Shanghai Daily Newspapers Association, 167, 184, 277; against censorship, 176, 244
Shanghai District Court, 40, 113, 182, 223, 227; enforcing regulations on lawyers, 111, 116
Shanghai District Procuratorate, 221
Shanghai Equity and Precision Stock Company, 30
Shanghai Federation of Medical and Pharmaceutical Associations, 197
Shanghai Flour Exchange, 32
Shanghai General Chamber of Commerce, 5, 84, 88, 169, 170, 176, 198, 247, 276–7; reorganization of, 97; supporting native medicine, 140
Shanghai General Chamber of Commercial Affairs, 84
Shanghai General Labor Union, 95
Shanghai Gold Exchange, 32
Shanghai Journalists Association (SJA), 19, 67, 96, 166, 170, 180, 277; efforts to revitalize, 179–80; fighting for freedom of speech, 185–6; founding of new, 178
Shanghai Local Post, 35
Shanghai Machine Weaving Plant, 26
Shanghai Medical Board, 153
Shanghai Medical Society, 152, 153
Shanghai Merchant Volunteer Corps, 90
Shanghai Merchants Association, Drug Trade Branch of, 196
Shanghai Municipal Council (SMC), 35, 91, 235, 256; and registration of doctors, 153

Index

Shanghai Municipal Government, and medical regulation, 143–6
Shanghai Native Medical Association, 149
Shanghai Native Medical Society (SNMS), 133, 197, 203
Shanghai Provision Exchange, 32
Shanghai Revolutionary Comrade Association, 103
Shanghai Shareholders Association, 30
Shanghai Stock and Produce Exchange (SSPE), 31–2
Shanghai Stock Exchange, 30; Japanese owned, 30–1
Shanghai Stock Trade Association, 30
Shanghai University Anti-Japanese National Salvation Society, 261
Shanghai Women's Association, 103
Shanghai Writers Association, 96
Shanghai-Wusong Garrison Headquarters, 103, 228
Shao Lizi, 177, 210
Shao Piaoping, 172, 185
Shao Yuanchong, 208, 209
Shen Bao, 46, 57, 69, 162, 164, 165, 167, 170, 171
Shen Enfu, 86
Shen Junru, 77, 265
Shenzhou Medical and Pharmaceutical General Association (SMPGA), 132, 149; fighting for native medicine, 138–41
Shenzhou Ribao, 89, 167
Shi Bao, 56, 167, 168, 170, 245
Shi Liang, 265
Shi Liangcai, 46, 86
Shi Ying, 209, 210
Shipping Administration, 24
Shishi Xingbao, 171
Sino–Japanese War (1894), 27, 85
Small Knife Society, 85
social associations, 98, 99, 125
Social Darwinism, 130
social identity, of professionals, 9
Society for Educational Research, 86

Society for Promoting National Goods, 198
Society for Promoting the Rule of Law (SPRL), 19, 246–9, 276
Society for Strength and Learning, 85
Song Jiaoren, assassination of, 226
Song Shixiang, 232
Soochow University, Law School of, 219
Southern District Citizens' Association, 89
Southern Manchurian Railway, 254
Specifics of Organizational Guidelines for Cultural Associations, 104
State Council, 136, 235
state building, 71, 97; *see also* modern state building
state–society interaction, 18, 19, 81, 148, 159, 266–7, 271, 273, 283; professionalization as, 13
state–society relationship, 13–18, 121, 162, 191
Study Society of Shanghai, 86
Su Bao, 87
Sun Baoqi, 117, 231
Sun Chuanfang, 93, 232, 233, 234
Sun Ke, 210, 258
Sun Yat-sen, 97, 202, 260–1, 268; Madam, 185
Supreme Court, 39
symbiotic dynamics, 3, 18, 158, 159, 271, 273–6, 278, 283

Taiping Rebellion, 85
Tan Sitong, 130
Tan Yankai, 151, 199, 200, 208
Tan Yigong, 238, 260
Tang Jiezhi, 169
Tang Yingsong, 246, 255, 260
tea gathering, and stock trade, 30
third force, 76–7
Three Principles of the People, 80, 97, 99, 102, 199, 202, 252
Tongji Medical School, 44
trade guilds, 4, 5, 83; called *gongsuo*, 13

Index

Treaty of Nanjing, 25
Treaty of Shimonoseki, 27

United States, 34, 133, 134, 222, 234, 237; missionaries from, 43; newspapers in, 163
University Professors Association, 96
urban culture, 66, 67; and professionals' life-style, 65–8

Van den Berg, Dutch diplomat, 236–7

Wang Baoji, 53, 64, 260
Wang Chonghui, 209, 231
Wang Daxie, 136
Wang Jingwei, 66, 71, 210, 258
Wang Kaijiang, 223, 232, 244, 246
Wang Qizhang, 146, 195, 210
Wang Xingyi, 198
Wang Zhaoshi, 265
Wang Zhongfang, 64
Wei Daoming, 71
Western medicine, 129; challenging native medicine, 130–1
Wu Jingheng, 86
Wu Jingxiong, 52, 219
Wu Kaisheng, 52, 53
Wu Liande, 153, 191
Wu Mai, 260, 261, 262
Wu Shiying, 226
Wu Xin, 90
Wu Zhihao, 198

Xi Yuchang, 246
Xia Yingtang, 133, 199
Xie Lihuan, 199
Xinwen Bao, 56, 57, 164, 165, 167, 181
Xu Erjin, 220
Xu Maoyong, 70
Xu Qian, 220
Xu Shiying, 118
Xu Weizhen, 224, 240
Xu Yuan, 233
Xu Zhucheng, 56

Xue Dubi, 200
Xunhuan Ribao, 45

Yan Duhe, 171
Yan Esheng, 180
Yan Huiqing, 210
Yan Shenyu, 183
Yang Jingbing, 220, 226–8
Yangzi River, 23–4
Yao Gonghe, 41
Ye Chuchang, 199, 200, 210
Ying Guixin, 226
Yu Botao, 132, 136
Yu Youren, 209
Yu Yunxiu, 192–3, 193–4, 195, 197
Yuan Shikai, 15, 51, 89, 90, 92, 93, 95, 117, 118, 119, 135, 181, 226
Yuan Xitao, 86
Yun Yiqun, 187

Zhabei Citizens' Association, 88, 90–1
Zhang Binglin, 86
Zhang Guotao, 72
Zhang Jiazhen, 123–4, 222, 246
Zhang Jingjiang, 199, 200
Zhang Jinglu, 165, 170
Zhang Junmai, 77
Zhang Mei'an, 199
Zhang Xun, 120
Zhang Yipeng, 116, 122–4, 222, 224, 233, 245–6
Zhang Zanchen, 199
Zhang Zongchang, 172, 173
Zhao Bingjun, 226
Zheng Rucheng, 92
Zheng Yuxiu, 71
Zhongwai Xinbao, 45
Zhu Jianxia, 103
Zhu Kewen, 54
Zhu Minyi, 149
Zhu Peide, 208
ziyou zhiye tuanti, 2; defined by Guomindang (GMD), 121–2
ziyou zhiye zhe, 1–2, 23, 38, 48, 49, 75, 76, 122, 179, 271; writers not recognized as, 71
Zongli Yamen, 35

Printed in the United States
83281LV00004B/1-60/A